Exploring Gender in Canada: A Multi-Dimensional Approach

Exploring Gender in Canada: A Multi-Dimensional Approach

Beverly Matthews
Mount Royal College

Lori Beaman
University of Ottawa

PEARSON

Prentice
Hall

Toronto

Library and Archives Canada Cataloguing in Publication

Matthews, Beverly
    Exploring Gender in Canada: a multi-dimensional approach / Beverly Matthews, Lori Beaman.

Includes bibliographical references and index.
ISBN-13: 978-0-13-127221-7
ISBN-10: 0-13-127221-7

    1. Sex role—Canada—Textbooks. 2. Sexism—Canada—Textbooks.
I. Beaman, Lori G. (Lori Gail), 1963– II. Title.

HQ1075.5.C3M38 2007   305.30971   C2006-905453-3

ISBN-13: 978-0-13-127221-7
ISBN-10: 0-13-127221-7

Senior Acquisitions Editor: Ky Pruesse
Executive Marketing Manager: Judith Allen
Developmental Editor: Jon Maxfield
Production Editor: Kevin Leung
Copy Editor: Nancy Mucklow
Proofreader: Sally Hall
Production Coordinator: Sharlene Ross
Composition: Laserwords
Art Director: Julia Hall
Cover Design: Julia Hall
Cover Image: Photostock

1 2 3 4 5   11 10 09 08 07

Printed and bound in the United States of America.

For Lori Beaman
To Lilly and Katie, may you live to see what I hope for
Bella, Emma, and Sierra, who are "doing it for women"
Gayle & Jo and Sally and Marny, who have paved the way

For Bev Matthews
To Sarah, Elinor, and Margaret Goldie,
not for what you do, but for who you are

Brief Contents

Contents

SECTION 5 CONCLUSION   283

Chapter 15 Crime as Case Study   284

Preface

On October 26, 2005, the two authors of this textbook were sitting at a dinner table in a fishing village in Mexico with our hosts, Larry and Reg, and their landlords (who had become our landlords for a month), Jorge and Carmen. Neither of us could speak much Spanish, but somehow we were able to understand as Jorge tried to explain *machismo* among Mexican men, an attitude that he traced back to fear. This experience struck us as a microcosm of everything we were talking about in preparation for writing this book: sexual identities, race, power, class, gender boundaries, and fluidity, and the profoundly complex intersection of gender identities and performances with institutional structures. Those discussions resulted in renewed consideration of our own ideas about gender. Moreover, we discovered that day how much cultural context, including historical moment, was central to thinking about gender boundaries.

The sociology of gender is a field that has changed a great deal over the last several decades. It is no longer an "emerging" field, but rather has taken its place with other essential areas of study in sociology. Socio-cultural shifts—egalitarian values, feminist movements, masculinist movements, the mobilization for same-sex marriage, changing work and family patterns, emerging health issues like HIV/AIDS, and ever expanding gendered media messages, for example—have changed the ways we think about gender in Canada.

As more scholars have explored the social components of gender, it has become clear that gender operates on many dimensions within society. Gender cannot be understood simply as a property of individuals. While most people perceive gender to be an integral part of their identity, they also *do gender* in interactions with friends and strangers. In addition, we live and work within gender regimes reflected in our legal, religious and economic institutions. These dimensions are fully integrated in the ways we do gender.

Introducing students to this growing area of sociology could easily fill many volumes, so we have been selective. Rather than developing an encyclopedic text covering the vast breadth of the field, we have chosen to provide an overview and then highlight specific topics. A variety of case studies are provided, as are guest essays from Canadian scholars working in the field to add further insight. We have used the best of what gender theorists have to offer. Judith Butler's notion of gender as performative, for example, has been helpful in defining how we see the working out of gender on the various dimensions. We have drawn from our own areas of expertise and research to provide discussions that will hopefully provoke debate and further analysis.

This book develops a unique multi-dimensional approach to the study of gender, exploring gender in four dimensions: individual, interactional, institutional, and socio-cultural. To facilitate student understanding of the complex nature of gender, we tease the levels apart and explore them separately. The final chapter of the book uses crime as a case study to pull the dimensions together and considers the links between them.

The introductory chapter introduces the multi-dimensional approach with brief explorations of patterns on each. In Section One, we consider the socio-cultural landscape: ways of thinking and studying gender, masculinities and femininities, as well as gendered language and media. Students are introduced to a variety of theories, from feminist approaches to Hall's conceptions of encoding and decoding mediated messages. A variety of measurement issues are also discussed to provide students with the tools to assess empirical research on gender differences and similarities.

In Section Two, we focus on individual gender experiences, including patterns of socialization in childhood and identity construction in adolescence. But we recognize that gender patterns in adulthood and old age are equally important. For this reason, Chapter Six is devoted to exploring the gendered lives of adults. Most importantly, intersections between gender and other identities—ethnicity, class, and mental health, for example—are considered. We briefly explore some of the issues that emerge in adulthood, including partnering and relationship breakdown, and we consider the gendered medicalization of the adult body.

Section Three of the text focuses on *doing gender*: the ways we present ourselves and interact with others. Specific topics of interest are friendships, sexual relations, and power. We have paid particular attention to the topic of power because it is an important factor contributing to the ways gender is and can be performed. The theory of power we present helps students see more clearly how gender works in society.

The final section examines some of the gender regimes in Canadian institutions: families, work, law and religion. Guest essayists have contributed discussions of volunteerism, the second shift, adverse impact discrimination, and men's participation in programs for men who batter. There is no separate chapter dealing with education, something we agonized over for many months. In the end, we decided to weave discussions of education throughout the book. We wish it had been possible to explore other topics in greater depth: HIV/AIDS, abortion, sexual practices, debates about reproductive technologies and forced medical treatment. Each deserves a detailed examination for which we simply did not have space. Moreover, feminist theory is a topic in and of itself, and we have barely scratched the surface. What we have done is provide enough information to generate discussion and to spark interest and debate among students, challenging existing notions and encouraging the exploration of new ideas. We hope this text provides a starting place, and we encourage you to explore more fully those areas which pique your interest.

The discussions that began in that Mexican fishing village not only resulted in this textbook, but it also inspired the two authors to revisit our own theories. In the process of writing this book, we have balanced our different perspectives: theoretical and empirical; qualitative and quantitative; postmodern and modern. Some of the topics have generated a great deal of discussion between us, challenging both of us to clarify and occasionally modify our ideas and positions. This interaction has enhanced our understandings of both sociology and gender patterns and has provided a broader consideration of the issues than might be found in other texts.

This textbook features the following pedagogical features:

1. Guest essays in most chapters, based on the current research of some of the best thinkers on gender in Canada. Each writer has expertise in her or his given field, and each prioritizes gender in research.

2. Review questions at the end of each chapter, which are intended to generate discussion of the issues raised and to encourage students to bring their own experiences into their analyses of gender.

3. A glossary, located at the end of the text to clarify some key terminology.

4. Summary statements at the end of each chapter, designed to highlight some of the key issues discussed in the text.

5. A bibliography, acknowledging sources and providing the reader with opportunities for further reading.

6. Tables, used to summarize important data and to clarify textual discussion.

Exploring Gender in Canada is accompanied by a Test Item File, which is available to instructors for downloading from a password-protected section of Pearson Education Canada's online catalogue (vig.pearsoned.ca). Navigate to your book's catalogue page to view a list of those supplements that are available. See your local sales representative for details and access.

Acknowledgments

We would like to acknowledge a number of people who were critical to the writing of this book. Nicole Saunders, our research assistant at Concordia University, who has worked tirelessly to find resources, to coordinate our efforts, and to comb our work with her critical editorial eye. Margot Millard, at the Mount Royal library, for tracking down research materials. Reg and Larry, who provided warm hospitality with boundless generosity. Gavin Matthews for his willingness to read early drafts and for all his valuable suggestions. Our guest essayists, who shared their work with us and gave this book life with their examples of gender and everyday life. Jon Maxfield, our editor at Pearson, has truly been marvelously patient and encouraging. We would like to thank him for keeping this book on track. The following reviewers, whose comments served to help us clarify our thoughts: Faith Richards, Georgian College; Gayle MacDonald, St. Thomas University; Sandra Rollings-Magnusson, Grant MacEwan College; Christina Meredith, Georgian College; Michelle Owen, University of Winnipeg; Pearl Crichton, Concordia University; Nicole Power, Memorial University of Newfoundland.

Lori Beaman would like to thank, again, Nicole Saunders, who especially during the last days of the preparation of the manuscript worked tirelessly to help to pull it together. I would like to thank Gayle MacDonald for her review of and comments on the last chapter. My co-author, Beverly Matthews, is a dear friend as well as a colleague. We've shared many adventures together, including a month together in Mexico to write this book. Thanks, Bev. Finally, thank you to Derek Mac Donald, who has seen first hand the stress caused by a book deadline and responded by doing all he could to diminish it.

Beverly Matthews would like to thank my daughters, for your encouragement, assistance, and cheerful willingness to forage when the cupboard was bare. My family has been wonderful, knowing when to listen, when to prod, and when to help me celebrate. Thank you to my friends for all of your constructive assistance and sharing many evenings of talk and laughter. Thank you, Lori, for being there for me through the highs and the lows and for learning to speak Spanish so we didn't starve in Mexico. And most especially, thank you, Gavin, for doing everything in your power to help me reach for my dreams.

chapter one

Exploring Gender: A Multi-Dimensional Approach

SEX OR GENDER?

What if you had been born a different sex? Think about how your life would have been altered. Would you now have a different job? Different friends? Different car insurance rates? Maybe it's easier to consider the things in your life that would not have changed if you had been wrapped in a pink blanket instead of a blue one (or vice versa). What would be the same—your perceptions? Your activities? Your hairstyle?

Asking these questions of our students in Canadian colleges and universities often results in lengthy discussions of all the things that would change. But students are hard pressed to identify things that would not change. For example, one of the few they can think of is their parents. On further reflection, however, most acknowledge that their relationship with their parents would likely be different if they had been born a different sex. They further note that their parents might not have grown into the people they are today if their offspring had been differently sexed.

We could conclude from these differences that our sex shapes every aspect of our lives. Many take this even further and contend that "anatomy is destiny." However, even though many people draw this conclusion, it is not entirely accurate. Our biological sex is only one part of a more complex picture.

A key concept in the study of gender is the separation of two terms often used interchangeably in common usage: **sex** and **gender**. For example, when filling out application forms, people are often asked to indicate their *gender* by ticking off the *male* or *female* box, as though *gender* were the same as *sex*. However, those who study in this area are not satisfied with this ambiguous use of language. To put it simply, we may be born with a sex-typed anatomy (our *sex*), but for most people, our *gender* is more fluid. Our gendered selves are largely shaped by the social world in which we live and with which we interact.

Think of the difference between sex and gender this way: when you look in the mirror, the face you see is partly based on biology—your bone structure, facial features, and colouring—and partly based on cultural norms. Your choice to colour, curl, or straighten your hair, to wear lipstick, to pierce your ears, eyebrow, or nose is largely influenced by societal expectations placed upon women and men. Look at your body: your basic anatomy is influenced by the number of X and Y chromosomes present at your conception, as well as your DNA; but your choices about diet and exercise are strongly influenced by societal expectations and these shape your body. (For example, in Canadian culture, boys and men are encouraged to eat heartily and to work hard to develop their upper body strength. Women, meanwhile, are more often encouraged to count the calories of every mouthful and to focus their food intake and exercise on achieving the thinnest possible physique.)

If you had been born an upper class female in medieval China, your feet may have been bound in childhood, severely reducing your ability to walk (this practice continued into the twentieth century). If you had been born male in some parts of Australia, your face, body, and penis may have been scarred at puberty as part of your initiation into manhood. In Canadian culture, some of our gender expectations are much less drastic (pink and blue baby blankets seem quite innocuous by comparison), but they can be equally powerful and potentially damaging. Consider the number of men who are killed by homicide or suicide and the number of women who live in poverty or in abusive relationships. Neither women nor men are immune to the consequences of gender in our society.

Historically, it was generally believed that men and women behaved differently because of their biological capacities. Textbooks used to discuss the "sexual division of labour" and "sex roles." The implication was that men and women were *opposite sexes*, which explained why women, for example, became nurses while men became doctors. The belief was that because sex was predetermined at conception and could not be changed (even those who have opted to surgically and hormonally change their bodies to resemble the other sex cannot change their chromosomes), the division of labour had to be biologically based. Thus, people believed that the sexual division of labour was unchangeable, a "natural" outcome of biological differences. In other words, they believed that "anatomy is destiny."

Since that time, many scholars interested in studying men and women have come to adopt the term *gender* to distinguish between the biological components (or *sex*) and the cultural components of human behaviour. Using the term *gender* instead of *sex* is a method of highlighting the reality that much of the division of labour—indeed, many of the challenges and obstacles that women and men face—result from cultural constraints rather than "natural" biological limitations. While it is obviously true that women cannot produce sperm, and men cannot grow fetuses or breastfeed infants, it is not biology that has kept women from becoming politicians, engineers, and priests, nor men from nursing the sick, rearing children, and fully participating in unpaid domestic work. The shift from the term *sex* to *gender* meant that the subordinate position of women could be challenged, not as an unfortunate side effect of a biological reality, but as a cultural creation based on gender.

Moreover, as some of the previous examples illustrate, many societal opportunities and challenges are also gendered. Getting a job at a construction site is harder for a woman than for a man; and getting promotions despite taking parental leave is harder for a man than for a woman. But these difficulties are not caused by the person's *sex*: the presence of ovaries or testes does not create these obstacles. Instead, the social construction of gender influences many of these social experiences. As a society, we create constraining normative expectations based on gender: expectations that say men who make their children their first priority are not good managers and that women are ill-equipped to handle the heavy labour required on a construction site. In short, in addition to individuals being gendered, the world we live in is also gendered. The combination of factors shapes our experiences.

In recent decades, the differences between *sex* (biology) and *gender* (culture) have been studied by scholars and taught in classrooms. The dichotomy has been particularly relevant for **sexual orientation** and **heteronormativity**. Many researchers now agree that while women and men do differ biologically, the social construction of gender determines the patterns of opportunity and experience that shape their lives. We learn those cultural expectations and regularly interact in gendered ways. Our lives are structured by gendered institutions, and we choose how to participate as gendered beings.

But more recently, the argument about the terms *sex* and *gender* has grown even more complex. Those scholars focusing on gender have challenged and largely rejected the notion that gender is a stable property of individuals, proposing instead that gender is fluid, resulting from both interaction and social context. In fact, some theorists argue that rather than residing within individuals, gender is actually a "system of social properties within society that constitutes people as different in socially significant ways and organizes relations of inequality on the basis of the difference" (Ridgeway and Smith-Lovin, 1999, p. 247). The very definition of gender is an issue for debate that we will explore throughout this text.

During this same period, academics have started exploring issues surrounding biological sex more deeply as well. They have noted that a surprisingly large proportion of infants are born with chromosomal or anatomical anomalies that make the determination of their sex problematic. While estimates vary, approximately 4 percent of infants have some sex-based anomalies—that is, they don't fit perfectly into the categories male or female. In addition, about 17 of every 1000 newborn infants have sufficient ambiguity to be identified as **intersexed** (Fausto-Sterling, 2000). For example, some people are born with additional X and/or Y chromosomes, some have ambiguous genitalia, and some have reproductive organs that do not match their chromosomes. In general, when these situations arise, the doctors and families seek to identify the dominant features of the infant and then assign the baby a sex, either boy or girl. Following this sex assignment, medical interventions may need to be used to refashion the person's body to fit the category. In essence, human decisions and medical interventions result in the recreation of the sex of the person. Thus, for some people, sex is also a cultural and medical construction from the moment of birth, when we are designated pink or blue.

Examining the contributions of biology and culture leads us to re-enter the nature/nurture debate, the age-old question that asks how much of who we are is predetermined by our physiology and how much results from our social experiences. This debate is also relevant for those who asked questions about the biological origins of sexuality: Is one "born gay" or does one "become gay"? For a time, the nurture argument was in ascendancy. The gender experts promoted the idea that humans were infinitely pliable and that men and women could be shaped entirely through environment, experience, and interaction.

To support this argument, they drew evidence from real experiences in one profound and well-known case study of a child whose birth name was Bruce Reimer. He and his twin brother, Brian, were born in 1968 in small-town Manitoba. Bruce's experience was a terrible example of what can result from a misunderstanding of sex and gender. And his case was used to justify the sex reassignment of other infants.

As described in the biography *As Nature Made Him: The Boy who was Raised as a Girl* (2000) by John Colapinto, the penis of Brian, a biologically male infant, was accidentally destroyed in a botched circumcision. Not knowing what to do, his family, with the support of their doctors, turned to a medical expert in the area of sex and gender. The expert's advice: turn Bruce into Brenda. This was to be accomplished by doing further surgeries, beginning when he was two (over a year after the circumcision attempt), to make his body parts resemble those of a female, providing the child with hormone treatments to "feminize" him, and by interacting with him forever and always as a girl. (This leaves aside the whole debate of how a particular reproductive part, the penis, is seen to symbolize the maleness of the person, or the issue of how much of a person's gender is established prior to the age of two.) So Brenda was dressed in girl's clothing and encouraged to play with dolls. As Brenda grew, the experts claimed that sex and gender were separate: a perfectly content woman could be produced from a human male through the power of medical technology and unrelenting feminine socialization. The case was written up in textbooks and journals to prove the power of nurture over nature.

But the experts were wrong. Brenda was miserable. He knew something wasn't right but had no idea what. The experts had insisted that the child never be told the truth about the situation, believing this would interfere with Brenda's ability to function as a woman. When Brenda was a teenager, his parents were unwilling to keep the secret any longer. In the face of Brenda's suffering, they told him the truth. From then on, Brenda was no more. He renamed himself David. He refused to pretend that he was a woman and opted instead to live life as a man. In a public interview, David said his overwhelming emotion that day was relief! He no longer had to wonder about what was wrong with him. He has since undergone more surgeries to "de-feminize" his body, and as an adult he married a woman and fathered his adopted children. Unfortunately, David became deeply depressed and committed suicide in 2004. The hardships David faced may have contributed to his early death. But his life experience offers proof that sex and gender are related—there is a critical nexus that cannot be ignored.

However, it must be noted that throughout his young life, David as Brenda was subjected to regular physical examinations of his body and genitals, undergoing intensive psychotherapy and surgeries and taking a regimen of pharmaceuticals. Any child undergoing such intrusive procedures, especially without knowing the reason why, would perceive that "there is something wrong with me." Continuous medical intervention has a profound impact on one's sense of self and body. As Colapinto points out (2000), many other aspects of David's story—such as homophobia, peer pressure, depression, family dynamics, and the power of medical professionals—likely played a role in shaping his life, but they are beyond the scope of this text. This case therefore doesn't actually *prove* that David's ongoing struggle with his assigned gender identity arose from some underlying sense of maleness, that his true biological sex was at war with his medically created gender, or that nature always trumps nurture in the arena of sex and gender. But it offers strong evidence that medical and social reassignment are not sufficient to prove that nurture can overwhelm nature either. What is clear is that we still don't fully understand the various contributions of nature and nurture to a person's gendered self.

We are not able to solve the mysteries of human development and the **nature/nurture debate** in this chapter. But keep in mind that, through environment, experience, and socialization, culture has an enormous influence on who we become and how we live our lives. As sociologists of gender, these are the mysteries that we continue to explore.

THE GENDER PERSPECTIVE: MULTIPLE DIMENSIONS

It would be simple if all sociologists and social scientists agreed on one theory of society—one overarching explanation that enabled us to understand why our social world unfolds the way it does. But this is not the case. A multitude of theories attempt to explain social phenomena, many of them contradictory. Even if we narrow our focus from the broader social world to consider only gender arrangements, we still find several theories. In part, this abundance results from differing research approaches: some scholars work to understand gender patterns through studying the actions and choices of individuals (a **micro approach**), while others seek to understand the larger structures that constrain and guide individuals (a **macro approach**).

A fruitful avenue of research and understanding that scholars are increasingly pursuing, and one that we utilize in this book, is a multi-dimensional approach known as the **gender perspective**. According to the gender perspective paradigm, gender should not be considered simply as a stable property of individuals that results either from biology or from childhood experience and then remains largely unchanged throughout life. Instead, the gender perspective theory acknowledges that while gender does shape individuals, it is also constructed and then reconstructed throughout their lives. In other words, beyond the **individual dimension**, we also *do gender* as we interact with others. That is, we act in gendered ways according to our perceptions of what is most appropriate in a given situation, even if that way of behaving doesn't reflect our personal views. In addition, we negotiate gendered interactions with others, as they too navigate through their own situational demands.

Beyond doing gender on the **interactional dimension**, we also live our lives in a social world shaped by gendered **institutions**. Our governments, religions, educational systems, and economies, for example, have been organized around gender. Remember that in Canada, equal opportunity in education, the right of women to vote, and equal pay for work of equal value policies are all relatively recent phenomena; and despite these legislative changes, women still have not achieved income equality in this country.

Another aspect of this multi-dimensional understanding of gender is **socio-cultural**. Think of the socio-cultural dimension as the cultural backdrop; the symbols, norms, beliefs, values, and ideologies that define our social world. Even the language we speak has resonances that influence gender. And the media, which continually disseminates these beliefs and ideas through words and images, is a powerful contributor to our socio-cultural landscape. (Socio-cultural influences are discussed in detail in Chapters Three and Four.)

This multi-dimensional approach to studying gender can be applied to any society. Each will have its own culture and institutions; and in each, all four dimensions—individual, interactional, institutional, and socio-cultural—will influence the genders of that society's individuals. Canada is no different. While some elements of Canadian culture and influences on gender (*e.g.*, the media) are shared with other nations, some uniquely Canadian socio-cultural patterns and social institutions shape how individuals living here do gender (*e.g.*, workplace policy, family patterns, and legal structures).

Thus, the gender perspective is based on the principle that a comprehensive understanding of gender can best be accomplished by examining individual, interactional, institutional, and socio-cultural components. But the gender perspective does not imply that the four dimensions are easily separable. They are fully interconnected, since change on one dimension has both immediate and long-term effects on the others. Our gendered selves change through interactions with others. Similarly, gendered institutions change as interactions and individuals define new ways of understanding and social practices. This book considers all four dimensions and their interconnections so that readers can gain insight into the complexities of gender and the profound impact it has on our lives, as well as the ongoing ways in which we participate in gender construction.

GENDER ON THE SOCIO-CULTURAL DIMENSION

A wealth of literature discusses the ways gender operates in the socio-cultural realm. The first section of this book explores the nature of our social landscape. By way of introduction to this dimension, we will consider the concept of patriarchy.

Most people have heard of **patriarchy**, the idea that society is hierarchically organized, with males dominating most of the positions of power and wealth and a disproportionate number of females filling subordinate positions with significantly less power and wealth. However, the concept of patriarchy is more complex than that. For example, in Canada, women and men are considered equal before the law. The **Charter of Rights and Freedoms** is designed to protect people from discrimination based on sex, and we readily acknowledge that spousal abuse is a crime. But does this mean that patriarchy does not exist here? There is a great deal of counter-evidence. For instance, the leaders of our governments, corporations, religious organizations, and the military are predominantly men. Very few women hold the ultimate decision-making power in these institutions. Moreover, women who have attained a degree of power and influence (at the time of writing, businesswoman and politician Belinda Stronach is an example) are often evaluated and denigrated based on their sex rather than their abilities. Canadian history is rooted in patriarchy. Less than 100 years ago, women weren't even allowed to vote, let alone participate in government. They were not even considered legal persons!

Even as we try to transform patriarchy by instituting legal equalities, it persists. A patriarchy is a value-based societal system that allocates people into specific positions based on an underlying value system and ideology. In this respect, patriarchy is not simply about "men oppressing women." Canada can be patriarchal even though many women would not accept the claim that they are oppressed, and even though most men would deny that they oppress anyone.

Perhaps the concept of patriarchal society is easier to understand if we compare it to a caste society based on racial and ethnic heritage. The **apartheid** laws of South Africa, which were not truly dismantled until the 1990s, were based on the ideology that some races of people were superior to others, and thus they were afforded specific privileges. Superiority was based on perceived racial characteristics, most obviously skin colour. The system gave people with light skin opportunities to live and work in relative freedom, while those with darker skin were restricted to locations and occupations with severely limited opportunities. The system was based on an ideology of white supremacy. Even though many light-skinned people did not directly oppress their darker-skinned fellow citizens, they still benefited from the system. Similarly, even though many Canadian men do not oppress women, they still benefit from patriarchal systems.

In his book *The Gender Knot: Unraveling Our Patriarchal Legacy* (1997), sociologist Allan Johnson discusses the continued existence of patriarchy in North American society. According to Johnson, patriarchy is a system that privileges males over females and entrenches structures which create and maintain the differential positions of the two sexes. It is built on the ideology of male supremacy and the core values of control and domination.

> It is like a tree rooted in the core principles of control, competition, dominance, and hierarchy. Its trunk is the major institutional patterns of social life as shaped by the roots—family, economy, politics, religion, education, music, and the arts. The branches—first the larger and then progressively smaller—are the actual communities, organizations, groups and other systems in which we live our lives, from cities and towns to parishes, marriages, and families. In all of this, individuals are the leaves who make possible the life of the tree and draw their form and life from it. (1997, p.14)

If our roots are control and dominance, these values will be reflected throughout every aspect of society. Johnson argues that the women's movement has been quite successful at rearranging the outer branches and leaves; but that the roots remain intact. We have not begun to alter the values that place us in competition with one another and drive us to subordinate others in our quest for control.

Johnson argues that patriarchy exists in North America. He says this socio-cultural landscape is **male-dominated, male-identified**, and **male-centred**. Canadian society is male-dominated in the sense that most institutions in Canada have far more men than women in powerful positions. This dominance can be readily observed in news coverage, the business section of newspapers, and photographs of federal or provincial leaders. Canada is also male-centred because we focus much more attention on the activities of men than we do on the activities of women. For example, if you watch the evening news or read the front page a newspaper, you will discover that there are "stories primarily about men and what they have done, or haven't done or what they have to say about either . . . if there's a crisis, what we see is what men did to create it and how men dealt with it" (Johnson, 1997, p.8). When women and their activities are covered in the media, commentary on their appearance and/or relationships is common and considered informative (for example, consider the media coverage of Belinda Stronach's political and personal choices). In the news this week, as we write this chapter, there is a story about a female Federal Cabinet minister who has been charged with very serious blunders (offering help with immigration issues in return for free pizzas!). You may see this as proof that our culture does pay attention to women's activities; but the coverage of this situation has referred to her as a "grandmother," even though being a grandmother is irrelevant to the issue at hand. The news rarely reports on men's familial status. (Are the other Cabinet Ministers grandfathers? Do we care?)

Test this for yourself. Is the media male-centred? When women and their activities are highlighted, what factors are included in the story? Do all the media outlets cover the stories in the same way?

Canadian society is also male-identified, because "core cultural ideas about what is considered good, desirable, preferable, or normal are associated with how we think about men and masculinity. The simplest example of this is the still widespread use of male pronouns and nouns to represent people in general" (Johnson, 1997, pp 5-6). Until fairly recently, the common practice when teaching medical students in Canada and the United States about the human anatomy was to use the male body as standard. Male figures and their systems (*e.g.*, digestive, circulatory) were used almost two-thirds of the time, while female figures were only shown 11 percent of the time. The only time female figures were used consistently was in discussions of reproductive systems, when approximately 45 percent of the images portrayed females. In essence, male anatomy was the norm by which humans were to be understood, and female anatomy only needed to be discussed in terms of its reproductive capacities (Giacommi *et al.*,1986). But the American National Institutes for Health took a stand on this issue by creating the "Office for Research on Women's Health." In doing so, they have encouraged new funding and research that focuses on women, rather than allowing medical research to remain male-identified (see http://orwh.od.nih.gov/). Another Canadian example showing both male identification and the movement away from it is found in the legal test for reasonableness. Courts are sometimes called upon to determine whether an individual's actions can be defended on the basis that they were "reasonable" in the circumstances. For many years, this was judged expressly on what the "reasonable man" would have done. But Canadian courts have recognized the limitations and biases built into such an approach. For example, it was particularly meaningless in determining what was reasonable for a woman suffering from battered women's syndrome. Thus, the courts now apply a "reasonable person" standard (see also Chapter Thirteen).

GENDER ON THE INDIVIDUAL DIMENSION

Even though some theorists argue that studying sex and gender differences reifies a misleading dichotomy, most sociologists and other social scientists with an interest in this area focus on asking questions about gender: what makes us gendered beings? How do we begin as biological organisms and grow into men and women, knowing how to act in ways considered appropriate to our gender? These are the types of questions about gender on the individual dimension raised and addressed in this text.

We know that socialization and interaction with others has an enormous influence on gender. If we raise our daughters to nurture others and our sons to strive for success, we recreate specific gender patterns. For this reason, until recently, a social psychological explanation of gender was widely accepted. Sex and gender identity was considered a relatively stable property of all individuals: nature and nurture combining to make gendered people, their lives reflecting this property. However, academics have openly questioned the "stability" of this identity. They now maintain that our "selfhood" evolves over the life course, and our gendered conception of "self" evolves along with it. While understanding early processes that lead to the development of gender identities is important, it is no more important than understanding how our **gender identities** change over time. Thus, sociologists see gender identity as an evolving, relational, situational, and fluid quality that intersects with other identities that shape the self. Beyond the issue of gender as a stable property, a further criticism of the earlier approach is the assumption that there is a specific set of qualities that define womanhood and manhood. The more academics study humans, the more variation they find. Thus, we no longer consider people who do not conform to societal expectations of gender "appropriate" behaviour as misfits who failed to achieve the appropriate sex identity. Rather, we recognize that there is a plurality of masculinities and femininities.

Joseph Pleck's now-classic work *The Myth of Masculinity* (1981) challenged one conceptualization of gender: the widely accepted belief that successful men and women developed appropriate **sex role identities** and that those with insecure identities were prone to engage in harmful activities (*e.g*, violent behaviour or promiscuity). Pleck argued that our understanding of sex identity was flawed. Failure to achieve the appropriate sex role identity was not an adequate explanation for many of the negative behaviours people engage in. Instead, he argued that the traditional "masculine sex role identity" is contradictory. For example, boys are encouraged to develop physical prowess; but men are more likely to be rewarded for intellectual and social skills. So which should a young male strive for? He also stated that the qualities of the male sex role identity are often beyond individual control. Living up to the expectation that a man should be a good provider for his family is largely dependent on external factors (*e.g.*, the economy, the unemployment rate, his race and age). Thus, the masculine sex identity is not achievable for many males. Men face great sex role strain as they strive to accomplish the impossible and then are judged as failures if they do not attain it.

According to Pleck, as long as we accept the idea of a stable sex identity, men who don't live up to expectation will tend to blame themselves, rather than challenging the paradigm itself. But refuting the paradigm promotes a new, more positive, understanding of masculinity, one with a wider range of behaviours that result from situational adaptation and social approval rather than an innate psychological need. Our gendered selves reflect normative expectations in concert with many other factors, including situational context, institutional gender regimes, and the intersection of sex with other statuses (such as ethnicity, age, social class, dis/ability, etc.).While Pleck's work is dated, it marks an important transition between two ways of thinking about gender on the individual dimension. More recent scholars have continued to theorize about the nature of gender and identity (see for example, Connell, 1987; Butler, 1999; Lorber, 1994).

Social constructionists have refocused our attention on the complexities of humans as gendered beings. Cynthia Eller, for example, has written an intriguing book that addresses some of these issues. In *Am I a Woman? A Skeptic's Guide to Gender* (2003), she discusses the ways people strive to live up to or resist societal expectations and how the emotions, actions, and judgments of others influence them. If our chromosomes and anatomy determine our sex, she asks, why do many of us spend so much time, energy, and often money trying to live up to the expectations placed on this biologically determined category? If we are born a particular sex, why do we have to prove our membership in that group?

Eller acknowledges that, physiologically, she fits into the category of "woman." She menstruates and has borne and breastfed babies. But she still questions what it is to be a woman:

> If being a woman is simply a matter of what genitalia I am sporting, why has it been so hard to pull it off gracefully? If I sprang from the womb genetically programmed to be sweet and considerate towards people, then why did I have to . . . learn how to encourage a boy to talk about his own interests while out on a date? And why have there been so many missteps along the way? For something so apparently natural as my sex, femaleness has turned out to be a depressingly huge and tiresome identity to carry around. (pp.5–6)

In exploring the question of what constitutes womanhood and how people come to see themselves as women, Eller notes that most people think about the sexes based on physiology, emotions, and actions. In each of these three areas, however, she documents the wide variations that exist: women with high levels of testosterone and men with observable amounts of breast tissue; men who are sensitive and women who are not; women who authoritatively direct large companies and men who lovingly nurture others. In short, she argues that our assumptions about gender are based on stereotypes. When we look at real people, we see that women and men are much more similar than different. In fact, she suggests that most of us, herself included, do not live up to our society's gender expectations, perhaps physically, emotionally, or in our actions. But Eller doesn't regard falling short of an unrealistic standard as a problem unless we become demoralized by perceiving this as failure. Instead, she argues that

> There's something really pitiful about us all judging ourselves against ideals of femininity and masculinity that, in my opinion, we've mostly invented out of whole cloth (or which, at least, don't truly come "naturally" to most of us, but have to be trained in). If we really feel compelled to measure ourselves against some standard so we can bemoan how unworthy we are, the least we could do is pick out something less trifling than our percentage of body fat or the width of our shoulders. (pp. 135–36)

She argues that trying to fit ourselves, or to pressure others to fit, into narrowly defined gender categories is harmful for all people, especially when the categories are not regarded as equal. Eller suggests that we would be more content if we could all be just humans without the pressures to live up to or down to a specific set of gendered expectations.

Despite Cynthia Eller's argument, however, most people do see themselves as gendered beings and do act accordingly. This has profound implications for how we see ourselves (on the individual dimension) and how we interact with others.

GENDER ON THE INTERACTIONAL DIMENSION

Even though the individual dimension of gender is important, we must also acknowledge that the gendered self, created in part through socialization, is not the only factor that contributions to gendered behaviours. We also *do gender*. What sociologists mean by *doing* gender is that we take cues from the social context and decide how to act and react based on our perceptions of what is appropriate in that specific situation. And, of course, sometimes we deliberately flout norms of "appropriate" behaviour.

We do gender every time we interact with other human beings, and sometimes we choose to highlight our membership in a specific gender category. One of the authors did gender recently when she had a flat tire out on the highway in the middle of winter. She acted out the part of the helpless woman who had no idea of how to use a jack or attach a spare tire. A man, also doing gender, came to her rescue (in an 18-wheeled Mack truck, rather than on a dashing white horse, but you can't have everything!) and changed the tire for her. He too was doing gender as he exhibited strength, protectiveness, and resourcefulness (the author's jack was defective). Had the author been a strong young man standing helplessly at the side of the road, it is unlikely that the trucker would have stopped. In conversation, he actually explained that in helping the author—the stranded woman—he was proving that most truckers were actually true gentleman and not uncaring, beer-drinking men as the stereotypes might suggest. In this tire-changing situation, the normative expectations of gender were recreated.

Even though the woman with the flat was anything but helpless, and the trucker was probably cold due to the winter weather and frustrated by the broken jack, he chose to live up to the normative expectations placed on him by virtue of being a man.

In the discussion that follows, we explore some of the most stereotypical ways in which people do gender in Canada, including bridal showers, bars, and sports teams. But don't misunderstand: people do gender in an infinite variety of ways. For this reason, many academics use plural forms to describe masculinities and femininities when they write about gender. In this section of the book, we have chosen these highly "traditional" examples because they are obvious and the gendered nature of the activities is unmistakable. In later sections of the book, we will explore masculinities and femininities much more deeply.

Canadian sociologist David Cheal (1989) discusses the ways women do gender at bridal showers. He suggests that "stereotypes are mapped onto the sexes from the typical activities that men and women engage in" (p. 87). He starts by explaining that we often find ourselves doing gender because of our statuses—for example, women often work in nurturing and service occupations. Thus, by doing their jobs, they are engaging in stereotypical behaviours and recreating the idea that women are nurturing. Nurturing may not be an underlying quality of a particular woman; rather, it may be simply a reflection of required actions in a specific situation. Cheal's explanations reflect ideas developed by Erving Goffman and the symbolic interactionists. Cheal suggests that "gender membership is neither an inherent trait of individuals, nor is it a property of social systems. It is, rather, accomplished during interaction. It occurs whenever an individual's claims (explicit or implicit) to belong to a gender category are accepted by others" (p. 88). Through interpersonal interaction and acknowledgement of our gender membership, we recreate gender based statuses and expectations.

In his study, Cheal examines the gendered nature of the social interactions that take place during traditional bridal showers. Showers have long been held before women marry and around the time of the birth of a new child to celebrate a woman's new status as either wife or mother. These showers are typically single-sex occasions, where women celebrate together and provide the guest of honour with gifts that will assist her with her new roles. Women do gender as they participate in the rituals, such as gift-giving. They recreate gendered stereotypes about women's responsibility for maintaining the family home, nurturing, and feeding family members by giving gifts such as kitchen appliances, bedding, and furniture. Men are rarely present at these showers recreating the idea that men need not be involved in activities related to homemaking and child-rearing. Certainly, rituals like gift-giving at an all-woman shower reinforce women's solidarity; but at the same time, they confirm the normative expectations of women as caregivers.

Cheal emphasizes that these gender rituals, created and expressed through interaction, do not arise from socialization into a gender category; instead they arise through our willingness to conform to the expectations of gender membership in order to be accepted by the group.

Since the time of Cheal's study, there has been an increase in popularity of showers at which both men and women attend. It appears that the activities and rituals, and the gifts exchanged, at these events are significantly different from those at all-female showers. Consider your own experiences at bridal and baby showers. Have you noticed different attitudes towards women at showers celebrating an impending wedding rather than those celebrating a new birth? Have you observed differences between single-sex and mixed-sex showers? Have you attended a shower for someone who is gay or lesbian? If so, are the rituals and gifts different? Are your friends more likely to have "stagettes" than bridal showers? As the Canadian social context changes, the multi-dimensional approach to gender posits that we should expect to see changes in such traditional "gendered" activities as bridal and baby showers.

In their studies "Hegemonic Masculinity, Friendship, and Group Formation in an Athletic Subculture" (Harvey, 1999) and "Negotiating Masculinities in American Drinking Cultures" (West, 2001), Harvey and West consider ways in which men do gender. Both authors note that masculinities are variable. But one form, **hegemonic masculinity**, tends to be acted out in certain all-male environments, such as sports teams, fraternities, and navy units. Hegemonic masculinity refers to the form of masculinity performed by cultural or group leaders, those who are most dominant. This type of masculinity oppresses those who don't conform to its standard.

After studying fraternities and military groups, West argues that drinking behaviours are one of the key ways in which hegemonic masculinity is enacted in some subcultures. She notes that there has been an historical link between masculinity and alcohol in American culture. "By 1830 hard liquor consumption averaged 9.5 gallons a year for every American male over fourteen, and by 1894, New York had one saloon for every 200 residents" (2001, p. 372). Alcohol continues to be a part of American life. As West describes, "what it means to be a man in society gets worked out in male alcohol use" (p. 372). By holding their liquor or consuming copious amounts without getting sick, men exhibit their masculinity. In particular, she argues that activities associated with alcohol—aggression, games, jokes, naming, and sexual negotiation—are all means for showing masculinity. Those who participate in these traditions are constructing their masculinity. Jokes are used to affirm sexual prowess and solidarity, especially when they denigrate women and people who don't identify with heteronormative culture, including gays, lesbians, bisexuals, transsexuals, and transgenders. Holding your own in a fight or attacking those who aren't part of the hegemonic group reaffirms this dominant form of masculinity.

Harvey's examination of a men's baseball team revealed similar patterns. The core group on the team exhibited hegemonic masculinity: they were strong baseball players, heavy drinkers, and loud and domineering partiers. Throughout the season, the central group on the team—that is, those not in the core group but who wanted to be accepted—tended to do masculinity in ways that would enhance their status: for example, by drinking with the core group or describing heterosexual exploits. In acting out these parts, they were often accepted by the core members and given a nickname, a symbol of their status. Other members of the team who did not participate in these activities and who did not successfully undertake hegemonic masculine displays were largely ignored, and some dropped off the team before the end of the season.

As these studies show, both sexes *do gender* in specific social contexts. We interact with others in ways that may enhance our position or undermine it. The examples above focus on "traditional" versions of masculinity and femininity in Canadian society, but it is important to acknowledge that many people choose not do gender in the ways societal norms seem to require. In fact, they resist the common notions of gender and present themselves in ways that challenge societal standards. Nonetheless, whatever our choices, to conform or to resist, our performance of gender plays a central part in determining the outcome of the interaction.

Of course, while we are theoretically free to choose the ways in which we want to do gender, our interactions take place within and are constrained by gendered contexts.

GENDER ON THE INSTITUTIONAL DIMENSION

As you may remember from an earlier sociology course, social institutions can be defined as "social practices that are regularly and continuously repeated, are sanctioned and maintained by social norms" (Abercrombie, 1984, p. 124). In most cases, institutions evolve as societies find ways to cope with ongoing needs and concerns. Systems of government evolve, for example, to make and enforce rules about how citizens may live their lives. Economies evolve to ensure that goods and services are produced and distributed. Education systems are created to enable younger members of society to learn the values and skills deemed necessary to become active members within society.

In fact, some sociologists have argued that gender itself is a social institution (see Patricia Yancey Martin's 2004 work, for example). Gender certainly fits the definition of a social institution. As Martin argues, "Framing gender as an institution is beneficial in drawing attention to its multiple features—ideology, practices, constraints, power—and affirming its complexities and multifacetedness. Recognition of this condition assures scholars that they need not 'study it all' and, also, gives those who work only on particular institutional features a framework for connecting their efforts to the bigger picture" (2004, p. 1264). While we don't use this conception—gender as an institution—in this book, preferring the multi-dimension perspective, Martin's argument can certainly provide a useful avenue for exploration.

Canadian institutions are unique: they are both reflections and components of the Canadian socio-cultural and physical landscape, and they shape the way in which we do gender in this country. For our purposes, the critical factor of institutions that we must examine is their gendered nature: how do Canadian social institutions create and maintain gender patterns within our society? And, more important, how have they evolved to alter gender arrangements? Some scholars use the concept of the **gender regime** to address these issues. A gender regime is the combination of features of an institution that create, maintain, or undermine specific gendered practices. In the final section of the text, we will discuss four key social institutions: family, work, law, and religion. Here we will examine the Canadian educational institution to illustrate how a gender regime works.

The two authors of this text have been involved in education, as both students and teachers, for over seven decades, in five provinces. We have seen fairly remarkable changes in gender patterns during this time span. In the 1960s, when we first entered school, very little attention was paid to gender and the curriculum. In Ontario and New Brunswick, children entered our schools through separate doors: one for the boys and one for the girls. We learned to read from a book called *Fun with Dick and Jane*. Dick had many fun adventures with his dog Spot, while Jane often helped her mother with the dishes or played quietly with her cat, Puff. Dad went off to work while mom stayed home. They seemed decidedly white, middle class, and heterosexual. We were too young to notice, and maybe the teachers were unaware, but the curriculum was sex-stereotyped. Traditional ideas of gender were recreated, and gendered stereotypes were not questioned. Also noteworthy is the homogeneity reflected in having the same book taught and the same school architecture used in two regions of the country. It wasn't until the second wave of feminism gained momentum that many of the gendered features of education were challenged in Canada.

A large body of research accumulated during the 1980s and 1990s that clearly showed the multitude of ways in which the gendered characteristics of education created obstacles for girls that boys did not face. The two well-known experts in this area are Myra Sadker and David Sadker. In their book *Failing at Fairness: How Our Schools Cheat Girls* (1994), the Sadkers discussed a great deal of research—their own as well the work of other scholars—that examined the negative impact of education on girls. In the opening paragraph, they commented on the fact that boys and girls learning in the same classroom with the same teacher did not receive the same education:

> From grade school through graduate school female students are more likely to be invisible members of classrooms. Teachers interact with males more frequently, ask them better questions, and give them more precise and helpful feedback. Over the course of years the uneven distribution of teacher time, energy, attention, and talent, with boys getting the lion's share, takes its toll on girls. Since gender bias is not a noisy problem, most people are unaware of the secret sexist lessons and the quiet losses they engender. (p. 1)

Throughout the book, the authors document the many ways in which this **discrimination** unfolds and the consequences that result. Examples include:

- overt sexism and discrimination by teachers in classrooms and lecture halls;
- sexual harassment that occurs in informal educational settings (*e.g.,* cafeterias, school buses, residences, and fraternities);
- the **micro-inequities** that undermine the confidence and abilities of female students by making them invisible or downplaying their educational accomplishments;
- the structure of standardized testing tools that favour male test-takers.

The Sadkers concluded that while great progress had been made in reducing sexism in formal curriculum materials, there was still a long way to go before education ceases to disadvantage girls and young women. And although there are now more women in post-secondary and professional schools than ever before, there is still much room for improvement.

Canadian sociologist Judith Blackwell (1998) studied the experiences of women in universities and points to a similar cause for concern. Specifically, she found that overt sexism still exists in some classrooms; that sexual oppression from other students was not rare; and that obstacles associated with family responsibilities prevented some women from continuing and completing their education. Blackwell stated that "the challenge to universities is to assure students that their problems will be taken seriously . . . Without overly dramatizing the situation, universities must bring gender related issues to the forefront and communicate the message that policies are in place to deal with them" (1998, p. 71).

A new debate on gender and education that provides a different perspective on the issue gained attention in the late 1990s. The new concern is that schools are failing boys. An increasing number of research projects focus on boys and their lack of success in school. Evidence is accumulating that shows boys are suffering: high dropout rates, low achievement scores, frequent discipline problems, and increased identification of learning disabilities. Some people are arguing that boys are the new gender problem. In his review of this literature, Marcus Weaver-Hightower (2003) calls it the **boy turn**. What he means by this is that a new wave of scholarship has emerged. Some of it is a backlash against curricular changes that seem to have improved education for girls. There is no shortage of "proof" that suggests boys are struggling, and there is increasing pressure to create a new curriculum to encourage success for boys (one of our students described this as a new movement to "guyify" education). Some of the conclusions that have been drawn from these patterns are fairly grim. They suggest that if we work to improve the classroom experience for girls, boys will pay the price. Meanwhile, if we work to change the curriculum to enhance the opportunities for boys to learn, girls will be disadvantaged. But there is no reason to think that there is a need to play off girls and boys, or that good education for one must sacrifice good education for the other.

Because education is such a critical institution—it is charged with the task of preparing our youngest citizens to actively participate in our society—its gendered nature is a matter for concern. The solutions to the concerns that have been raised are not simple. Some have suggested that we should return to a model of **single-sex schools**, where boys and girls learn separately (an approach already being provided on a small scale in some communities, such as Calgary). Others argue that this kind of segregation is a step backwards, a step that may result in the institutionalization of a new gender regime.

The preliminary explorations in this introductory chapter are intended to show that gender does operate on a variety of dimensions. It shapes our sense of self, influences the way we interact with others, structures the social institutions, and colours the cultural landscape upon which all social life is based.

This text explores in detail these aspects of gender and considers their ramifications for the individual and the Canadian society. In the first section, the chapters on sex differences and similarities, normative expectations, language and media examine the socio-cultural landscape. The second section's chapters on childhood, adulthood, and intersections with other statuses study gender on the individual dimension. In the third section, chapters on interaction, sexuality, and power examine gender on the interactional dimension. And in the fourth section, chapters on family, work, law, and religion consider gender on the institutional dimension. As emphasized throughout this introduction, however, such divisions should not be regarded as distinct and separate compartments of information. In our view, gender and doing gender operate on all dimensions at the same time, with each influencing the others. For example, sufficient change on the individual dimension is likely to affect institutions in this country; alterations in the structure of the education or legal systems will likely bring about some change for individuals.

We invite you, throughout the book, to consider and challenge the illustrations and examples provided and think about whether and how gender shapes you and the society in which you live.

CHAPTER SUMMARY: KEY POINTS

1. While humans have sex-based characteristics, due to chromosomes, anatomy, and hormones, they also have gender-based qualities that influence their opportunities and experiences.

2. In order to fully understand the impact of gender on our lives, we need to recognize that gender operates on four different dimensions within our society: individual, interactional, institutional, and socio-cultural dimension.

3. The socio-cultural dimension of society is like a landscape upon which all action occurs. It consists of our values, norms, beliefs, and ideologies and is transmitted through our language and mass media.

4. Patriarchy is a sex-based, hierarchical, socio-cultural landscape that privileges males over females. Canadian society has patriarchal roots, though our Charter of Rights and Freedoms has made discrimination based on sex unacceptable.

5. On the individual dimension, people internalize gender. There is some debate as to whether they develop a stable gender identity or whether gender is a fluid quality that is performed in interaction with others. The authors of this text recognize the importance of interaction and the situational context for influencing the ways we enact gender.

6. Whether they regard gender as fluid or stable, most people see themselves as being gendered, and this awareness influences their self-perceptions and their assessments of others. Eller argues we should actively resist gender categories because of their limitations.

7. On the dimension of interaction, we **do gender**. That is, when we communicate with others, we are influenced by our perceptions of their gender and our own.

8. **Hegemonic masculinity** is a particular kind of gender behaviour performed by men in powerful positions. It is acted out in many environments, including sports teams and bars.

9. Social institutions evolve over time to meet the needs of a social community. Most institutions exhibit a **gender regime** that creates, maintains, and/or undermines gendered patterns.

10. The education system in Canada, as an institution, has exhibited a sexist gender regime where girls and boys have inequitable experiences in the classroom. Efforts have been made to eliminate sexism and have met with some success, though there are still problems faced by both girls and boys.

DISCUSSION QUESTIONS

1. Why is the possession of a penis seen as central to the life of a boy or man in our society? Why was it assumed that Bruce Reimer would be better off living as a girl because he did not have this anatomical part?

2. What gender-based explanations can you think of to explain why there is such a significant difference in suicide rates (higher for men) and poverty rates (higher for women)?

3. Do you think single-sex schools would or do solve the problems boys and girls face in their ability to learn in school? What are the arguments for seeing this kind of gendered arrangement as a "step forward" or a "step backward"?

4. Given what you know of the four dimensions of gender, think briefly about how these dimensions are reflected in your life and experience. How is heteronormativity created or maintained on each of these dimensions?

5. Think of examples when you "do gender." On a first date? At a job interview? Why do some situations encourage us to engage in this behaviour? When and how do you resist "doing gender" by ignoring societal expectations?

KEY TERMS

apartheid

boy turn

Charter of Rights and
   Freedoms

discrimination

gender

gender identity

gender perspective

gender regime

hegemonic masculinity

heteronormativity

individual dimension

institutional dimension

interactional dimension

intersex

macro approach

male-centred

male-dominated

male-identified

micro approach

micro-inequities

nature *vs.* nurture debate

normative expectations

patriarchy

second wave of feminism

sex

sex role identity

sexual orientation

single-sex schools

socio-cultural landscape

Gender on the Socio-Cultural Dimension

chapter two

Lenses of Gender

Very few of us think about the air we breathe or the fact that we need it for survival. Unless there is something wrong with the air or with our lungs, we usually take it for granted and barely notice the role air plays in our daily lives. Culture, for many of us, is equally invisible. We grow up in families and learn how to interact with others, how to work and play and rest, without ever really questioning why we do it this way or that way or who made the rules. Our culture is almost invisible to us—that is, unless something is wrong with it, or something marginalizes us within it.

Many students, for example, are barely aware of the socio-cultural landscape or the ways it shapes their world. For example, if you grew up in mainstream Canadian society, you probably accept the principle of democracy (the election of leaders and the right of all adults to vote) and the importance of a universal social safety net (pensions, employment insurance, and healthcare) without questioning them. These are taken-for-granted features of our Canadian socio-cultural landscape.

Gender is a major part of this landscape. Surprisingly, many people don't realize this. When the two authors told friends that we planned to write a book about gender, many, many people asked, well what is the book *really* about? There are men and there are women, so what's to talk about? They found it difficult to conceptualize their world as a gendered place, until we started pointing out some examples—features of their social context that they had never really paid attention to before. It was easier for them to recognize gender on certain dimensions—for example, thinking about the behaviour of men and women in a bar, or the opportunities and limitations for women and men in the workplace—than on others. The landscape itself, though, was still difficult to comprehend. What are the pervasive beliefs about women and men in our society? Where do these ideas come from? How are they maintained? If you grew up recently in mainstream Canada, you likely believe that women and men should have the same rights to participate in public activities like education or politics. We take this belief for granted, but we must realize that it is not universally held, that it is a part of our landscape not shared by numerous other cultures and subcultures. In the opening chapter, we spent some time discussing patriarchy because patriarchy is a particular type of socio-cultural landscape based on inequality between the sexes. We can recognize and analyze other cultural landscapes as patriarchal; but it's more challenging to actually see and critique the patriarchy in our own cultural milieu. This first section of the book focuses on three elements of the socio-cultural landscape: 1) prevailing beliefs about the innate differences and inequality between the sexes; 2) gender-based normative expectations; and 3) the cultural landscape as created by and reflected in language and the media.

Sandra Bem (1993) describes socio-cultural gender perceptions using the analogy of eyeglasses, which she calls the "lenses of gender." She argues that we are so busy looking *through* these lenses that we have difficulty looking *at* them or thinking critically about them. The two key lenses that shape gender in our culture are 1) the popular belief that men and women are innately different, and 2) a general acceptance that a degree of inequality is inevitable. Keep in mind, though, that not everyone shares these core gender lenses. But because these two notions are accepted uncritically by many people, most people ignore any counter-evidence. For this reason, students of gender must examine the knowledge and beliefs accepted in our culture—our gender lenses—as they relate to difference and inequality. We begin with a discussion of sex differences.

BIOLOGICAL SEX DIFFERENCES

The significance of biological sex differences has long been a topic of study for academic disciplines such as biology, sociology, and psychology. In part, the goal has been to unlock the mysteries of nature and nurture, to prove the real ways that the sexes differ in order to explain their differential positions in society. Many sociology of gender texts used to devote significant space to exploring and challenging what were considered significant differences. But what is becoming increasingly clear from empirical research is that the innate differences between the sexes are relatively rare and small. In fact, sociologists increasingly argue that the vast majority of differences are social in origin; thus, researchers are now paying more attention to similarities between sexes and to the construction of gender rather than to innate differences.

Inherent sex differences are in many ways obvious. The reproductive systems of human beings vary depending on their arrangement of X and Y chromosomes and their anatomical development. As explained in the introductory chapter, the notion that there are actually only two types of sexes and that everyone fits into one or the other category is faulty. Approximately 1.7 percent of humans have significant physical anomalies which makes their "categorization" into one of the two main alternatives problematic (Fausto-Sterling, 2000). However, given that over 98 percent of people do fall into the main categories, for the purposes of this discussion, we focus primarily on these two groups.

The issue considered here is the extent of similarities and differences within and between the two main groups. If we accept that most people either have ovaries or testes, vaginas or penises, we must then recognize that these two groups of people play different reproductive roles. But do these specific differences predispose people to a larger range of emotional and social differences? Are women truly better nurturers than men? Are men innately more rational than women? Is this because their reproductive capacities make them so? Many people believe the answer to these questions is yes, men and women are innately different in a whole range of behaviours and abilities, predisposing them to excel at different occupations and activities. But many of the misconceptions about biological sex differences arose as a result of faulty science or as a result of the ways that science becomes popularized and disseminated.

In her text *Biological Politics: Feminist and Anti-Feminist Perspectives* (1982), Janet Sayers explores some of the so-called "science" that has been used historically to prove that women are innately different (or inferior). One such area of research in the late nineteenth century was brain size. Doctors and researchers began to systematically autopsy corpses to try to understand the mysteries of human physiology. After examining and measuring everything, they concluded that female brains were measurably smaller than male brains. This they accepted as proof that females were not equipped to understand more complex ideas or to participate in higher education and public affairs and that they were intellectually inferior. However, after further investigation, scientists were forced to reconsider their argument. Measurements indicated that since female bodies were also smaller, the ratio of the size of the body to the size of the brain indicated that female brains were actually relatively larger and heavier than male brains! But even though scientists no longer had proof that women's brains were smaller, no scientist made the argument that females' larger brains were actually superior or that maybe men should not be active in education and politics. Since this early research, more refined measurements and studies have shown that male brains are larger than women's brains relative to body mass. More importantly, however, recent research also shows that brain size is simply not predictive of intellectual performance or ability.

A second way that science was used to justify keeping women limited to nurturing activities and out of the public realm was through theories about energy. The gist of the argument was as follows: human beings have a limited amount of energy that they expend on the activities they engage in. If this energy is squandered on unnecessary activities, then there is less available for other possibly more essential activities. Nineteenth-century medical practitioners expounding such theories accepted the notion that for women, the primary activity should be reproduction. Engaging in other activities, such as higher education, for example, would reduce their biological capacity to reproduce. Evidence to support the argument was based on the fact that educated women had fewer children (failing to consider a multitude of other factors that could explain this pattern). These beliefs were used to keep women out of schools and out of public activities.

Thus, the predominant gender lens in the late nineteenth century was that women were inferior. Scientists did research and developed theories to explain this perception and to substantiate this belief.

Since then, science has become more sophisticated. Rather than simply weighing brains or theorizing on the expenditures of energy within the human body, we have developed tools to measure much more finely a range of differences in brain function, cognition, and perception, not to mention behaviours, emotions, and abilities. As a society, Canadians also like to think that we are far more objective than nineteenth-century society. We believe that instead of searching for ways to prove the superiority of one sex, our scientists just measure the differences and seek to explain their origins without prejudice. Our current gender lens is the belief that modern science is objective and value-free, and that scientific findings apolitically support the position that women and men are significantly different beings. However, critical scholars challenge these notions, arguing that science is always political and always immersed in the socio-cultural landscape in which it is situated.

Noted philosopher Sandra Harding takes direct aim at this notion that science is apolitical in her book *The Science Question in Feminism* (1986). She argues "that despite the deeply ingrained Western cultural belief in science's intrinsic progressiveness, science today serves primarily regressive tendencies; and that the social structure of science, many of its applications and technologies, its modes of defining research problems and designing experiments, its ways of constructing and conferring meanings are not only sexist, but also racist, classist, and culturally coercive" (1986, p. 9). Her book provides significant evidence documenting sexist and racist elements of scientific research practice. Thus, when considering scientific, empirical research, students of gender must always approach it critically, assessing the research rather than simply accepting its findings as "truth."

In addition, the ways that scientific research is disseminated reinforces the notion of sex difference. A surprisingly large amount of research has been aimed at assessing the "real" differences between the sexes. This research has been the project of thousands of academics interested in documenting sex differences in cognition, behaviour, temperament, and ability. In fact, during the twenty-year period of the 1970s and 1980s, more than 16 000 psychology articles describing research into human sex differences were published in refereed journals (Unger & Crawford, 1992). Note that the policy of most refereed journals, then and now, is that studies should make a valuable contribution to the knowledge base in order to be chosen for publication. This selection criteria contributes to a problem known as the *alpha bias* (studies that find significant differences are more likely to be published than those that show there are no differences). The alpha bias arose because studies that did *not* find significant differences between the sexes were not seen as making the requisite contribution—thus, they seldom appeared in the journals. This refereed journal system, then, seriously under represented all the work that failed to prove difference.

This phenomenon occurs in the popular media as well. Not too many headlines announce that scientific researchers found no differences between women and men—this wouldn't be deemed newsworthy. So researchers and journalists both have a vested interest in focusing on and discovering difference, since that is the best way to get work published. See, for example, the cover story of *Time* magazine, March 7, 2005 (Ripley, 2005), the subtitle of which reads, "Yes women's and men's brains are different. But new research upends the old myths about who is good at what" (p. 35).

The human brain continues to be a site for study and controversy. As described by Fausto Sterling (2000), a spate of articles in the popular media in the 1990s reported on the new scientific research proving a difference in the brains of males and females. These reports claimed that researchers had found a measurable difference in the corpus collosum. The corpus collosum is essentially the bridge of cells that join the two halves of the brain. According to this research, the female brain has a thicker corpus collosum. Is this a good thing? Well, that depends on your interpretation. Some scholars proposed that this different thickness explained measured differences in ability: females use both sides of their brain for verbal tasks, while males are more "specialized." This specialization, they argued, predisposes the male brain to excel in visuo-spatial tasks, potentially accounting for men's greater participation in the fields of engineering and mathematics. There has not been public discussion suggesting that this thinner corpus collosum might actually be a limitation, keeping males from fully accessing various areas of the brain simultaneously. Interestingly, there has also been no reciprocal suggestion that the female's great ability to verbalize from both sides of her brain should predispose her to outperform males in language-based occupations like law, politics, and international relations. Because this research was discussed in the popular media, including the *New York Times* and as the cover story in *Newsweek*, as well as in the scientific research journals, it had an impact on our gender lens. It appeared to be proof that brain differences are at the root of these measured skill differences. But while the potential advantages for male brains received attention, those for female brains remained largely undiscussed. Our socio-cultural landscape continues to be shaped by this new "evidence" that the sexes are profoundly different. (Even though the *Time* article referred to earlier emphasized the critical links between experience and biology, the focus was still on difference.)

Moreover, while the groundbreaking research on brain sex differences is disseminated to the general public, the controversies surrounding this research do not reach the general media. In fact, there is much debate within the scientific community as to whether the corpus collosum of female brains actually *is* thicker—apparently it depends on how you measure it. And more significantly, there is little evidence to suggest that the possible difference in thickness explains difference in the visuo-spatial abilities of women and men. The research community is still actively exploring these questions; to date, there is no clear evidence from which we can draw firm conclusions (Fausto Sterling, 2000). Yet regardless of the ongoing debate, the preliminary discussion already has had an impact on people's general beliefs about women and men. Most of us fail to appreciate the tentative and ongoing nature of such scientific findings. Instead, we tend to believe what we read in respected newspapers and magazines.

You might think that measuring any sex differences would involve a relatively simple research design. Measure a random representative sample of men and women for a particular quality (for example, verbal skills), then undertake a statistical analysis to see if significant differences exist between the two groups. But, in fact, comparative research is more complex than that, as the examples discussed above illustrate. Even if two groups score differently, the question remains: Is this an innate sex-based difference, or a result of differential experience? Are the observed differences in the behaviours and emotions of boys and girls (and of women and men) based on sex or gender? Is it nature or nurture? How do we understand this distinction? And what are the biases built into the scientific methodology and media that might overemphasize sex differences?

MEASUREMENT ISSUES

As the brain differences example revealed, empirical research assessing innate sex-based differences so far has not been conclusive. Even though beliefs about these differences are widely held (contributing to our gender lenses), they are contradictory enough that we cannot say for certain whether significant innate sex differences truly exist. Clearly, there are measurable differences in performance, and our gender lens encourages us to attribute these differences to sex-based biological capacities. In reality, the issue is much more complex than that. And the research that has been undertaken to measure these differences must be carefully examined. Thus, we must assess the research designs used to test these differences and the interpretation of results. In their book *Thinking Critically about Research on Sex and Gender* (1994), Paula Caplan and Jeremy Caplan provide a brief guide to aid those who are assessing research literature. They challenge commonly held assumptions and offer tools to reassess our gender lenses.

One central issue in empirical research is **causality**. Did you know that when ice cream cone sales increase, so do drowning deaths? This phenomenon occurs consistently across time and locations. Because this same pattern repeats each year, a seemingly obvious conclusion is that eating ice cream cones is linked to drowning. Maybe people eat too much and then go swimming. Maybe they are more prone to stomach cramps after eating ice cream cones, and this affects their ability to swim. This hypothesis could explain the link. Or maybe there is a simpler explanation—that hot weather contributes to both. When the temperature goes up, more people eat ice cream, and more people go swimming. With more people swimming, there is a greater risk of drowning. Thus, while there is a **correlation** between sales of ice cream cones and drowning (the two events do occur together), there is no *causal* link. Eating ice cream cones does not increase your risk of drowning; swimming does. This example illustrates the difference between a correlation and causality, a distinction too often misunderstood by the general population.

Scientists judge true causality based on three criteria. In order to *prove* that X causes Y, three conditions must be met:

a) Consistent pattern: there must be a frequently measured correlation between X and Y (ice cream and drowning);

b) Consistent time order: X must always occur before Y (eating ice cream before drowning); and

c) No alternative possibility can satisfactorily explain the relationship.

Thus, even though a consistent pattern occurs for ice cream and drowning, an alternative explanation more satisfactorily explains the correlation.

Similarly, to prove that innate sex differences cause different outcomes in males and females on any particular measure, we need to satisfy these three causality criteria. For example, consider the hypothesis that girls are better at verbal skills than boys. Some empirical data certainly supports this hypothesis. In Ontario's province-wide testing of the writing and reading skills of Grade Three and Grade Six students, approximately 10–15 percent more girls than boys met the provincial standard (see Table 2.1).

To test the hypothesis that girls have superior verbal skills, we would need to devise an unbiased test of verbal ability. (This task alone would be very difficult, which is why there is so much controversy surrounding IQ tests and measures of scholastic ability.) Then we would test a sample of students to measure their abilities. If we compared the scores of the girls to the scores of the boys and found that girls scored significantly higher, we might be tempted to conclude that they scored higher *because* they were girls. But is this a reasonable conclusion, keeping in mind the difference between correlation and causality? Have the three criteria for causality been met?

If X is sex and Y is verbal abilities, the data can easily meet the second criteria. X did come before Y (the sex of the participants existed before they wrote the test). However, we can't fully prove the first criteria if we administer only one test. But what if we did the test every year, as the school system does in Ontario, and we kept finding similar results? Then we could meet the first criteria. Have we proved a causal relationship? Not yet. The real issue is the third criteria. We must consider competing explanations.

TABLE 2.1	Percentage of Students Meeting or Surpassing Provincial Standards			
	Grade 3		Grade 6	
	Male	Female	Male	Female
Reading				
2001/2	45%	56%	47%	64%
2002/3	44%	56%	48%	69%
2003/4	48%	59%	55%	65%
2004/5	54%	68%	58%	68%
Writing				
2001/2	47%	64%	44%	64%
2002/3	47%	64%	44%	64%
2003/4	50%	67%	45%	64%
2004/5	54%	68%	50%	68%

Source: EQAO, 2005, p. 19

One sex scoring consistently higher on a series of tests than the other sex does not necessarily prove that that the first group is innately superior at that particular skill. For years, American boys have outperformed American girls on the math portion of SATs (scholastic aptitude tests written by all American high school students who wish to attend university). This consistent gap (currently boys score 7 percent higher than girls) was taken as proof that boys are better at math than girls (another cover story in a popular newsmagazine). But interestingly, when researchers compared the boys' and girls' actual performance and test results in any given math class, this same pattern did not emerge (see, for example, Cherian & Siweya, 1996). The girls did not always, or even often, score significantly lower than the boys. The conclusion some scholars have drawn is that using the SATs as proof of an innate difference ignores a key alternative explanation (the third criteria). All students who wish to attend university must write SATs. But not all students who wish to attend university take the same number of math courses. In fact, because more American boys than girls take a full complement of math courses (for example, 60 percent more boys take calculus than girls, according to Persell, 1999), it is not surprising that girls don't fare as well on the standard test. Significantly less education in math would easily explain significantly lower test scores.

The results of the verbal skills testing can be examined in a similar way. Clearly, a great deal of learning and experience occurred before these students sat down to write the test. If the boys and girls have had different learning experiences, then they will likely score differently on the test. We would be measuring a *learned* difference rather than an innate sex difference. And as was noted in the introductory chapter (to be explored further in later chapters), we know that boys and girls do have different opportunities to learn. From a very young age, girls are talked to more than boys, and boys are encouraged to be more physically active than girls (Lytton & Romney, 1991). This alone allows different opportunities to speak, learn, and read. All three of these activities help to develop vocabulary and verbal comprehension.

In addition, as the first chapter explained, girls' and boys' experiences are different in the classroom. Even when they are exposed to the same teacher, the same curriculum, in the same classroom, they don't receive the same education. This difference in experience can contribute to differences in learning.

Finally, socio-cultural influences may persuade some boys not to develop their reading and writing skills. If reading and studying are defined as passive, feminine activities, then boys may be less inclined to engage in them (see, for example, Pirie, 2002). If boys do not engage in activities likely to develop reading comprehension, it is hardly surprising if we find that boys don't fare as well as girls on empirical writing and reading tests. The fact that the gap betweens boys' and girls' abilities shifts over time (see Table 2.1) proves that the differences are not solely caused by innate sex differences. Social factors, like opportunities to learn, clearly play a role.

But most people are uncritical when they read or hear about sex differences and do not go through the type of analysis set out here. They see that boys are outscoring girls on science tests and assume a causal relationship, without considering the possibility that other factors might be involved. Even when people do look beyond the surface impressions, they still may be misled, since many studies in this area are accompanied by statistical results which are frequently misunderstood. Several common errors contribute to misinterpretations of statistical results.

First, to understand statistics, you must also understand the concept of **statistical significance**, a very specific term, often misused by non-academics. Statistical significance refers to a pattern found in a sample population that has a high probability of being true for the population as a whole. Thus, a researcher may test her findings and report that they are statistically significant at 95 percent. This means that there is a very high likelihood that what she measured in her sample is also true for the general population; but it does not mean that the findings are *socially* significant.

To illustrate the difference between statistical significance and social significance, consider the following hypothetical example. A test shows that there is a difference in the average number of kilometres men and women can walk within a certain time period (endurance walking was an athletic event in which women competed during the nineteenth century, when they were excluded from marathon running events). In this hypothetical test, we find that women, on average, can walk 48.11 kilometres, and men can walk 47.93 kilometres. Even if this difference is a statistically significant finding (meaning that it most likely reflects a difference in the population, rather than just a difference in our sample group), that does not make it an *important* difference. Men and women can both walk a very long way, and after nearly 50 kilometres will be within the length of a football field of one another, a difference of less than one-quarter of one percent. Frequently, the statistically significant relationships reported in the media are as small as those in our hypothetical situation—the relationship they reveal is incredibly weak. But the finding is considered "real" and is thus erroneously interpreted as if it is important. Therefore, while statistical significance is important (a result that is likely confined to the sample group has limited value), a result can be *statistically* significant without being *socially* relevant.

Second, people run into difficulty with statistics because they do not know how to interpret average scores. If we learn that men on average score 2 percent higher on their drivers' tests, and that this is a consistent finding over decades of standardized driver testing, how should we interpret this? Does it mean all men are better drivers? No. It means what it says: on average, men score higher on driving tests. It does not imply *within-group* unity. There is a wide variation in the level of skill of drivers of both sexes. Simply because, on average, one group scores higher than another, you cannot draw the conclusion that everyone in that group scores higher than everyone in the other group. It is not an absolute difference. In most sex-based testing, there is more **within-group variation** than **between-group variation**. This means that there is a huge range of skill among women drivers, as well as a huge range of skill among men. The gap between the best and worst drivers of a single sex is markedly larger than the skill gap between the sexes. Knowing what group someone belongs to tells little about their specific abilities. In fact, on the math SATs, significantly more American males scored in the *lowest* percentiles than did females, even though on average men scored higher. Often, variables other than sex can reveal a great deal more useful information. For example, if we actually undertook a driving study, we might find more marked differences comparing people by age categories than by sex categories.

Here is another example that helps to illustrate within-group and between-group variations in average scores. If we tested 1000 students, half girls and half boys, on their science skills, knowing that 200 of those students went to an expensive private school with a student-teacher ratio of 1:6 instead of the 1:30 of the public school system, we may or may not find a significant difference between the sexes. But if we never ask the question, "Where did these students go to school?" then we miss a much more important variable. We would probably miss the fact that the students from the private school scored markedly higher on the test than did those from the public school. In this case, student-teacher ratio—and the ability to pay for an elite school education—would be far more important for explaining science ability than would sex. When considering examples related to education, researchers tend to miss the powerful importance of social class. Too often in gender research the narrow focus on sex differences overlooks other, potentially more important, social differences. To interpret average scores, then, we need to consider the differences within and between groups, as well as other factors and biases built into the research design.

The third significant area of misunderstanding in statistics is time. We forget that any particular study is typically a snapshot of one point in time. Even if there is a statistically and socially significant difference between the sexes on a particular test, if we only measure it at one time or over one short period of time, we may miss important information. If we only test only once, we cannot learn about the consistency of our findings. We must test the relationship over a lengthy period of time to see if the measured differences are stable, growing, or disappearing. What we find with academic skills is that differences do change over time. The gap between boys and girls on math skills is narrowing, but boys are not narrowing the gap in terms of their verbal abilities. Relative to girls, they are now scoring worse than they did two decades ago. This tells us that social factors are involved. We must consider these social factors if we want to understand the patterns. And when examining empirical research, we must be very careful to assess the limits of the research design and its findings.

OVERLAPPING NORMAL CURVES AND GENDER POLARIZATION

Patterns of sex difference can be conceptualized and understood by using a tool called **overlapping normal curves**. If you have ever studied statistics, you will have studied the

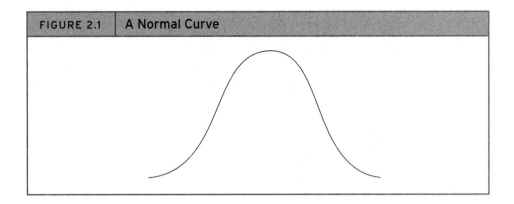

FIGURE 2.1 | A Normal Curve

concept of the **normal curve**. A normal curve illustrates the distribution of a particular quality. For example, if we measured the heights of 5000 people and plotted those heights on a graph from the shortest to the tallest, we would likely create a normal curve (also known as a *bell curve*). The majority of people would fall in the middle range, with fewer and fewer people occupying the extreme positions. The high point of the curve represents the average of all the scores. (In a normal curve, the mean, median, and mode— three ways of measuring average—are all the same score.) Figure 2.1 shows an example of a normal curve.

If we measure IQ, the ability to do sit-ups, or averages on Law School Aptitude Tests, we would likely see this same normal curve. The normal curve reflects the fact that more people are average, and fewer people score extremely high or extremely low on any given measure.

But if we then separated our sample into two groups—men and women—and plotted two curves, one for each category, we would likely see two separate curves that share a great deal of overlap. If we measure verbal ability, we would have two normal curves with two peaks indicating slightly different overall averages (See Figure 2.2).

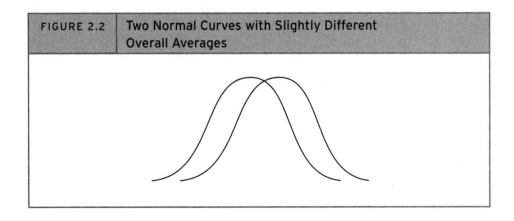

FIGURE 2.2 | Two Normal Curves with Slightly Different Overall Averages

Thus, if females scored 2 percent higher on a test than did males, the overlapping normal curves would allow readers to picture both the average difference and the high degree of overlap. We would see that there is actually great similarity between the groups—a great deal of overlap. In much of the empirical research on sex differences, the shared area under the two curves is growing greater, and the number of cases that fall at the extreme ends of the distribution is diminishing.

Normal curves show what is, not what has to be. While there may indeed be universal sex differences in the brain or bodies of humans that predispose one group of people more than another to excel at a particular skill, these differences are still subject to social influences in the majority of cases. If people with XY chromosomes have innately better visuo-spatial abilities, this difference does not have to be limiting for those with XX chromosomes. If we cared enough about the difference, we could train XX people and help them develop their visuo-spatial capacities to their maximum potential. This would greatly expand the degree to which the normal curves overlap. In effect, we would minimize the difference between the two sets of people. Most people would accept the idea that the male anatomy has the potential for greater physical strength than the female anatomy. But if we chose to, we could create an environment that undermined this biological propensity. Consider an extreme example useful in illustrating this point. Imagine a boarding school for junior high students at which the boys got to have unlimited pizza, doughnuts, pop, and access to computer games and DVDs, but had no gym privileges; and girls had healthy diets and daily rigorous exercise, including weight training. By the end of the school year, it would not be surprising to have a group of XX people who were, on average, stronger than their XY classmates. The social environment could be manipulated to exaggerate differences, with girls outperforming boys on physical tasks. Figure 2.3 illustrates how such results might look on a normal curve.

Even though this illustration is extreme, it echoes a pattern of historical gender-based discrimination. Women have often been disadvantaged, kept from realizing their potential by limitations enforced within their particular cultural milieu (except these women typically

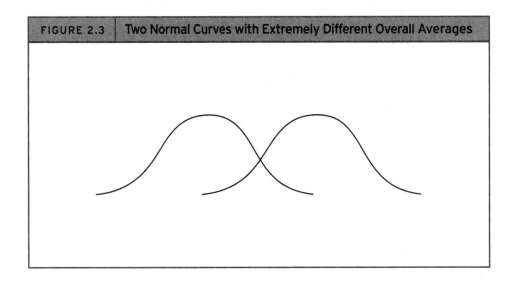

| FIGURE 2.3 | Two Normal Curves with Extremely Different Overall Averages |

weren't enjoying pizza and computer games; more likely, they were working hard, nurturing children while feeding and clothing their families). Women have been excluded from participating in physical activities (for example, female Olympians were not allowed to compete in track events longer than 200 metres until 1960), from higher levels of education (Canadian woman were not admitted into the University of Toronto's medical school until 1906), and from legal, religious, and economic activities (see Chapters Twelve, Thirteen, and Fourteen). This kind of differential treatment has been widespread and has resulted in many of the measurable differences we still see today between the sexes. Yet the gender lens of many Canadians supports the notion that these patterns are evidence of innate differences rather than evidence of unequal opportunities.

Alternative explanations for understanding the gender differences we measure and the larger inequalities in our society do exist. Bem (1993) argues that we do not have to look to differences in brains or hormones to explain sex differences: cultural arrangements provide sufficient explanation. First, in past centuries, reproductive requirements combined with limited technology gave rise to a necessary division of labour, a division that is becoming less relevant in modern culture. Second, whatever innate differences there might be, our inability to clearly identify socially significant patterns is proof that these innate differences are likely to be relatively minor. Third, given our ability to create cultural arrangements to accommodate our biological capacities, we do not need to be limited by sex-based differences if we choose to create a social world that does not allow it. In short, Bem argues we shouldn't focus all our energy on trying to pinpoint underlying physical differences. Instead, we should seek ways to redress inequities, whatever their origin.

The historical division of labour has certainly had a marked effect on women's social and economic advancement. Because women's historical role has been to mother and to produce goods for her family's consumption, women's participation in non-family activities has been limited. This arrangement led to a specialized division of labour that some people now regard as inevitable. However, now that we have a remarkable ability to plan fertility (access to contraception, reproductive technologies to aid conception, abortion, and sterilization gives us more control than ever before to conceive or avoid conceiving offspring), and now that technology exists to raise thriving babies without relying on breast milk, reproductive tasks that restricted women's activities in the past are now less time-consuming and less critical for the survival of the community. Conversely, men's physical prowess that had been valuable for protecting and providing for communities throughout much of human history is now less relevant than their other capacities. We have machines that undertake many of the most physically demanding tasks. Technology enables women and men to share similar work and to compete for jobs on a much more even playing field than ever before (as long as discrimination does not intervene). In addition, Bem makes the case that we have the technology and the knowledge to successfully address any innate sex differences that might be identified and confirmed in the future. Human culture has enabled us to successfully adapt to all manner of challenges. Should we actually find socially significant innate sex differences, we are capable of creating social arrangements to accommodate them without recreating unequal positions for women and men. Thus, the specialized division of labour that emerged because of reproductive roles and differences in strength is no longer necessary, though it is still being propped up by our socio-cultural beliefs—our gender lenses.

What we have been describing is a phenomenon called **gender polarization**. Gender polarization is the pervasive organization of social life around gender differences. One key element of gender polarization is the exaggeration of difference between the sexes. Focusing primarily on reproductive and providing roles, as Bem described, emphasizes differences between the sexes. The specialized division of labour led women and men to develop unique skill sets, which over time came to be seen as inevitable. Human beings are quite willing and able to emphasize and exaggerate differences—in fact we have long-standing traditions that do exactly that. For example, women's fashion was often designed to highlight physical differences. Corsets were designed to emphasize a narrow waist and thrust breasts forward and upward; high heels position women's breasts forward with their backs arched; and, most recently, breast implants create the illusion of large, gravity-defying breasts. The effect of such fashions has had an impact on digestive and reproductive health, mobility and skeletal deformity, and on sexual health and pleasure. For example, implant surgery reduces sensation in the nipple, causing augmented breasts to look like the cultural ideal while limiting the sexual pleasure of the women who have undergone such surgery. When the socio-cultural landscape highlights differences rather than similarities, these exaggerated positions are reinforced in our institutions, in our interactions, and within our gendered selves. Thus, our cultural milieu is silently gender-polarizing us, and the effects of this gender polarization play out on every level of social life.

Many sociologists and other scholars have challenged the acceptance of gender polarization in our society. By critically examining the gender lens itself—both the ways in which gender polarization is reinforced within the social milieu and the empirical research evidence—scholars are learning how the idea of gender accentuates differences and contributes to inequality. But gender polarization is not inevitable, and there are increasing challenges confronting it. The very fact that you have an opportunity to take a course on gender means that post-secondary institutions have made room for the critical study of these issues (sociology of gender courses and women's studies programs are relatively new). The publication of books, such as those mentioned in this chapter, has permitted the widespread dissemination of ideas that challenge the current gender lens.

GENDER INEQUALITY

In addition to promoting the notion of profound sex differences, gender lenses also shape ideas about inequality. Canadians don't share identical beliefs about the relative positions of women and men in society. In effect, Canadians view the sexes through multiple gender lenses. From conservative thinkers who believe that innate sex differences naturally flow into hierarchical gender arrangements, to feminists who seek to explain the differences and redress imbalances, to those who believe there are no inequalities left to be concerned about, each lens contributes to our cultural milieu.

Some sectors of society accept the notion that sex-based differences are innate. To them, the idea of gender inequality seems inevitable and quite possibly desirable. Therefore, instead of challenging the differential positions of women and men in society, they actively work to protect the separation and oppose those who challenge it.

For example, religion has played a role in highlighting, emphasizing, and reifying the differences between sexes (see also Chapter Fourteen). Because many religions accept the differences as "natural" and "god-given," they have emphasized the role of women as mothers and connect this role to divine purpose. In contrast, they often link men's calling or purpose to leadership. This "divine plan" is evident in these families and religious communities with men as the "head" of families, and women excluded from leadership roles in the larger communities. Religion has also played a role in the condemnation of sex (except for procreation) and sexualities (except for male-female monogamy). The issue of same-sex marriage continues to cause rifts in Canada and between Canada and the United States among some denominations even as we write this.

Similarly, conservative Christian churches have influenced the development of the Canadian women's group REAL (Realistic, Equal, Active, and for Life) Women, which pursues a specific socially conservative agenda, focusing on parenting issues, as well as anti-abortion and anti–same-sex marriage activism. While their mandate and policy statements have shifted over the years, REAL Women identify themselves as "Canada's alternative women's movement." They state: "REAL Women speaks for women who support traditional family values. Society may change, but society's need for strong, stable families remains" (www.REALwomenca.com). When the Canadian government raised the issue of funded, universal, and affordable daycare in Canada, REAL Women voiced concerns about the potential impact on families. At one time, their opposition to daycare was based on the argument that the ideal arrangement is for children to be raised at home by their mothers and that government-subsidized daycare would undermine this possibility. In addition, they claimed that being a stay-at-home mother would become less financially viable because parents using daycare would receive an unfair subsidy. But REAL Women has since modified this position. The statement on the REAL Women website now suggests that there is a place for women who choose to enter the workforce, and that government policy on daycare should support both stay-at-home mothers and those who enter the paid labour force. Nonetheless, the underlying emphasis in their carefully worded statements on the subject of "traditional family" arrangements and "pro-family" values has not changed and emphasizes the importance of women focusing on mothering while men focus on the marketplace.

This socially conservative position represents one gender lens in Canadian society. Importantly, though, several sets of beliefs can exist simultaneously within a culture. So while some people believe that inequality between women and men is inevitable and even desirable, others are actively pursuing alternative explanations and theories for enacting change.

In her classic book, *The Creation of Patriarchy* (1986), feminist historian Gerda Lerner proposes an explanation of the gender division of labour that challenges the conservative view. Lerner argues that inequality is not innate and uses ancient Mesopotamian history to explain its emergence. She states that one of the main reasons why women's inequality can be reproduced so easily is that women are largely absent from history. They remained invisible because history has been written by men and has recorded what men have done and have deemed to be significant (Chapter Ten discusses the question of why there are no great women artists). Equally important, women have been excluded from the symbol-creating systems that give meaning to human life, such as philosophy, science, and law. Lerner's basic argument is that there may be biological differences between women and men, "but that the values and implications based on that difference are the result of culture" (p. 6).

Lerner maps the creation of patriarchy and the institutionalization of women's inequality through history. She locates the roots of this inequality in two meaning systems developed by early human societies. First, the "symbolic devaluing of women in relation to the divine becomes one of the founding metaphors of Western civilization" (p. 10). By this, Lerner means that over time, the goddesses that celebrated female sexuality and procreativity were replaced by a male god or god-king, and the mother-goddess became his wife/consort (p. 9). Think for a moment of god images with which you are familiar, and remember their gender.

Imagine for a moment that these god images are female. God images and human interpretation of the divine have had a powerful impact on the shaping of Western civilization, even if we hold to the notion that we live in a secular society.

The second founding metaphor identified by Lerner is one based on Aristotelian philosophy, which assumes as a given that women are "incomplete and damaged human beings of an entirely different order than men" (p. 10). Like the god-image, this concept remains largely invisible now, but it formed the foundation of many of our cultural ideas. Thus, medical research has focused on the male body, taking it as the template for all human bodies. Legal language to this day still uses "he" to include men and women. Use of words such as "mankind" remains pervasive; and when women contest this usage, they are criticized for being "politically correct" or oversensitive. The exclusion of women from our cultural symbols has had long-term effects and has entrenched the subordination of women and their inequality as "natural," invisible, and unassailable. Lerner's extensive research in this area led to a new understanding of the place of women and men in history. Her work has caused those who study history or gender or feminism to rethink their notions about the beginnings of patriarchy.

FEMINIST GENDER LENSES

Understanding inequality and seeking to rearrange the positions of women and men in society has been the major project of *feminists* for over a century. The **first wave of feminism** began in the late 1800s when women worked to secure voting rights and the legal right to be considered persons (see Chapter Thirteen). The **second wave of feminism** emerged in the 1960s as women worked to achieve equal opportunities, reproductive freedoms, and solutions to violence. The current **third wave of feminism** arose in the 1990s with the recognition that being a woman intersects with other statuses, such as class, sexual orientation, and ethnicity. Thus, feminists must addresses a broad spectrum of issues. The notion that they are "women's issues" oversimplifies the reality of women's lives in the twenty-first century. Feminists certainly don't all agree on the character of patriarchy or the ways to scounteract it, though they do share three common features:

a) a (not necessarily exclusive) focus on the inequities, strains, and contradictions inherent in gender arrangements;

b) an assumption that gender relations are not immutable but rather changeable social creations; and

c) a normative commitment that societies should develop equitable gender arrangements. (Chafetz, 1999, p.4)

Interestingly, when we ask students if they agree with the ideas that (a) gender inequality is not inevitable and (b) it should be changed, many of them say yes. These ideas reflect their own experience and beliefs, even though they might not call themselves feminists.

There are many strands of feminism, though we only discuss four in this chapter: *liberal feminism, radical feminism, cultural feminism,* and *socialist feminism*. There are many variations because women are not a monolithic group, and their needs and priorities are not all the same. Different ways of responding to women's inequality are reflected in the various theories. When we ask our students about feminism, many mention radical feminism, yet very few actually know what radical feminism is (see below). Moreover, in terms of public policy and women's participation, radical feminism plays a relatively minor role. The fear of radical feminism may have been perpetuated by a male-dominated, male-owned media with a corporate agenda that does not want to deal with equal pay for women or paternity/maternity leaves. The bra-burning feminist is a somewhat mythological creature created to alienate both women and men from the feminist movement as a whole. The reality is a lot less fantastical. Like all social movements, feminism has more radical and more moderate elements. All these elements are important to the movement as a whole; but not everybody can identify with the beliefs or goals of every group within the movement.

The dominant strand of feminism in Canadian society is **liberal feminism**, which, following liberalism more generally, sees the human being as an autonomous self who is able to make choices in a "free and democratic society." To this end, liberal feminists argue that women have largely been excluded from positions of power in the workplace and social institutions. They have challenged the lack of equity in pay and have fought to equalize access for women, who can then choose whether to follow opportunities open to them. Equality of opportunity is the key focus of liberal feminism.

But the real challenge is to enable women to achieve substantive as opposed to formal equality. That is, liberal feminists strive to achieve true equality in daily life in addition to the legal recognition of equal rights. As discussed in Chapter Thirteen, women make up at least half of all law school classes but have a very high rate of departure from the profession. Why? Because the climate in many law firms does not account for the fact that women often need accommodation for childbearing and -rearing responsibilities. Only women can bear children; and yet the response of much of the labour market is to grant women maternity leave and then expect them to carry on as though all their parenting obligations have been accommodated. Thus, aspiring female lawyers have formal equality but not substantive equality. Equal access is relatively meaningless if nothing else about the culture or workplace changes. Thus, a second focus of liberal feminism is to address these substantive inequalities.

Those known as **radical feminists** take quite a different position. They focus more on issues of power and oppression in all elements of the social system. They sometimes suggest that liberal feminists ignore the fundamental values of dominance and control that shape our culture. Rather than trying to enable women to act more effectively within the existing arrangements, radical feminists challenge the very nature of those arrangements. They would like to end hierarchies and explore the social construction of both sex and gender. An important goal of their work is to guarantee women control over their own bodies. Thus, reproductive control, sexual freedom, rape, intimate violence, and pornography are focal issues in radical feminism.

A third strand of feminism is **cultural feminism**. Instead of arguing that women will prosper only when they have the same opportunities as men, or that women share the same qualities as men, cultural feminists argue that women have unique and valuable characteristics that should be celebrated. Women are different; they speak and feel differently, and their ways should be acknowledged as equally valid instead of being denied. Of course, some people believe that this position just reinforces existing stereotypes that keep women from thriving in the larger society. However, cultural feminists argue that women must continue to promote their unique virtues—connection, nurturance, and compassion—and this can be done by creating women-centred environments where the "masculine" values of competition, self-interest, and dominance are excluded.

A fourth dimension of feminist theory is **socialist feminism**. Socialist feminists believe that both patriarchy and social class combine to oppress women. The reciprocal relationship between these two systems reinforces both—patriarchy is enhanced by socio-economic divisions, which, in turn, are buttressed by male dominance. Although patriarchy exists in other economic systems, socialist feminists focus their attention on women in capitalist societies. In essence, socialist feminists argue that women are doubly "exploited" in capitalist societies because of their unpaid work in domestic households (see Chapter Eleven), and their over-representation in badly paid, marginal jobs (see Chapter Twelve). Chafetz states: "Capitalists foster an ideology of patriarchy (male supremacy) that justifies women's nonwaged domestic and childrearing work with reference to biologically rooted reproductive differences between sexes and justifies labor market inequities based on women's domestic obligations" (p. 10). At the same time, men are doubly advantaged because they are not held responsible for participating in domestic labour—women are doing this work for them—and they have more access to well paying, upwardly mobile jobs because women are less likely to compete for them.

Dorothy Smith (1987, 1990) is often regarded as an important figure in Canadian socialist feminism. Her early work focused on the intersection of class and gender and the ways in which class/gender was institutionally reproduced. In other words, Smith examined the organizing power of social institutions, such as the education system, considering the ways in which class and gender played into the work that mothers were expected to do behind the scenes.

From this very brief overview of four of the theoretical strands (see Tong, 1992, for a more thorough discussion of the range of feminist theories), it is evident that feminists do not all agree on the nature of gender hierarchies. However, their ongoing debates certainly do filter into the general public, adding new dimensions to existing gender lenses.

THE BACKLASH LENS

A final position that must be considered is the belief that equality has already been achieved and there is no need for further concern or study. This position can take two forms. First, people often claim that women are not discriminated against, and that those working to improve women's position in society are actually disadvantaging men—an argument that is often referred to as the **backlash** against feminism. To support the claim that equality has already been achieved, this group focuses on issues such as the equal numbers of young women and men gaining professional educations in fields like medicine or law. They cite hiring practices in many careers; for example, in law enforcement, where managers make a concerted effort to find qualified women to join the police force. In addition, this group points out that there are women in positions of real power. Condeleeza Rice, for example, serves in one of the highest positions in the United States government. (It is noteworthy that Canadian examples of women in positions of real power are few.)

These pieces of evidence certainly do indicate that the second wave of feminism has been successful at opening doors for women in a variety of occupations, some with high incomes, prestige, and authority. But they do not prove that equality has been achieved. Women are not equal in the world of work. As discussed in Chapter Twelve, Canadian women still earn only approximately 71 percent of what men earn. A higher proportion of Canadian women than men are poor: 17.1 percent of women and 14.7 percent of men living in families are poor, compared to 42 percent of women living alone and 34 percent of unattached men (Statistics Canada,

2006). Because of this pattern, the "feminization of poverty" has become a serious concern for social workers and policy makers. Certainly, many gains have been made to expand the opportunities for women in Canadian society; however, to argue that equality has been achieved is simply not supported by empirical evidence. In particular circumstances, a woman may be in a more beneficial position than a man regarding salary, authority, or prestige, but these particular instances do not prove that women in general have equality. As long as a significant majority of poor people are women, because of lack of job opportunities and/or family responsibilities, equality has not been achieved. But this gender lens reveals only the ways in which women have succeeded, ignoring the ongoing economic and social disadvantages many women face.

The second form of the backlash lens is the "I made it by my own merits and so should you" strand. This approach sees any attempt to even the playing field for women as an accommodation to a "special needs group." (They somehow perceive half of the population as a "special needs group.") This lens is used by both successful women as well as men, because it employs a classic liberal *laissez-faire* philosophy—that success (or lack thereof) is entirely dependent on individual effort. Thus, if women really wanted to succeed, they could. This perspective ignores the structural inequalities that create an uneven playing field for many women. If we all had the same opportunities to gain an education and the same obstacles standing in our way, then we would likely agree that those who excel did so by dint of their own merit and hard work. But the opportunities and obstacles that exist in this world remain gendered.

For instance, unskilled men and women don't have access to the same jobs (see Chapter Twelve). Unskilled men get hired for jobs that typically pay more than jobs for which women are hired. In addition to having to deal with work segregation and pay differentials, women continue to be expected to take the primary role in rearing children. Thus, their work aspirations and opportunities reflect this reality. In a heterosexual couple, salary differentials giving men more earning power than women often lead them to choose different paths: he focuses more on work because he can earn more, and she focuses more on raising the children because it costs them less in lost wages. This continuing difference in earning power influences people's choices. And these factors are gendered: even though many powerful women excel in the world of work, they are not proof that inequality has disappeared, and that all women have the same access to that kind of opportunity.

CONCLUSION

These examples highlight the fact that our socio-cultural landscape reflects many perspectives about sex and gender. Most likely, your own beliefs have been influenced by your experiences and those of the people you know. They are also shaped by the ideas you have been exposed to through the media and in your communities. Further shaping these perceptions are the more long-standing gender lenses of innate sex differences and the inevitability of inequality. These two gender lenses in particular have led to an overemphasis on and distortion of the "science" showing differences between sexes.

Ask yourself questions about your perspective on gender. How is it influenced by your family of origin? Who are your role models, and what do they say about men and women? The first step in gender analysis is to critically examine how we do gender. Then we can look to the world around us to identify gendered patterns and their impact, as well as the ways in which we can shift or resist them.

CHAPTER SUMMARY: KEY POINTS

1. The socio-cultural landscape is gendered. Laws (discrimination on the basis of sex is not legal), ideologies (women and men are equal), normative expectations (women should be primary care givers for children), and beliefs (male and female physiological differences explain differential opportunities and achievements) shape our experience.

2. One feature of the socio-cultural landscape is the dominant belief that there are only two sexes and two genders. Empirical research provides evidence that there are more than two sexes: 1.7 percent of people have physiologies that do not fit into the male/female categories.

3. In the nineteenth century, the disadvantaged position of women was explained by biology: women were considered weaker and less intelligent and therefore undeserving of equal rights and opportunities.

4. In the late twentieth century, a great deal of scholarly research has measured "sex differences." But despite the media attention, innate differences between males and females appear to be very few, and those that do exist are minor.

5. Correlations (measured relationships between variables) on tests of sex differences, such as IQ, do not prove one sex is intellectually superior to the other. A measured difference between two groups should not be accepted as causal unless it has met the three criteria of causality.

6. Those who interpret statistical findings must be careful to avoid three common problems: (1) Statistical significance does not equal social importance. (2) Differences in average scores do not imply within-group unity. (3) A relationship must be measured over a period of time to determine whether there is a changing relationship between the variables.

7. On most variables, there is a great deal of overlap between the sexes. Women and men are more alike than they are different. Some of our social arrangements polarize the genders and exaggerate difference.

8. Reproductive requirements and limited technology are rational explanations for historical sex differences in the division of labour. But our current ability to control fertility and to use technology in place of physical strength can successfully offset innate differences and create equal opportunities for all.

9. Feminist theory focuses on the origins and maintenance of gender inequality. Different strands of feminist theory have unique explanations for gender power imbalances, but all agree that we must develop more equitable arrangements.

10. Some people believe that equality between sexes has already been achieved and that there is no need to re-organize social relations. However, this position ignores the unequal earning opportunities and structural challenges that disadvantage women.

DISCUSSION QUESTIONS

1. Why is it difficult to create an unbiased, gender-neutral, standardized test of verbal abilities?

2. Why do girls tend to take fewer math courses than boys?

3. Think of historical and current examples of gender polarization. How have they shaped your social context and experiences? Do you resist gender-polarizing influences in your social milieu? How?

4. Have you encountered people who argue that working for equality between the sexes is unnecessary, either because it has already been achieved or because it is undesirable? How did you or how would you respond to these arguments?

5. Assume for a moment that there truly are innate cognitive differences between males and females—that males' specialized brains give them enhanced mathematical skills and females' more substantial corpus collosum gives them superior language skills. Why aren't females the predominant sex in fields that utilize such skills (law, religion, international relations)? What would the world look like if such "natural" differences were allowed to play out without discrimination?

KEY TERMS

backlash	gender polarization	socialist feminism
causality	liberal feminism	statistical significance
correlation	normal curve	within-group variation
cultural feminism	overlapping normal curves	between-group variation
division of labour	radical feminism	

chapter three

Shaping the Socio-Cultural Landscape: Stereotypes and Normative Expectations

STEREOTYPES, ROLES, AND EXPECTATIONS

We've all heard the stereotypes: men are rational, while women emotional; men are competitive, while women are more inclined towards co-operation. Ideas like these are so ingrained in our socio-cultural landscape that many people don't even notice them. It is absolutely normal to hear people comment on stereotypical behaviour patterns as if they were stating facts. As we write this book, our country is involved in a federal election campaign. During a debate when leaders were questioned about the rude, adversarial, and unproductive behaviour during parliamentary question periods, two prime ministerial hopefuls suggested that the solution was to elect more women. They expressed the belief that female parliamentarians would not engage in such foolish behaviour, and that male MPs in the House of Commons might moderate their behaviour if there were more women present. Of course, we realize that this argument is based on the stereotypical notion that women are more polite and less aggressive than men. However, as we discussed in a previous chapter, even if this stereotype were based on empirical fact, there is no reason to believe that a *particular* woman would be less rude or adversarial than a *particular* man. We certainly have examples of women parliamentarians willing to engage in verbal duels (for example, Deb Gray and Elsie Wayne), as well as men who are not confrontational. Thus, an increase in the number of women in the House of Commons certainly would not guarantee that our MPs will behave more civilly during question period. Nonetheless, many people accept and promote this stereotypical belief, and few Canadians bother to question their assumptions.

Stereotypes are standardized impressions of the characteristics that typify a group of people. They are mental constructs that we use to understand the world we live in. Stereotypes are not always problematic; in fact, we use them to frequently to interact with others. If you have ever met a person for the first time, knowing that he belonged to a particular social group—for example, he was a Baptist minister—you would likely have moderated your behaviour accordingly. Based on the stereotypes you hold about religious leaders, you would probably have avoided engaging in or discussing any potentially "inappropriate" activities in his presence, such as swearing, consuming alcohol, or telling off-colour jokes. In this way, we rely on our stereotypes to interact with other people. But they become harmful when we treat the stereotypes as complete, factual representations of all the people belonging to that category. For example, not all Baptist ministers would react the same way to the consumption of alcohol. When we treat stereotypes about groups as facts, we become blinded to the real individuals. Stereotypes that apply negative characteristics to a particular social group are even more serious: for example, "all _____ are stupid," or "_____ are alcoholics." In essence, a stereotype is damaging when it becomes a **prejudice**: a rigidly held, adverse belief or judgment about an entire category. The more extreme and absurd prejudices are easy to identify: blondes are dumb, lawyers are crooks (one of the authors of this book is actually blonde and a lawyer!); but subtle stereotypes are harder to perceive. Their hidden nature can make them even more dangerous. For example, the widely held assumption that women are less rational than men is an adverse judgment about half the human race that undermines women's authority and ideas and has been used throughout history to keep them from engaging in a variety of activities. Sex-based **discrimination**, known as **sexism**, is often based on these stereotypes. For example, for centuries, the assumption that women were not as strong or as tough as men justified the discriminatory practice of excluding them from military careers.

Think about the gender stereotypes that you have heard. Men are _____, whereas women are _____ (for some examples, see Table 3.1). In class, we often list these notions on the board (usually accompanied by a great deal of laughter).

Now think about the women and men that you know. Do they fit the categories? All the time? Think about your own actions and characteristics. Do you fit? When do you make an effort to conform, and when do you ignore expectations? Can you think of anyone who always and only exhibits the expected qualities identified with their particular gender? In general, very few people consistently exhibit all the qualities attributed by

TABLE 3.1	Common Gender Stereotypes	
Men	**Women**	
Tough	Gentle	
Independent	Dependent	
Aggressive	Passive	
Rational	Emotional	
Competitive	Co-operative	

stereotype to their own gender and none of the qualities of the other; in fact, most of our students cannot think of a single such person. The most nurturing people are capable of toughness and aggression when they deem it necessary. (For example, nurturing caregivers may appear tough and/or aggressive when protecting the vulnerable people in their care.) Similarly, even the most rational individual likely responds emotionally to intense loss or severe pain. In short, humans are not walking gender stereotypes. They share a wide of a range of behaviours and characteristics and exhibit those qualities in specific times and places. Moreover, our gender behaviour is often situation-specific. We may be more nurturing when looking after vulnerable people, more passive when in situations where we have less invested, and more competitive when there are rewards available for success or achievement.

The two stereotypes set out at the beginning of this chapter are a part of our socio-cultural landscape; we have named these stereotypes **masculinity** and **femininity**. We perceive these qualities as *mutually exclusive* groupings, like the columns in Table 3.1. But when we observe real human beings, we see that the categories are clearly generalizations: most people don't fit completely into only one category at all times. Masculinity and femininity describe stereotypical patterns, but they don't reflect the reality of most of the people we know. When we look at typical behaviours, we might well see more men enacting the *masculine* qualities and more women appearing to follow the *feminine* expectations. But instead of acknowledging that these are stereotypical behaviours, we tend to see them as more concrete divisions, leading us to question what is *wrong* with people who don't fit neatly into "their" category. Men who are perceived to be passive and women who appear to be aggressive are considered problematic because they don't fit with our societal expectations.

In addition, most people also understand masculinity and femininity to be *opposites*. If you look at Table 3.1, you'll see this opposition: if feminine people are expected to have a certain characteristic (*e.g.*, gentleness), then masculine people are expected to have the opposite quality (*e.g.*, toughness). Seeing the gendered qualities as opposite ends of a continuum reinforces the notion that a woman who seems less feminine must therefore also be more masculine. Similarly, a man who seems less masculine must by this logic be more feminine.

But these gender stereotypes are not mere neutral descriptors of behaviour; they are also *prescriptive*. As prescriptive descriptors, stereotypes not only indicate what masculine and feminine people *are* like but also create expectations about what people *should* be like. Stereotypes are thus **normative expectations** against which people are measured. Normative expectations are elements of the socio-cultural landscape that guide our behaviour and our assessments of others. *Gender-based normative expectations* define cultural standards of masculinity and femininity. They reinforce the pressure to conform, rather than promoting the notion that there are ranges of behaviour, and even ranges of femininity and masculinity. People feel pressure to suppress non-stereotypical activities and characteristics in order to avoid being judged as deviant. Normative expectations illustrate Bem's idea of gender polarization that was introduced in Chapter Two:

> Gender polarization operates in two related ways. First it defines mutually exclusive scripts for being male and female. Second, it defines any person or behaviour that deviates from these scripts as problematic—as unnatural or immoral from a religious perspective or as biologically anomalous or psychologically pathological from a scientific perspective. (Bem, 1993, pp. 80–81)

As long as our gendered socio-cultural landscape is both polarizing and prescriptive, we will likely feel pressure to conform to expectations, knowing that by challenging them we risk being regarded as "problematic." People who do not reflect these standards may face social pressure or sanctions for their non-compliance. For example, high school males who are not physically strong and aggressive are often subjected to bullying and ridicule. High school girls who don't achieve gender expectations are also subject to harassment (see *Case Study: Adolescent Girls, Peers, and Appearance* on pp. xxx). Failing to meet gender expectations in the teenage years can be particularly harsh, but the pressure to conform continues into adulthood. The media exacerbates the problems by playing into people's fears about gender expectations (see also Chapter Four).

Fortunately, these stereotypes and the accompanying normative expectations are being challenged. In academic circles, the study of gender has continually recognized both the power of stereotypes and the harm that arises from sexism and discrimination. Stereotypes are also being challenged by people in their daily lives as they increasingly strive to portray their true selves and to create social arrangements that suit their needs and temperaments, rather than conforming to a preconceived set of normative expectations. Women who pursue military careers and men who choose stay home to nurture their young children are two obvious examples. As stereotypical notions of gender are challenged, the polarized expectations diminish. That is, there is increasing acceptance of those who do not conform to the stereotypes.

Even though all humans have a broad repertoire of behaviours and qualities, gender stereotypes and the accompanying normative expectations do continue to guide many of our actions. They also influence our assessments of other people. One way to explain these gender-based behaviours is to describe them as **gender roles**. Roles are the behavioural expectations associated with any particular status. Your role as a student includes several rights and obligations, including expectations from instructors and the student body; and while there are variations in the ways you enact the role, there is also a degree of homogeneity with other students. Gender roles are the expectations based upon a person's perceived gender. The term is derived from Talcott Parsons' concept of **sex roles**. Parsons argued that society links overarching attitudes and activities to each sex, thereby identifying and defining appropriate behaviour for each sex. He believed that we learn these roles through socialization and enact them in order to effectively participate as women and men in the larger society.

However, Parsons' discussion of gender-based roles has been sharply criticized. One concern is that enacting learned roles fails to account for situational variation. Learned roles imply that once we adopt a set of behaviour patterns, we follow them regardless of the social context in which we act. But this is a highly limited vision of human activities. Another serious concern about Parsons' explanation is that it failed to effectively address power differentials, as if masculinity and femininity were separate but equal roles associated with the statuses of man and woman. His theory obscured the gender issues of dominance and subordination. It also ignored the ways in which the gendered activities were valued by the larger society. A third flaw is his failure to consider that while roles are attached to various statuses, the membership of some groups is so diverse that no set of role expectations can effectively describe them. For example, *females*, *Aboriginal persons*, and *millionaires* are such broad categories that defining a common role for each of these statuses is simply not possible. It is not worthwhile to attempt to define *ethnic roles* or *upper-class roles* or *gender roles*. The people holding those statuses are so heterogeneous that it would be a disservice to try to lump them into a single set of behavioural expectations.

Despite the flaws in Parsons' work on gender roles, we still can learn from his concepts. In fact, theorist Helena Lopata has developed a version of role theory that addresses many of these limitations. She defines a social role as "a set of patterned, mutually inter-dependent, social relations between a social person and a social circle involving negoti-ated duties and obligations, rights and privileges" (Lopata, 1994, p.4). This definition highlights relationships in social contexts, rather than focusing entirely on an individual's actions. The "negotiated" duties and obligations address power differentials within the social circle and the different ways in which roles are performed. She argues that assuming homo-geneous behaviours among women or men is faulty because it ignores social context. Instead, she recommends approaching gender in a way that considers both roles and identity:

> Sexual identification at birth, or at the time of sexual change, seems universal. This becomes a gender identification and identity into which people are socialized and remain involved as they enter different social relations and roles through the life course. This pervasive identity becomes an important characteristic in some roles (*e.g.*, mother or father), but less so in other roles (*e.g.*, physician, or store clerk). . . . It is part of the "package" that we carry with us in our social inter-actions, as are race, religious, and ethnic identities. (Lopata, 1999, p. 232)

Certainly, it is useful to recognize that we are socialized to adopt particular activities, atti-tudes, and roles (see Chapter Five), and that we may act out these gender roles as we inter-act with others. However, even though socialization has an impact on social relations, it does not determine them. Other factors also make significant contributions.

STATUS EXPECTATIONS THEORY

Status expectations theory is a micro-structural theory, meaning that it focuses on small-scale interactions and looks for explanations of behaviours that arise out of situational con-texts rather than searching for qualities inherent in individuals. Thus, this theory downplays both socialization and innate qualities.

Status expectations theory states that people base their expectations about individuals on the status ranking of the group to which those individuals belong. As we interact, we are very much aware of the status of other people. If they belong to a social group that it is considered superior or inferior to our own, we judge their actions accordingly, even when that particular status is not relevant. For example, in a medical emergency, people may defer to a man rather than a woman, even though gender has very little connection to knowledge of first aid. As another example, a well-groomed, fashionably dressed adult asking for help on the street is more likely to be assisted than a badly groomed person dressed in ragged clothing, because a business person has higher status than a homeless person. Similarly, a group of young males in jeans and Doc Marten boots may be perceived as more threatening than a group of middle-aged women in dress clothes and high heels, because age and clothes indicate particular statuses about which we have expectations. Age and social class indicate status—and so does gender.

In mainstream Canadian culture, more value is attached to the status *male* than to the status *female*. These values influence our behaviours and our perception of the behaviours of others. Even when men and women behave identically, their statuses influence us to inter-pret their actions differently. If we expect males to be more vocal and assertive than females, this influences our perceptions of both men and women. As Risman and Schwartz explain, "If you are a man, people tend to stop talking when you raise your voice just because you are a man. No matter what you say, it is taken seriously, even if it is repudiated. But when you are a woman, you always fight to get the floor, and it is hard to be taken seriously . . . In this way sexual stratification organizes interaction even though people believe they are giv-ing fair weight to the abilities of each person in the room" (1989, p. 5). Even if a man and a woman assert their rights with equal force, expectations determine that only the male will be regarded as acting within his normal role, and therefore his message will be more widely accepted. A woman using the same words and tone may be seen as overly aggressive or described as a pushy bitch for forcefully asserting herself.

Same behaviour + different statuses = different perceptions

Because status expectations reinforce gender and power differentials, women tend to moderate their actions to avoid negative judgments.

Moreover, when a group of people work together on a task, status expectations play a role. Ridgeway and Smith-Lovin found that "both a man and a woman will implicitly assume that he is a little more competent and has a little more to offer than she. Lower performance expectations for her compared to him make her less likely to offer task suggestions and more likely to ask for his ideas, to evaluate his ideas positively and hers negatively, and to accept his influence in task decisions, creating a behavioral power and prestige order that advantages him over her" (1999, p. 252). Women and men in this example are operating on the basis of gender expectations, which influence their performances and become self-fulfilling prophecies. Empirical research supports the theory: gender-based status expectations do influence performance and experience. Of course, we all have many statuses (such as age and social class) that play a part in any interaction. Frequently, gender is less important than another status: for example, in a hierarchical organization, people in higher positions (upper management executives, elected politicians, high ranking military officers) assert more power and are afforded more deference than people of lower statuses, regardless of their gender. But the empirical research also shows that status expectations lead people to assume that women are less able to fulfill those positions of authority. This assumption reduces the likelihood of their being promoted to such positions in the first place. In their research, Ridgeway, Johnson, and Diekema (1994) found that the gender expectation that men are more appropriate candidates for positions of power created a **legitimacy effect**. Men are expected to be assertive and are judged by that standard. Women striving to prove their abilities and overcome low expectations are more likely to meet with resistance and be judged negatively because they are acting outside of expectations. One long-term result of these gender status expectations is that men are more likely to attain positions of power and prestige (Wagner and Berger, 1997).

GENDER-BASED NORMATIVE EXPECTATIONS

Notions about gender—stereotypes, roles, and expectations—have a profound impact on the way we act and the way we judge the actions of others. Studying those notions is therefore essential. Even though we *do gender* on the interactional dimension, the ideas themselves are part of our socio-cultural landscape. Certainly, we can challenge and resist them, but they already exist within the culture, and our actions and choices will be influenced and judged by them.

The common terms for these stereotyped concepts are **masculinity** and **femininity**. Dictionary definitions of these terms refer to qualities associated with *being male* or *being female*, as though masculinity and femininity were natural extensions of our biological selves. But we know that real biological sex differences, beyond anatomical differences, are relatively few and rather minor.

Our understandings of masculine and feminine are largely cultural in origin: they are shaped by social structures and social context, rather than by innate qualities; they are learned in part through socialization; and they are played out as people interact with one another. Most of us give very little thought to the terms *masculinity* and *femininity*. We know what they mean, and we can identify their common qualities. But, as those who study gender argue, they are actually rather complex concepts. Picture someone who is masculine. Are you picturing a relatively young, strong, heterosexual man? What about a businessman in his early sixties—is he masculine? The point is that there is more than one version of masculinity, just as there is more than one version of femininity. Think about the people you know. They probably exhibit a wide range of behaviours that could be considered either feminine or masculine, with a few exceptions (depending on your circle of acquaintances). Scholars typically use the plural form of the words—*femininities* and *masculinities*—to express the range of possible qualities that fit the categories.

But the fact that there are many ways to *be a man* or to *be a woman* does not mean that all versions of masculinity or femininity are equal. Some types of masculinity and femininity are considered more desirable than others. The term **hegemonic masculinity** is often used to describe the dominant form. The introductory chapter discussed two specific contexts where hegemonic masculinity figures prominently: athletic teams and drinking subcultures. The authors of both those studies described ways in which hegemonic masculinity shape interactions and experience. In essence, there are many ways to be masculine; but one set of characteristics is the idealized norm, and other patterns are typically devalued and/or oppressed. When we asked you to picture a masculine person, chances are that you envisioned the hegemonic version of masculinity. The idealized version is usually a reflection of the most powerful group of men within a particular society—in our society, this is white, middle/upper class, heterosexual men. Those who fit the category are advantaged over those who do not (non-white, non-heterosexual, poor). You are much less likely to hear the term *hegemonic femininity*. Though there is still an idealized version for how to be feminine, it is not typically associated with the same degree of power as masculinity. Connell (1987) uses the term **emphasized femininity** to describe this dominant form. This version of femininity reflects sociability, empathy, and nurturance, rather than power or physical strength. Connell suggests that emphasized femininity is based on compliance with gender inequalities, accommodating others' needs rather pursuing one's own. Some scholars do explore the notion of **hegemonic femininity**, particularly in the area of sport. They argue that a specific version of femininity, largely based on appearance, is highly valued over other patterns. Female athletes perceived to be more masculine, or non-heterosexual, or who participate in "male sports" are devalued by coaches, judges, and sport administrators, and also by sponsors, the media, and the public at large (Choi, 2000). Choi argues that because athleticism is often considered to be masculine, female athletes are expected to behave in ways that reinforce their femininity through appearance and heterosexual desirability. She believes that strong and athletic women challenge hegemonic masculinity, but reinforcing an appearance-based femininity minimizes this challenge and ensures male domination.

Masculinities and femininities change over time and from place to place. In addition, there are always women and men struggling—more or less successfully—to resist or challenge the societal gender norms. Such efforts, however, do not diminish the power of the norms as ideals. The hegemonic masculinity and enhanced femininity at play in Canada early in the twenty-first century are an integral part of our socio-cultural landscape, even as each is under greater pressure to shift and change than at any time in the country's history.

MASCULINITIES

While there are multiple ways to be masculine, society still measures men according to *normative expectations*. These normative expectations are linked to the stereotypes discussed earlier: "men are supposed to be _____." You can certainly create your own list, based on your experiences, but most mainstream Canadian lists of masculine ideals include the following qualities:

1. Competition, success, achievement: the act of striving to do one's best and out performing others when possible.
2. Self reliance, assertiveness, strength, toughness: pressure to act in control in any situation, to solve problems and to fight for what is right, defending against those who challenge their position; not showing weakness or emotion, or other qualities deemed to be feminine.

The common thread in these expectations is performance: men's masculinity is judged by their actions. Moreover, like norms, these expectations are culturally specific. They change over time and place, depending on the needs and features of a particular culture. Behaviours expected of men in other cultures might be considered completely non-masculine in twenty-first-century Canada. For example, British noblemen openly wore wigs in public, but men wearing hair pieces in our communities today are often subjected to scorn. Men should look a certain way, but it is not masculine to be anxious and uncertain enough about one's appearance to wear a wig.

Of course, in addition to being culturally specific, notions of masculinity (and femininity) are open to challenge. As we saw in Chapter One, hegemonic masculinity exacts costs from men who don't conform, but it also exacts a price from men who do conform. The important thing to remember is that when we critique masculinity, we are not attacking people who are masculine or even people who are male. Instead, we are examining a particular cultural construction, probing its parameters, strengths, and weaknesses. *Masculinity* does not equal *maleness*. We must recognize that many men feel compelled to follow cultural standards to be "tough" or to be "competitive" even if this has negative consequences.

Scholars from several disciplines have explored this question of gender-based normative expectations. Anthropologist David Gilmore (1990) undertook a cross-cultural analysis to understand the ways in which masculinity manifests itself in a variety of cultures. He raises an important point: in many cultures, *manhood* is not automatically attached to any person who is male and is not an inherent quality of maleness. In fact, in most cultures, masculinity is something that must be earned. Manhood is proven and maintained by actively living up to certain normative expectations. Gilmore argues that in most cultures, proof of masculinity involves providing, protecting, and procreating. In order for communities to thrive, those three activities are essential. But the physical environment in which the community exists determines the degree of danger or urgency associated with those requirements. Gilmore argued that cultures existing in more difficult physical environments, where men's activities are both necessary for the economic good of the community and highly demanding or dangerous for individuals, afford higher rewards to men who live up to expectations. For example, a low-technology culture that relies on the ocean for food needs adult men able to fish in dangerous waters or people will go hungry. In order to encourage men to engage in such dangerous activities, the culture highly values and rewards masculine courage. In short, men who engage in this work and provide for the community are considered to be the most masculine and they are rewarded through prestige and power in the larger community. If they do not, they lose their "manhood" and their position in the community.

Interestingly, Gilmore argues that in such difficult environments, the script for manhood isn't really in the best interests of individual men. It would be easier and safer to let someone else brave the elements to provide food for the community. But the masculine script is good for the larger community because it generates the willingness among men to put their individual interests aside for the good of the group. Masculine norms, then, serve to meet the community's needs for provision and protection.

One of the often-voiced concerns about masculinity in Canada today is that it is in a state of "crisis." The root of this so-called crisis is the fact that men's traditional roles—providing, protecting, and procreating—are being challenged. The increased participation of women in the paid labour force means that women can provide for themselves. The advances in reproductive technology mean that women can choose when or if they wish to have children, and their choices do not require consent of a male partner. Women also participate in the military and in police forces, eliminating the masculine monopoly on protection. Thus, the perceived need for traditional masculinity is diminished. Of course, individual men can and still do protect and provide for their children; therefore, the crisis, if there is one, isn't entirely about the loss of a particular set of roles. Nor has it been the case that women in the past played no role in procreating, protecting, or providing—they too made valuable contributions. As noted throughout this text, stereotypical masculine and feminine qualities are rarely unique to a single gender. Nonetheless, the hegemonic masculine gender role, with characteristics often defined in opposition to feminine characteristics, provides a measure—however false or harmful—of what it means to be a man. Because of the fundamental opposition in the stereotypical definitions of masculine and feminine, it might well be a "crisis" if one cannot clearly define and limit the feminine against which masculinity is defined.

Andrew Kimbrell (1995) sees a different aspect of this crisis of masculinity. He focuses on current North American culture and argues that our perception of masculinity and the expectations placed on men are actually quite harmful, not just for individual men but for the community at large. Over time, Kimbrell says, masculinity has become destructive. Again, he isn't blaming men for adopting these potentially harmful normative expectations; rather, he is challenging our current notions of masculinity. Competition, success, and control norms have become so demanding that too much must be sacrificed to meet the expectations. He examines the evidence showing how much harm men currently experience. For example, he notes men's shorter life expectancy and higher suicide rates. He attributes these health risks not to a fundamental weakness in maleness but to a distorted understanding of how men are supposed to be, to the flawed normative expectations of masculinity. Three brief examples from his work, *The Masculine Mystique* (1995), illustrate his concerns:

1. Men must compete and continually prove their manhood. This leads to aggressive and exploitative attitudes that erode relationships. Men win or lose everything in the attempt (or die trying).

2. Men are "trapped in the harness" of working to provide (make as much money as possible). They come to see everyone as a potential customer, always trying to sell or profit from relationships, foregoing opportunities for other intimate relationships.

3. Men gain power (the ability to be dominant, to control or coerce) through success in attaining the masculine ideal. Achieving this masculinity requires intense pressure and sacrifice. Not all men achieve this power, and many end up feeling frustrated and angry in their powerlessness.

One of Kimbrell's key concerns is that our culture has tended to blame men for these problems and the larger problems in society, rather than focusing on the true culprit—a distorted version of masculinity. Instead of blaming men for the current crises in individuals, families, and communities, he contends that we need to understand men's struggles with a destructive set of cultural ideals. Kimbrell argues that the feminist movement has contributed to this placing of blame on men by polarizing gender roles, characteristics, and definitions. Accepting such gender-polarized assumptions leads also to the valorization of one over the other. Praising women, according to Kimbrell, appears to necessarily involve blaming men.

Kimbrel would like to see masculinity evolve into a set of normative expectations that are healthier for everyone. He calls this ideal "husbandry":

> Husbandry implies caring for others, one's family and community as well as the larger biotic community with whom we share the natural world. Moreover, husbandry also suggests a sense of pride for men, a pride gained in the purposeful care of their own health and that of their families and friends, and in the stewardship of the earth's land and its limited resources. Husbandry reflects the ultimate expression of masculine generativity and power. (pp. 300–01)

This evolution towards husbandry is Kimbrell's solution to the problems of masculinity.

Canadian scholar Michael Kaufman (1993) argues that masculinity is already evolving in more positive ways. He uses the powerful image of a suit of armour to describe traditional masculine normative expectations. Armour served to strengthen and protect knights in competition and in battle. It was a valuable tool, but it had major drawbacks. The armour itself was incredibly heavy (the headpiece and attached chain mail weighed well over 12 kilos), and carrying this burden precluded many other activities. Armour also isolated the wearer and made effective communication much more difficult. Kaufman suggests that the traditional masculine normative expectations are like armour. They are protective because when "wearing" these expectations, men can hide weaknesses and pain beneath a mantle of strength and power. But behind the mask is isolation. Kaufman works as a consultant and activist to help men remove their armour. He argues that until men effectively communicate with one another and show their full range of human emotions (including sadness and pain as well as anger), they will continue to be heavily burdened by the armour—limiting their relationships and activities.

While masculinity has evolved towards more freedom in expression of emotion, some shifts have been harmful. One emerging pattern is a growing emphasis on appearance. Masculine expectations have traditionally been based on actions and achievements rather than appearance, but some research indicates that this is changing. Men are increasingly subject to appearance norms. In their work, *The Adonis Complex*, Pope *et al.* (2000) produce evidence suggesting that there has been a harmful increase in the pressure on men to work towards a body image and appearance standards that are unrealistic, unhealthy, and limiting. They argue that men are "increasingly surrounded with media images of masculine perfection—not just in the gym, but in advertisements, on television, in the movies . . . they are also bombarded with messages from burgeoning multi-billion dollar industries that capitalize upon their body insecurities" (p. 5). Because of the other normative expectations that do not grant freedom to discuss fears and concerns, men are subjected to these pressures with little support from others. Rather than working together to challenge them, they face the pressures alone. "Many women can now recognize and voice their appearance concerns, speaking openly about their reactions to ideals . . . But men still labour under the societal taboo against expressing such feelings. . . . To a degree unprecedented in history, men are being made to feel more and more inadequate about how they look—while simultaneously being prohibited from talking about it or even admitting it to themselves" (p. 5).

The end result of this pressure contributes to several harmful trends, such as:

- an increase in the use of anabolic steroids that can have short-term psychiatric effects and a long-term risk of heart disease and cancer;
- increasing numbers of men with disordered eating patterns (restricting, binging, purging);
- "body dysmorphic disorder" which involves "health-threatening worries that something is wrong with the way that they look" leading to depression and isolation (Pope *et al.*, 2000).

Because the authors of *The Adonis Complex* are medical practitioners and psychological clinicians, they work regularly with men experiencing some of these difficulties. Thus, their findings should not lead us to conclude that all men are currently experiencing these troubles. But they do shed light on a relevant concern. Men are increasingly facing these appearance pressures as body image industries—supplements, diet aids, fitness programs, hair growth remedies—grow more numerous and pervasive.

As provocatively discussed in the following guest essay "In Praise of Men" by Anthony Synnott, masculinity and masculine gender roles have taken quite a toll on the lives of individual men. As the definitions and roles change, Synnott suggests that we would do well to move away from viewing masculinity and femininity as opposites. The existing gender polarization means that recognition of and support for women automatically involves criticism and devaluing of men. An underlying theme in Synnott's essay is the need to move away from this oppositional categorization and the almost inevitable valorization of one over the other.

BOX 3-1	In Praise of Men

by Anthony Synnott

There seems to be considerable confusion these days about the current status and future prospects of men, and even about their moral value. Men are widely stereotyped as pigs, violent, idiots (in the media from sitcoms to *The Simpsons* to *Trailer Park Boys*), deadbeat dads, misogynists, though most men are none of these things. Minorities are used to scapegoat the majority. Joke books satirize men, as in *Women are from Venus, Men are from Hell* (Newman, 1999), "*101 Reasons Why a Cat is Better than a Man*" (Zobel, 1994), "*Men and Other Reptiles*" (Contemporary Books, 1993). T-shirts are equally rude: "PMS: Putting up with Men's Shit," and one I saw at the University of Winnipeg: "I like sensitive men: who cry when I hit them." And a popular series of T-shirts, gloves, purses, and posters of the series: "Boys are smelly. Throw rocks at them." This advocacy of violence against men in popular culture is disconcerting, given that men are the majority of homicide victims.

In academia, the same male negativism is apparent. Sociologist R.W. Connell, author of numerous books on men and on gender, refers to men as the "hegemonic sex" and oppressive of women, and opines that all men benefit from a "patriarchal dividend" (2000; 2002). Michael Kimmel, the leading American sociologist on men, is particularly male-negative. He opens his text *Manhood in America* with a long list of male villains (1996:vii), not a hero in sight, nor a good husband, father or worker. And in the sixth volume of his

popular reader, co-edited with Michael Messner, he just adds to the list, and comments that "Not a week seems to go by without another in the seemingly endless parade of men behaving badly" (2004: 565). Well, you find what you look for, but the same could be said about women, of course. And not a week goes by without another in the seemingly endless parade of men behaving well, even heroically, as at 9/11, which he did not even mention.

While some see men as hegemonic and having all the power as problematic (Kimmel, 1992), Warren Farrell, author of the *The Myth of Male Power* (1993), challenges the whole idea of hegemony, describes men as relatively powerless in many domains, and refers to men as "the disposable sex." While many authors have been concerned with the victimization of women, quite rightly, Farrell has drawn attention to the victimization of men: by societal norms, by other men, and by men themselves. He discusses the draft, the war deaths, deaths by homicide, suicide, at work, in accidents, the failures of the justice system, the penal system, the family system, the health system and more. There is nothing hegemonic about incarcerations and early deaths in war and peace, nor homelessness. David Thomas (1993) refers to men as "the suicide sex." We might label all this as the "patriarchal tax" (contrary to Connell), and compare dividends and taxes for both sexes.

But how people identify the "problem(s)" and solutions varies widely.

(Continued)

BOX 3-1	In Praise of Men (*Continued*)

Trendspotters and advertising executives concluded their recent book *The Future of Men* as follows:

> Does modern man have a future? Yes, indeed. And he has the power to shape it just as women shaped theirs in the last century. Man's greatest battle is not against women or other men or even changing times. It's against the inertia that falsely tells him he's on top and will always be on top. It's against the false sense of security that what forever has been will always be. (Salzman, Matathia and O'Reilly, 2005:219)

How interesting even to ask that question; and to diagnose the problem as men's "false sense of security." We might agree that it is time men defended their own interests better than they have done, and that in post-modernity men and women have to be adaptable and flexible in changing times. But to suggest that men believe they are on top is silly: some are, as are some women; but most are just working to support their families, and many are homeless, unemployed, injured, incarcerated, have lost their wives, children and homes, are victims of war and violence and eventually suicide, or ill-health and premature death. And many fought hard battles for women's rights. Indeed, surely it was men as controllers of the "system" who opened the system to women. For this too we might praise men.

Robert Bly, whose book *Iron John* (1990) inaugurated the field of Men's Studies, diagnosed men today as "soft," having lost their sense of self and purpose due primarily to two factors. First, the widespread alienation of men from the family (by work, drugs, alcohol, prison,

divorce and separation, etc), and second, the raising of a generation of men by their mothers who, he said, can raise boys but not men, nor give them a sense of male identity. He recommended more male mentoring and deeper male bonding.

In a time of doom, gloom, and misandry, it is also time to be male positive, which—despite our cultural definitions of men and women as opposite sexes, Mars and Venus, yin and yang—does not mean being female negative. We can be human positive, and humanistic, if we try. So herewith some words in praise of men.

In Praise of Men

The beginning of a new century and a millennium is an excellent occasion to look back and reflect, and to assess the contributions of men and women over these long time spans. Any such assessments are bound to be controversial and political, but they do open the door to a discussion of the realities of men and women. Rather than debate comparative victimizations, and the merits or demerits of misogyny and misandry, here we will cut through these knots and suggest that male-positive attitudes are indeed evidence-based.

The Nobel Prizes are a measure of human achievement; they are offered in five scientific disciplines, and the Peace Prize. In the new millennium, almost all the disciplinary prizes have been awarded to men, as they were in the past. The significant exception was Mme. Curie, who won two Nobels in two different disciplines—the only person ever to do so. The Nobel Peace Prizes are more evenly distributed. From 2000, the Peace

BOX 3-1	*(Continued)*

Prize has been awarded successively to South Korean President Kim Dae Jung, Kofi Annan and the United Nations, former U.S. president Jimmy Carter, and in 2003 to Shiran Ebadi, a lawyer and the first Iranian and the first Muslim woman to win the prize. In 2004, Wangari Maathai, a forestry conservationist, won, and in 2005 Mohamed El Baradei and the International Atomic Energy Agency won. Of the six Peace Prizes won in this millennium, four were won by men—these and the dozens of men and women who won before deserve our praise and gratitude.

We recognize and reward contributions to civilization in many domains; and contributions to scientific disciplines with Nobel prizes, contributions to Peace with the Peace Prize, and we sometimes recognize personal bravery.

The first iconic case was the RMS Titanic, which sank off Newfoundland in 1912. Of the 2223 passengers and crew, 1517 (68 percent) were lost; but 70 percent of the women and children were saved, and 80 percent of the men were lost (Kuntz, 1998: 559). And the 1360 men were lost precisely to save the women and children. "Women and children first" was the order, and it was carried out peacefully. The men, some of them the wealthiest and most powerful in Europe and the United States, gave up their lives for total strangers. Such heroic altruism and bravery was no doubt laudable, but much of it was, sadly, unnecessary.

The other classic case was 9/11. The 9/11 Commission Report stated: "On September 11, the nation suffered the largest loss of life—2973—on its soil as a result of a hostile attack in its history" (2004: 311). This was a higher casualty rate than Pearl Harbour and included 343 FDNY fatalities, 37 PAPD fatalities and 23 NYPD fatalities: 403 men. They lost their lives doing their jobs, saving lives, protecting strangers. Thanks to them, very few of those below the impact sites on the two towers lost their lives. And thanks also to the bravery of the passengers of United Flight 93 (Todd Beamer's "Let's roll!"), this aircraft came down before hitting its intended target of either the Capitol or the White House.

The loss of the *Titanic* and 9/11 were perhaps isolated incidents in terms of scale, but men's self-sacrifice and altruism is part of the bedrock of male identity.

In the United States and Canada, the Carnegie Medal is awarded "to those who risk their lives to an extraordinary degree while saving or attempting to save the lives of others." Ninety-two medals were awarded in 2005: 85 to men, and seven to women. Eleven medal winners lost their lives—all men. Six of the medal winners were Canadian, one of whom died. The bravery of all these men and women is remarkable, as they rescued total strangers from burning houses, planes and cars, floods, assaults, drowning, attacks by dogs, and, in one case, a mountain lion, and a gas explosion. The costs in terms of lives lost and injuries sustained are high (www.carnegiehero.org). Men do not have a monopoly on bravery—there are brave women out there too—but the balance is clear.

Though English historian and feminist Rosalind Miles (1991) referred to men as "the death sex," she might equally have referred to men as "the life-saving sex"—not only for their bravery, but

(Continued)

BOX 3-1	**In Praise of Men (*Continued*)**

also for their services to medical science. How many lives our medical researchers, male and female, have saved is impossible to calculate, though the global population "explosion" from 1.8 billion in 1900 to 6.1 billion in 2000 and 6.5 billion in 2006 suggests that the numbers are in the billions rather than the millions. Among the greatest researchers were William Harvey, Edward Jenner, Louis Pasteur, Alexander Fleming, Jonas Salk, as well as James Watson and Francis Crick (Friedman and Friedland, 2000). More recently, *Newsweek* has eulogized U.S. Navy Dr. Richard Jadick, "Hero M.D." who saved an estimated 30 lives in the battle for Fallujah in 2004 (Wingert and Thomas, 2006). Engineers may have been equal or even more important in life saving and the elimination of diseases with the provision of clean water and sanitation facilities.

Male bravery may or may not be hard-wired; but boys are socialized and trained to be brave and altruistic, usually more than girls. Parents instruct their sons: "Don't cry!" "Be brave!" "Don't be a baby!" And the comics, television shows and children's films are full of superheroes: Superman, Spiderman, Batman, the Six Million Dollar Man, and more recently in the films: Luke Skywalker, Peter Pan, Harry Potter, and Frodo Baggins. The role models of bravery, stoicism, and self-sacrificing heroism are everywhere for boys to emulate, and girls to admire and to expect.

War is difficult to theorize in any way other than as a sometimes necessary evil. Yet over 100 000 Canadian military men have been killed, and even more injured, in the wars of the last century. Over 60 000 were killed in World War I and over 42 000 in World War II in the war against fascism, and over 100 so far in U.N.-mandated peacekeeping operations around the world. The protection of the nation and international peacekeeping has until recently been an exclusively male duty and responsibility, with high costs, even life itself; and the sacrifices continue to be offered. This enormous altruism and love we remember on November 11 every year.

Men learn very early what masculinity is; and though in post-modernity there are now many models and options available, and we talk of masculinities; plural, not a monolithic singular, core values, expectations and behaviours persist and remain worthy of recognition and respect. Negativities exist among both sexes, but we do need to remember the positives.

Conclusion

In sum, the prevalence of misandry requires a response. The misandry may itself be a response to an earlier sexism, misogyny; but the new sexism is hardly superior to the old. It is embedded, so to speak, in much popular culture, generated by both men and women, in joke books, sit-coms, on T-shirts and in novels, films, and even sociology texts; so something in praise of men may be a useful antidote. Indeed, faced with such polarized, binary, and valenced analyses: powerful/powerless, hegemonic/decline, violent/soft, misogyny/misandry, dividend/

BOX 3-1	*(Continued)*

tax, and the trinitarian perspective of men as villains/victims/heroes, there is clearly room for middle ground, balance, and more nuanced discussions. They tend, however, to be conspicuous by their absence, and we certainly lack consensus.

The *Titanic* and 9/11 illustrate the extraordinary bravery and courage, and altruism and self-sacrifice, of ordinary men. The Carnegie and Canadian medals for bravery are overwhelmingly awarded to men. Instead of portraying men as violent, rapists, pigs, the enemy, or the death sex, we can look at another side of the coin and recognize men as the heroic, life-saving, productive, and constructive sex. We might even sing a song in praise of men.

Bibliography

Bly, Robert. 1990. *Iron John*. New York: Addison-Wesley.

Connell, R.W. 2000. *The Men and the Boys*. Berkeley, CA:University of California Press.

Connell, R.W. 2002. *Gender*. Cambridge: Polity Press.

Farrell, Warren 1993. *The Myth of Male Power: How Men are the Disposable Sex*. New York: Simon and Schuster.

Friedman, Meyer and Gerald W. Friedland. 2000. *Medicine's 10 Greatest Discoveries*. New Haven: Yale University Press.

Kimmel, Michael. 1992. "Reading Men: Men, Masculinity, and Publishing". *Contemporary Sociology* 21:2:162-71.

Kimmel, Michael. 1996. *Manhood in America: A Cultural History*. New York: The Free Press.

Kimmel, Michael and Michael Messner, eds. 2004. *Men's Lives*. 6th Edition. New York: Brown, Allyn and Bacon.

Kuntz, Tom (ed.) 1998. *The Titanic Disaster Hearings. The Official Transcript of the 1912 Senate Investigation*. New York: Pocket Books.

Miles, Rosalind. 1991. *The Rites of Man*. London: Grafton Books.

Newman, Amanda. 1999. *Women are from Venus, Men are from Hell*. Holbrook, MA: Adams Media.

9/11 Commission Report 2004. Final Report of the National Commission on Terrorist Attacks upon the United States. New York: Norton.

Salzman, Marian, Ira Matathia and Ann O'Reilly, 2005. *The Future of Men*. New York: Palgrave Macmillan.

Thomas, David. 1993. *Not Guilty: The Case in Defense of Men*. New York: William Morrow.

Wingert, Pat and Evan Thomas. 2006. "On Call in Hell." *Newsweek*. 20 March: 34-43.

Zobel, Allia. *1994. 101 Reasons Why a Cat is Better Than a Man*. Holbrook, Mass.: Bob Adams.

FEMININITIES

Just as there has been criticism of traditional masculinities, so too has there been concern over traditional notions of femininity. While exploration and discussion of masculinities is a fairly recent phenomenon, attention has been focused on the limitations associated with traditional notions of femininities for several decades. The most commonly accepted notion of femininity that has been sharply challenged by the women's movement was the

belief that women should focus their attention on making successful marriages and raising their children. The emphasized femininity of the 1950s and 1960s was the "motherhood mandate." During these decades, the normative expectations for femininity revolved
around marriage and children. There was also an expectation of dependence rather than
self-sufficiency. In fact, many of the feminists writing during this time felt that notions of
femininity were oppressive to women: as long as women strove to live up to these expectations, they recreated patriarchal relations in their own home and internalized their own
oppression.

Betty Friedan (1963) was one of the first writers to publicly critique this notion of femininity. In her book *The Feminine Mystique*, she argued that the limitations of femininity
were harming homemakers. By focusing all their energies on looking after their husbands
and children, female homemakers failed to develop their own interests and abilities, leaving
them feeling empty and depressed. She felt they should become active participants in the
paid labour force, pursuing economic opportunities instead of restricting their activities to
the household. Of course, Friedan's ideas had weaknesses. For example, she really was only
speaking of middle-class married women who could afford to live out the feminine normative expectations, rather than of working-class women who held low-wage jobs and raised
families. More importantly, she essentially valorized masculine norms over feminine by encouraging women to focus on careers instead of families and reinforcing the notion that paid
work is valuable and family work is not. Nonetheless, her argument was widely discussed.

Susan Brownmiller (1984), in her classic work entitled *Femininity*, also addresses the
problems with this dependent notion of femininity. In her assessment, being feminine
meant sacrificing dreams and potentials in order to live down to a limited set of behaviours
that were judged appropriate for women. The pay-off for these sacrifices was male attention, societal approval, and the possibility of becoming a mother:

> The world smiles favorably on the feminine woman . . . one works at femininity by accepting
> restrictions, by limiting one's sights, by choosing an indirect route, by scattering concentration
> and not giving one's all as a man would to his own, certifiably masculine interests. It does not require
> a great leap of imagination for a woman to understand the feminine principle as a grand collec-
> tion of compromises large and small, that she simply must make in order to render herself a suc-
> cessful woman. (p.16)

Her basic argument is that fear of being judged unfeminine has kept women, individually
and collectively, from exploring their potential and achieving great things. In short, this
kind of femininity has been debilitating for women.

Brownmiller was not alone in her critique of femininity. Some feminist scholars suggested that femininity was a form of internalized patriarchy: women are colonized by these
notions and thus became implicated in their own oppression. Kate Millet (1977) argued
that women should actively resist being feminine, but she didn't advocate that they adopt
masculine norms either. Millet believed that the ideal arrangement was to do away with
gender expectations altogether and to adopt androgynous characteristics.

In part because of the efforts of many feminist writers, femininity has not received a
great deal of attention in recent decades. To illustrate this, try looking in the table of contents
and indices of books on gender. *Masculinity* figures prominently in most texts, while *femininity* rarely even appears. It is as though *femininity* were something to be ashamed of and
therefore remains largely undiscussed. But the normative expectations for women are still present, even if the term *femininity* is seldom used. As we already noted, normative expectations are

time- and place-specific. Because women's activities have changed substantially since Friedan and Millet challenged traditional ideas about femininity, our notions of appropriate expectations for women have also changed. Create your own list of expectations about women's appearance and behaviour and of actions that are likely to receive negative attention or sanctions. You may find that your list reflects two prominent sets of expectations:

1. Nurturance, empathy, and interdependence: Women are expected to express care and concern for others, often putting the needs of others ahead of their own, and are expected to be relationship oriented.

2. Appearance: Women are expected to be concerned about their appearance, especially beauty and slenderness.

These two elements of femininity shape the lives of women. The first—empathy and nurturance—is discussed in Chapters 8 and 11. While there is increasing recognition that women deserve opportunities to pursue education and careers and their own interests, they are still expected to put other people before themselves, not necessarily by focusing primarily on their husbands and children (as in the past), but certainly on maintaining relationships and nurturing people around them.

The second element of femininity in twenty-first century Canada—appearance—has been growing in importance. Sandra Bartky (1998) discusses the normative expectation of appearance in great detail. Like Millet, she links elements of femininity with **internalized oppression**. Women discipline their bodies to achieve the emphasized ideal, regardless of the cost. Bartky argues that three key activities make a body appear feminine: size, comportment, and ornamentation. These appearance norms change over time and place. What was deemed desirable in the 1950s—Marilyn Munroe's voluptuous curves, for example—would now be considered overweight. The current fashion is extreme thinness to the point of emaciation—a body type that does not come naturally to the majority of women. By dieting and exercising, women discipline their bodies' appetites to live down to these unrealistic standards. Bartky argues that women's comportment also is highly restricted: they train themselves to keep their arms and legs close to the body in order to take up a minimum amount of space. Women's bodies as ornamented surfaces also require great discipline (not to mention time and money). Signs of aging are to be defied through the use of creams and dyes, lasers and botox. Cosmetics and hairstyles are employed to create beauty, as if women without artifice were deficient. The irony of all this effort and self-policing is that it does not earn women respect. Those who don't conform are devalued for "letting themselves go," and those who do comply are ridiculed for their vanity or obsession with clothes and shoes. In addition, Bartky argues that almost everyone woman who strives to achieve this model of femininity will fail, at least to some degree, because of the difference between real people and the stereotyped ideals. Women are living, breathing humans who cannot reach the perfect ideals against which they are judged. Media models have typically spent hours being groomed and clothed, and then the images are usually enhanced via computer technology to create truly unreal beauty standards. As Bartky describes it, "a measure of shame is added to a woman's sense that the body she inhabits is deficient: she ought to take better care of herself" (p. 34). Those who succeed to some degree gain attention but little significant social power: succeeding at this feminine task wins social approval but requires great self-discipline.

It is not simple vanity and blind compliance with normative expectations that encourages women to pursue these beauty ideals. There is a concrete benefit attached to meeting expectations. Empirical research suggests there is a real **beauty bias**: good-looking people are treated better in our society. Attractive babies are cuddled more; attractive toddlers are punished less; teachers give more attention to better-looking students; strangers are more likely to offer help to attractive people; jurors show more sympathy to good-looking victims; and attractive applicants are more readily hired for jobs (see Freedman, 1986). But the beauty bias is *not* a gender-neutral pattern:

> Because beauty is asymmetrically assigned to the feminine role, women are defined as much by their looks as by their deeds. To be womanly is to be beautiful, and, conversely, to be unattractive is to be unwomanly. Good looks are prerequisite for femininity but incidental to masculinity. This asymmetry produces different social expectations and different psychological consequences for each sex. (Freedman, 1986, pp. 1–2)

Women much more than men are judged by their appearance, and they are more severely rejected if they are considered unattractive. Consequently, it seems in their best interests to maximize their attractiveness. Women striving to achieve this feminine expectation spend enormous amounts of time, energy, and money on it. But the irony is that as more women seek to enhance their appearance, the measurement standard moves ever upward. Women's appearance standards aren't measured against a real person, but against an inflated norm. This theme of the cost of femininity is echoed by Wolf (1990), who argues that the continued pressure on women to comply with appearance norms takes away other opportunities. So much effort is expended on appearance that there is little energy left for developing their other potentials. She calls this the **beauty myth**: women have been freed from the expectations of domesticity, but the demands of appearance norms continue to limit women's potential.

Meyers argues that we are surrounded by cultural images and myths that "encode various meanings of womanhood and norms applying to women" (2002, p. 25). These *figurations of womanhood*, as she calls them, are a means of internalized oppression. But they can't just be wished away by discussing them. Becoming aware of the tremendous costs associated with extreme thinness (physical and psychological), as well as the financial and emotional costs attached to striving for an unattainable beauty standard doesn't stop most women from measuring themselves against that standard. This is not surprising: appearance expectations are part of our socio-cultural landscape and become part of women's own self-portraits. Meyers suggests that this internalization occurs because the "culturally entrenched representations of womanhood" are so compelling that they facilitate "the transmission and retention of these messages. Thus girls are often inducted into cultural expectations, their attitudes and behavior shaped" (p. 26), even when parents try to raise their daughters in nonsexist ways. For most women, denying the power of these normative expectations and ignoring the pressure to conform involves re-conceiving their self-portraits—not an easy task by any means.

Nonetheless, recognition and acknowledgment of the gender-based normative expectations—for both women and men—is a necessary starting point for understanding ourselves as gendered beings. The women's movement evolved out of a recognition of and challenge to the socio-cultural *femininity* that valorized a certain set of feminine qualities and roles over all others.

CONCLUSION

Gender-based normative expectations are a part of our socio-cultural landscape. They are ubiquitous in the media (see also Chapter Four), and they influence our self-perceptions and interactions. Of course, we don't all choose to strive to live up to or down to such expectations; but they are a cultural standard by which we are typically measured or against which we struggle. Some scholars (Lorber, 2000, for example) have argued that we need to do away with such social constructions—that people would be better off if they were not measured according to gender standards. Lorber says participation in a **de-gendering movement** by resisting the categories and reveling in the freedom this affords us is preferable to performing normative gender in our daily lives.

Maybe you can see a certain appeal to such an argument. Wouldn't it be nice if we could just be ourselves without the pressure of being measured against a gendered standard? But is it really that easy? Can we just exist outside of gender constructions? A colleague of the one of the authors does exactly that. She is a woman in her 40s who likes to describe and present herself as a teenaged boy. A sociology professor, she challenges everyone's notions of gender, sexuality, age, and social class. This frees her from societal expectations, because she resists them at every turn, but it also exacts a price. Some people around her do not understand or accept her choices, condemning her lack of orthodoxy and questioning her professionalism. They wonder how a person who looks and acts as she does can effectively fulfill the requirements of her job. (If they saw her teaching evaluations, they'd realize how incredibly successful a gender resistor can be!) But is this option available to all of us? We are born into a gendered world. We do not choose our sex, any more than we choose our ethnicity. We can do gender as we choose, but from infancy, gendered expectations are thrust upon us, and our choices are constrained by our social context.

Meyers argues that gender is not only internalized but also individualized. We don't have to be slaves to gender expectations, but we can't avoid them entirely either:

> It is a mistake to picture attributes like gender as toxic capsules full of norms and interpretive schemas that individuals swallow whole and that lodge intact in their psychic structure. The diversity of individuals' experience of gender belies this view. But it is also a mistake to picture attributes like gender as systems of social and economic opportunities, constraints, rewards, and penalties that never impinge on individual identity. (2002, p.10)

There is an interesting tension between the performance-based explanation of gender—such as Judith Butler's—and the theory that our gendered society has an impact on the shape of our identities—as Diana Meyers argues. Many of the most interesting debates in gender studies at this time (including one between the two authors of this text) focus on this tension.

CHAPTER SUMMARY: KEY POINTS

1. Humans use *stereotypes* to organize information and to facilitate interaction. But stereotypes become problematic if they are rigid, adverse beliefs (*prejudices*) which blind them to the diversity of real people.

2. Canadian society has stereotypes about the qualities of women and men, which it categorizes as *masculine* and *feminine*. These are normative expectations against which people judge themselves and others.

3. Our gender-based normative expectations are polarized: whatever women are supposed to be, men are not supposed to be, and vice versa. People who do not live up to these normative expectations are often subject to negative sanctions.

4. Roles are sets of rights and obligations attached to particular social statuses. *Gender roles*, a concept used to explain the activities of women and men, are negotiated in specific social contexts.

5. *Status expectations theory* suggests that when we interact with others, we take into account their status and they ours. Because we judge each other and our actions according to gender-based expectations, status expectations influence interaction. In general, men are typically afforded higher status than women.

6. Specific versions of masculinity and femininity, known as *hegemonic masculinity* and *emphasized femininity*, are the dominant patterns of behaviour expected of men and women.

7. *Hegemonic masculinity* emphasizes performance. Qualities of hegemonic masculinity include competition, achievement, self-reliance, strength, toughness, and avoidance of anything considered feminine or weak.

8. Some people believe there is a *crisis in masculinity* because they believe the normative expectations for men are not healthy. These expectations create intense pressure and demand unreasonable sacrifice, harming men, their relationships, and the larger community.

9. The notion of *femininity* was challenged by many feminist writers, who argued that it was a form of internalized oppression. Women who conform to ideas of femininity by focusing on nurturing others and undertaking domestic activities and self beautification reinforce and recreate unequal relations between the sexes.

10. The current feminine ideal, known as *emphasized femininity*, focuses mainly on appearance: women are supposed to be thin and beautiful. Achieving this ideal requires a large investment of time and money; and many women experience shame for not achieving the beauty ideal.

DISCUSSION QUESTIONS

1. Do you believe there is a "crisis" in masculinity, or that misandry is a serious problem? What evidence have you seen for and against this notion in your social milieu? If you could alter normative expectations for masculinity, what would you change?

2. In his guest essay, Anthony Synnott notes that men are more likely to have earned many more medals for bravery and Nobel Prizes and have made more scientific discoveries than women. While men deserve praise, we must also consider the reasons underlying these patterns. Why haven't women earned such accolades or been as prominent in the past?

3. Can you think of examples where status expectations have advantaged or disadvantaged you in a social situation? Have they operated as self-fulfilling prophecies in your life?

4. Do you see emphasized femininity as "internalized oppression"? Can you think of a counter-argument? In what ways do you challenge hegemonic masculinity and/or emphasized femininity?

5. Do you think a "de-gendering movement" is possible? Is it desirable? How could it be achieved?

KEY TERMS

beauty bias	gender polarization	normative expectations
beauty myth	gender roles	legitimacy effect
de-gendering movement	hegemonic masculinity	prejudice
discrimination	hegemonic femininity	sexism
emphasized femininity	internalized oppression	status expectations theory
femininity	masculinity	stereotype

chapter four

Shaping the Socio-Cultural Landscape: Language and Media

How did you spend your day yesterday? Did you watch TV? Chat with people on MSN? Read a book? Meet friends at Tim Horton's for coffee? Write an essay? If you think about your day, you will likely find that, except for the time spent sleeping, the majority of your time was spent using language, and a large portion may also have been spent using some form of media. When I thought about my day, I realized that the only waking moments I spent *not* using media or language were spent swimming laps in the pool and walking my dog. (Actually I used language to communicate with the dog too; I'm just not sure whether he was listening.) These are normal patterns for the majority of people living in Canada at the beginning of the twenty-first century. With iPods and computers, televisions, and telephones, we are almost constantly using language, media, or both. This means that both language and media have a profound impact on our lives. They play a key role in shaping the socio-cultural landscape. This chapter will discuss the impact of language and media on gender issues. How are they gendered? What messages do we give and receive simply by communicating with others and using media?

LANGUAGE

Language operates in two key ways in our lives. The most obvious is communication. We use words, symbols, and gestures to interact with other people, to explain our needs and feelings, and to participate in economic and social life. Language and communication will be discussed in greater detail in Chapter Nine, which examines the ways that gender influences communication patterns. Many people use gender-specific language patterns, both verbal and nonverbal. Empirical research shows that women are more likely to smile frequently and ask questions to further the conversation, while men are more likely to interrupt and use slang. In fact, these language patterns can contribute to or reflect differing positions of power. Our perceptions of others are in part based upon the ways in which people choose to communicate. In this chapter, we are going to focus more directly on language itself—that is, the links between words, their interpretation, and gender.

Does language shape the way people think? It certainly shapes the way we understand the social world. All our social relations involve symbols and the interpretation of those symbols. In this sense, language provides the basic building blocks for social life. Children are socialized into the culture through language: they learn the symbol system necessary to act and interact within their social group. The language system they learn, then, shapes their understanding. Moreover, that language reflects the biases and prejudices of the culture. If the language itself is sexist or racist, then through socialization, we are predisposed to interpret words and actions in sexist or racist ways.

Whenever a symbol is used, it carries with it the meaning intended by the user. But it is also interpreted by the one who hears or sees it, and this transfer of information is not precise. Symbols can be interpreted in many ways. Often a person's interpretation is based on his or her prior experiences and accumulated knowledge. An eleven-year-old known to one of the authors was describing her new friend: "She has long brown hair, likes to play basketball, is a slut, and has an older brother." When questioned on the slut descriptor, she explained that her twelve-year-old friend had already had three boyfriends. In Grade Six in Alberta, apparently a girl that has gone out with more than one boy can be labelled a slut. Importantly, the child doing the labelling was not using the term in a pejorative sense: she didn't mean it as an insult or as a value judgment on her friend's sexual activities. Her understanding of the word was limited to "having several boyfriends." The author, however, had a very different understanding of the word; and had she not questioned the statement, she would have been worried about sexually precocious grade-schoolers. (This text discusses the word *slut* in more detail in a later section, for it has implications for understanding gendered language.)

Long-standing language theory suggests that language limits our perceptions: we can't comprehend ideas if we don't have meaningful symbols for them (Sapir, 1956). The classic example is the word *snow*. If a culture has only one word for snow, then when white precipitation is falling from the sky, they use that word, and those around them who share their language know what they mean. But some cultures, such as the Inuit in the far north, might have many words for snow and use these words to be much more precise: is it granular, sticky, about to melt, drifted? For those who live in urban environments where snow has a limited impact on survival, one word is sufficient. But for those whose livelihoods and safety depend on snow conditions, precise words might be much more critical. If city-dwellers and southerners know only the one word, they are far less likely to see a difference between types of snow. Their perceptions are limited by their inadequate language. Having few specific words limits what people perceive.

Other linguists have suggested that if we don't have words to describe concepts, we even have difficulty remembering them. Think of the example of classical music. If you don't have much musical training but you go to the symphony, you might enjoy the music immensely; but how would you describe your favourite part to someone else (the loud part? the fast part? the part with the trumpet solo? the part where the drums sounded like thunder?)? And when you think back on it a day or a week later, you will likely have difficulty remembering what you experienced, because you don't have words to meaningfully organize your experience. Those who understand the intricacies of orchestral music have words to organize their memories and can think back to specific sections and recreate the sounds in their heads more readily. In fact, some argue that the reason most of us do not have clear memories from early childhood is that we didn't have adequate language skills to organize our experiences; thus, we are unable to recall them later.

The link between language and thought has been explored thoroughly. Two of the first well-known scholars in this field were Edward Whorf and Benjamin Sapir. Whorf and Sapir sought to understand the ways in which language shapes understanding. In essence, they argued that our perception of the world is shaped by the language habits of the community. The ways a group uses the language influences the ways its members interpret what they hear (Sapir, 1956). In short, what we see is limited to that which we are capable of understanding, and our understanding is influenced by our language. This argument is called **linguistic determinism**. Whorf argued that different languages cause people to live in different worlds; and thus translations between language groups are virtually impossible. But other scholars strongly criticized this hypothesis. They point out that people are capable of learning a variety of languages and thus can learn to comprehend the world in a variety of ways. We are not limited to understanding the world through our own vocabulary: if we need to know more, we'll learn existing terms or create new vocabulary to describe and understand our experiences. But despite this criticism, the argument that language and understanding are linked still has merit. Just try remembering an experience you had without using words. You certainly can't share the memory with others without words, and you may not be able to even experience it in your own head without framing it in words.

In addition, post-structuralists and postmodernists focus on language as a significant factor in shaping social arrangements. Theorists like Michel Foucault (1978) and Dorothy Smith (1990) (neither of whom self-describes as postmodern) use the term *discourse* to mean both language and frameworks within which meaning can be constructed. Discourse— or texts, to use Smith's conceptualization—is as important for what it excludes as for what it includes. Quite simply, some ideas are inexpressible within particular discursive frameworks. Think about being asked to participate in a survey, as one of the authors was during the process of writing this book. She was offered three choices and found that her experiences did not fit within the categories that were offered. The experience was similar to being asked: what is your favourite colour—blue, red, or green? If your favourite colour is yellow, then your experience (or preference, in this case) is excluded from the collection of responses. In this way, language and discourse shape experiences by presenting "facts" from a particular standpoint.

So if language shapes our thoughts, perceptions, and interactions, we need to think about the ways in which language is gendered. Do you think language reinforces inequality? If that eleven-year-old child had told me about her new friend and said *he* had "long brown hair, likes to play basketball, is a *stud*, and has an older brother," would her words have had the same impact? Does *stud* equal *slut*? They both refer to people who are sexually active; but we use one word almost exclusively for males and the other for females. For most people, the term *slut* has strong negative connotations, while *stud* is understood as a neutral or even a positive descriptor. Are there any neutral or positive words for highly sexually active women? How many negative words can you think of for men that are equivalent to *slut*? If we don't have positive words for highly sexually active women, are we naturally predisposed to think of such women in negative ways? Conversely, if we don't have negative words for highly sexually active men, are we inclined to see them positively? The Sapir-Whorf hypothesis would support the notion that words shape perceptions and that the available words for sexually active men and women incline us towards positive and negative assessments.

Does language in fact create or reinforce inequality between women and men? Many scholars have argued that patterns of **linguistic sexism** devalue women. In 1850, a British Act of Parliament legally entrenched a language convention that defines the **masculine generic form** as the inclusive form. In all legal documents, using the terms *man* or *he* would from then on refer to all people, regardless of their sex. This use of the masculine form had already been the common practice; but by creating a law declaring that all official documents must follow this form, Britain institutionalized a practice that made women less visible. And this practice was reflected in most English writings until the 1970s. One of the most remarkable consequences of this practice was its ambiguity. If the words *man* and *he* are supposed to represent all people, then laws should be interpreted accordingly. But, in fact, the reverse held true: women were excluded in many cases because they were not considered to be included when the term *man* was used. For example, when a document indicated that all *men* should have the right to vote, it was interpreted *not* to include women. The interpretation of so-called generic language was used to deny women the franchise. The language and its interpretations had powerful consequences for women and for men—subordination and privilege.

In her essay "Masculine Generic Language and the U.S. Women's Rights Movement, 1850-1920" (1998), Lou Ann Matossian explores this contradiction in depth.

> Because its ambiguity could be and often was used to marginalize women—effectively denying them social and political rights, in particular the right to vote—feminists found themselves engaged in the politics of language as a matter of practical necessity. (Matossian, 1998, pp. 5–6)

Even in the 1800s, it was abundantly clear that legal documents were often interpreted to exclude women. Matossian reviewed many speeches and documents of the era to show that this exclusion went beyond the word *man* to include *society*, *class of persons*, and *citizen*. A language convention, then, had real political and social consequences—women were even jailed for participating in activities that only *persons* had a right to engage in. Canadian women obtained legal status as *persons* in 1929 after a prolonged legal struggle, finally settled by the English Privy Council (see Chapter Thirteen).

After 1929, the concern about male generic language became muted until reactivated with the second wave of feminism in the 1960s. Renewed efforts since then have been directed towards identifying and rectifying linguistic sexism. The efforts are based on the belief that changing our language conventions is a powerful strategy for undermining inequality. Some feminists, though, are less convinced about the importance of this issue, arguing that economic vulnerability and economic inequality should be the focus of activism (Blaubergs, 1980). However, there are certainly features of the English language and the way it is conventionally employed that contribute to differential perceptions of gender. In addition, significant changes in recent decades have altered the gender-based language conventions. The two key concerns about linguistic sexism are the *invisibility* and *deprecation* of the female in our language.

A. Invisibility

Invisibility refers to the ways in which our language conventions highlight one group of people (males) while diminishing or disappearing another group (females). When legal language was based on masculine generic language, the invisibility of women in the language ultimately contributed to the subordinate position of women within society. The masculine generic form, though, extended well beyond legal documents and included a variety of elements. Here are three simple examples: (1) Society and official organizations accepted that the word *man* included all people. Thus, phrases like the "ascent of man" or the "rights of man" were supposed to refer to all people. (2) When discussing a person whose sex has not been stated, the correct pronoun has traditionally been *he* or *his*. (3) Many of the terms used to describe specific statuses include *-man* in the title: businessman, mailman, and chairman, for example. For well over a century, these male generic forms dominated our spoken and written communication. Only in the last three decades has a serious effort has been made to change these patterns. If you look at journals and books written before the 1970s, you will see how pervasive these patterns were. You can probably still think of many examples where these conventions are still used. The question is: does it really matter? Who cares if someone uses the term *fishermen* to refer to all people who fish for a living? Does it make a difference if people who control committees are sometimes called *chairmen*, even though many of them are women?

A survey of the empirical research would suggest that the answer is yes, it does make a difference. In one study, Hyde (1984) asked a cross section of students to write about an "average student." When the instructions used the male generic pronoun, the vast majority (over 85 percent) wrote about a male; whereas when the pronoun phrase *he or she* was used in the instructions, less than 60 percent wrote about a male student. Quite simply, from elementary school to college, the majority of students who saw the pronoun *he* did not interpret this as a generic pronoun—they thought it referred to a male. Research shows that the majority of people think of males and men when they see or hear masculine generic language (see Silveira, 1980; Wilson & Ng, 1988). In her review of the issue, Henley (1985) concludes that male generic language is not generic at all. It diminishes the position of women, leading most people to regard women as being excluded from the category being described, or as exceptions rather than full participants.

Other language patterns also contribute to this invisibility, such as the use of pronouns in particular contexts. We often see pronoun sexism in language about occupations. When we don't know the sex of the actual individual, many people make assumptions: they refer to lawyers, judges, doctors, and other similar professionals using masculine pronouns. Nurses, teachers, and clerical workers, on the other hand, are most often referred to using feminine pronouns. Many people would accept the argument that these conventions just reflect reality: more doctors and judges are men, and more nurses and secretaries are women. While this is true (and we'll explore gender segregation and work patterns in detail in Chapter Twelve), the use of gendered pronouns linked to occupations of higher or lower prestige reinforce gender inequality. In fact, some research indicates that the use of masculine terms (*fireman* and *chairman*), as well as masculine pronouns, has an impact on the self-concepts of women and men (McConnell & Fazio, 1996). Not surprisingly, these differences are beneficial for boys and men and more detrimental to girls and women.

Spotlighting is another practice connected to language conventions, gender, and social positions. When discussing a person whose gender does not match traditional notions, we add an adjective—*female* pilot, *male* nurse. While this gives additional information about the individual filling a particular role, it also marks her or him as an anomaly. This convention indicates that female doctors or male nurses are exceptions and that the profession itself is gendered. Spotlighting reinforces the notion of differential positions for women and men.

Naming conventions also reinforce this pattern of invisibility. Upon marriage, it has been the convention in Canada that women adopt their husband's name. From then on, she would be known as Mrs. *husband's name.* This pattern arose because of the historical legal right of husbands to assume ownership of any property that their wives brought into the family, and of the husband's legal responsibility for their wives, as well as any children. In effect, legally, wives were the property of their husbands. Subtracting a woman's surname from her family of origin and substituting her new spouse's surname significantly altered that woman's public identity. The roots of this name changing convention are clearly patriarchal, and the practice continued because it was considered "traditional." In the late 1970s, the wife of then Prime Minister Joe Clark was Maureen McTier (the name of her family of origin). Her choice to retain her "own name" was considered an unusual deviation from tradition, sparking questions about Clark's ability to lead the country if he couldn't even lead in his own family. However, since that time, more and more women have chosen not to change their names upon marriage. In fact, in Quebec, women cannot change their names on legal documents: they retain their birth surname all their lives. However, women who continue to follow the old naming tradition argue that it shows commitment to their new family (Kaplan & Bernays, 1997).

After reading this section you may be thinking that these concerns are no longer relevant in the twenty-first century. After all, these conventions have been challenged and changed so that the masculine generic form is no longer commonly used. Instead of always using masculine pronouns, it is more common to see persons of unknown gender referred to as *he or she*, or *he/she* or even *s/he*. In fact, the practice of using words formerly reserved for the plural case—*they* or *theirs*— to refer to a single person is becoming more and more acceptable. For example, the following usage is understandable, even though it mixes singular and plural: "The driver of the red car caused the accident. They drove right through the stop sign." Just as pronouns have changed, so have other conventions. Good writing and speech does not use the masculine form for occupations, since most occupations have now adopted gender-neutral generic forms, as the Table 4.1 shows.

TABLE 4.1	Masculine and Generic Names for Occupations
Masculine Form	**Generic Form**
Fireman	Firefighter
Mailman	Letter Carrier
Policeman	Police Officer
Chairman	Chairperson
Alderman	Councillor
Businessman	Businessperson

Nor do we typically use masculine words like *man* or *mankind*, substituting instead *humanity* or *humankind*. Even legal conventions have changed: where once the "reasonable man" standard was used, the "reasonable person" standard has replaced it. And finally, women are less likely to change their names when and if they marry.

So why do these old patterns matter? For two reasons. First, it is always valuable to have some insight into historical patterns: knowing how patterns originated and developed helps us to understand how and why they persist. Second, and more importantly, these changes did not occur on their own. People within the second wave of feminism highlighted concerns with sexist language, arguing that it did not just reflect but actually created and reinforced inequality. Their argument was supported by empirical research proving that masculine language forms tended to diminish or disappear women. As a result, projects were undertaken do undo sexist language patterns. Handbooks for non-sexist writing were produced and distributed. Dictionaries and academic journals adopted non-sexist language policies avoiding masculine generic patterns and spotlighting. Individuals chose to alter the language conventions that they use and to challenge sexism in their daily conversations. These changes required effort from diverse sources. But on the whole, they have been successful—so successful, ironically, that many students now question whether the issue is still relevant. They don't know or remember a time when these sexist conventions were the norm.

B. Belittling, Deprecating Language

A second element of sexism in English is belittling, deprecating language. There are three key elements to this pattern. Consider the lists of words in Table 4.2.

These words are roughly equivalent in their denotations, but the words in the left column are used to describe females while those on the right refer to males. More importantly, notice the associations or connotations attached to the words. In your mind, picture a bachelor; now imagine a spinster. What did you visualize? Were your images equally desirable? What about governor and governess? Most people assess the words differently: the words linked with males create images that are much more desirable than the ones for females. When we ask our students to undertake this exercise, they often see spinsters as lonely old ladies with cats (another stereotype), while bachelors are pictured as young and free, with lots of opportunities and relationships. These differences in connotation illustrate an element of sexist language known as **semantic derogation**. Semantic derogation refers to a process where meanings change over time. The patterns that emerge typically attach negative connotations for female words and positive or neutral connotations for male words. So the *master* is powerful, while the *mistress* is the immoral "other woman." This kind of

TABLE 4.2	Semantic Derogation
Mistress	Master
Governess	Governor
Spinster	Bachelor
Madame	Sir
Witch	Wizard

linguistic sexism is more subtle than the masculine generic language because it relies on connotations and associations, but still harmful, perhaps even more damaging because we are less conscious of it. As discussed earlier, with the stud/slut pairing, if gendered language has differential values associated with it—words for women consistently less powerful and more negative than words for men—then simply using the language reinforces inequality.

A second element of deprecating language we need to consider is **slang**. Slang refers to non-standard, informal words and language, often used in particular situations or subcultures and often developing over long periods of time. In English, slang words for women are often trivializing, associating them with food or animals: *honey, cupcake, dog, cow, chick*. But words for men tend to connote power: *hunk, jock, stud*. In fact, negative slang words for men frequently use feminine words: *sissy* (sister), and *wuss* (pussy). Sexual slang, as we discussed earlier, carries this pattern even further. Words for sexually active women are far more negative than those for sexually active men (*slut, whore (ho), cougar versus stud* or *player*).

To illustrate the ways in which our language can be deprecating for women, try the following exercise. Go to Dictionary.com and compare the definitions for *slut* and for *stud*. You'll find that slut is defined as "promiscuous woman" or "prostitute." *Stud*, on the other hand (excluding references to building materials), is slang for men who are "virile," "sexually active," and "attractive." From the same webpage, you can then go to the thesaurus to see what other words are associated with the first two. *Stud* is linked to words such as *womanizer, heartbreaker, ladies' man, playboy*, and *wolf*; while *slut* is associated with *hooker, whore, loose woman, floozy*, and *tart*. These words are clearly not equal in power and prestige, and the connotations associated with them are more positive for males and more negative for females. To carry this exercise further, we can look at synonyms for less controversial words like *girl* and *boy*. The same thesaurus defines girl as *female* while boy is defined as *young man*. There are 29 synonyms listed for boy including *child, guy, youth*, and the less desirable *runt, puppy*, and *squirt*. There are 49 terms listed under girl, and while some are neutral—*female, maiden, woman*—many more are deprecating, such as *babe, chick, cutie, jail bait, piece*, and *wench*. Once again, this evidence shows that our language does not value the two sexes equally. Even the most innocuous words *girl/boy* are associated with positive and negative connotations.

In addition to the nouns we use to identify women and men in particular roles, the adjectives we choose to use with gender often promote inequality. These adjectives typically encourage polarized thinking, diminishing women by making them seem overly emotional or irrational while elevating men with adjectives that connote power (see Table 4.3).

Certainly, the words in the left column are used to describe both women and men, though more frequently men. The adjectives in the right column, on the other hand, are almost always associated with women and very rarely with men. How often have you heard men

TABLE 4.3	Comparison of Adjectives
Assertive	Pushy
Outraged	Hysterical
Cautious	Hesitant

described as *pushy, hysterical* or *hesitant*? These are everyday examples of linguistic sexism that most of us don't even notice.

A third element of linguistic sexism is the use of **diminutives**. Diminutives are suffixes like *-ess, -ette,* or *-ienne* (*e.g.*, actress, waitress, comedienne, heroine, majorette, and suffragette) added to words to distinguish between the sexes. The masculine version is seen as the standard form, and the feminized alternate version is the non-standard or exceptional form. Use of diminutives is another form of *spotlighting*, which reinforces normative expectations of gender (Weatherall, 2002).

In the following guest essay on female athletes at her university, sociology graduate student Melanie Muise considers the importance of language and gender. Her research speaks directly to the issue of diminutive language and its links to our perceptions of women athletes. It also introduces other elements of normative expectations of gender discussed in other chapters.

| BOX 4-1 | **Proof by Performance: Subjectivity in Sporting Practices** |

by Melanie Muise
Laurentian University

Introduction

The lived body experiences of female varsity athletes at Laurentian University are organized through cultural ideas of sex and gender: the female athletes are labelled as *Lady Vees* as opposed to *Voyageurs*, a label reserved for men. Although female athletes are proud that they subvert the image of "femininity"— they are strong, competitive, confident, and empowered—female athletes are institutionally organized as deficient to male athletes and are constructed as not the "real thing."" There is a precarious subjectivity that you are able to be masculine within this particular context, but this departure from the linear construction of sex and gender is not permanent: female athletes cannot be female and masculine, a *Voyageur*. The institution has a particular historical context where women were excluded and then instituted under the label *Lady Vee*. The preservation of these labels confuses and perpetuates unequal gendered power and is problematic for achieving equality.

Methodology

This qualitative research investigated female student-athletes' experiences and realities of gender, sexualities, and body practices in the institutional setting of Laurentian University. Examining the social meaning of being a "female" body in a sporting context that has demonstrated formal equality, I explored the notion of being embedded within a masculinist institution and the embodiment of gender. Beginning from the lived reality of being a varsity athlete, I participated and observed the local context. In 2004, I conducted 10 in-depth interviews with female athletes competing on or training with women's interuniversity athletics at the university in all five sanctioned sports. A thematic analysis of field notes, interviews and the Laurentian

BOX 4-1	*(Continued)*

2003 student-athlete handbook was conducted. An open coding system was used to identify meaningful pieces of information as they emerged. Each interview was coded prior to the next while also coding field notes and textual data.

The Local Sport Culture

The University itself is located in Northeastern Ontario with a total enrollment of 4,869 in 2003. In order to be eligible to compete, athletes must meet the Ontario University Athletics (OUA) and Canadian Interuniversity Sport (CIS) student-athlete requirements as full-time students. The 2003–2004 season marks the forty-fourth anniversary of Voyageur Athletics. Women's history of competition is absent in the official discourse of the institution as the Lady Vees began competition just over 30 years ago. There are 135 athletes on nine varsity teams: women's and men's basketball, Nordic skiing, soccer, swimming, and women's cross country running. There are 81 female athletes and 54 male. All head coaches are male. A voyageur is a man and therefore the male athletes are known as Voyageurs; the women are "Lady Vees."

The Experiences and Realities of Female Athletes

Managing the Contradiction in 'Female/Athlete'

All the participants identified as athletes and considered themselves to be highly competitive in superior athletic performances. They live in an athletic culture where they experience the physicality of their own bodies. The meaning of competition in female sport is seen as performing the role of an athlete; however, this is generally qualified with the male competitive ideal.

> I always get the comment, "You play like a guy... you're so good". I take it as a compliment . . . well you know guys are superior . . . but at the same time why can't I get a compliment as a female who plays really, really well?

As athletes on an interuniversity team, academics also play a role in the assumed roles of athletes. Athletes are institutionalized as students first, as suggested by the student-athlete handbook, having to meet academic regulations to be eligible as an athlete. Some felt there was a double standard of being a student-athlete.

> Athletes are stereotyped as jocks. The funny thing is that we are all student–athletes, not just Voyageurs or Lady Vees, and I think the men think they are just athletes. The females definitely challenge the jockism in sport, we have to be smart and get good grades, prove that we belong here.

Although they train hard, put in the same hours of training and intensity of competition, they subvert "femininity" but the contradiction of being "female" and "athlete" remain.

Whose Measure of Equality?

Many of the female student athletes acknowledged that Laurentian is unique in terms of the athletic department and varsity athletics. The university itself is seen as the guardian of equality.

> I think its pretty fair at Laurentian . . . everything is kinda equal . . . but I actually know at another

(Continued)

BOX 4-1	**Proof by Performance: Subjectivity in Sporting Practices (*Continued*)**

school the football team is the center of the athletic departments, and men's teams get better practice times . . . things like that don't happen at Laurentian.

The institutional definition of equal numbers/opportunities is clearly understood to be achieved; however, "less measurable" forms of inequality exist.

Many of the female athletes stated that their abilities and skills in sport are comparable or superior to many males', thus they had proof by their performance that they belonged here. Sometimes social experiences are taken for granted until verbalized.

> The guys always complain that we get more media attention than them. I guess that's true . . . I think things should be equal . . . even in the reverse.

She further adds:

> If it were the reverse, and the women's team were losing we wouldn't even exist . . . .I think the men are uncomfortable with being in the position female athletes are usually in . . . this could teach them a lesson.

In general, the female athletes felt that male athletes, fans, and students dismiss and devalue female athletes' status, achievements, and work to be an athlete.

"What the hell is a 'Lady Vee'?"

In part, the trivialization and inequality in official status is embedded in the institutional organization of varsity athletics: men are "Voyageurs" and women "Lady Vees." There is a sense that being called a "Lady Vee":

is a subtle yet powerful message that we are glad you are active and fit . . . you have a nice body . . . but you won't beat us (referring to male athletes).

Being a "Lady Vee" is not the only practice of differentiating and devaluing female athletic performances. The cavalier notion of "ladies first" supports the scheduling structure that women's teams compete first, establishing women as opening acts and not the real show.

> With fan support there tends to be more people coming in towards the end of our game. People come to watch the guys' warm-up. They usually watch the last little bit of our game.

Men's sport becomes the version that "really counts." The word *Lady* does not embody the experiences of the athletes, nor does *Vee*; it naturalizes the production of female athlete as inferior to male athletes.

Hot Bodies, Chilling Realities

Despite being called "Lady Vees," many female athletes physicality celebrated their body's skill and accomplishment within this sport culture. The women were not always apologetic or docile when it comes to gendered social behavior. There is a desire to show the bulging muscles and physical power in public.

> I like wearing t-shirts that show off my arms . . . I'm starting to get definition. It makes me feel strong.

In debating private/public bodily practices there is the issue of when to wear just a sports bra or not. To wear clothing that displays the power of the

---

BOX 4-1	*(Continued)*

body often reveals the sexuality of the female body.

> It was hot one day and I took off my "jersey" and wore just my sports bra. At the end of practice the female trainer came up to me to say 'coach' doesn't think it's appropriate for us to wear just a sports bra at practice.

The male coach then instituted a "practice jersey rule" disallowing sports bras to be worn as practice attire.

The displaying of the body also reveals another dimension of sexuality: if one does not appear feminine, one's sexuality is called into question.

> I was going up for my award . . . I had just won the biggest race of my life . . . and someone in the crowd shouts "dyke" overtop the cheering. At first I wondered if I was the only one who heard this. Then there was some laughing and sneering. I feel uncomfortable going up for awards now.

Women in sport must negotiate their bodily appearances in terms of perceived values of the female body. These experiences are brushed off as meaningless; however, they reveal systemic rules which attempt to devalue and/or exclude women from institutional sport competition.

Conclusion

Being competitive for female athletes is seen as challenging traditional gender norms of femininity and the "proof by performance" that female athletes belong within the male arena of sport. There is a gap between the subjective empowering experiences and the objective equality based on performance standards; the embodiment of unequal gender practices within a masculinist institution. Within sport the body has an objective identity. The cultural meanings given to the body maintain that a female body can not be attached to "masculinity." Female athletes become participants in perpetuating the "naturalness" of gender by being "Lady Vees." It is crucial to recognize that if we are not critical of the natural assumption of difference between male and female athletes the organization of sport will continue to place these cultural differences in a social order where women are deficient to men.

Muise's essay highlights many of the themes and concepts discussed in our text thus far, including the ways in which language—the name *Lady Vee* in this case—creates or reinforces a diminished role for women.

MEDIA

The majority of Canadians use some form of mass media on a regular basis. We turn on radios or televisions, read books and magazines; in urban settings we see advertisements on buses and billboards; and many of us use computers to access information and entertainment. In many ways, media is ubiquitous—it's becoming hard to avoid. **Mass media** is defined as an impersonal form of communication directed towards a large audience.

Imagine all the earlier human societies that did not have televisions and computers, or even books. In those societies, information was passed from individual to individual, directly and personally. But since the media has become increasingly prevalent in technology-laden societies, it plays a significant role within our socio-cultural landscape—not just as a means for disseminating information, which it certainly is, but also as a means for shaping the culture itself and, by extension, our notions of gender.

The degree to which media plays a role in shaping behaviour and culture and the way it does this has been the subject of considerable debate. One position holds that the media mirrors the values of the mainstream culture, rather than actually shaping that culture. This is known as the **reflection hypothesis**. In essence, the reflection hypothesis argues that the creators of media develop their messages based on what their audiences want to see and hear in order to sell products and make profits. If they did not reflect the dominant ideals of their audiences, then there would be no viewer demand, and they would fail to attract the necessary consumers. On its face, the reflection hypothesis seems like a viable argument: if a particular medium does not please its audience, that audience will quickly abandon it in favour of something else (remote controls for televisions have made this incredibly easy). But the audience is very diverse and divided into "niche markets," where a media creator can profit from a small, targeted audience. Thus, there is no reason to believe that mainstream or dominant ideals and values must be disseminated in order for a profit to be made. While the media may reflect the values and interactions of many segments of society, it is not limited to simply portraying already existing facets of mainstream culture.

In contrast, a second theory about media argues that the media shapes culture by structuring information and defining "normal." It *creates* culture by influencing its viewers and shaping their behaviours and choices, therefore contributing to beliefs, norms, and values. I am influenced by what I read. If I read a report indicating that a certain product is produced by enslaved children in sweatshops, I will actively avoid purchasing this product. Thus, knowledge gained from the media shapes my behaviour. But I am not foolish—I don't believe everything I read or see in the media. I like to think that I critically assess all that I am exposed to, and therefore it only shapes my thoughts and behaviours when I choose to accept its messages. Or does it?

Ask yourself: what role does the media play in your life? What impact does it have upon you? We like to think that it doesn't have a huge impact, that we are independent thinkers, not swayed by its messages. But right now, you are taking a university course on gender (unless you are reading this book just for fun). What you are reading here shapes your knowledge and may have an impact on your notions of gender. And the authors, editors, and producers of this text all have a voice in determining what you are reading. The book was written to accomplish a specific goal: to provide a stimulating but concise introduction to the many dimensions of gender in Canadian society. The publishers wanted a book that would be appropriate for a certain target audience (you), and thus they provided guidelines and suggestions for us (the authors). A very basic guideline is the chapter structure and target length: given the target audience, we were strongly encouraged to aim for a specific number of pages and to include chapter summaries and glossaries. This meant that we needed to choose what concepts, theories, and examples would fit the format and set aside ones that would not. The editors gave feedback on early drafts of the chapters, based on comments from peer reviewers, making suggestions about which topics to include or expand. Fortunately, our publishers gave us a great deal of freedom in the writing of this book, but they did retain the ultimate authority to decide the final shape and format of the book. The publishers' goals, then, shaped the book you are reading right now. Thus, they have influenced what and how you are learning about gender. This is the way the textbook industry works, and it is an example of how all media works. Someone is making decisions about what you see and hear and what you don't see and hear. Often the underlying principle in determining what gets disseminated is economic: will this material draw an audience and make money?

Since media is ubiquitous and evidently powerful in our society, it is the subject of many sociological and communications theories. Several are relevant to gender issues.

A. Cultivation Theory

One theory explaining the impact of media on our beliefs and behaviours is **cultivation theory**. This theory focuses primarily on television viewing, but it applies to other types of media as well. Cultivation theory suggests that the more television/media we are exposed to, the more likely it is that our understandings of the world will be skewed by it. Our worldview starts to resemble the television version, rather than the world in which we actually live. In essence, cultivation theorists believe that the media provides stories that are not complete or accurate representations but that many viewers accept as real. Mass media creates a symbolic environment in which virtually all of us participate. We have been born into societies in which the media provides mass-produced stories. Children are encouraged to watch programs aimed at their age group; some are pro-social, encouraging learning and promoting specific values; and others are designed simply to entertain. From a young age, children learn about their world through these programs. But adults too tend to watch a great deal of television: 99.2 percent of households have televisions, and Canadians view an average of 21.6 hours of television per week (Koop, 2005). In fact, to date, television is the most pervasive disseminator of information in human history. It exposes us to an ongoing story about the world, a story that is reasonably coherent and repeated across a broad range of television genres (stories in the news often appear later on talk shows, in fictionalized dramas, in crime shows, and on soap operas). Even the imagery is repeated across genres: specific types of women and men (as well as people from different social classes and ethnicities) are frequently portrayed, and those who deviate from the cultural ideal may be shown as less desirable, either as a source of humour, or as an example of deviant behaviours. For example, across a range of media genres large women tend to be the object of ridicule, such as Roseanne Barr; or they are portrayed as dangerous, like the evil witch Ursula in Disney's *Little Mermaid*; or they are shown to be worthy of pity, such as the women in the "before" pictures in weight-loss advertisements.

Empirical research shows that cultivation theory has validity. Heavy consumers of media do tend to hold beliefs and values similar to television beliefs and values more often than do lighter consumers of media (see, for example, Gerbner, Gross, Morgan, & Signorelli, 1986; Signorelli, 1991). The most common images of women on television are young and thin, made up to appear blemish-free. In her study of appearance and beauty standards, Stern (2004) measured kindergarten girls' television habits and then interviewed them about their perceptions of beauty. She identified those who watched less than 14 hours a week as light viewers and those who watched 14 or more hours as heavy viewers. Stern found clear evidence that girls who are heavy viewers of television have narrower perceptions of beauty: they believe that beauty is a feminine trait, and that people with wrinkles or who are overweight can't be beautiful. Interestingly, she found that both groups of girls were likely to define what makes someone beautiful based on products (clothes, make-up, and jewelry, for example). She found it significant that in a culture rife with appearance-oriented messages, a measurable difference in beliefs could be found between light and heavy television viewers.

B. Encoding and Decoding Mediated Messages

While cultivation theory supports the notion that media influences audience perceptions, not everyone experiences media images and messages the same way. Viewer characteristics and the content of the message itself combine to influence our perceptions. For example, consider occasions when you and someone else have watched a movie or heard a song, and you had very different reactions to it. You might have thought it was unrealistic and cheesy, while your friend may have found it emotionally compelling. In his research into media, Stuart Hall developed two key notions to help explain the links between the viewer and the materials viewed: **encoding** and **decoding**. Encoding and decoding explain why we don't all hear or see the same messages, even when we are exposed to the same content (Proctor, 2004). Two people might play the same video game, with one barely noticing the violent imagery and the other distracted by the lethal moves to the point of losing concentration. (For those of you who do not play video games, the lethal move is the signature technique the main character uses to kill his/her opponent. In *Mortal Kombat*, Tanya kills her enemies by wrapping her thighs around their necks and twisting herself around until the neck snaps.) Hall's theories help us understand why some people are offended by certain images (women posed provocatively in alcohol advertisements, for example) while others remain undisturbed.

Hall argues that all media messages are encoded. What we see and hear is not accidental. Scripting, editing, and posing are integral parts of virtually every form of media. Producers meticulously structure every word and image they create and disseminate. Even the content of so-called reality television programs is controlled. The people portrayed in these programs are taped day and night for weeks. We see only a few hours of their activities—tightly edited to make interesting television—and clearly not reflecting all the events of the week. The producers want us to have "favourites" and "enemies." They want us to be fully engaged in the contest so we will keep tuning in and they edit their materials accordingly. Books, video games, advertisements, and computer websites are all designed to keep us engaged by creating the most compelling messages possible. However, just as we discussed in the section on language, everyone interprets the symbols through the lens of their own knowledge and experience.

As Hall explains, the audience decodes the messages. We are not passive receivers of information. We bring our own interpretive skills into play as we consume the media messages. Distortion is built in to the communication process. Think about the famous court case involving O.J. Simpson, who was acquitted of the violent murder of his ex-wife and her friend. The events surrounding both his arrest and his trial were televised in such great detail that everyone in the viewing audience felt they had accurate information about the murders and the guilt or innocence of the accused. While there was strong evidence linking Mr. Simpson to the crime, there was also evidence suggesting that some incriminating information may have been planted by police officers. His acquittal was very controversial: many people did not share the perception of the jurors, who found the "planted evidence" theory more compelling than the DNA evidence. Meanwhile, many people who are well versed on issues of spousal assault and murder saw evidence indicating that this was a classic case of an abused wife, killed as she tried to move ahead with her life, separating from her abuser. We all saw the same images and heard the same testimony, but people drew dramatically different conclusions. Those whose position in society leads them to be suspicious of police officers (including some members of the jury) perceived the "facts" and "evidence" differently from those whose position led them to have first-hand knowledge of abusive relationships and spousal homicide.

Hall argued that there are three basic ways of interpreting mediated messages: **dominant/preferred** meanings; **negotiated/resistant** meanings; and **oppositional** meanings. The dominant or preferred interpretation typically reflects the mainstream cultural order. The audience sees what the encoders were overtly trying to portray. When viewers see an alcohol advertisement with artfully posed women, they may just see it as an attractive commercial for a desired product. Those who decode with a negotiated interpretation see the dominant encoded meaning but can also see other possibilities. They may oppose some elements of the advertisement but find ways to make it fit with their understanding of the social world and their particular context. For example, they realize that the alcohol advertisement is trying to play on sex appeal to sell its product, but at the same time, they acknowledge that the ad is attractive and compelling—the images succeed in linking alcohol consumption with beauty. The final interpretation is an oppositional one. That is, the viewers see the dominant message, do not accept it, and challenge it instead. They may believe that the media messages are deceptive and harmful and bemoan the fact that many audiences are blind to the harm. In the case of the alcohol ad, they would note the harm that arises from the objectification of women and the degradation arising from using women's bodies to sell products. In their discussion of Hall's theory, Shields and Heinecken (2002) use the example of the television program Ally McBeal to illustrate differences in decoding meaning. This program was about a female lawyer, her legal cases, and her relationships with other women and men (see Table 4.4).

TABLE 4.4	Three Interpretations of Ally McBeal
Dominant Interpretation	Ally is a talented professional woman meeting the challenges of career and relationships in a highly demanding environment.
Negotiated Interpretation	Ally has talent and ability as a lawyer and should succeed in her career; but the ridiculous storylines and foolish choices she makes would never be tolerated within an actual law firm.
Oppositional Interpretation	The show is completely unrealistic, undermining women's professionalism, minimizing the real challenges of balancing work and life, and implying that thoroughly ditzy women can get by on their looks and charm.

Source: Shields & Heinecken, 2002 p. 2

In his theory, Hall notes that not only do individual viewers have various interpretations, but so too do social groups. For example, women are more likely to be offended when female characters are portrayed as brainless sex objects; Asian ethnic groups are more likely to be offended by repeated images of Asian characters as violent gang members; old people are more likely to be oppositional towards images of the elderly as frail, vulnerable burdens on their families and society. Thus, different social groups aren't all going to see the same gender representations in the media or interpret them in the same way.

C. Content Analysis

In the 1970s, research into gender (then called *sex roles*) and the media focused on a technique known as **content analysis**. In essence, content analysis evaluates the messages disseminated through the media, focusing on the encoded symbols rather than on the decoded interpretation of those symbols. For example, if you undertook a content analysis of your favourite television program, you might focus on the physical appearance of the characters, the roles that they undertake, or the dominant/subordinate positions in interaction between the sexes. The findings from the early content analysis research were unequivocal: the media overwhelmingly presented the sexes in gender-polarized ways:

1. In a simple count of characters, men far outnumbered women in most genres of television programming, news stories, movies, and books.

2. Women were most often portrayed in a limited number of roles associated with nurturing and homemaking, while men were more likely to be working outside the home.

3. Men were more likely to be portrayed in authoritative, decisive, rational and powerful behaviours, while women were more likely to be portrayed as dependent, indecisive, unintelligent, or subservient.

4. Women were often portrayed as decorative objects (sexually attractive) rather than as active participants. (see Pachecco & Hurtado, 2001; Shields & Heinecken, 2002)

While there have been some changes over time, content analyses continue to document similar patterns. Advertising targeted at children, teenagers, and adults shows a marked disparity between the sexes. In terms of behaviours and activities, while women are less likely to be portrayed as homemakers than they once were, they are still portrayed as sexual objects and are often the subject of violent images as well. The physicality of females in the media is tightly restricted to a specific body type that normalizes an unhealthily thin ideal (Pachecco & Hurtado, 2001).

Just as there has been a long history of measuring gendered symbols in the media, so too has there been a great deal of research theorizing and measuring the impact of such imagery. One of the first widely read discussions of this was Betty Friedan's book *The Feminine Mystique* (1963). While this book was a thorough accounting of the limitations of the middle-class woman's homemaker role, Friedan also critiqued the media for supporting this narrow version of womanhood. She argued that advertising was structured in such a way as to play on women's vulnerabilities and insecurities. By questioning their domestic prowess and their feminine appearance and then offering products as solutions to "fix" these weaknesses, the media and their advertisers were able to make profits. Widespread use of this strategy reinforced the cultural standards for women: to be beautiful and nurturing as they undertake their domestic roles. While there is certainly merit to her argument, Friedan's analysis is flawed in that it implies that women are merely passive receivers of media messages—that they absorb and decode the dominant meanings of the symbols uncritically. But clearly, not everyone was swayed by their content: Friedan herself was able to take an oppositional stance towards such messages.

Susan Douglas (1995), in her detailed study of media culture over a span of four decades (1950s to 1990s), raised concerns similar to Friedan's, but she drew different conclusions about their impact on the audience. She examined television programs, popular music, magazines, and comic books, documenting the ways in which portrayals of women diminished and restricted them, valorizing the homemaking role, and ridiculing women outside of that narrow range of activities. For example, she discusses the popular 1970s television program *Charlie's Angels*. You may have seen movies spun off from the original show: women working as private investigators, relying on their employer/mentor/patriarch Charlie to find the work, to guide and support their activities, and to acknowledge their successes. In the original show, the Angels typically avoided real violence and relied upon their "feminine wiles" and sexuality to catch the bad guys and solve the crimes. Douglas points out that this program perfectly captured the feminist/antifeminist tensions of the day. Women should be encouraged in nontraditional activities, but only under the authority of a man; and their sexuality and beauty should be valued over their actual intelligence and skill. Though she doesn't directly use Hall's three measures for identifying ways of interpreting symbols, Douglas does address them in her discussion. The dominant reading is that women can successfully engage in nontraditional activities if an enlightened male population gives them the opportunity to prove themselves. The negotiated interpretation applauds the Angel's teamwork and success in solving the crimes, acknowledging their accommodations to a sexist world, while regretting the sexual titillation as a necessary part of a successful, unconventional television program. The oppositional interpretation concentrates on the blatant misogyny that perpetuates the myth that women use sex to get what they want—both in the show as Angels solving crimes and as actresses using their appearance to become television stars. Importantly, though, Douglas notes that the show was hugely popular, even amongst those, like herself, who criticized it. She says,

> I was as outraged as other feminists over its objectification of women and its celebration of patriarchy through the use of invisible Charlie's instructing voice. But you know what? I watched it regularly, and not just for work. At the same time that I hated it, I loved it. (p. 21)

Douglas's argument is that even though the media appeared to perpetuate the sexist arrangements of the dominant culture, it also contributed to the development of feminists who challenged that traditional order. The women who grew up watching *Charlie's Angels* (and I confess that I was one of them) are the same women who have challenged the status quo and are now working outside the home for pay and are active in politics and in their communities. We didn't just absorb the dominant message. We may have enjoyed the entertainment value of even the most facile of programs; but we didn't necessarily buy into their messages. Douglas's work clearly shows the importance of considering the ways in which messages are decoded, as well as encoded.

This research touches on two issues that are widely discussed today: the link between media portrayals of extremely thin women and the prevalence of eating disorders within our society, and the impact of video games on the people who play them. The common approach to studying these relationships is to measure the strength of the correlation between them.

As the media has inundated its consumers with images of emaciated women, eating disorders amongst girls and women have also increased. Empirical research shows a connection. For example, in their summary of the research, Pacheco and Hurtado state "frequent viewers of soap operas tended to be more concerned about their body weight than viewers who watch less frequently or nonviewers" (p. 705); and "undergraduate women who view fashion magazines are more likely to prefer lower body weights, be less satisfied with their bodies, feel more frustrated about their bodies, be more preoccupied with 'thinness,' and be more concerned with weight gain than undergraduates who viewed only newsmagazines" (p. 706). But Gilbert *et al.* (2005) reviewed the empirical research on this subject and found that the messages themselves are not sufficient to *cause* eating disorders. They argue that two other factors related to viewer characteristics play as important a role as the encoded message. First, they found that the tendency to engage in **social comparison** was significant in women who absorbed the thinness message. Social comparison theory suggests that people are inclined to compare themselves to others in a form of self-evaluation; but not all people who engage in social comparison do it to the same degree. In general, people who have a tendency to compare are more likely to develop disordered eating patterns. The second important factor is **internalization**. Internalization refers to the degree to which we accept cultural ideals. If we don't internalize the extremely thin ideal, we are less influenced by the abundance of images that surround us. If we internalize the ideals, we judge ourselves accordingly and are more likely to strive to achieve them or feel dissatisfied when we do not. Our decoding of the images, whether we internalize them, compare ourselves to them, or oppose them, appears to have a profound impact on our behaviour. The decoding of the symbol is as important as the image itself.

In their summary of the recent empirical research measuring the impact of gendered media on its audience, Ward and Caruthers (2001) conclude that the research clearly documents the power of media models for influencing notions of gender. The cultivation theory is supported by evidence. "Greater exposure to mainstream media portrayals increases support for sexist attitudes, reinforces stereotyped associations about what the sexes do and how they should act, strengthens preferences for traditional occupations and activities, and colours evaluations of women and men encountered subsequently"(p. 696). But the research also shows that non-stereotypical images have the opposite effect: viewing these images "encourages more flexible associations about the sexes, strengthens preferences for non-traditional roles and activities and leads to increased self-confidence in young women" (p. 696). Clearly, the media is an integral part of our socio-cultural landscape: the gendered messages that it disseminates have an impact upon all of us.

While some mediated symbols may reinforce gender polarization and others undermine it, we must remember that people don't all interpret these symbols the same way. Therefore, it is not enough for those who decode critically and oppositionally to dismiss the role of the media. Media's role in influencing viewers and both shaping and reinforcing popular ideas about masculinity and femininity—for good or ill—is profound for most of the Canadian population.

CASE STUDY: COMPUTER GAMES

One of the most recent changes in modern mass media is the rapid technological development of video and computer-based games. Within the last few decades, this medium has advanced from the most simple of games, like Pong (two players hit a sphere back and forth across a black and white television screen), to incredibly developed life-like graphic games giving players access to countless complex actions. Video games have not only become increasingly innovative and realistic, they have also become incredibly pervasive. Approximately 60 percent of Americans over the age of five years play video games (that's 145 million people); and the sales of these games in the year 2000 was valued at over six billion dollars (ISDA, 2001). Forty-nine percent of American youth have the equipment to play video and/or computer games in their rooms. It is estimated that boys in Grade Seven and Eight play an average of 13 hours a week, and similar-aged girls play about five hours a week (Dill *et al.*, 2005). For this reason, we shouldn't underestimate the significance of these games in our socio-cultural landscape. However, this medium is not experienced equally by the sexes. As noted above, boys are more than twice as likely to play these games as girls. A survey of adult video game usage shows that only 23 percent of heavy users are women (reported in Yates & Littleton, 2001).

Much research has explored the gendered nature of both video games and their users. A content analysis of the gendered features of the most popular video games reveals how polarizing these games actually are. In fact, women are largely absent from these video games. When women are present, their roles are very narrowly defined (Dill, *et al.*, 2005). Violence against women is a common theme in over 20 percent of these games; and sexualized imagery and unnaturally buxom female characters appear in 28 percent. The male characters are hyper-masculinized—their bodies, chest and arms are impossibly massive. Their roles revolve around aggression, dominance, and power. Physical prowess over opponents/enemies is rewarded in most of the game worlds.

In her studies of video games, Nina Huntemann (2004) argues that there are three typical roles for women in video games. First is the "damsel in distress" whose entire role is to be rescued. She is a passive character who is often a victim of violence and abuse at the hands of her captor. She remains invisible throughout the actual playing of the game, only appearing at the beginning and end, just in time to reward the hero for saving her. (In *Duke Nukem* games, the rescued damsel sometimes shows her appreciation by stripping down for his pleasure.)

The second role of females in video games is the "femme fatale." Gamers are able to choose the characters they wish to portray in the game. They sometimes have the option of choosing a female character. These women are fighters of equal ability to their male counterparts, having their own lethal moves (like the neck-snapping thighs mentioned earlier). However, these women are highly sexualized. While male characters are dressed reasonably appropriately for their exploits, the females wear body armour and very little clothing.

The third category evolved from the femme fatales into what Huntemann calls the "buxom babes." With technological advances, the main focus of the games transformed from first-person shooters (where you looked through the eyes of the hero but did not typically see him/her throughout the action) to third-party characters (where you were the character, but you could also watch every move and action). Lara Croft in the *Tomb Raider* games epitomizes this genre. (To date, over 30 million of these games have been sold, at a cost of over one billion dollars.) The *Tomb Raider* creator explained that he chose a female character rather than a male because he thought the gamers would prefer to look at a beautiful, sexy woman rather than a man as they played this new format. Thus, these females were not designed to encourage female gamers; they were created to please male gamers. As a technologically mediated male fantasy, Lara Croft's sexuality was used to promote the game in posters and advertisements. The most recent version of Lara Croft video games, *Tomb Raider: The Legend*, has actually recreated the image of Lara's body to reflect a more realistic form: she has shrunk from a 32DD bra size to a 36C. Models were hired to enact the role of Lara Croft at promotional events (Herbst, 2004); and, of course, Angelina Jolie portrayed her in two film adaptations.

The question why girls and women are much less likely to play computer games has been explored by a variety of researchers. Initially, they hypothesized that females were just less comfortable with the technology, but the empirical findings have not supported this argument. No evidence indicates that the differences in playing patterns is related to either physical (dexterity) or psychological (spatial) abilities (reported in Yates & Littleton, 2001). A second argument suggests that the problem is that the images and context alienate female gamers: the winning traits are strongly associated with masculine gender normative expectations. In addition, the characters tend to objectify or trivialize women. This certainly appears to be part of the explanation; women gamers when interviewed about their likes and dislikes don't necessarily appreciate the scantily clad buxom babes. But some do prefer them to the male characters, claiming it is easier to visualize themselves as the female character, despite the flaws (Yates & Littleton, 2001). These differences result from decoding. Most of the women interviewed tended to take a negotiated stance in their interpretation of the game imagery. They didn't necessarily like the portrayal of women, but they enjoyed the challenge and the action and simply recognized that the sexist stuff was there to popularize the game—it didn't particularly offend them. Those that were offended, taking an oppositional position, presumably would be much less likely to play.

Because only a limited number of women play these "masculine" video games, the industry has specifically created a genre of games designed to appeal to female players, in essence catering to feminine gender expectations, such as nurturing. Jenkins (1999a) describes games for girls, such as Purple Moon's *Secret Paths in the Forest*, that involve solving problems through exploration and careful observation rather than through physical prowess. They also involve solving emotional dilemmas. These games have been quite successful, but they raise another concern. By creating two separate gender-oriented gaming genres, the creators of video games have essentially catered to gender polarization, rather than challenging it. And many women don't want to be in what they perceive to be a feminine gaming ghetto (Jenkins, 1999b).

In two empirical tests designed to explore the gender patterns more fully, Yates and Littleton (2001) challenged boys and girls to play specially created computer activities. In one study, two randomly assigned groups of children were asked to play the same puzzle. One group was told the puzzle was a game, and the other group was told it was a skills test. There were no gender differences amongst the scores of children who believed they were participating in some kind of test, but in the group who thought it was a game, the boys scored significantly higher. In a second study, two games with identical challenges were developed with different story lines and graphics. One story involved a quest for a treasure and fighting pirates, while the other story involved bears trying to recover their missing honey from some "honey monsters." The boys performed equally well on both versions of the game, but the girls scored much higher on the honey bear version. The researchers concluded that the nature of the challenge (a game or a test) as well as the themes and storylines clearly had an influence on the players, even though the actual puzzles were identical. This work supports the notion the perceptions of the players has an impact on their gaming success, reinforcing the idea that separate game genres may be most suitable for the majority of gamers. Decoding appears to be a factor in these gender-based interpretations of mediated symbols.

CONCLUSION

This chapter has focused on two very powerful (and not mutually exclusive) symbol-making systems in the Canadian socio-cultural landscape: language and the media. In each case, there are multiple levels of meaning, both in the sending and receiving of messages. Not all people in an audience will react the same way to each communication; but a pervasive presence or absence in the language or media does more than reflect the gender values of the society: it shapes and reinforces those values. This section has also considered gender lenses and normative expectations, which are recreated and disseminated through language and media. All these elements are integrally connected, and they combine to create the socio-cultural landscape within which we live our lives. Section Two focuses on the individual dimension of gender—how we learn and experience gender within this larger dimension.

CHAPTER SUMMARY: KEY POINTS

1. Our socio-cultural landscape is constructed through symbols and language. These are the tools we use to think, understand, and to communicate ideas. Therefore, the language we use shapes the way we think.

2. A traditional convention in the English language was the use of the male generic form. That is, we used to use words like *he* and *his*, like *man* and *mankind* to refer to all people. This pattern of linguistic sexism resulted in women being excluded from legal rights and led to a concerted effort to change language conventions.

3. Our language continues to be sexist in that it tends to render women invisible. This occurs through persistent use of the masculine generic—*firemen* and *chairman*—as well as through the use of masculine pronouns.

4. A second concern with the English language is the way it tends to belittle women. Patterns of *semantic derogation*, as well as the use of adjectives and slang, all contribute to negative perceptions of women.

5. The mass media is ubiquitous in Canadian society. Therefore, it plays a major role in transmitting culture and shaping our gendered socio-cultural landscape.

6. The *reflection hypothesis* argues that the media merely mirrors the culture, without shaping our ideas, norms, or values. However, by controlling what information and ideas get disseminated, the media has the power to shape the socio-cultural landscape.

7. *Cultivation theory* suggests that mass media is the most pervasive disseminator of information that has ever existed in human society. Media tells a relatively coherent, though not entirely accurate, story about our society, which in turn shapes our understanding of the world we live in.

8. Producers and writers meticulously create and develop media messages and images, a process known as *encoding*. However, not all media messages are *decoded* by the audience in a uniform fashion. The media audience is not passive: we interpret what we see and hear.

9. An audience interprets mediated messages in one of three main ways. Some accept the *dominant* message as it was encoded by the media producers. Some follow a *negotiated* pattern, in which they view the media critically, accepting some components of the message but challenging others. A third possibility is an *oppositional* interpretation, in which the audience directly challenges the dominant message.

10. *Content analysis* is a method for examining the media by assessing all its images and scripts to measure the encoded messages. Most research reveals that gender-polarizing messages are prevalent in the media.

DISCUSSION QUESTIONS

1. Do you believe linguistic sexism is problematic? Why or why not? Listen to the conversations of people around you. Do you hear pejorative slang or gender-based adjectives? Some have argued that men are also harmed by such language patterns. What did you observe?

2. Are there sports teams at your university or college? Do women's and men's sports teams receive equal attention and support from the administration and student body? Are the team names gender based like the *Lady Vees* and the *Voyageurs*? If so, canvas your fellow students to find out if they think this is problematic.

3. Take a critical look at your favourite television show (or music genre or movie). Can you identify the encoded messages? Are these messages based on gender normative expectations? How do you decode the messages? Now think about a program/music/ movie that you really don't like. How is it encoded and decoded?

4. Do a brief content analysis of all the advertisements you are exposed to during one day. Do you see the same patterns as those outlined in this chapter? Or is there a wider range of gendered images? Were the advertisements for some products more stereotypical than others? Which products had the most and the least sexist encoded messages? Why do you think these patterns exist?

5. If people you know play computer games, ask them about the gendered images. Do the women gamers ignore or enjoy the gender stereotypes present in these games? What about the gamers who are men? Does anyone take an oppositional interpretation when decoding the images? Who adopts a dominant interpretation?

KEY TERMS

content analysis	invisibility	reflection hypothesis
cultivation theory	linguistic determinism	semantic derogation
decoding	linguistic sexism	slang
diminutives	masculine generic form	social comparison theory
dominant/preferred meaning	media	spotlighting
encoding	negotiated/resistant meaning	
internalization	oppositional meaning	

Gender on the Individual Dimension

chapter five

Being Gendered: Childhood and Adolescence

SOCIALIZATION

Do you ever think about how infants born helpless and dependent grow into gendered beings? Humans are born physiologically ready to grow and mature. They have sex-based physiologies, but they lack the ability to survive independently. Through interaction with others, they survive and develop language skills and a knowledge base. And, importantly, they also develop a sense of their gendered selves through interaction with others. As we have already discussed, gender is a central element in our lives and has an impact on our relationships and choices. The previous chapters have introduced you to the ongoing debate about whether gender is a stable property of selfhood or an evolving identity that adjusts to shifting social contexts. This chapter focuses on the ways people learn gender through the process of **socialization**. Socialization can be defined as a complex learning process through which individuals develop selfhood and acquire the knowledge, skills, and motivations required for participation in social life. It is both intentional and accidental, both blatant and subtle. We do not propose that socialization necessarily creates a permanent gender identity that guides our choices and actions. Instead, we explore the many ways that gender arrangements are learned and maintained.

If we were not socialized, we would not know how to interact with others, how to interpret their emotions, or how to function in the social world. There have been cases—fortunately relatively rare—where children have been forced to grow up in profound isolation. They physically matured to some extent, but they had no significant interactions with humans. Even after these children had been discovered and efforts made to teach them how to speak and act in the social world, their capacity to learn was limited. From this, researchers conclude that socialization is critical to human development generally and specifically to the development of gendered ways of being.

Gender is a key part of the socialization process. We begin life with no sense of ourselves as gendered beings. We start as biological entities with various sex-based characteristics. The humans around us categorize us as either boys or girls and sometimes use medical technology (see Chapter One) to recreate us if they don't think we fit sufficiently into one of the predefined categories. Even though approximately 1.7 percent of people do not fit neatly into one of the two biological sexes, society makes little or no accommodation for them and organizes its social structures and symbolic interactions as though there were only two sexes. However, because this book is an introductory text, and because even the two-gendered, two-sexed societal relationships are complex, we focus the majority of our attention on these two main sexes, always remembering that many more sex and gender possibilities exist.

From the moment of our birth, people interact with us based on our membership in society as boy or as girl. **Gender socialization** is already underway when we are wrapped in a pink or blue blanket, as is still common practice in Canadian hospitals. Students often question how much impact the colour of a blanket can have on an infant only minutes old. The baby cannot possibly see well enough or understand enough to be influenced by the colour of a blanket. But empirical research tells us that these earliest experiences actually do make a difference—not because the baby perceives anything from its blanket, but because the humans that surround the baby know what pink and blue signify. They believe that a baby wrapped in blue is a boy, and without even thinking about it, they interpret what they see based on their knowledge of boys in general. In a classic study by Rubin, *et al.* (1974), new parents were asked to describe their babies. The infants chosen for the study, all less than 24 hours old, were similar in size, weight, muscle tone, and alertness. But the parents described them very differently depending on the sex of their newborn. All parents described their children in positive terms, such as alert and easygoing; but parents of girls were more likely to perceive them as softer, smaller, and less attentive than the boys, while parents of boys perceived their infants as stronger and better coordinated. Even though objective assessments of the infants did not show these differences, the parents believed them to be true. So how do the parents' perceptions influence socialization? If a parent interacts with a child in certain ways because she is a girl or he is a boy, that parent's expectations are influencing that child's experiences and thus their understanding of the world. If this only happened once in infancy, it would not be particularly important. But these early signifiers of gender begin a lifelong pattern of separation and distinction between the sexes. Consider this: if everyone in your world treated you as a fragile being in need of protection, you might be less likely to have the freedom to explore your world and discover your own abilities. You might also be less likely to get into trouble. Conversely, if everyone around you thought you were tough, strong, and capable, you would likely be less protected and might be expected to fend for yourself—more freedom and more potential for disaster. This example is a reflection of the way many girls and boys have been and continue to be raised (Lytton & Romney, 1991). When we are children, the expectations of others shape our worlds.

A great deal of research has examined gender patterns in parenting. In a meta-analysis (*meta-analysis* is a statistical re-assessment of the data and findings of a large number of research projects) of 170 research projects, Lytton and Romney (1991) found that parenting patterns have changed over time, and that there is noticeably less specific gender socialization than there was during the 1950s and 1960s. However, they did not find that boys and girls are now being raised identically. Observe children in the playground or at the mall with their parents. How easily can you identify the gender of the child? Usually a determination of gender is obvious by the child's clothing or by the parents' interaction with him or her. (We think of this difference in treatment as the *tiger/princess dichotomy*. Many parents unwittingly use nicknames that are highly gendered, evoking stereotypes. For example, *tiger* implies strength and fierceness, while *princess* creates images of beauty and preciousness.) This differential treatment is a form of gender socialization. Much of the research literature shows that boys are still more likely to be encouraged in physical activities (*e.g.*, sports), and girls are more likely to be restricted, both by the clothes they wear and by their parent's rules (*e.g.*, kept from independent activities, such as using scissors and tools, or walking alone in the mall or the street until they are older). Also, although parents most often discourage aggressive behaviour in children of any sex, they tolerate more from their sons than from their daughters. When parents do punish their children's misbehaviours, sons are more likely to be physically disciplined than daughters. In short, there are still significant gendered differences in parents' treatment of their children (see Lytton & Romney, 1991; Mitchell, 1992).

The socialization that occurs in earliest childhood is often called **primary socialization**. Primary socialization is our initial learning about the world and our place in it. Young children learn rapidly, and their ability to learn language is astonishing. Moreover, children are typically uncritical of the information they are learning. Early in life, humans do not have the capacity to assess information; they just absorb it. When people get a little older, they develop the ability to evaluate ideas and information. If someone gives you a piece of information, you evaluate it against the wealth of knowledge you already have before making a judgment about its validity. So if someone told you that all women were bad drivers, you would think about your experiences with drivers of both sexes, good and bad, and probably conclude that this is nonsense. But a young child who has always and only heard that women are bad drivers and has only ever seen their dad drive, that child would have no reference points against which to judge this "fact." That child would likely just accept the idea.

We've used this example to illustrate an important point: early socialization has a powerful impact on our understanding of the world and consequently on our understanding of gender. We think of primary socialization as a foundation: it lays the groundwork for everything a person later observes and experiences. Subsequent learning usually builds on this foundation, though occasionally, it also undermines it, crumbling the base to rebuild it into a different shape. So if you grew up in a home where your parents held traditional views regarding the appropriate behaviours for women and men, then traditional views would be your foundation: everything you later learned about how to be a woman or man would be influenced by this foundation.

At one time, it was commonly accepted that early gender socialization provided a growing child with a long-term, stable gender identity. That gender identity was understood to be a relatively permanent, unchanging component of selfhood that was then reflected in all subsequent choices and actions. Thus, a person's gender identity served as a guide throughout life. Most sociologists today are less accepting of this conceptualization for two key reasons. First, most believe that while socialization *begins* in childhood, it is a *lifelong process*. We are continually developing a more complex self, which can change significantly over time. We learn about ourselves as gendered beings and new ways for participating in our communities throughout our lives, whenever we move into new work roles, new family roles, and new intimate relationships, for example. People are still being socialized when they move into senior citizen residences and nursing homes. Second, sociologists are deeply aware of the importance of social context: situations affect gendered behaviour. Gender identity shifts and adjusts to the situational demands that shape our daily interactions. This explains why many people act in ways that don't seem consistent— why women who perceive themselves as competent occasionally present themselves as helpless or confused; or why men who believe fully in gender equality might laugh at sexist jokes or participate in activities that objectify women.

Social Learning Theory

We have already identified primary socialization as the initial learning process that occurs in early childhood and arises from our first interactions with others. Many sociological and psychological theories explain primary socialization and define the parts of the process.

Perhaps the simplest theory is **social learning theory**, the idea that we learn gender the same way that we learn other things—through observation and interaction. Specifically, we learn through **reinforcement** and **modeling**. For example, when teaching a child to say *please*, parents can use reinforcement. When the child whines, they ignore her; but when she says *please*, they give her what she has asked for. By reinforcing the desired behaviour, the child learns that a specific pattern of behaviour works. She also learns that whining does not get her anything, so after a while, she stops whining.

Gender expectations are often learned via reinforcement. People might train their young sons to be strong by telling them to "be a man" and that "big boys don't cry." Frequently, when sons show their pain or fear, parents ignore them, or worse, sometimes belittle them, saying: "Don't be such a baby." We might give them positive rewards when they handle their troubles without showing "weakness." Because girls are more likely to be comforted when they are afraid or in pain, they learn that they don't have to hide their feelings. Empirical studies show that the perceived sex of a child influences the way adults interpret the child's emotions and behaviour. In one classic study, adults were shown a videotape of a nine-month-old child (dressed in neutral clothing so the child's gender was not readily apparent) playing and then reacting tearfully to a surprise event. The adults who believed they were observing a girl said she was afraid and that they should comfort her, but those who thought the child was a boy interpreted his reaction as anger and said there was no need to intercede (Condry & Condry, 1976). This kind of reinforcement is a feature in the lives of many children, subtly shaping their behaviour and interaction patterns.

A second component of social learning theory is *modeling*. Modeling means that children emulate the behaviours of people around them, especially people who they know share the same gender. Girls supposedly copy the actions of other girls and women while boys copy other boys and men. When children play house, the girls may want to be the mommy to emulate their own mother's actions. This modeling can be combined with reinforcement if dressing up in mommy's clothes and high heels gets a positive reaction from the adults. Boys in the same skirts and heels might receive negative reinforcement, teaching them that dressing up like mommy is not appropriate. In short, social learning theory claims that we reward children for gender-appropriate behaviour and ignore or punish inappropriate behaviour. Through reinforcement and modeling, children learn about gender. Observation, combined with direct and indirect reinforcement, creates gendered people.

Interestingly, while this theory makes intuitive sense, empirical research testing this theory yields contradictory results. The meta-analysis by Lytton and Romney showed that parents do not typically treat their sons and daughters differently regarding achievement and encouragement. However, other individual studies have indeed found that reinforcement from adults influences children's behaviour. For example, Fagot and Leinbach (1993) found that the children of parents who follow fairly traditional divisions of masculine and feminine behaviour are more likely to positively reinforce gender-stereotyped play. They also found that interacting differently with boys and girls does correlate with the development of gender-based behaviour differences (Fagot, Hagan, Leinbach, & Kronsberg, 1985). Social learning theory can be useful for explaining some elements of gender socialization, but not all. In her more recent summary of socialization research, Stockard (1999) argues that there has been little empirical support for the theory that modeling is a source of early gender socialization. "Parents who exhibit traits that are highly stereotypically associated with one sex group or the other are not more likely to have children who exhibit such strongly stereotyped behavior" (p. 218). Part of the problem with social learning theory is that it treats the child as a relatively passive receptor of stimuli, as though the child had very little to contribute to the process (a situation that really only exists in the first few months of life). Further, research on parents as reinforcers and models showed that the importance of other socializing influences in each child's life may be undervalued. As discussed in earlier chapters and the introduction, the education system and the media play a significant role in the development of gender, as do a child's individual ways of decoding messages.

Cognitive Development Theory

A second theory—cognitive development theory—addresses some of the shortcomings of social learning theory. **Cognitive development theory** regards the socialization process as one of *self-socialization*. That is, rather than being relatively passive, children learn through mental effort. They seek to make sense of their social world and find their own place within it. Then they act in accordance with their understanding of that place. As children's thinking capacities develop, so too do their perceptions of gender. In essence, cognitive development theory argues that young children make sense of the world in part by creating categories to organize information. Sex is a simple category because, as far as most children understand, there are only two groups, and all people are members of one or the other. At this point in their development, they think in very concrete terms, and their ability to organize information is based on obvious clues, such as clothing, hairstyles, and anatomical differences. They later develop a sense of what is gender-appropriate and what is not. As their intellect develops more fully, they realize that their sex/gender (they don't yet differentiate between the two) will not change. Recognizing the unchanging nature of their sex is known as **gender constancy**. Children who have achieved gender constancy typically monitor themselves, striving to ensure that their appearance and behaviour reflects their gender category. Thus, if a child believes she is a girl, she seeks to be "a girl" by wearing make-up, for example, to prove her girlness. Activities that she perceives to be "gender-inappropriate" threaten her membership as a girl and for this reason, she will avoid them.

Cognitive development theory is not without problems, however. Certainly, examples suggest children actively try to understand and identify gender arrangements and to categorize people but they appear to do so earlier than the theory would suggest. The children of one of the authors, at three and five years old, were in the room while she was watching a tennis match featuring Andre Agassi. He was a teenager at the time and wore his hair very long; but his face showed the beginnings of a beard, and he also wore an earring. Her children engaged in a lengthy discussion about whether he was actually a man or a woman. They were looking at what they perceived to be contradictory evidence—beard, long hair, and an earring (in the early 1990s, it was much less common to see men wearing earrings). They finally concluded that he must indeed be a man, though not very good at manhood, given his appearance. The decisive factor in their minds was that the organizers of the tournament wouldn't let a woman play in a men's tennis match. Young children do think about sex and gender markers and do try to understand what they see. But the cognitive development theory posits that a child's sense of their own gender remains unclear until their intellect has reached a state of gender constancy at the age of five or six years. When we attempt to measure the theory empirically, we find that many children exhibit signs of constancy and engage in gender preferences (for example, playing with trucks or dolls) at an age much earlier than the theory would predict.

Gender Schema Theory

Sandra Bem addresses constancy and self-identity issues more fully in her **gender schema theory**. Gender schema theory goes beyond reinforcement and self-socialization to recognize the importance of culture in influencing gender socialization. In our society, which often highlights gender differences, children develop *gender schema* from a very early age. **Schema** are cognitive categories created for organizing information. These schema become increasingly elaborate as children mature. As they gain new information and experiences, they integrate them into existing schemas. In Bem's words, a person's understandings of their gender is "more than a particular collection of masculine or feminine traits; it is also a way of looking at reality that produces and reproduces those traits during a life time of self-construction" (1993, p. 154).

The gender schema theory helps to explain why children behave in gendered ways earlier than cognitive development theory suggests they should. Some empirical research shows that children as young as 12 months can distinguish masculine and feminine qualities (see Leinbach & Fagot, 1993). Gender schema theory also helps address weaknesses in social learning theory. It shows that parents are not the only models or reinforcers in a child's socialization. No simple, direct causal relationship exists between parents' actions and their children's understanding of gender. Everything children encounter and experience gets filtered through their schema as they seek to make sense of the world. The child's social context, then, is an integral part of their gender socialization: the ideas and experiences they are exposed to shape their schemas and influence their subsequent actions. Not only do they learn "facts" about gender (*e.g.*, that men have beards and women do not), but they also evaluate what is good or desirable for women and men. In a long-term study that followed young children for two and a half years, regularly assessing their understanding of gender and their ability to identify it, researchers found a vast array of differences among the children. Instead of seeing a common developmental path for all the children, they found unique patterns among the children and varied connections between elements of gender cognition within each individual child (Hort *et al.*, 1991).

Bronwyn Davies (2003) uses a post-structural approach to analyze children's gendered behaviour. She argues that an **incorrigible male-female binary** develops out of our linguistic structures: that is, we engage in discursive practices that position people as belonging to one of *only* two possible categories. In learning language, children can't help but learn this pervasive two-sex gender model. When they try to locate themselves in one of these two categories, they adopt the most obvious signifiers they have come to recognize: behaviours, activities, speech patterns, and appearance. These adopted signifiers prove not only that they are boys or girls but also that they are quite definitely *not* the other sex/gender. Importantly, when adults try to minimize obvious gender stereotypes for children, possibly by providing gender-neutral toys and clothing, children tend to work even harder to maintain the signifiers. Thus, instead of raising children to be free of gender constraints, adults may actually be encouraging them to embrace stereotypical behaviour even more enthusiastically. It is not uncommon for adults actively working to raise children in non-sexist ways to be surprised that their efforts do not succeed. The children's fervor at maintaining gender-based signifiers lead perplexed adults to conclude that sex differences must truly be innate. Nature seems to have triumphed over nurture. But Davies provides an equally plausible conclusion: it is not nature, but a pervasive linguistic and social binary that creates an imperative for children to both understand and present themselves as clearly belonging in one sex/gender category or the other.

Identity Construction Theory

The development of our gendered selves is a complex, ongoing process; and as Hort *et al.* (1991) reveal, we do not all follow an identical path. Nor do we do achieve a specific *gender identity* at one point in time that reflects our gendered selves forever after. This project of becoming gendered is a lifelong activity, though adolescence is a time of particularly intense questioning and exploring. Developmental theorists sometimes describe adolescence as a time of **identity construction**. During adolescence, people seek to discover for themselves who they are and where they fit in. If you think of adolescence as the phase of your life when you changed from a dependent child into an independent adult, when you stopped defining yourself in terms of your family and their expectations and started defining yourself in terms of your own accomplishments, you will realize that adolescence is a time of significant personal development. A large part of this identity construction involved your understanding of yourself as man or woman, as queer or straight; and your choices about conforming or resisting the societal gender expectations delineated within the sociocultural landscape.

While adolescence is a time of identity construction, it is also a time of physical maturation, intellectual growth, emotional growth, and sexual development. Individuals attain new social statuses and a whole new set of rights and obligations. Your own adolescence likely felt wonderfully exciting, terrifying, and lonely, as it does for many Canadian teens. With so much change, feeling insecure is the norm. While all adolescents face similar challenges, they do not go through the changes in lockstep. I'm sure you remember the boy who grew to be six feet tall in Grade Five and also the one who was still five feet tall in Grade Ten. You may remember the friends who seemed very mature in junior high and the others who still seemed very immature in high school. We each underwent these changes at our own pace, facing the challenges alone together. Most of us turned to our peers, rather than to our families, for information and support, because we were also striving for independence from our families.

Both social learning theory and gender learning schema are relevant for explaining gender in adolescence. Teens follow new models and gain new reinforcement from a wider variety of sources; and their gender schema continue to develop based on their increasing interactions and experiences. Vivian Seltzer (1989) suggests in her psychosocial theory of adolescence that the importance of peers during adolescence cannot be overstated. From our age mates, we learn about a broad range of possibilities for appearance, actions, and relationships. Seltzer calls this adolescent world the **peer arena**. The peer arena is the social milieu in which young people evaluate, model, imitate, experiment, critique, observe, and judge the people around them. Seltzer argues that young adolescents need to socialize with each other in large groups to gain insights into the array of possibilities and the consequences of acting on some of these choices. This she calls the **comparative act**. Psychological research shows that early adolescence is the time of greatest conformity. People are more inclined to go along with group expectations during early adolescence than at any other time in the life course: there is some urgency to finding one's place in the gendered world and adopting the normative expectations. Once young people reach later adolescence and have developed a stronger sense of themselves, they may be less in need of the large circle of peers. They both experience and create less pressure to conform as they reach adulthood.

Gender and Social Context

Reviewing some psychological theories, notwithstanding the fact that this is a sociology textbook, is fruitful because gender operates on multiple levels and psychologists contribute greatly to our knowledge of child development. Gender schema theory is especially useful because it integrates many theories and helps us comprehend the infinite variety of gendered understandings people create. Gender schema theory also highlights the importance of studying the social realm for understanding gender: each person's gender schema develops based on the specific ideas and experiences to which she or he is exposed. Thus, considering the social context in which these patterns unfold is essential.

Throughout this chapter, we have referred to some of the adults and peers who participate in the socialization of children. But now we need to examine the social contexts and the role other people play more directly. Beyond the theories, we need to pay attention to the content and context of socialization—not just how we become gendered beings, but what being gendered entails, and where and why it occurs. Many sociology texts refer to these influences as **agents of socialization**. However, there has been some critique of this conceptualization, since it creates the impression that outside agents act upon the individual being socialized in a unidirectional rather than reciprocal manner. In addition, studying *agents of socialization* does not enable us to consider the interrelationships between various elements of the socialization process. To consider these relationships, we examine three specific social contexts as well as some of the empirical research that illustrates the process of becoming gendered.

LEARNING GENDER: FAMILY

For small children, the key arena of socialization is their family. This is where they spend much of their time; these are the people with whom they have the most meaningful relationships; and this is where ongoing attachments develop. In addition, family members raising that child determine what other socializing influences enter her life. Does she go to daycare? Does he belong to a religious community? Is there a television in the house? Family's crucial role in a child's first learning experiences is called the **primacy effect**. As children get older, they have more non-family experiences, such as those at school, with their peers, or on sports teams.

Of course, families are not all alike. They vary by structure (membership), social class, and ethnic heritage, for example. In earlier sociological research (1950s–1960s), one particular form of family, the two-sphered homemaker/breadwinner model, was commonly considered superior to others (see Parsons, 1949). While Chapter Eleven discusses this model further, it is important to note that this notion has been soundly critiqued (for example, see Eichler, 1988). However, there are groups that still believe this "traditional family" is the *ideal* family form. (Recall the discussion about gender lenses in Chapter Two. Belief in the superiority of the "traditional family" is a pervasive gender lens.) Accordingly, these factions believe that any family that does not conform to this "ideal" may be dysfunctional and prone to problems (neatly avoiding the issue of problems within "ideal" families).

Abundant popular interest has focused on questions about family type. Do children in lone-parent families, post-divorce families, or gay or lesbian families fare better or worse than those raised in "traditional" families? What about children with a working mom or a stay-at-home dad? Do children in families that belong to specific cultures—ethnic, faith-based, or geographic—have developmental advantages or disadvantages? The research addressing these questions has supported contradictory conclusions. For example, some research reports that children who grew up in families where a divorce occurred fared worse than those in so called "intact" families. Others have critiqued these findings, arguing that children's experiences reflect the degree of conflict and economic stresses in their lives, rather than effects of divorce itself. Some research, most notably by the Roman Catholic Church, has claimed that children in same-sex households will suffer because they will not be exposed to *sexual complementarity* (role models of each sex). Others, including the Canadian Psychological Society, have reviewed all the empirical literature and concluded that the Catholic Church's claims have absolutely "no support in the scientific literature" (CPA, 2003). We would ask you to keep one thing in mind as you think about families and the gendered socialization that occurs: all families are different. Assuming that a particular family structure, income level, or religious heritage automatically implies that the children within that family will be raised in identifiable ways is simplistic. Every household represents an intersection point between a variety of statuses (see Chapter Seven). Thus, the experiences of that family's members are unique. The dynamics within the family (*e.g.*, the degree of stress and conflict, or the quality of interactions) are more likely to influence the children's development than is the "type" of family. Nevertheless, we do see patterns in gender socialization influenced by the gendered arrangements created and maintained within the household, though not usually based on "type" of family.

Physical context often reflects and recreates gender patterns. Research conducted on children's rooms, toys, and clothing to assess the gendered nature of their content shows that gender polarization is evident in many families (see Etaugh & Liss, 1992; Fagot & Leinbach, 1993). Boys' rooms are much more likely to be decorated in primary colours with athletic or warrior themes. Girls' toys often include dolls and homemaking equipment (such as the famous Easy Bake Oven). The differences are encapsulated by a dichotomy we call *Barbie vs. G.I. Joe* (one of the earliest action figures for boys). Barbie's purpose is to look good in different outfits and accessories (even Doctor and Astronaut Barbie), while action figures use their strength and skill with weaponry to kill bad guys. In a similar fashion, boys' clothing is much more likely to be comfortable, while girls' clothing is often pretty and impractical, limiting physical activity. Some people may question the importance of these findings: do clothes and colours and toys really make a difference? The research suggests that they do. If groups of people (boys and girls) are constantly surrounded by materials that are clearly gendered, they learn what is considered right and appropriate for people "like them." Whether the individuals ultimately accept or rebel against such normative expectations, this early gender socialization has an impact.

In addition, the roles and relationships within the family context influence a child's socialization. Research on mothers and fathers indicates that they often play different roles. Fathers who are not the primary caregivers for their children are more likely to sex-type them, particularly their sons (Hardesty *et al.*, 1995). This means, for example, that they would be more likely to comment on their daughter's appearance and encourage her to participate in "girls'" activities, while they would be inclined to throw the ball or play hockey with their sons. Interestingly, fathers who are major caregivers, single fathers, or stay-at-home dads are less likely to engage in those stereotypical patterns (Parke, 1996). Some researchers have suggested that this difference results from very involved dads getting to know their children as well-rounded persons, rather than thinking of them simply as "my son" and "my daughter." In addition, discipline patterns differ depending on the parents' notions of gender roles. Research shows that fathers are more likely to punish gender-inappropriate behaviour than are mothers, especially from their sons. In general, parents who do not follow a traditional gendered division of labour are less likely to raise their children in stereotypical ways. One study observed parents telling stories to their children. It found that traditional parents told stories about achievement more frequently to their sons than their daughters, while non-traditional parents were more likely to tell their daughters such stories (Fiese & Williams, 2000).

Studies show that the games parents play with their children also reflect gender patterns. Daughters are much more likely to be handled with care, while sons are considered more sturdy and often handled more vigorously. As the infant grows, the differences in play patterns persist (Lytton & Romney, 1991). Research shows that sons are allowed more physical freedom and opportunities to explore. Parents are more likely to talk and cuddle with daughters and to discourage rowdy behaviour. Communication with children reinforces these gendered patterns. Girls are encouraged to be co-operative and helpful, while boys are rewarded for assertiveness and competitiveness. Parents also have fewer conversations with sons about feelings than with their daughters (Fivush *et al.*, 2000).

Even this brief review of some of the research literature on gender socialization in families illustrates that gender polarization continues to be a factor in most households. For many children, sex-typed socialization is the norm; and as gender schema theory shows, these experiences shape their understanding of their selves and the gendered nature of the social world.

LEARNING GENDER: SCHOOL

Another social context that plays an important role in the socialization of most children is school. Certainly in Canada, the vast majority of children attend schools from about age five until at least age 16. Schools are charged with the responsibility of preparing students for active participation in the economy and civic life of the community. Ideally, they provide opportunity for every child to maximize his or her intellectual potential. This learning is not gender-neutral, however. Analyses of most schools and classrooms show that while there is much less sex stereotyping than there was in the past, gender polarization still occurs (Sadker & Sadker, 1994).

When considering schools as a forum in which gender is done, we need to recognize that the learning that takes place extends beyond the subject matter. One way to conceptualize this is to think of two distinct curricula. The **formal curriculum** is a set of subjects officially and explicitly taught to students in school. The informal or **hidden curriculum** involves the values, norms, and beliefs that are not deliberately taught, but underlie the formal curriculum. So, for example, in history class, students might learn about a series of conflicts and treaties between Aboriginal people and European explorers in Canada—this is the formal curriculum. But if the course materials ignore the motivations and actions of Aboriginal people, while focusing on those of the European people, the students learn through the hidden curriculum that Aboriginal people's motivations and actions, not to mention the consequences they experience, are unimportant. While not explicitly stated, the message in the hidden curriculum is that the actions of some people matter and those of others do not. Thus, both the formal and hidden curricula have implications for gender.

The formal curriculum in Canadian schools has changed a great deal. The physical space and materials are less sex-typed than they were in previous decades. When the authors went to school, even though we lived in two different provinces, Ontario and New Brunswick, the architecture and textbooks were the same. At our schools, there was a boys' door and a girls' door, with labels engraved in granite over each entry. The materials, such as the *Fun with Dick and Jane* reader, overtly supported gendered roles and a sharp division of labour. Moreover, it was the norm in the 1960s and 1970s for boys and girls to take different courses: girls in the home economics room typically equipped with kitchen appliances and sewing machines; boys in the industrial arts shop filled with power saws, blow torches, and mechanic's tools. Physical Education classes were also divided by sex, while those sports restricted to boys (such as football and hockey) received a much larger share of the equipment budget. Quite simply, at that time, the formal curriculum itself was gender polarizing. In the wake of the second wave of the women's movement and the critiques of education, much has changed. Texts and educational materials have been rewritten to minimize sexist teaching. Skill development courses, such as home economics and shop, are now open to and in some cases required for both sexes. Efforts have been made to more equitably fund boys' and girls' athletics programs, including having mixed-sex football and wrestling teams in some jurisdictions. However, despite these changes, the hidden curriculum frequently continues to create differential experiences for girls and boys. Consider Melanie Muise's guest essay on university sports in Chapter Four. Given her research, how much has actually changed in the past 30 years? Are the Lady Vees and other female athletes treated differently than the male athletes?

Meanwhile, a hidden curriculum teaches girls and boys that they will have different opportunities in life. The staffing of many schools supports this idea. The main positions within schools are the teachers, administrators, and support staff. The most typical pattern reveals women teaching younger grades and arts and language courses, while men teach the higher grades and the maths and sciences. Upper-level administrators are more likely to be male, and support staff is more likely to be female (Cusson, 1990). In short, the roles played out within schools reflect a larger pattern of gender polarization, wherein girls and women are more involved in nurturing younger children and supporting people in positions of authority, while men fill positions of authority and occupy more "prestigious" positions.

Interaction and activities within classrooms that reflect gender differences are also considered part of the hidden curriculum. As discussed in Chapter One, the empirical research shows that many classrooms still provide differential learning opportunities for girls and boys. The ways in which teachers interact with students tends to be gendered. Boys are more likely to be both praised and criticized for their work. Girls are less likely to be noticed; and when they do receive attention, it is less likely to be an acknowledgment of their scholastic ability and more likely to be focused on their compliant behaviour (Sadker & Sadker, 1994).

Obviously, activities in classrooms make up only one part of the interaction that occurs at school. Students' experiences in the hallways, cafeteria, and on the bus also contribute to their socialization. There is evidence to suggest that these interactions are even more likely to be gender polarizing than are the classroom activities.

LEARNING GENDER: PEERS

For young children, family is the most important socializing influence. But during adolescence, peers become increasingly important. While adolescents still participate in family relationships, they also expand their non-family relationships, with peers, teammates, and classmates. From age-mates, teens see a broad range of possibilities—how to act, how to adorn oneself, how to interact with others of different sexes, ages, and sexual orientations—and they observe the reaction of others to those individuals who do or do not conform to expectations.

The gender normative expectations discussed in Chapter Four (appearance for girls and toughness and success for boys, especially in athletic activities) have an impact on adolescents' popularity. As the boys get a little older, the sexual normative expectation—"young men are expected to have heterosexual experience"—also plays a role in their peer groups. Those who are able to successfully conform to the expectations are less likely to be excluded or bullied. Many teens who are subject to bullying are those who are unable to or who choose not to conform to gender or sex-based normative expectations. (Bruce Reimer, discussed in Chapter One, was subject to this type of harassment.) Boys who aren't competitive or who don't present as anti-feminine or heterosexual enough are often singled out for maltreatment. This harassment can involve name-calling: the pejorative language may challenge their masculinity (*wuss*) and/or their sexual orientation (*fag*). In a fascinating study of school shootings, Kimmel and Mahler (2003) found that the shooters had been routinely teased and bullied, specifically about their sexual orientation. The researchers describe the shootings as retaliation for challenges to their manhood. Girls and young women, on the other hand, are less likely to be punished for behaving like boys, since there is no corresponding anti-masculine expectation. But they often become targets of teasing or aggression based on their appearance and their perceived sexual behaviour. Even the types of bullying behaviour people engage in are shaped by gender. While boys are more inclined towards physical aggression, girls more often show **relational aggression**. That is, girls are less likely to physically hurt someone than they are to bully through gossip, rumour, and social exclusion.

CASE STUDY: ADOLESCENT GIRLS, PEERS, AND APPEARANCE

In a qualitative study of the appearance norms and social experience of adolescent girls, Matthews (2000) found a strong connection between gender expectations and interaction within the peer arena. Specifically, the young women in the study (age 14–21) were very candid about the link between having success within the peer group, having the ideal weight (extremely slim), and/or either discussing or engaging in weight-loss activities. The social hierarchy in junior high and/or high schools across Canada over several decades seems remarkably similar: some were outsiders by choice or exclusion, and some young people fit more easily into the "popular" social groups than others. (At one of the author's high school in the 1970s, these popular girls named themselves "the clique.") The young women in this study made it quite clear that they were not blindly trying to live up to or, in this case, down to a socio-cultural expectation to be thin. While they certainly were inundated with media images of beauty and slimness, they argued their actions were conscious choices. Avoiding food, discussing weight-loss techniques, and/or being thin typically enhanced their popularity. Girls who did not strive to achieve this particular version of beauty also said that they were making conscious choices about appearance and resisting cultural expectations.

Girls who interacted heavily in the peer arena were judged by the appearance standard and were rewarded or punished through popularity or relational aggression, based on their ability to conform to the ideal. Those who chose not to spend as much of their time on their social lives often had other interests—sports, jobs, academics, or music, for example. These girls were less likely to judge themselves by their appearance and more likely to withstand or ignore challenges from other teens about their appearance.

Let's examine four specific young women in this study (names have been changed to ensure the anonymity of the participants). First, meet Reva, who is now in college. She enjoyed popularity in high school, but it was not easy for her to achieve. She recognized that popularity was based on "material things, the way things look, everything on the outside." Many girls in her group were what she called "backstabbers." In other words, they used relational aggression to maintain their position by excluding others. At one point, when she felt that her position in the group was insecure, she decided that focusing on dieting and losing weight would resolve the problem: "There were a couple of us that wanted to like starve ourselves, try to lose weight, so we just wouldn't eat." Their friendship remained strong, but Reva said she was "unsure of her *self*" and struggled to feel good. Binging and purging became an issue for her. Maintaining her position in the peer arena was not easy or fun, but it was accomplished by conforming to a particular gender normative expectation: appearance.

Kim is still in high school and wants to be popular. She has a clear understanding of how the social hierarchy works. "The pressure increases as you move towards the popular group. You always have to prove yourself, based on how you look." Like Reva, she acknowledges that judgment and exclusion are part of the peer arena. She says bluntly, "Popular people are jerks, they don't care about others [and] are very competitive." She also says that "trying to fit in is limiting" and she feels "insecure, [I'm] always beating myself up." But she still wants to be one of them, and she perceives that meeting the ideal beauty standards will help her achieve this. So she and her friends are focused on weight—they all started smoking on the same day when they were told that it would help suppress their appetites. Once again, conforming to normative expectations is understood as a measure of social success within the peer arena.

By contrast, Una has little time for dwelling on gender-based normative expectations such as appearance or on the pressures of the popular girls. She's an athlete and a musician who says, "I just don't have the time or the money to keep up" to the expectations popular girls have to deal with. Her teammates and coaches are interested in performance rather than popularity. Una finds that it is hard to "be yourself" in junior high because it is a choice between trying to fit in or pursuing her own goals. She formed a close circle of friends among whom appearance was less important than other skills. She believes that not being part of the popular group allows her to see it clearly—to avoid its traps.

Terry had a very different experience. When she was in high school, she was marginalized because she did not conform to the cultural ideal—she was considered overweight by her peers. While she had some close friends, "the rest just left me out." Like other young people who don't "measure up" in the peer arena, she was subject to some cruelty. Her solution was to use all her energy to conform to the appearance norms. Terry just stopped eating. Her strategy worked. She lost weight and people noticed the change. She got much more attention; in fact, she became a member of the most popular group at her school. At first, she enjoyed her new status, but Terry says, "I felt better for a while but then I came to realize that my life still sucked. Even when I was skinny I wasn't happy." Terry now believes that the reason for this was because the distinction was so artificial. In the peer arena, others only her saw her appearance and didn't truly know her or care about her. Her close friends and family could see how much she was struggling and did not support her food limitation strategy. Terry began eating again, and although she gained weight, she now feels truly comfortable with herself. By choosing not to conform, she moved out of the popular circle once again—she lost status but became stronger. When she graduated from high school and left that group of peers behind, accepting herself as she was became much easier. She found that people were less likely to focus on her appearance than on her skills when she began a new job.

Each of these four young women connected appearance norms with both social status and selfhood. Finding ways to be themselves while being measured by unrealistic normative expectations within the peer arena was challenging. Like many adolescent girls, they do not believe they are or were blindly following normative expectations promoted within the socio-cultural landscape; rather, they see themselves as self-aware actors making choices based on the realities of their social milieu. In this case study, we see three dimensions of gender—individual, interactional, and socio-cultural—combining as these young women actively make choices about gender and construct their identities.

This case study focused on one social context: the peer arena. But of course, people participate in many social contexts in their daily lives. Not surprisingly, mixed messages are common. For example, Terry's parents and Una's coaches encouraged different goals and expectations than those of their peer arenas. The athletes studied by Melanie Muise also received mixed messages. Each adolescent faces such contradictions and must find their own way. For example, your family may promote the idea that you should not have sex until you are married, but the mass media inundates you with images of adolescent sexual activity. Your school may teach safe sex and/or abstinence; meanwhile, your friends may encourage participation in sexual activities. Each individual must navigate between these conflicting alternatives. Social experiences in a variety of locations and interactions with a variety of people influence the development of people's sense of self and their gender schemas and identity in childhood and adolescence. This is a lifelong process, which we will explore in the next chapter on adulthood and late life.

CHAPTER SUMMARY: KEY POINTS

1. Humans grow from biological organisms with sex-typed physiologies in infancy to members of a social group where they participate as gendered individuals. Theories about gender identity have shifted from believing it is a relatively permanent, unchanging property to believing it is a more fluid identity that is relational and influenced by context.

2. People learn about gender through a process known as socialization. Empirical research shows that despite progress in reducing sexism, children continue to be raised following gender polarized expectations. Girls are more likely to be encouraged to communicate and express a range of emotions, while boys are afforded more independence and are rewarded for assertiveness.

3. *Social learning theory* suggests that children learn to be gendered through *reinforcement and modeling*. They see gendered behaviour enacted by those around them, and they are rewarded when they conform to expectations and punished when they do not.

4. *Cognitive development theory* suggests that children play an active role in their socialization, actively striving to portray what they see as gender-appropriate behaviours.

5. *Gender schema theory* integrates ideas from both social learning and cognitive development theories. It suggests that children organize ideas about gender into schemas based on their experiences and observations. These schema guide their ideas and actions.

6. *Post-structural theory* focuses on language and symbols. Linguistic structures highlight a male-female binary that children learn. They then locate themselves in their social context according to their understanding of this bipolar arrangement by adopting signifiers of their sex.

7. Adolescence is a time of *identity construction*—figuring out who we are and how we fit in. Gender plays a large part in this process as adolescents come to understand themselves as women or men, queer or straight; and they choose to conform or resist gender expectations.

8. Family is the most important arena for socialization in childhood because this is where most long-term, emotionally meaningful relationships occur. In addition, families act as filters determining what situations and ideas children are exposed to prior to starting school.

9. School is also an important site for gender socialization, both in the *formal* and *hidden curricula*. While an effort has been made to reduce the sexist elements of education, boys and girls still face different opportunities and challenges within the education system.

10. The *peer arena* is a central place for learning about gender (among other things) during adolescence. This arena is a place for evaluating, imitating, experimenting, observing, and critiquing the appearance and actions of others. Through this comparative process, adolescents construct their own identities.

DISCUSSION QUESTIONS

1. Can you think of examples from your own experience where reinforcement and modeling (from social learning theory) influenced your choices and behaviours? What happened when you did not follow expected behaviour patterns? Was your resistance to normative expectations socially punished?

2. Think about the content of your gender schemas. In what ways are they similar to or different from the gender normative expectations we discussed in Chapter Four?

3. Sport and athletic activities influence our gender identities. Many people argue that sport for boys and men help to create and maintain masculine qualities. Explain how this masculinization might work. How are female athletes affected by this focus on male athletics? Re-read Melanie Muise's essay on pp. 70–73. Does it support or challenge your conclusions?

4. Looking back on your earlier educational experiences, do you see examples of hidden curriculum? How was your schooling gendered? How did it support heteronormativity? In what ways did it resist or reduce normative expectations for gender and sexual orientation?

KEY TERMS

agents of socialization

cognitive development

comparative act

formal curriculum

gender constancy

gender schema theory

gender socialization

hidden curriculum

incorrigible male-female
  binary

identity construction

modeling

peer arena

primacy effect

primary socialization

reinforcement

relational aggression

social learning theory

socialization

chapter six

chapter six

Gender in Adulthood and Late Life

The previous chapter on gender in childhood and adolescence focused on the process of "becoming gendered." The socialization process and our interactions with others are an integral part of how we learn about the categories of gender, how we define gender-based normative expectations, and, most importantly, how we choose to be and/or become gendered. When we consider gender throughout adulthood, we see that socialization becomes less central. Most adults have already come to understand the basic nature of the gendered world, even if we are not always conscious of it, and have developed at least a sense of their place within it. That sense of place may require conforming to normative expectations or resisting them. Middle adulthood and late life focus less on becoming gendered and more on understanding what it means to be gendered while living life in a gendered society. Whatever your response to the gender normative expectations—compliance or resistance—you live in a gendered society, and this gendered environment has an impact on your opportunities and your challenges.

The authors of this text sometimes hear our students insisting that their lives are not bound by society's notions of who they should be as women and men. And yet their gendered behavior persist despite their confidence that they are not bound by the gender limitations of past generations. Previous chapters have discussed some of these issues, including work, sexuality, and intimate relationships. But gender infiltrates many—if not all—aspects of our lives. And as we enter adulthood and live our adult lives, we often have to negotiate gender in the process.

This chapter is a quick survey of some of the gender issues facing adults during the life course. Many of these issues are raised in other chapters of this book, specifically in the chapters on sexualities, families, and paid work. This chapter focuses on a few issues that illustrate how gender at the individual level is manifested in adulthood.

GENDER IN ADULTHOOD

Adulthood is the stage of life that marks the end of adolescence and the beginning of the second phase of life. The markers of entry into adulthood are socially constructed and vary from culture to culture. Adulthood brings many choices that are in part constituted through power relations that are woven through gendered sedimentation. As we make choices about university or college courses, employment, and career options, we face these sometimes shifting gender expectations. Think about the reactions to choices made by men, such as becoming a stay-at-home dad or a nurse, or to choices made by women, such as becoming firefighters or fisherpersons. We may see examples of people making these choices, but they are still within the realm of the "exceptional" rather than the "normal."

Many people believe that ideas about who an adult is are framed exclusively by age, such as the "age of consent" and age-related rites of passage, including completing high school, finding full-time employment, getting married, and having children. But the association of these rites of passage with adulthood is socially constructed; and this short list of rites of passage is neither comprehensive nor fixed. Nor, as is obvious, does everyone move through all these specific rites. For example, does the fact that a 15-year-old has given birth to and is raising a child render her an adult? When do boys become men and girls become women? When do they become adults?

Beaman's research on religious freedom (2005) shows that age alone does not make one an adult in this society and that gender significantly impacts on the notion of age of consent. She analyzed legal discourse about consent in cases involving the refusal of blood transfusions by Jehovah's Witness youth. The question in each case was whether the court would support the young person's desire to refuse transfusions that were deemed necessary for their treatment. The courts tended to characterize young men as serious, mature, and capable of refusing to consent (even though they were under the legal age at which they were able to do so). But the courts tended to characterize the young women as immature, childlike, and unable to understand or appreciate the consequences of their decisions, and therefore as being incapable of refusing consent. In these decisions with possible life-and-death consequences, young women were perceived as having been brainwashed by their religious group, whereas young men were perceived as having made a serious commitment to their religious beliefs. This example illustrates the gendered nature of the process of becoming and of being identified as an "adult."

Adulthood often brings both the beginning and end of intimate relationships. There is much we could talk about here, including shifting courtship rituals that now include Internet dating services. The impact of intimate relationships remains relatively under-researched, but we encourage you to think about the gendered ways in which people present themselves. Look at personal advertisements in a newspaper and examine the desirable qualities highlighted by women and by men. Are there differences in descriptions according to age? How do those seeking same-sex relationships differ from those seeking heterosexual relationships? Why do many men seek women who are younger than they are? Personal ads are interesting because they reveal both gendered presentations and the ways in which individuals seek to negotiate their identities.

In her analysis of the movie *Leaving Normal*, Rebecca Johnson (2000a) examines how popular and legal discourses shape societal notions of the family. While she points out that the family tends to be conceptualized in fairly narrow terms, there are **counter-hegemonic** moments. Counter-hegemonic actions are those that resist or go against the hegemonic order or the status quo. Even when we live in families that do not fit the model of a heterosexual couple with children, we often think about the "normal family" or "traditional family" in those terms. As adults, we often seek to form those types of families, without considering alternative models. As Chapter Five and Chapter Eleven show, families both produce and reify gendered notions about their members. Terms such as "head of the family" and "breadwinner" still have gendered currency. "Husband" or "wife" is most often pictured as an opposite-sex partner rather than a same-sex partner. Think about your models for family and the way you replay or intend to replay them in your adult life. Are you married, or do you intend to marry? Have children? Will you stay or have you already stayed at home to raise your children? These issues are often addressed during the first phase of adulthood, and they are imbued with gendered notions about "how we should be."

A. Same-Sex Adulthood

Research on same-sex relationships is still a relatively new field. It is rendered even more challenging to study because of the social stigma attached to being gay or lesbian, as well as the diversity of ways in which same-sex couples work through gender and sexuality in their relationships. Some same-sex relationships approximate their heterosexual counterparts, but others have sought to avoid gender expectations (Adam, 2006, p. 6). Barry Adam (2006) explores the ways in which male couples construct their relationships. The monogamy issue is complicated among male couples: those in *open relationships* do not necessarily engage in sexual relations with men other than their primary partner; those in *closed relationships* often do engage in sexual relations with men other than their primary partner. Barry points out that definitions of open and closed relationships differ from one couple to another. So even if men say, "We're in an open relationship," they may never exercise the option of seeking relationships with others; and even if they say, "We're in a closed relationship," they may have what might be termed "casual" sex with other men. "Non-monogamy is not an indicator of relationship failure among gay men" (2006, p. 8). Unfortunately, much of the research on gays and lesbians seems to focus on sexual patterns, rather than on gendered patterns or on the innovative ways in which gender is reconstituted.

Gary Kinsman's (1995) research is an important contribution to the study of the link between gender and sexuality. He explores masculinity and our perceptions of its impact on our sexual self-identification. He argues that hearing words like *queer*, *faggot*, and *sissy* "serve to define, regulate, and limit our lives, whether we consider ourselves gay or straight" (1995, p. 406). Thus, masculinity/gender is profoundly implicated in sexuality. Kinsman argues that masculinity is associated—indeed equated—with heterosexuality. The fact that many men have had sexual experience with other men yet define themselves as straight "has demonstrated that contradictions can exist between our actual experiences and desires and the rigid social categories that are used to divide normal from deviant" (1995, p. 407). Kinsman argues that these rigid categories and the negative messages about men loving men are harmful to all men (1995, p. 408). As males move into adulthood, they often start out with rigid notions about masculinity and its implications on the boundaries of their relationships with other men.

Moreover, **HIV/AIDS** affects relational patterns, especially among gay men. The extent to which AIDS has shaped the ways gay men engage in relationships has to some extent been framed by broader responses to the disease. Maticka-Tyndale (2001) states that sociological attention needs to be paid to AIDS "as an epidemic of changing social conditions that is characterized by several persistent and recurring social responses" (2001, p. 13). These changing social conditions include refusal to acknowledge that a particular group will be affected and urgency/panic that something must be done to "stop AIDS." As Maticka-Tyndale points out, "HIV is not an equal-opportunity virus when it comes to gender and age. Nearly 90 percent of new infections are those in their most productive stage of life, between 15 and 49 years of age. Men continue to represent the majority of cases" (2001, p. 17). How does this context shape adult relationships, especially those between men?

Joseph O'Shea (2005) has studied this issue through his interviews with 40 gay men. He found that, surprisingly, gay men are demonstrating a shift toward risk-taking behaviour in relation to their sexual activities. He found that the reasons for this trend are different for younger gay men and older gay men. Younger gay men have not yet lost friends and partners to AIDS. Moreover, this cohort no longer views an HIV diagnosis as a death sentence. Medical advances have resulted in hope for those who have HIV and the development of a discourse of life with HIV. As a result, these men have a different relationship to the gay community and feel freer to make choices about their self-definition and identities. O'Shea contrasts this perspective with that of older men: "For older gay men, those who lost many lovers, friends, and acquaintances during the HIV epidemic, changes in gay men's sexual risk-taking are both surprising and inevitable. These men are dealing with issues of ageism, loss and lack of visibility in a changing gay community" (2005, p. 4). O'Shea argues that aging is difficult in a community that defines itself in terms of youth, and that for older gay men, the willingness to engage in condom-free sex is an enhanced opportunity for intimacy.

B. Gendered Health Issues

In addition, general health issues that are gendered in ways that have a significant impact on the adult life course. HIV has been predominantly characterized as a gay men's disease, even though the global picture of AIDS looks quite different. Moreover, despite the use of men as the baseline for medical and social scientific research until relatively recently (and, some would argue, still even today), Marshall and Katz (2002) point out that "relatively little attention has been paid to male bodies." However, no attention has perhaps been so consistently paid to men's bodies as that related to "male sexual functioning." Marshall and Katz argue that male sexuality has been problematized in terms of the ability of the penis to penetrate the vagina (2002, p. 44). (They also acknowledge the use of "vascular flow" model in female sexual dysfunction as a problem that needs to be pharmacologically treated.) They review a wide range of medical and quasi-medical beliefs about male sexual functioning historically. They mention in particular the idea that if men were too sexually active, they would wear out their ability to function sexually; and the belief that as men and women age, they make a transition into a neutered or man-woman state.

Marshall and Katz map the gradual shift from the language of impotence to the use of "erectile dysfunction" to name the issues of male sexual functioning. This shift marked a transition to the idea that there was a normal male sexual body that could be medically identified. This new definition allowed the abnormal or pathological male sexual body to be identified and treated. Thus, penile erectile dysfunction was born as a disease and as such became something to be monitored and treated. However, as Marshall and Katz note, erectile dysfunction was framed not only as a medical problem but as a social one as well. "It is this framing that illustrates the extent to which anxieties about penile erectility crystallize broader social anxieties about masculinity, sexuality and agency and foster a particular mobilization of social resources" (2002, p. 56). The medical profession began reporting rates of impotence in order to support the notion that there was a sexual function epidemic that they needed to address. Researchers defined "stages" and "signs" of this "disease" (2002, p. 57) from which men were "at risk." Tests were developed to let men determine their level of risk. Men were thus charged with responsibility to ensure that they remain "forever functional" (2002, p. 59). Marshall and Katz argue that the 1998 arrival of Viagra secured "this view of male sexual fitness." The parameters of the medicalization of penile erectile dysfunction were further expanded to include men "whose erections could be 'improved.'" Stress, illness, and life course events were minimized as potential causal links to sexual functioning, as was the possibility of sexual satisfaction occurring without a perfectly erect penis. The original target group for diagnosis and treatment intervention through medication shifted from older couples to the young, single male. With this development, argue Marshall and Katz, "The pill becomes one more tool in the project of constructing the sexually functional male body—with both its maleness and its functionality defined by penile erectility—as an ageless body, a project which must now begin earlier and earlier in the lifecourse" (2002, p. 61). They further concluded that "the functional penis remains the visible indication of interior character and successful living" (2002, p. 63).

Like erectile dysfunction, the lubricated vagina in women has become another site of medical problematization. Perhaps, though, we might argue that for men, the "erect penis" is more profoundly a representation of their masculinity and their abilities to be men than women's sexual functioning is for them. For women, perhaps their reproductive functioning is more clearly a social and cultural measure of their womanliness.

C. Gendered Adults in Relationships and Families

Women and men experience marriage and partnering in heterosexual relationships differently. These differences are even more profound if the couple has children. Having children is generally considered to have a negative effect on the relationship, predominantly because of the ways in which children interfere with the primary relationship between the couple. Couples pre- and post-children are generally more satisfied with their relationships than couples with children. Women tend to experience more overall change and greater stress than do their husbands after the birth of children, whereas men "perceive more change than wives in their marital lives" (Worthington & Buston, 1986, p. 446).

Rosemary Gillespie's (2003) research on women's choices to remain **childfree** recounts traditional attitudes as well as what she identifies as an emerging shift in the attitudes of women who decide not to have children. As Gillespie notes, "The notion of motherhood as constitutive of feminine gender identity, of women's social role, and as desirably and fulfilling for all women remains entrenched in industrial, urban and rural societies"

(2003, p. 122). Women who remain voluntarily childless are characterized as deviant, self-ish, and unfeminine (2003, p. 124). But Gillespie argues that this attitude may be shifting. She interviewed 25 women who were voluntarily childfree to explore the attraction of remaining childfree. Several themes emerged from these interviews, including the freedom to make choices about one's time and leisure activities, closer intimate relationships, and financial advantages. However, Gillespie also found that participants in her study rejected the notion of motherhood as a gain—instead, they framed it as a loss. To them, mothering and motherhood represented "a sacrifice, a duty and a burden" (2003, p. 130). Gillespie's findings are important because they document a shift among women themselves who are rejecting cultural norms that link motherhood to definitions of femininity and woman-hood. Gillespie also notes differences in responses based on class: expectations for upper-class women were different from those for "poor, single and lesbian women [who] have generally been framed by others as unfit mothers and expected to remain childless" (2003, p. 133). Thus, upper-class women who do not wish to have children are often described as "selfish," and impoverished women who have children are sometimes described as "irresponsible." Gillespie also acknowledges that there are racial dimensions to expectations around childbearing as well, with women of colour more likely to be condemned for wanting children.

Despite the fact that *only* women can have children, the "choice" to have a child is framed within the liberal model of the freely choosing citizen who independently makes the decision to do or not do something. This model ignores the fact that women make the decision in the context of relationships. Parenting is challenging at the best of times; but it becomes especially challenging for those who do it outside of traditional expectations, such as lone parents and gay and lesbian parents.

Wachholz explores the **ideology of motherhood**, which includes the "core assump-tions that motherhood is a natural, desired and ultimate goal for most women, that women should be largely responsible for the care of children and that motherhood should function within a heterosexual family framework" (2000, p. 180, Wachholz citing Kline). Wachholz notes that because lesbian mothers step outside of the assumption of heterosexuality, they are subject to accusations and scrutiny of their mothering that other women do not have to deal with. Indeed, lesbianism and motherhood are often construed as "mutually exclusive choices" (2000, p. 183). Wachholz points to the practice in some clinics of the screening-out of lesbians as ineligibile for reproductive technologies as an example of this assump-tion in action (2000, p. 183).

But research has shown that there are few differences between lesbian mothers and het-erosexual mothers and that their children demonstrate the same development of gender identity and gender role development as do children raised in heterosexual households (Wachholz, 2000, p. 185). Lesbian mothers also report that they sometimes minimize information about their sexuality as "part of a strategy to shield their children from harm" (2000, p. 188). Gay men face similar challenges. They also must deal with the opposite side of a stereotype noted by Wachholz in her discussion of the ideology of motherhood—that is that "women should be largely responsible for the well-being and care of children. Childcare has been constructed as an obligation that is both normal and inevitable for most families" (2000, p. 182). Men, then, are largely assumed to not do this sort of work. And thus, the question arises of the lone-parent male or gay parents—how can they raise a child? Embedded in assumptions about family life are gendered ideas about who does the work of caring for children.

D. Divorce and Relationship Breakdown

Because adulthood is the time of intimate relationships, it is also the time of relationship breakdown. Moreover, breakdowns are gendered. A great deal of research examines the disadvantaged financial position of women after marriage breakdown: while women's standard of living goes down, men's go up. The severity of this disparity differs according to one's life stage, race, and class. Ross Finnie's 1993 research was important for drawing attention to the profound negative economic impact divorce has for women. Drawing from tax files, he found a modest rise in economic well-being for men after a divorce, contrasted with a drop of 40 percent in income for women. He also found that women's labour market activity shifted after a divorce, while men's careers remained stable (1993, p. 206). Ross concluded that "these results paint a picture of divorce where, on average, women experience steep declines in economic well-being while men enjoy moderate increase. And while there is some recovery for women in the post-divorce years, three full years after the split they remain well below their pre-divorce levels, as well as the current levels of their husbands" (1993, p. 228). Of particular concern are those women who stayed at home with their children during their marriage. While the decision to stay at home is often made jointly by both partners, the economic consequences of that decision are often borne by women after a divorce. This is especially true for women whose marriages end in their late forties and early fifties. This group is vulnerable because of their lack of work-related skills and their need to retrain or find employment that pays more than minimum wage (Beaman, 2000, p. 138). As Margrit Eichler so simply put it, these women are "only one man away from welfare" (1990, p. 62).

Nakonechny (2003) discusses the patterns of the Supreme Court of Canada's decisions regarding the impact of marriage on men and women in heterosexual relationships. She defines three phases of court responses during the past 25 years. First, in the early 1980s, the courts recognized that a spouse who had worked in the home (usually the woman) needed to be financially supported after the marriage ended, perhaps on an ongoing basis. In the second phase, the courts adopted a "self-sufficiency" model, which expected financial independence in women after divorce or marriage breakdown. This "self-sufficiency" model reflected society's growing belief in equality in relationships between men and women (2003, p. 103). However, this model "proved in some cases to be too onerous and unrealistic an obligation to place on some spouses" (2003, p. 103). Thus, in the third phase, "the court saw cases where a spouse who had been out of the workforce for a long period of time due to child and family responsibilities, could never become self-supporting in a way that was reasonable, based on the circumstances of the parties' marriage" (2003, p. 103). The courts returned to a model that recognized that "the role of homemaker and caregiver was as integral to the family as was the role of breadwinner, entitling the non-income earning spouse to ongoing financial compensation for this role" (2003, p. 104).

These relationship breakdown issues relate only to heterosexual relationships. It is too early to be able to determine legal patterns related to same-sex marriages, although the courts have begun to consider division of assets in same-sex relationship cases. The first important Supreme Court decision on this matter was *M. v. H.*, [1999] 2 S.C.R. 3, which expanded the definition of "spouse" in the Ontario Family Law Act to include same-sex couples. This expansion of the definition meant that the same rules about division of property would apply to both heterosexual and same-sex couples who cohabit outside of marriage. In the future, the courts will also have to consider the financial and work-related contributions of partners in both same-sex and heterosexual relationships, especially the ways each has contributed to the household.

On balance, some of the shifts in gender relations may give hope that there is a generational difference that will mean that future generations of women are not as economically vulnerable, but there is good reason to be pessimistic, especially in this era of backlash against feminism. There is still a great deal of cultural support for the myth of the knight in shining armor and the rescue of the damsel in distress.

GENDER IN LATE LIFE

Even though this chapter is called "Gender in Adulthood and Late Life," the distinction between these two statuses is not clear-cut. When people are in "late life," they are still adults; and, as noted above, the Viagra culture can blur the adult/late-life line even further. The line one crosses when entering "late life" is not obvious for most people. Aging is a gradual process, unique to every individual. Unfortunately, the language around aging is not sufficient for adequately describing the process. Some people refer to this time of the lifecourse as *later life* or *older age* (as opposed to *old age*) because it seems kinder than to bluntly categorize a group of people as *old* or close to death. Being old in our culture carries a stigma. However, while *later life* may seem like a less pejorative term, it is not. Using the terms *older* or *later* reinforces the idea that there truly is something inherently negative about simply being *old* because it avoids naming it openly, as if there were shame attached. In this book, we use the terms *old* and *late life* not in a pejorative, stigmatized sense, but with the simple recognition that as the years advance, we do become old and reach the latest stages of our lives. Using the word *old* without associating it with negativity is a way of neutralizing the term and removing the stigma. However, there are problems inherent with the terms *old age* and *late life* as well: they label a specific time of life in such a way as to create the impression that a truly diverse population can be easily lumped into one category, sharing the same experiences. The category *old* spans several decades (60s to 90s and beyond). Do you share the same activities, challenges, and needs as people 20 years older or 20 years younger than yourself? The term *old age* reifies a category that cannot actually reflect the people it is trying to identify. Even more problematic is that the terms appear to set boundaries, implying the old age can easily be separated from middle age. We must take care not to ignore the various pathways through which people age, recognizing that there is great diversity in both the timing and experience of *getting old*.

One of the most basic variations in these experiences is associated with gender. Women and men do not have the same opportunities or face the same challenges as they age. (And, of course, there is great variation among women and among men also.) The experience of women and men in the last segment of their lives is shaped by their previous activities and interactions, as well as by the gendered nature of social institutions and socio-cultural landscapes.

One of the challenges of studying the oldest Canadians is that those who are now senior citizens were born prior to 1940—many of whom followed the "traditional" homemaker-breadwinner family model (see Chapter Eleven). They have led relatively gender-polarized lives, with men taking the major responsibility for providing financially and women caring for family members (children and/or parents). Their late life experiences reflect this division of labour and social position. However, when we discuss future patterns, we recognize that this gender division of labour is disappearing in other generations. More women are earning paid incomes, and men's family responsibilities are shifting (to some extent). In addition, there is more diversity in family patterns than ever before, including same-sex relationships and common-law unions. As we examine the current patterns, we must remember that most Canadians who retire in the future will have a different set of challenges and opportunities than those who are old today.

Regardless which generation of old people we consider, gender stereotypes and normative expectations have an impact on their lives. Consider the expectations associated with late life. Men supposedly become more distinguished as they age, while women just get older. Men get character lines, while women just get wrinkles. Scholars have gathered evidence supporting this notion by documenting the greater pressures and challenges that women face as they age. Because of the normative expectations associated with appearance, women tend to be judged more harshly as they lose their "youthful appearance." This may be compounded by the fact that women in patriarchal societies have often been valued for their reproductive capacities. Once they are no longer fertile (usually experiencing the menopausal transition in their forties or fifties), their value to society diminishes (Gannon, 1999). In their discussion "Bodies in Old Age," Calasanti and Slevin (2001) note the links between ageism and sexism which put increasing pressure on older women to engage in a war on aging, attempting to make their bodies appear more like those of their younger selves. They find that negative body image is greater for women than men and that this problem is increasing. "Women of all ages are more invested in their looks than men" (p. 57). Further, the stigma associated with looking old is capitalized upon by those who stand to make a profit from it. Anti-aging products are continually marketed to women (try watching TV or reading women's magazines and assessing the prevalence of these messages for yourself). And everywhere in Canada the media surrounds us with images of young beautiful women. The few women in their fifties or older that continue to be a presence in the media are typically flawless (unless they are caught by tabloid photographers without their make-up, in which case they are castigated for their appearance). Most old women characters in television or film are portrayed as frail and vulnerable (although there are a few wonderful exceptions where old women portray vital, creative, and active characters—several roles played by Dame Judi Dench spring to mind).

One harmful result of this intense pressure to appear young is that "internalizing the cultural norm of youthful appearance discourages solidarity forming between young and old women. Young women learn to dread growing and looking old. In learning to be ageist toward women older than they are, they also learn to turn against their future selves as old women" (Calasanti & Slevin, 2001, p. 67; see also Woodward, 1999). A second harmful result is that engaging in the "anti-aging war" is expensive, often painful, and time-consuming. And ultimately, unless one dies young, this war is not winnable—we all grow older. In the effort to look forever young, we end up constantly managing our bodies, which results in a war against ourselves (Biggs, 1999). The intersection of gender and age certainly has an impact on how many women see and present themselves. It can also have an impact on their experiences in the workplace.

Because our culture is youth-focused, particularly for women, older women are judged against the standard of youth. Bernard *et al.* (1995) found that there is a **glass ceiling of age**, after which women are no longer hired and/or promoted; and this glass ceiling occurs at a much earlier age for women than for men. They estimate this gap to be ten years; that is, male employees are judged to have reached their peak levels of efficiency and skill approximately ten years later than women. The result is that many managers described female employees in their forties—and even some in their thirties—as "older workers." Once they have been defined as "older," these women reach a plateau where upward movement within the organization is extremely difficult. This perception creates an employment obstacle for women.

Research suggests that inequities that women experience throughout their life typically worsen with age. If they were discriminated against in terms of paid employment and compensation for unpaid labour throughout their adulthood, they are much more likely to experience poverty in late life. This pattern of privilege and challenge in early life being reflected in late life is not true just for women, however; it intersects with other factors, such as class and ethnicity. For example, working-class men whose incomes barely covered their costs throughout their adult lives are likely to have little income beyond old-age pensions in their old age. The working poor in middle adulthood become poor pensioners in late life.

While some of the challenges linking sexism and ageism for women have been well documented, less attention has been paid to the challenges faced by old men. There is less pressure about appearance for old men than there is for women, since appearance has not been one of the defining normative expectations for masculinity in the same way it has been for femininity. Nonetheless, men do experience this pressure to some degree, frequently having to deal with negative associations with hair loss or a growing paunch. An examination of the trend in cosmetic surgeries indicates that more and more men are challenging the signs of aging through surgical intervention (Calasanti & Slevin, 2001).

Of greater importance to men than appearance, though, is the link between aging and activity. Normative expectations of masculinity are frequently measured in terms of performance. But men's ability to achieve these expectations frequently diminishes with age. As Arber, Davidson, and Ginn summarize, retirement often leads to the end of a significant role, economic decline, as well as loss of relationships with co-workers; these changes can certainly have a negative impact. "In addition, possible loss of sexual potency, diminishing physical strength and the onset of ill health can further reduce his esteem in both his eyes and those of society" (2003, p. 5). In short, it's not easy to be an old man if you measure yourself according to the expectations of society. Gender and aging, then, intersect for both women and men.

A. Defining Old

In order to understand the links between gender and old age, we need to define age itself. Quite simply, people don't all understand or measure age in the same way. My daughter thinks that I am old; but I don't feel old, and some of my friends think I am young. I have many friends who are my age, some of whom act and look much older than me, while others act and appear much younger. Being old isn't simply based on the number of years we have lived; it is more complex.

Consider three different measures of age: chronological, physiological, and social. The simplest measure, which has been adopted and institutionalized in our society for practical purposes, is **chronological age**, which measures age based on the calendar. According to chronological age, we all grow older at the same pace, day by day, year by year. Society recognizes certain points on the calendar as socially significant, as indicative of a person's level of maturity. We accept the notion that people are capable of driving at age 16. At 18, we call a person an adult and allow that person to vote, smoke, and join the military. But the requisite number of years for official adulthood is arbitrary. Some jurisdictions make people wait until they are 21 years before allowing them to drink or gamble, and others allow them begin driving at 14 years. The arbitrariness of these age grades becomes obvious when we consider the people we know, some of whom are far more mature at 17 years than their legally adult friends in their early twenties.

In Canada, people are understood to be old when they reach their sixty-fifth birthday. But truly, people are only a few hours older than they were the day before. In terms of health and social relationships, very little has changed overnight, but this date is imbued with significance and privileges (pensions and discounts, for example) and sometimes enforces economic changes (in jobs where mandatory retirement is still in effect). Using chronological age as a measure means that some people who are in wonderful physical and mental health are treated as though they are not capable of working, or as if they are in need of public support. By the same token, many people who experience age-related challenges before their sixty-fifth birthday are denied those privileges. (For example, some provinces offer free drug plans for people over age 65; but 63-year-olds with age-related health problems are not eligible.)

In general, a person's chronological age is only loosely related to that person's actual aging experience. Chronological age is a weak predictor of activities, needs, and interests. Moreover, while the magic number in Canada is 65, in other countries, it's a different age. In the United States, the age of retirement is gradually being raised, such that by the time the authors retire, it will probably be 67. (And who knows what it will be by the time you retire?)

Of particular interest is Britain, which has different retirement ages for women and men. Men retire at 65, but women are considered old at 60 years of age—an interesting gender inequity. The rationale for this arrangement is that since women typically are married to older men, the differential retirement age results in their both receiving pensions at about the same time. But some observers believe that this arrangement reinforces the financial dominance of the husband by ensuring that his wife is unlikely to earning an income higher than his pension once he retires (Ginn & Arber, 1995). Some women see this differential in retirement age as negative, since it means they are expected to stop working earlier than they would like, which might in turn have harmful financial implications if their pension is significantly lower than their salary. Other women see it as a wonderful advantage: they get to start collecting their pensions and may actually experience an increase in their income if they had previously worked in low-paying or unpaid positions. In this case, a social construction—retirement age—intersects with gender and social class to yield real economic consequences.

While chronological age makes it easier to label someone as *old* or *not old*, that age is only an approximation of their actual place in the life span. Increasingly, we see people ignoring the chronological age grade and making individualized choices about retirement (such as retiring early or late, depending on their needs, health, and finances).

A second way of measuring age is based on **physiological factors**. As people age, their bodies undergo physical changes. This process begins very early in life: you may have started noticing some changes as early as your twenties, as hearing often begins to diminish in this decade. The obvious cues to physiological age are external (gray hair, wrinkles, stature, and gait), though the internal changes (skeletal, muscular, cardiovascular) are usually much more significant for a person's health.

As already noted, the external changes of aging intersect with gender because of the way society evaluates women. Women are considered older at a lower age than men are, prompting many of them to "defy aging" through cosmetic interventions. Importantly, life experiences have an impact on physiology as well. The activities people engage in, their diets and consumption patterns, can have an impact on aging. Engaging in extremely intense physically activities can take a toll on the body. Similarly, using certain substances, such as tobacco, tends to age the body more rapidly. In contrast, healthy living can extend the biological aging process, keeping bones, joints, and cardiovascular systems strong. Because gender typically has had an impact on people's activities throughout their life-times, it also has an impact on physiological age. As long as tobacco use was primarily seen as a men's activity, its damage was much more profound for men than for women. In fact, differential rates of tobacco and alcohol use have been linked to differential life expectancies for women and men. But now that women and men have much more similar patterns of tobacco and alcohol use, the health advantage for women has disappeared. In addition, work and activities have been segregated by sex: until recent decades women did not participate in many of the most hazardous of activities, such as jobs in the military, in mines, or on fishing boats. This workplace barrier protected them from some of the nega-tive biological impacts of such occupations. Of course, childbearing, an activity limited to females, also has an impact on physical health.

Social aging involves the social constructions and social experiences attached to the physiological and chronological reality of becoming old. It involves norms and values, sta-tuses and roles, changes and transitions. And, importantly, social aging intersects with gen-der in significant ways. From a multi-dimensional perspective, social aging is of much greater interest than the physical changes that accompany aging, because it is in the social realm that the most significant gendered experiences occur.

One aspect of social aging is the phenomenon known as **gender depolarization**. Gender polarization is the process whereby the behaviour of old men and old women tends to become less polarized over time. Men seem to become more nurturant and mellow, and women seem to become less dependent and more assertive. This pattern has been noted by a variety of scholars in different decades (see Neugarten, 1968; Gutman, 1987; Sheehy, 1995). In short, women and men are less likely to conform to gender-based normative expec-tations in late life. The polarized expectations are most prevalent throughout adolescence and adulthood, when our gendered landscape and institutions encourage conformity to masculine and feminine qualities and activities. However, once we reach old age and are less involved in the paying workforce and in the daily raising of children, the pressures of gender polarization seem to be less pervasive. Thus, when we are old, some of the societal expectations for gendered behaviour appear to diminish. This gender depolarization exists, in part, because of the patterns of polarization that exist within our socio-cultural landscape.

B. Being Old in Canada: Demographic Patterns in the Early Twenty-first Century

The most significant change in Canadian aging patterns over the last century has been the dramatic increase in **life expectancy**. Life expectancy refers to the number of years a per-son can expect to live, measured from their current age. At the beginning of the twentieth century, life expectancy at birth was only 60 years, whereas infants born today can expect to live to be 80 years old. Many factors explain this increase in the length of our lives, some related specifically to gender activities and others not. More infants and children survive to adulthood; fewer women die in childbirth; fewer men are killed in work-related accidents. In addition, better nutrition and a higher standard of living in Canada mean we are all less susceptible to disease because modern medical advances afford those who are ill or injured more possibilities for survival. The impact of these factors is that far more people are living into old age in Canada than ever before. But one of the unique features of this old cohort is that there are far more old women than there are old men. This imbalance is due to a gender-based **mortality differential**.

Women in Western countries typically outlive men by approximately five years. In Canada, a typical 65-year-old woman can expect to live until she is 85.6, while life expectancy for a 65-year-old man is only 82.2. Some research suggests that certain features of being female have a protective effect. For example, prior to menopause, the hormonal balance in most women reduces their likelihood of heart disease. But historically, women's life expectancy was not significantly higher than men's, because women were much more likely to die through childbearing activities than they are today. With increased standards of living, better diets, better public health, and access to relatively safe contraception and abortion, not to mention the advantages of medical intervention for high-risk pregnancies and deliveries, the death rates for childbearing women have declined dramatically.

But gender is not the only—nor even the most significant—mortality differential. For example, Canadian aggregate statistics show that rich people outlive the poor; and Aboriginal people die much earlier than non-Aboriginals (Statistics Canada, 2000). Moreover, these patterns, like the patterns associated with gender and life expectancy, are not entirely based on physiological factors, though those may play a part. (For example, Aboriginal people appear to be genetically more prone to diabetes.) The larger concern is differential social experiences, such as nutrition, standard of living, and access to health care, rather than biology.

While some biological factors are involved, much of the gender-based differences in life expectancy are linked to the different life experiences of women and men. As noted earlier, in the past, women were much less likely to use tobacco or to participate in military campaigns, which had a positive impact on their life expectancy (though of course they were subjected to second-hand smoke and were frequent civilian casualties of military actions). In addition, women are more likely to engage in help-seeking behaviour—going to the doctor, for example. This tendency has meant on the one hand that women are more

TABLE 6.1	Population by Age and Sex, 2004		
Age	# of Women	# of Men	% Women
45-54	2 419 100	2 386 800	50.3%
55-64	1 716 600	1 670 100	50.7%
65-74	1 162 100	1 050 800	52.5%
75-84	858 500	601 900	58.8%
85+	324 900	142 800	69.4%

Source: Statistics Canada, 2006b, p. 28

likely to be diagnosed as ill, depressed, or disabled; but on the other hand, they are more likely to receive help with health issues, thereby increasing their chances of a positive outcome. (For example, getting a lump checked early significantly increases one's survival relative to someone who delays a check-up until the last possible moment.)

Men are much more likely to die of suicide throughout the life course: 19.6 of every 100 000 men compared to 5.1 of every 100 000 women. After age 65, the difference is even greater because the risk of men for suicide increases and the risk for women decreases: 23 out of 100 000 men compared to 4.5 out of 100 000 women (Statistics Canada, 2005). Gender patterns in suicide are paradoxical: more women attempt suicide, but more men succeed in ending their lives. Some have suggested that men are more determined to die while women are actually seeking help (Stillion, 1995). Others have focused on means of suicide: men are more inclined to use "masculine" methods, such as guns, which are more lethal than pills, which women are more likely to use (Kushner, 1985). Suicide in older men is linked to a number of factors: health problems, isolation, or the death of a spouse. In his discussion of this phenomenon, Kilmartin argues that gender role stress also plays a role. Ill health, reduced economic productivity, and increased feelings of dependence may limit the opportunities for men to fulfill masculine normative expectations, which contribute to depression and increased vulnerability to suicide (1994).

Interestingly, over the last two decades, the life expectancy gap in Canada has begun to narrow. Between 1981 and 2002, women's life expectancy has increased 1.5 years, while men's has increased almost 2.5 years (Statistics Canada, 2006b). Some explanations for this change relate to changes in gender patterns: women are more likely to smoke and drink; they are more likely to work in dangerous sectors; and they engage in higher risk recreational and adventurous activities than they once did. Meanwhile, men are more inclined to care about their health and seek medical advice when necessary than in the recent past. Indeed, a recent advertisement campaign on Spike TV, a channel aimed at a masculine audience, encouraged viewers to go to the doctor and not "die of embarrassment."

Even though the gap is narrowing, the differential life expectancy means that the older segments of the population still include more women then men. Of all people over age 65 in Canada, 57 percent are female. In higher age groups, the proportion of women grows larger, prompting some to be concerned about the "feminization of later life" (Arber & Ginn, 1991). This imbalanced ratio of women to men has profound implications for older people. For heterosexual married women, outliving a male spouse and thus living several years as a widow is a common pattern. But partnered or not, women predominate in the older age categories, creating unique opportunities for new social interaction and relationships. Men, on the other hand, are a significant minority in these later years. They are more likely to have lost their peers and are less likely to have a social support network (see *Social Aging* below).

Health and disability patterns also vary by sex. (For a concise summary of these patterns, see Belsky, 2001.) Some problems are sex-linked. For example, men are more susceptible to hearing loss, though this is linked to previous life experiences, such as greater exposure to damaging levels of occupational noise. This loss of hearing can interfere with social interactions because it undermines the ability to converse easily. Hearing loss is often associated with both isolation and depression. In contrast, women are much more susceptible to osteoporosis than men because of smaller bone size and the estrogen depletion that occurs after menopause. This bone loss hampers women's mobility; and if it is very severe, the deteriorating skeleton may no longer be able to protect vital organs.

Because of the higher levels of estrogen prior to menopause, women are also somewhat protected from vascular disease. This actually gives them a slight intellectual advantage in early old age (into their 70s). But by virtue of their longer lives, women are more susceptible to certain age-related health challenges. Dementia is one such serious problem. A German study (Baltes, 1999) found that by age 90, 60 percent of the population was demented. Moreover, because more women reach these ages, they are at higher risk of dementia. In fact, women are almost twice as likely to develop Alzheimer's disease. While there is a possible link to neuron deterioration associated with estrogen loss after menopause, women are generally just more likely to reach very old age, when dementias become more prevalent. Moreover, age-related problems, such as arthritis, cataracts, and cardiovascular disease, are more common in women because of their longer life expectancy. By age 85, almost 20 percent of the population experiences a limitation in their ability to undertake daily activities. Called ADLs (activities of daily living), these activities include eating, bathing, and dressing. Because there are far more old women than old men, more women experience challenges associated with ADLs.

These demographic and health patterns show that women have a greater chance of survival and that the oldest age groups are dominated by females. But because of aging in greater numbers, women have a much greater chance of experiencing health challenges, losing a spouse, and living in a nursing home or other care institution.

C. Social Aging: Retirement

Retirement means the exit from paid employment. When most people think about retirement, they like to picture themselves healthy, free from alarm clocks and rush hours, financially comfortable, without having to work. It's a wonderful dream, but it doesn't really reflect the reality of late life. Prior to the twentieth century, there was no expectation that the average person should be allowed to withdraw from productive labour at a specific age and live in relative ease. Women and men worked at economic tasks as long as they were able; and as their strength and abilities declined, so too did their labour. If they had been fortunate enough to accumulate wealth through their working years, these assets could fund the years when work for economic compensation was not possible. Those who were unable to accumulate wealth relied on the good will of their children and community to provide for them. But back then, the life expectancy in Canada was so low (near to age 50) that most people died before they reached what we now consider to be old age.

But even though today both men and women benefit from retirement, the whole notion of retirement is itself gendered. Retirement was created when the "traditional family" was most common (see Chapters Eleven and Twelve). So the vast majority of people doing the retiring were men. All the unpaid work of maintaining a household and its members was largely accomplished by women, both before and after the age of retirement. In effect, you don't get to retire from laundry, cooking, and vacuuming.

Retirement, then, has been experienced quite differently by women and men. Of course, the patterns discussed here are merely general patterns, because neither all women nor all men experience the same conditions and opportunities. Other statuses, such as ethnicity and social class, have just as a profound an impact on the retirement experience as gender. But in general, for men, retirement typically is a transition out of the dominant activity of their adult years. They are much more likely to have followed a typical path: education, then employment, then retirement. Though the timing of retirement depends largely on health, finances, and career opportunities; blue-collar workers are more eager to retire early than are those in professional jobs (Hayward *et al.*, 1998). In contrast, women of retirement age in Canada are more likely to have had a disrupted career path, shifting in and out of unpaid, part-time and full-time work (Han & Moen, 1999), depending on other responsibilities.

For men, one of the key issues of late life is the timing of retirement. Increasingly, men are not making an abrupt and permanent exit from the paid labour force on their 65th birthday. Instead, they are following patterns of increasing individuation. Some are retiring early and beginning second careers or taking up major volunteer commitments. Others are retiring later, choosing to remain in the workforce. Still others are gradually decreasing their paid labour over a period of years. In their research on this subject, Mutchler *et al.* (1997) refer to these as *blurred* versus *crisp exits*. As the words imply, a **crisp exit** is a definitive departure from the paid workforce, while a **blurred exit** involves at least two changes in labour force status over two years. The blurred exit pattern was more frequent among adults under age 65, often involving a *bridge job*. Bridge jobs are jobs at which an employee works after leaving a career job but before retiring fully and permanently. The phenomenon of bridge jobs is not new, but there is some evidence that they are becoming more popular. First, early occupational retirement incentives have encouraged people to leave career jobs before they might have otherwise chosen to. These people are taking up bridge jobs until they are eligible for their full pensions. Second, there is evidence of more involuntary job displacement (job loss) among older workers, increasing their need to find a bridge job until they are financially prepared to permanently retire (Henretta, 2001). In addition, structural factors may influence the timing of retirement:

- The aging population is expected to create an increased demand for old workers.
- Life expectancy is increasing, and the health of old people is also improving. Thus, there will be more healthy, able-bodied people in their late sixties and seventies available to work.
- More people have higher educations and professional careers than in the past; and, men in professional careers are more likely to work past age 65.
- Changes in pension benefits and mandatory retirement rules actually encourage later retirement.

Henretta (2001) reviewed the trends and argued that in the future, retirement patterns will be more diverse than they have been in the past. But he cautions that despite factors which appear to encourage later retirement, we should not assume that these external factors will be deterministic. The retirement decision is made by individuals who, while *influenced* by other factors, make their choices based on individual needs and desires.

As more women participate fully in the paid labour force, they will increasingly be subject to the same issues of timing of retirement that men face. However, one retirement concern that women are more vulnerable to, both now and in the future, is poverty in late life. Even women who have worked full-time have significantly lower incomes and pensions than their male counterparts (see also Chapter Twelve). Current data shows that old women are twice as likely to be poor than old men.

This pattern results in part from women's working life experiences in the second half of the twentieth century in Canada. In one report on the income of older women, the British Columbia Human Rights Commission (2001) identifies many of the reasons why women

TABLE 6.2	Percentage of Population below Low Income Cut-off by Sex and Age, 2004	
	Women	Men
All ages	16.6%	14.4%
Over 64	17.8%	9.3%
Unattached	38.1%	29.1%
Source: Statistics Canada, 2006c		

are more likely to be poor in their old age. First, women typically earned less than men, and they were more likely to have family-related work interruptions. Thus, they have had lower incomes and were less able to invest in RRSPs or to save for retirement. Their lower incomes influence their post-retirement income because pension incomes are calculated based on income and years of work. Women are also less likely to be in union jobs and jobs with pensions and more likely to be working part-time or for only part of the year—jobs that typically pay less and have fewer benefits (pensions, health, and dental plans). Second, women are more likely to live alone in their old age (differential mortality means married women typically outlive their spouses), which reduces their income through the loss of their partner's pensions. Elderly couples with little income beyond their government pensions are close to the low-income cut-off; and upon the death of their spouses, the reduction in pension often pushes women below this poverty line.

Improving the financial position of old women is integrally linked to increasing their paid work activities throughout their adulthood. Increasing economic opportunities and incomes by reducing gender-based discrimination and occupational segregation (see Chapter Twelve) will greatly improve their financial positions. Moving away from the gender-polarized expectation that women are primarily responsible for the majority of unpaid family work (see Chapter Eleven) will also have a further beneficial impact on their incomes, decreasing the likelihood of poverty in their old age.

D. Social Aging: Widowhood

Just as differential working lives have an impact on men and women's timing and economic positions in retirement, so too do differential family patterns. Living into old age with a spouse is much more likely for men than women (see Table 6.3).

Men are more likely to remarry after divorce or the death of a spouse and are more likely to die sooner than their spouse. Women are more likely to be widowed and less likely to marry either after divorce or after the death of their spouse. This pattern accounts for the dramatic gap: almost 40 percent of senior women live alone, and less than 20 percent of senior men do. The numbers are even more dramatic in the oldest age category: 55 percent of men over age 84 live with their spouse while less than 12 percent of women do. These patterns are significant: men have the advantage of a live-in partner to provide social, emotional, and practical support. Women are more likely to age alone

TABLE 6.3		**Living Alone or with a Spouse by Age and Sex**			
		65-74	75-84	85+	All People over Age 64
Alone	Women	28.9%	47.3%	59.4%	38.3%
	Men	14.3%	19.4%	29.3%	16.8%
With Spouse	Women	55.2%	33%	11.7%	43.2%
	Men	76.4%	71.2%	55.6%	73.5%
Source: Statistics Canada, 2006b					

and to spend their last years in some form of institutional living (such as seniors apartments or nursing care).

This data may lead you to think that elderly women are a sorry lot, bereft of husbands and abandoned to assisted care living. If this is your vision of elderly women, the research shows that you are mistaken. Of course, not all women thrive after the death of their spouse. If the spouse dies early, it is actually more difficult for the surviving widow. In part, this is because older couples are more likely to expect death, and it can be a relief if it ends the spouse's suffering. But in general, while the transition to widowhood for women is difficult, research suggests that after a period of grieving, most widows tend to recover emotionally and continue on with social activities. A husband's death does not typically lead to social isolation. In fact, some research suggests that activity levels actually increases within two or three years of the death of their spouse, possibly because they are freer of care-giving responsibilities (Ferraro, Mutran & Barresi, 1984). Some researchers use the phrase **society of widows** to describe the strong practical and **social support** network in which many widowed women participate (Gallagher & Gerstel, 1993).

In contrast, men whose spouses die tend to fare worse than women. The empirical data suggested that widowerhood is relatively rare, a non-normative life event. Just under 72 percent of elderly men live with their spouse; and even after age 85, 55 percent still live their wives (see Table 6.3). Compared with widowed women, widowers show a greater decline in life satisfaction because they suffer more social isolation and loneliness (Lopata, 1996); and they are more likely to die of natural causes or to commit suicide soon after their spouse dies (Lee, Willetts & Seccombe, 1998). These patterns are in part linked to gender-based normative expectations throughout the life course. Because men have been more likely to focus on careers while women have typically undertaken more of the relationship work, this leaves older men with few or no support networks. Losing a wife means a man is also more likely to lose his social network, his connection to family, and his connection to the larger community. Of course, not all widowed men suffer such dire outcomes, just as not all women thrive after their spouse dies.

In her guest essay on old men, Deborah van den Hoonaard interviewed many men who have adjusted to living alone after the death of their wives. But she finds that they feel compelled to deal with gender-based normative expectations. Caring for themselves can undermine their sense of masculinity, since they must engage in work that for their generation has been perceived as "women's work."

BOX 6-1	Older Widowers do Gender

by Deborah K. van den Hoonaard
Gerontology Department, St. Thomas University

When I told people that I was doing a study[1] of older widowers, they usually joked about how quickly men remarry[2] or their inability to cook, clean, and do laundry.[3] These remarks reflect widely shared stereotypes. This essay reports on an in-depth interview study of twenty-six widowers over 60 who lived in New Brunswick or Florida. The study did not originally look at older widowers through the lens of masculinity and doing gender, but participants' efforts to frame their responses as men was striking. This essay focuses on how participants described cooking and doing housework in ways that protect their sense of masculinity.

Most of the men knew how to cook. However, their descriptions of cooking shed light on its potential to undermine their sense of themselves as men. Participants emphasized that their cooking was limited in some way and cooking was an issue of necessity rather than enjoyment. Al explained:

> I think your body is a machine that does need certain elements to feed it properly, just like an automobile does.[4]

Others described "opening a can" and reheating food as challenging.

Several men who knew how to cook linked it with very masculine activities. Ralph talked about cooking during the war:

> My mother . . . taught me how to cook . . . even during the war . . . the commanding officer would come down and get a home-cooked meal. (Ralph)

Marc complemented his cooking ability with athletic activities, pointing that he played or coached:

> senior hockey . . . senior basketball . . . volleyball . . . softball. . . . hockey . . . baseball, you name it, . . . and I'd say, "Hey, come on home; I'll cook you a steak.

Men also described their cooking as "basic" or "plain." Matthew is a good cook but does not make pies or cakes. Some widowers highlighted "masculine" meals:

> I make sure to cook a big dinner every night: meat and potatoes and all that stuff. . . . the core of your meal. (Marc)

Almost no one admitted making casseroles or desserts[5] although a few did have specialties, for example, fruit cake or pickles. Several men used a Foreman Grill, which is not only promoted by a retired prize-fighter but also replicates a barbeque, an appliance often used by men.

In contrast, a few affirmed that they were good cooks or liked cooking. Marcel, a European immigrant, had learned to cook the meals he remembered from his youth, while Bernie, who had cooked for his disabled wife, had a girlfriend[6] who:

> keeps telling everybody what a good cook I am. Actually, I'm not that great a cook, but . . . there are certain dishes I'm great. . . . I have no problem.

Bernie takes great pride in making special dishes for his friend who has trouble swallowing. He accompanies his self-deprecating language with

BOX 6-1	*(Continued)*

"agency speech" in which the "speaker adopts the identity of an independent actor" (Kirsi, Hervonen, and Jylhä 2000: 161).

A few participants did talk about cooking with a sense of competence and pride. Marc jokingly challenged me to a "cook off," turning it into a competition, while a few others compared their ability to cook with men who could not cook:[7]

> Nobody tells widowers how to get along, how to cook for one. Most . . . have no idea how to cook. (Matthew)

Angus explained that some widowers rush to remarry because they can't even boil water.

One widower's comments were different. He was younger than the other widowers (in his late 40s when his wife died), and still had had children at home. Leonard had had a "pretty traditional relationship" with his wife but found that cooking recreated the "home" his family lost when his wife died:

> And I found a book that my wife had started. . . . all the recipes that she made . . . And I started baking . . . and all the smells . . . and warmth [came] back into the house . . . [T]hat opened up cooking for me . . . And I really enjoyed it.

The participants also talked about other types of housework, particularly: (1) buying housework and (2) having a low standard.[8] Buying housekeeping was a common strategy. Tim used "home care" that included housekeeping and cooking:

> I get home care; the girls come in two hours a day . . . five days a week and do

my housework for me. And if I've got any cooking, they'll do that.

Leroy communicated his ignorance of housework:

> I have a housekeeper . . . **I don't know what she does.** . . . She stays about 2, 2 $\frac{1}{2}$ hours . . . and cleans me all up and washes the windows, or **whatever she wants to do**. [emphasis added]

George and Samuel provided the most extreme descriptions of poor housekeeping. George was adamant that we not meet in his home because it was too messy. Samuel associated his not caring about housekeeping with the early days of widowerhood and men's lower standards:

> The days seemed to be meaningless. . . . I . . . didn't care at all about what the house looked like. . . . one of the things about men is that they're not as fussy about the house as women.

Even men who knew how to keep the house clean had lower standards than their wives. Chad "helped" his wife when she was alive; his comments are typical:

> I do housework stuff. . . . I got two shelves full of chemicals in there. **I don't know what the hell she used that for** . . . I'm starting to get a little bit tired of housework. . . . I don't always do a good job of it.

A few participants saw housework as part of the discipline of getting on with life, developing a routine, and keeping busy. Two men conceptually linked housework with work around the property, minimizing the feminine nature of what they were doing.

(Continued)

BOX 6-1	**Older Widowers do Gender (*Continued*)**

Only after their wives were no longer there did some widowers recognize the extent of housework. Keith, whose remarks are particularly poignant, talked about the everydayness of housework and "sentient care" (Mason 1996, cited in Davidson, et al. 2000: 543) that he took so for granted it was virtually invisible.

> I used to help her... but... I never realized the amount of work to keep a house going.... You clean the bathroom one day and have a shower the next [day]... you have to dust again.... Or just a little lunch... You've got to wash the dishes... It's the planning that always gets me.

A few participants had shared the housework. Ed's comments are most striking although his wife was the expert:

> Whoever got home first would start supper. [My wife] taught me very well. She taught me to be self-sufficient.... Taught me how to clean the house.... We were in business so we shared everything.... It wasn't... "I'm the man of the house."... It was an equal partnership.

Discussion

These widowers' efforts to demonstrate their masculinity during the interviews are striking. Other subjects, including being pursued romantically and enjoying a sense of freedom often associated with bachelorhood, highlighted their desire to portray themselves as men.

West and Zimmerman's classic 1987 article, "Doing Gender," sheds light on this case of "impression management" (Goffman 1959). It makes the point that gender is "constituted through interaction" which serves as 'testimony to our 'essential natures'" (129). These

widowers may have been in a precarious position in terms of their gender because most were not in a heterosexual relationship, were retired, and were emotional during the interview while they were discussing "women's work." Perhaps the men's obvious efforts to show that housework is not a part of their "essential nature" as men was an attempt to redress the precariousness of their identity in this particular interview with a woman who was about the age of any woman they might be interested in.

Endnotes

This study was supported by a grant from the Social Sciences and Humanities Research Council of Canada.

See van den Hoonaard (2002) for a discussion about repartnering.

Lund, Caserta, and Diamond (1993: 246 quoted in Moore and Stratton 2002: 112) found older men "deficient in a predictable set of skills, including cooking, shopping, and housecleaning."

All names are pseudonyms and all quotations are taken verbatim from interview transcripts unless otherwise specified.

Single women whom some widowers perceive to be chasing them are often characterized as arriving on the doorstop bearing casseroles.

Having a girlfriend may make the issue of masculinity less salient. Thanks to Marianne Skarborn who brought this to my attention.

These descriptions are reminiscent of the way widows (see van den Hoonaard 2001) talk about women who "didn't even know how to write a cheque."

Kate Davidson reports similar findings among British widowers (1999: 120).

BOX 6-1	*(Continued)*

Bibliography

Davidson, Kate 1999 *Gender, Age, and Widowhood: How older widows and widowers differently realign their lives.* Unpubl. PhD Dissertation, University of Surrey.

Davidson, Kate, S. Arber, & J. Ginn 2000 "Gendered Meanings of Care Work within Later Life Marital Relationships. *Canadian Journal on Aging* 19 (4): 536-553.

Goffman, Erving 1959 *The Presentation of Self in Everyday Life*. NY: Doubleday.

Kirsi, Tapio, Antti Hervonen, & Marja Jylha 2000 "'A Man's Gotta Do What a Man's Gotta Do': Husbands as caregivers to their demented wives: a discourse analysis." *Journal of Aging Studies* 14(2): 153-169.

Moore, Alinde J. And Dorothy G. Stratton 2002 *Resilient Widowers: Older Men Speak for Themselves*. NY: Springer.

van den Hoonaard, Deborah Kestin 2001 *The Widowed Self: the older woman's journey through widowhood*. Waterloo, ON: Wilfrid Laurier University Press.

van den Hoonaard, Deborah K. 2002 "You Have to Have Someone': Widowers' Attitudes and Experiences with Repartnering." A Paper presented to Studying Life Ethnographically, 19th Qualitative Analysis Conference, McMaster University, May 23-24.

West, Candace and Don H. Zimmerman 1987 "Doing Gender." *Gender and Society* 1 (2): 125-15.

CONCLUSION

This brief overview of the gender issues of adulthood demonstrates the importance of gender analysis of the life course. We enter adulthood with particular notions about who we are as gendered beings. Often, we aren't aware of the extent to which we perform gender in the course of making decisions about our lives as adults. The relationships we enter, the work we do, and our financial circumstances are all linked to our gendered identities, as well as to gender divisions in society. Our own identities as gendered beings are not static but shift over the life course and in relation to life events. This discussion is intended to encourage you to think about gender critically, both in your own life, in the lives of those you know, as well as in relation to social expectations.

CHAPTER SUMMARY: KEY POINTS

1. Adulthood brings about many life changes through which individuals perform gender. Career choices, intimate relationships, having children, parenting, medical issues, and relationship breakdowns involve choices that invoke gender scripts.

2. Masculinity is equated with heterosexuality, meaning that gay men are excluded from definitions of what it means to be a man.

3. Health issues are often gendered. Male erectile dysfunction has been medicalized and created as an illness for which men must take responsibility and seek treatment. Maleness thus becomes defined by the erect penis.

4. For women, the definition of womanliness remains associated with the ability and desire to mother.

5. Upon marriage or relationship breakdown, women generally experience a greatly reduced standard of living, while men experience a modest rise in standard of living.

6. Our experiences in old age reflect our activities throughout the life course. Our health, financial position, and relationships in late life are built upon our earlier choices and opportunities. Because our experiences are gendered, the lives of old people reflect gender differences.

7. There are three key ways to measure aging: chronological, which involves the actual passage of time; physiological, which is based on the health of individuals (some people's bodies age more rapidly than others); and, social which is based on statuses, relationships, and transitions.

8. Demographic patterns have a profound impact on gender and age. More people are living into their 80s and 90s than ever before. And many more women than men are achieving these great ages. However, this increased life expectancy means that more women face problems with dementia and disability.

9. One major life transition in old age is *retirement*. Women are less likely to have pensions and therefore are more vulnerable to poverty in late life. Men face different challenges as the hegemonic normative expectations seem to be unachievable in retirement.

10. A second major life transition is *widowhood* for men and women who have been partnered. This is a normative experience for women, and empirical research suggests that women are better equipped to thrive post-widowhood. Men are much less likely to be widowed. Moreover, research suggests that they have less social support and are more vulnerable to suicide and early death.

DISCUSSION QUESTIONS

1. We know that late life experiences reflect a lifetime of physical, emotional, and financial arrangements. Given that our society is less gender polarized now, and that your generation will have a much more egalitarian division of labour and power, what do you think the gender patterns will look like when you are in your 70s?

2. If you had the power and resources to create change within Canadian society, what two programs or policies would you implement to address the mortality differential and the feminization of poverty amongst the elderly?

3. Think about your own life course. How is gender implicated in the history of your life? How did you dress when you were a child? How have you defined your gender since then? How does that define who you are today in your day-to-day life?

4. How does family influence the way gender is communicated and taught to children? Again, think about your own family of origin. What are the gender patterns you saw as a child and teenager?

5. Is masculinity associated with heterosexuality?

6. What do think we mean when we say that the medicalization of penile erectile dysfunction has contributed to the equation of "real man" with an "erect penis"?

7. In your opinion, do most people think about the reasons for having children beyond feeling as though it is a normal expectation?

KEY TERMS

adulthood	gender depolarization	social aging
AIDS	glass ceiling of age	social support
blurred exit	ideology of motherhood	society of widows
childfree	life expectancy	retirement
chronological aging	mortality differential	
counterhegemonic	pathologized	
crisp exit	physiological aging	

chapter seven

Intersectionality

Think about how you describe yourself—woman? Student? Son? Boyfriend? Partner? Gay? White? Muslim? Young? Canadian? Think about the multiple hooks on which you hang your identity and on the ways in which your description shifts depending upon the context. Chances are you chose more than one descriptor from even this short list above. Maybe you are the person who articulates the perspective of a single mother when you speak out in class, or the perspective of a feminist or gay man. Or maybe these are perspectives that you choose not to share or embrace. Whatever the case, as you think about identity, remember its fluidity, from situation to situation, over the course of your life thus far, and imagine how it might change in the future (for example, from single to married to divorced). Moreover, consider how the elements of your identity *intersect* with other elements of your identity and your environment.

Thinking in terms of intersections is not easy. We social scientists often build discrete categories to help explore the social world, only to find ourselves so wedded to the categories we have created that we reify them, refusing to let go of them even when they do nothing to enhance our understanding of social life. *Intersectional thinking* pushes us to think beyond one-dimensional categories. While acknowledging the sedimentations that structure our social world, this way of thinking attempts to opens up a space for us to incorporate the richness and complexity of peoples' lives and the ways they link to each other.

The multiple and shifting ways that people construct their identities has been the focus of considerable debate in social science. Moreover, the use of identity categories to define populations has proven to be especially contentious. What does it mean to talk about *women* or *men*? And how are these categories **essentialist**? Essentialism refers to theoretical assumptions about a group of people based on an identifying characteristic (such as *man* or *woman*). Essentialism assumes that all members of that group share the same characteristics or that there is some unifying element to being *men* or *women*. But because not all women or men share similar experiences, we must then ask: can individual identities be used as a starting point from which to build collective or group identities? And how do those group identities become politicized?

Although this chapter discusses identity at the individual level, we want to be clear that identity is a *heuristic* or *analytical* device only. This chapter focuses on identity and its construction at the individual level; but it acknowledges the importance of the *agency-structure relationship*, which assumes the primacy of neither the individual nor the social structure. Thus, the observations in this chapter are always made with an understanding that structural influences also influence identity. While social structure shapes our actions and beliefs, individuals also make choices about which beliefs they accept and how they choose to act. The manner in which people construct identities does not come out of a void. Rather, identity categories draw on condensations of meaning, such as the "good mother," the "bad girl," or the "ADHD boy." These bundles of meaning weave together in complex ways.

People construct identities as an ongoing process, with life stages and experiences influencing how they see themselves and others. For example, being gay and the process of "coming out" alter both self-perception and the perceptions of others. Some identity shifts occur simply because of the life course. For example, for some women, menopause brings changes in identity that are both positive and negative, both perhaps based on social scripts that define women in terms of their ability to bear children. Pre-menopausal women who are unable to bear children may experience this identity point at a different time, seeing themselves as "infertile" women who are "less than" the ideal woman or unable to fulfill their socially defined roles. In their anxiety about childbearing, these women may adjust their identities to focus almost exclusively on what they perceive as their own inadequacies. Thus, their identities shift to negative self-perceptions because of a particular identity point they and society have created: being a "mother."

In addition, intersections of race with class, gender, ethnicity, sexual orientation, and ability move identity theory out of an exclusive "gender as identity" or "gender as role" manner of thinking. Intersectional thinking considers the ways that gender is woven through other dimensions of domination, such as **race**. Race is a socially constructed term that accounts for differences in external human features. It has no basis in biology but is often used as an identifying characteristic, frequently in negative ways. Thus, by considering race as an intersection, intersectional thinking permits the exploration of multiple factors in power relations. Note that the experiences of women of colour or working-class women (or both together, in some cases) are not captured by an essentialist reading of *women* as a gendered, disadvantaged group. In short, the way gender works for a middle-class, white woman lawyer living in the suburbs whose first language is English is different from the way it works for an immigrant woman from Haiti working in the garment industry and living in an urban core.

This race- or class-gender intersection revealed itself in the case of Beth Symes in *Symes v. Canada*. Lawyer Beth Symes, who took her argument all the way to the Supreme Court of Canada, argued that the Income Tax Act discriminates against businesswomen because it does not allow them to deduct childcare expenses as a business-related cost. She based her argument on the equality provisions of the Canadian Charter of Rights and Freedoms. Short of taking their children to the office with them, women like Symes must either hire childcare or have a stay-at-home partner. Symes also argued that a disproportionate burden of childcare falls on women (which is certainly borne out by all of the available evidence). But the courts held that women "choose" to have children. By focusing on the *choice* issue, the courts ignored the social and relational context in which that *choice* happens (for an excellent book-length analysis of this case, see Rebecca Johnson, 2002). Remember our earlier comments about the agency structure relationship. This is a good example of the way courts highlight agency. In this case, the courts ignored or downplayed the structural pressures and context in which women, as the only possible child-bearers, make decisions about reproduction.

But more important, some commentators held that Symes was a woman of privilege who was seeking more privilege on the backs of less privileged women. The result of this case was highly contested within the feminist community in Canada, with some people arguing that to have allowed Symes' claim would have advantaged privileged women while giving policy makers an excuse to claim they had dealt with the problem of child-bearing and -rearing among working women.

Unfortunately, Symes was unsuccessful in her argument, and the *misery justice* approach prevailed. **Misery justice** is a term coined by Ruth Morris (1995), a Canadian prison abolition activist who wrote a great deal about inequality and just societies. Morris talked about misery justice specifically in relation to our retributive (punishment-oriented) justice system, but she also recognized that it was a pervasive way of thinking about justice and fairness. "Retributive justice is based on a philosophy that you can only create justice by taking away. If one person has more than another, *misery justice* always looks at ways of taking away from the one with more, not giving more to the one deprived. Thus, misery justice never looks at improving the lot of the victims, but only victimizing offenders so they will be equally miserable. In the same spirit, if any prisoner is said to like prison because a heated though wretched cell is better than freezing to death on the street, we must take heat and food away from all prisoners to make sure they are as miserable as the most miserable frozen wretch on the street" (1995, p. 72). Misery justice often functions as the dominant approach to gender issues as well.

But in *Symes v. Canada,* Symes was not positioning herself against less privileged women; rather, she was positioning herself against a patriarchal tax structure in which golf club memberships are deductible while childcare expenses are not. To deny Symes the benefit of a legitimate expense does nothing to improve the lot of less privileged women. Intersections acknowledge the profoundly disadvantaged position some women are in because of their race or ethnicity. The *Symes* case illustrates the fact that intersections are also important tools for critical thinkers to assess privilege and advantage.

Intersectional thinking allows and indeed compels us to consider the individual's position within structures of domination. It also encourages us to examine the means by which individuals rework and resist their positions within those structures. Aker summarizes intersectional thinking this way: "These dimensions of domination or discrimination are neither obviously discrete nor structurally analogous. Class relations do not function in the same way as gender relations; race relations are still another matter. Yet all of these come together in cross-cutting ways for particular individuals and at particular historical moments" (1997, p. 566). Intersectional thinking allows us to move past simplistic statements such as "men oppress women" to a more complex analysis and understanding of inequality and privilege. To characterize all men as oppressing all women, for example, misses the relative privilege of some white women over men of colour. The matrix of **intersectionality** facilitates an examination of both disadvantage and privilege that can emerge from the intersections of race, class, and gender. Ransford's *multiple jeopardy, multiple advantage hypothesis* (1980), as cited in Browne and Misra (2003), holds that the most disadvantage will be experienced by those individuals who are in the lowest position in two or more categories (such as *Aboriginal* and *female*). On the other hand, those who are in the highest levels of two or more social categories, specifically white men, have the greatest privilege or advantage. There is, argue some theorists, a multiplier effect of advantage and disadvantage that surpasses the simple addition of one category to another (2003, p. 493).

Thus, the intersection of race and gender is certainly important, but it must be situated in the social context of class, education, and even geography (which is a rarely mentioned but important variable). Sherene Razack (2002) powerfully argues that we continue to reproduce colonial space as raced space. Razack uses the case of Pamela George to illustrate her point. George, who worked as a prostitute several times a month in the area known as the Stroll in Regina, was murdered by two white middle-class male university students. Steven Kummerfield and Alex Turnowetsky took Pamela George to an isolated area outside of the city, and after she had performed oral sex on each of them, they severely beat her and left her lying face down in the mud. The two were eventually convicted of manslaughter.

Razack argues that "because Pamela George was considered to belong to a space of prostitution and Aboriginality, in which violence routinely occurs, while her killers were presumed to be far removed from this zone, the enormity of what was done to her and her family remained largely unacknowledged" by the courts, the media, and society generally (2002, p. 125). Razack argues that the fact that George worked as a prostitute was scrutinized, as though in part explaining and justifying her murder; while the fact that Kummerfield and Ternowetsky approached her twice (the second time, one of them hid in the trunk of the car) to "hire her services" was normalized—that is, this is how men behave. Interwoven with race and class in this case are assumptions about white middle-class masculinity and the activities that reproduce it. For the two men who murdered George, this masculinity included crossing into the "dangerous" space of the Aboriginal "Other," consuming large amounts of alcohol, and participating in a hypermasculine sports culture. In addition, white complicity in this case is astounding, from the police who looked first in the space of the Other (the Aboriginal community) for suspects, to the friends of the accused (who minimized and normalized the murder, reassuring them with statements (such as "You shouldn't assume you killed her"), to one of the suspect's mothers who offered to call Crimestoppers and give a false tip when her son confessed the murder to her (in addition to washing his jeans and cleaning his shoes).

Ironically, as Razack argues, the trial process worked to eliminate the relevance of race, class, and gender, preserving a model of *justice as sameness*—a model that is justice-blindfolded in the worst possible sense. George's race, class, and gender were indeed relevant to the case, as were the race, class, and gender of the two men convicted of manslaughter, but the court disqualified these as relevant factors in George's murder. One of the justices wrote, "Every effort was made during the trial by counsel and myself to deal with the case strictly on the basis of relevant evidence and not on the financial and social positions of the accused and their victim or their race" (Razack, 2002, p. 154). But Razack calls attention to the purposes served by racialized spaces. They allow the beneficiaries of colonialism and patriarchy to collect their dues, so to speak. "Moving from respectable space to degenerate space and back again is an adventure that confirms that they are indeed white men in control who can survive a dangerous encounter with the racial Other and who have an unquestioned right to go anywhere and do anything" (2002, p. 127).

In addition, Razack emphasizes the role of colonialism in George's murder. She contextualizes George's murder in light of other white man/Aboriginal woman murders and in the light of the broader history of white abuse of Aboriginal peoples. The importance of intersections and the use of an intersectional perspective is key to Razack's analysis. "Police described the Stroll as a world of drugs and prostitution, and most of all, as a space of Aboriginality. Steven Kummerfield and his friends visited the Stroll 'out of curiosity.' Alex Ternowetsky and his friends took their girlfriends on an adventure to the Stoll 'sort of seeing who was there,' as his lawyer put it. The young women hid under the blankets while the young men negotiated for the services of an Aboriginal prostitute: a thrilling excursion into the slums that would have helped these young white people to know their own place in the world" (2002, p. 141). The intersection of whiteness, gender, and class came together to mark privilege and disadvantage. And yet, as Razack points out, it is whites who are often portrayed as being vulnerable and in danger during such encounters (2002, p. 142). In a similar manner, in other well-documented occasions, police have abandoned Aboriginal men outside town in the winter to make their own way to a safe place. Some of them have frozen to death (2002, p. 143). Razack weaves together these intersectional identities to highlight the importance of race, class, gender, and history in viewing the case of Pamela George as not "just" one murder of one Aboriginal woman, but as the continuation of an ongoing historically rooted oppression. At the same time, as she situates Pamela George's murder in its broader context, Razack also includes information about George beyond the fact that she worked as a prostitute. She was the mother of two children and, by all accounts, a good mother. She was a loving daughter and had helped her father to overcome an addiction problem. She was also a good cook and liked to do crafts.

Pamela George did what she had to do to survive. If we displace moral judgment from prostitution, which tends to be the dominant lens through which law and society view it, and adopt a prostitution-as-work framework, we can shift from a one-dimensional picture of Pamela George to one that brings to light the full horror of her murder and its tragedy for her and her family. Jeffrey and MacDonald (2006) position prostitution as work, according agency to the women and men who choose to work in the sex trade. Such an approach normalizes the sex trade and de-stigmatizes it. This lens opens the door for discussions about improved working conditions for sex trade workers and arguably exposes the raced assumptions that frame cases like that of Pamela George. Intersectional thinking allows analysis of many causes and explanations that a focus solely on gender may miss.

Sometimes intersections take us by surprise, often because we simply haven't thought about them. For example, Sandra Kirby (2000) documents the difficulties faced by elderly gays and lesbians as they attempt to deal with the aging process. She points out that as a cohort, gay and lesbian seniors are relatively new. (This doesn't mean that gays and lesbians haven't existed as a group with needs in the past, but that for the first time in modern history, they are claiming a public identity as a group with needs.) Until extremely recently,

gays and lesbians have not been able to marry, which meant that medical and estate decisions about aging and dying gays and lesbians remained legally in the hands of relatives,
even if a same-sex couple had been in a lifetime relationship. Kirby also points out that
many nursing homes are church-sponsored, and that many churches teach that homosexuality is a sin; thus, many elderly gays and lesbians find themselves alienated from care possibilities, perhaps even closeting themselves in order to find appropriate housing and care.
"The destructiveness of 'passing' as heterosexual is multifaceted. It includes not speaking
in public in the first person plural, not speaking about important things in one's life such as
significant relationships and events. It means hiding who one loves, and ultimately in hiding oneself as if it is shameful to be gay" (2000, p. 116). The intersection of sexual orientation and age results in both unique needs and an inequality that results from the
intersection of being both gay and elderly. In effect, the way individuals self-identify intersects with the ways others identify them.

IDENTITY AND THE OTHER

People construct identity and its intersectional points not only in relation to self but
also in relation to others—people unlike themselves. People regard others in terms of
particular identity points, sometimes those that have been selected by the others themselves, but more often in terms of physical characteristics that have been socially constructed around race or ethnicity. People who adopt sexual identities that are not readily
discernable—for example, the biologically female "bois" discussed in Chapter Nine,
who eliminate outward evidence of their sex and gender by having their breasts removed
and taking hormone treatments—create one of the interesting challenges to this method
of identifying others.

In general, challenging gender boundaries makes people nervous, as is demonstrated
by a short story by Lois Gould called "X: A Fabulous Child's Story" (1992). Gould creates
a story in which Mr. and Ms. Jones bring home Baby X and refuse to disclose X's sex (or
gender) to others. This scientific experiment (Xperiment, as Gould calls it) explores the
extent to which we socialize children into gender, and the extent to which we rely on external markers to adjust our perceptions and expectations of others when we meet them.
People become confused, distracted, and indeed sometimes angry when they cannot categorize others. And indeed, Baby X encounters problems from the other children when X
goes to school. But then, following X's example, the other children start breaking gender
rules and causing anxiety for their parents, demonstrating the extent to which gender categories and expectations are built into everyday interactions. "The worst came when the twins,
Joe and Peggy, decided to share everything with each other. Peggy used Joe's hockey skates,
and his microscope, and took half his newspaper route. Joe used Peggy's needlepoint and her
cookbooks and took two of her three babysitting jobs. Peggy started to run the lawn mower,
and Joe started running the vacuum cleaner" (1992, p. 46). Gould's fantasy story is an
insightful statement about how people construct and rely on categories when they relate to
others and when others relate to them. Gould's point applies intersectionality to other
situations. How do we construct other such categories based on skin colour, language,
and age? Even when we think these factors don't matter to us, that we aren't racist or
sexist, or that we don't hold stereotypical notions about others based on outward characteristics, our collective histories and cultural context are part of the way we negotiate our
way through day-to-day life.

Barbara Trepagnier (2001) has researched the insidious nature of racism. She interviewed white women who considered themselves "not racist," as many people consciously do. All the participants described themselves and were perceived by others as being "not racist." She then asked the women to also keep journals in which they were to record their thoughts about racism. Trepagnier found that many of her participants had negative thoughts and attitudes about African American and other racial minorities, a phenomenon she describes as *silent racism*. From her findings Trepagnier argues that the racist/not-racist binary is not particularly useful in defining and dealing with racism. Trepagnier's research reinforces the point that people bring stereotypes and prejudices into social interaction even when they think they do not. Perhaps by recognizing silent racism, people can then develop creative strategies for dealing with it.

Some theorists go further, arguing that race is completely socially constructed, an unstable category that political struggle and power relations are constantly renegotiating and reforming. There is no biological basis for the division of human identity on the basis of race because there is only one human race. Omi and Winant propose the following definition of race: "a concept which signifies and symbolizes social conflicts and interests by referring to different types of human bodies. Although the concept of race invokes biologically based human characteristics (so-called 'phenotypes'), a selection is always and necessarily a social and historical process" (1994, p. 55). However, Omi and Winant point out that race does play a role in ongoing social relations (and in self-construction and negotiation of identity). As a result, race is very real. They argue that social scientists need to examine race more critically and to "avoid both the utopian framework which sees race as an illusion we can somehow 'get beyond' and also the essentialist formulation which sees race as something objective and fixed, a biological datum" (1994, p. 55). In short, when considering race in patterns of oppression, students of gender must avoid reifying it as a "given."

Identities of the Other are part of a society's institutional markers as well. For example, schools identify children using gender, race, ability, and IQ. In addition, the law sometimes uses racial or ethnic identity in negative ways: the police can decide to target racial minorities for increased surveillance; or in this post-9/11 world, airport security can institute tacit racial profiling policies (while insisting, of course, that they do not). The law can also use the Other in a positive manner, such as s. 714 of the Criminal Code of Canada, which provides that in sentencing Aboriginal offenders, courts must take into account their status as a disadvantaged group in Canadian society.

We don't want to reduce identity here to "gender and . . ." categories, which tend to obscure the effect of multiple strands of identity and gloss over differences that are key to understanding and addressing inequality and oppression. How does being an Aboriginal woman differ from being an Aboriginal male? What are the assumptions that go with each of those descriptions? Identity bits play a role in terms of self-definition and Other-definition. The pieces of one's identity that one defines as important at any given moment may not be the pieces that other people emphasize. In short, other people do not always see us the way we would like them to, especially when we are members of marginal groups in society.

One of our students once made this point rather vocally by stating that she resisted identifying herself as a First Nations person in certain circumstances. She felt that even when there was a named advantage, there was inevitably a hidden price to be paid for assuming the status of the Other in relation to the hegemonic white community. She did not want what she described as "special" treatment because she felt it inevitably marked her as less capable. Although she very strongly identified with being Aboriginal in some situations, she wanted to maintain control over the terms of that identity and its negotiation. Partly, she wanted to manage perceptions of others and her treatment as an Aboriginal person. Her observations about how First Nations peoples are treated led her to select the situations in which she was willing to allow "First Nations woman" to be the group with which she was identified. Sometimes, such management of Otherness is negotiable, and sometimes it is not.

Of course, while people may recognize the importance of taking into account multiple and shifting identities, the challenge for social scientists is to actually account for these shifts. This task might be summed up as: how do we theorize intersectionality without essentializing the categories from which we draw—that is, *woman*, *man*, *gay*, *elderly*, and so on? Moreover, while intersectionality at the level of the individual is important, in what ways do patterns of identity intersections matter? For example, what does it mean to be a First Nations woman?

Of key importance is listening to the voice of the person who is experiencing the intersection. This was one of the central points made by bell hooks. In the women's movement of the 1970s and 1980s, white middle-class women failed to recognize that for women of colour, gender was often not the primary experiential locus of their oppression. The "sisterhood" was much less important to women of colour than solidarity with other people of colour. Moreover, as hooks pointed out, "while it is true that white women have led every movement toward feminist revolution in American society, their dominance is less a sign of black female disinterest in feminist struggle than an indication that the politics of colonization and racial imperialism have made it historically impossible for black women in the United States to lead a women's movement" (1981, p. 161). The exclusionary politics of race are not limited to the United States, and bell hooks' work has relevance in Canada as well.

Margaret Anderson (2005) points out that criticism by women of colour during the second wave of feminism resulted in a shift in analytical focus from "gender" to "race, class and gender." This shift recognized that "gender is constructed differently in different social locations because of its relational character. But race/class/gender studies also conceptualizes all three as realms of power and exploitation. Thus, gender can never be studied in isolation from race, class, and related social conditions" (Anderson, 2005, p. 444). Patricia Hill Collins named these intersections *the matrix of domination* (1990). An important component of matrix of domination theory is that no one component is consistently primary. In other words, a First Nations woman's identity as a First Nations person may be primary for her understanding of her own social location in dealing with contaminated water in her community (and the lack of government assistance to deal with it); but her identity as a woman may be primary in her fight for status as a First Nations person under the *Indian Act*. Social theory must be flexible enough to account for these shifts.

But despite acknowledging the complexity of grounding gender analysis in multiple constructions of identity, social science has not yet found a way to capture this complexity. Postmodern feminists such as Judith Butler (2004) have challenged the essentialism of categories such as *woman*, calling into question their analytical and political usefulness. But the counter-argument maintains that such changes would eliminate the possibility of political action based on those categories. One cannot challenge gender inequities if such categories do not exist or cannot be used. In other words, how can women insist on equality if there is no notion of *woman*?

A. Women with Disabilities

The complexity of talking about *women* is illustrated by Howland and Rintala's work (2001) on women with physical disabilities. While women with disabilities do share the physical vulnerabilities of women to sexual assault, for example, their experiences cannot be subsumed under those of women who are not physically disabled.

In their qualitative study of the dating behaviours of women with physical disabilitites, Howland and Rintala document the painful experiences of women who have attempted to push past stereotypes about disability and sexuality. "Men, and often the women themselves, view women with disabilities as 'damaged goods'" (2001, p. 41). According to their study, this perception has two major consequences. First, women with disabilities are viewed as asexual or as undesirable. This is not to say that men with disabilities do not experience a similar problem; but there is a significant difference between the consequence of men's and women's desirability in relation to partnering and sex. "Several sources . . . report that women with disability are less likely than women without disability to marry later, and more likely to be divorced. According to the Current Population Survey's data from the early 1980s, 60 percent of men with disabilities and 60 percent of women without disabilities are married, but only 49 percent of women with disabilities are married. Among women with severe disabilities, 37 percent who were once married are no longer married, compared to 22 percent of men with severe disability, for reasons other than death of spouse . . . According to Sandowski (1989) more men than women abandon marriages when their spouse becomes ill or disabled" (2001, p. 43).

The second consequence identified by Howland and Rintala is that women with disability are seen as easy targets: because they are less desirable, some people believe they should be grateful for any sexual attention, however brutal or unwanted. Women report being sexually assaulted because they have found themselves in situations that an able-bodied woman might have been able to escape. Moreover, women are sometimes simply abandoned, left in dangerous situations. "Jennifer had an epileptic seizure after having sex with a date in a hotel room. He was so shocked by the seizure that instead of getting help, he left her alone in the hotel room. When she woke up the next morning, her face and pillow were soaked in blood because she had bitten her tongue so hard. After this incident, she endured the humiliation of her friends making fun of her because the man told them that she acted like she was possessed "(2001, p. 59). The vulnerability of women to sexual assault is exacerbated by disability. Moreover, the women in Howland and Rintala's study also measured their self-worth in gendered ways that were compounded by their perceptions that their disabilities impacted on their desirability as women.

B. Women of Racial Minority

Race intersects with gender on numerous fronts, such as in media portrayals of the dangerous black man or the irresponsible black woman. In her study of media portrayals of crack mothers, Marian Meyers (2004) argues that the superficial manner in which the news covers such stories misses the complexities of race, gender, and class. She analyzed a television series that portrayed "the battle to save the children of crack mothers. This narrative of redemption, viewed through the lens of gender, race and class, is one of a white professional middle-class working to rescue women and children of the black underclass" (2004, p. 194). Meyers names this phenomenon *paternalistic racism* and argues that such portrayals reinforce negative stereotypes about African American women.

In their research on gender and race in the labour market, Browne and Misra identify domestic work as the space in which race-gender intersections are most striking because "[d]omestic work is deeply imbedded in hierarchies of class, gender, race, ethnicity and nationality. Not only are domestic tasks associated with one gender (women) but gendered norms of childcare and housework being seen as 'natural' for women devalue domestic work and workers" (2003, p. 502). Browne and Misra argue that domestic workers, who are almost always ethnic minorities, are constructed as Others who are unworthy of decent pay or good working conditions. The combination of race/ethnicity, gender, class, and citizenship status effectively puts domestic workers in a uniquely disadvantaged position. Domestic workers are often employed for extremely little pay and essentially on-call hours because of promises of support for sponsorship held out as enticement.

Finally, it is important to emphasize that *race* is itself a constructed category, which can reify the racism society seeks to eliminate. In other words, simply by identifying people using racial categories we support the idea that those categories have some basis in reality. Race, though, is not an objective category that can be measured; rather, it is a social construct that shifts in meaning according to historical period and social context. For example, many white ethnic groups have been identified as the racial Other, including the Irish when they immigrated to Canada in the nineteenth century. The guest essay by Tanya Titchkosky, author of a new text entitled *Reading and Writing Disability Differently: The Textured Life of Embodiment* (University of Toronto Press, 2007), explores the intersection of disability and race.

| BOX 7-1 | **Pausing at the Intersections of Difference** |

By Tanya Titchkosky

It was the late summer of 2005. I watched television coverage and read newspaper accounts about the poor and black people in the midst of the US gulf coast devastation that followed hurricane Katrina. Black people were being described as looters, white people as securing provisions; a white male senator said that the behaviour of the people of New Orleans is "shaming America," a white female *New York Times* writer spoke of the "United States of Shame" given the government's lethal lack of response (Dowd, *New York Times,* Sept. 3, 2005). I watched this human degradation unfold during a gentle summer in Eastern Canada. From the Scottish Highlands of rural Nova Scotia, I watched the CNN coverage; I watched in all my middle-class whiteness; I watched black, poor women and men suffering and dying in New Orleans.

In our attention to such matters, we find the making of the meaning of people. It is not just that we "all have our differences;" it is, instead, that we attend to difference differently, making them *intersect* in particular ways. One form of attention can lead to compelling news stories for some. Another form of attention leads to reviling trauma for others. Our identities are forged, in part, by how we attend to these intersecting differences. Between all our identifications, of both ourselves and of others, lies the possibility of uncovering how we constitute a

(Continued)

BOX 7-1	**Pausing at the Intersections of Difference** (*Continued*)

sense of the world. "Intersectionality," then, is a call to watch our watching, to read our readings, and to uncover a few of the ways we identify differences, including disability.

Responses to the storm represent identifications of disability—disabled people are present everywhere and disability is one thing cultural endeavors always bring into being. Many wheelchair users appear in the media coverage of Katrina; blankets draped over them, blanketing signs of gender and race but not of death. Through images and words, disabled people are depicted as stuck outside of the big sports dome or stuck inside some attic awaiting transfer to a habitable environment. These people are referred to as the "special needs" people, "the elderly, the infirmed, and the weak," or simply as "the vulnerable."

Vulnerable is a term that can allow blackness, poorness and disablement to intermingle as if these differences are merely individual fates. *Vulnerable* can be used so that people do not have to imagine how the intersections of some social differences are made to appear as if natural, like unwanted storms. But keeping close to the concept of intersectionality, we could ask what it means to interpret the intermingling of some social differences as "the vulnerable" and who is thus constituted as "the strong"? From this more social perspective, *vulnerable* can draw attention to daily life as it is tied up with collective ways of interpreting embodiment. A deep vulnerability lies in the ease with which we can forget that embodiment is always a mediated

social phenomenon. Embodiment appears through intersecting interests of self and other. During the aftermath of Katrina, it seems that people try to remember this; some say, "Just because they were vulnerable, doesn't mean they deserved to die." More than identity politics is at stake here, since people are never in their bodies alone.

Disability appears in other ways too. I read in the newspaper, "Why does this self-styled 'can do' president always lapse into such lame 'who could have known?' excuses." Or, " . . . they were deaf for so long to the horrific misery and cries for help of the victims in New Orleans–most of them poor and black" (Dowd, *ibid*). Blind to the levee issue, deaf to the anguished calls, lame in their responses, and needing to stand up and run with some courageous leadership. This disability discourse serves something other than the interests of disabled people. Disability is made viable as a metaphor to express only that which is unwanted and that which is devastatingly inept. What might be made of the intersection between disability as a taken-for-granted metaphor for "big problem" and disability as a blanketed dead body slumped in a wheelchair outside the sports dome?

It is provocative to think about how disability is both excluded *and* included simultaneously in the interstices of our lives. It is essential to think about how we do and do not notice these forms of exclusion *and* inclusion.[1] The different expressions of disability found in media accounts of Katrina demonstrate that the meaning of embodiment is made by

BOX 7-1	*(Continued)*

people. One meaning constituted today is that disability is the metaphor of choice to express problems while often disappearing from the social landscape as a form of human existence. The meaning of disability is composed of conflicts of inclusion and exclusion as this intersects with our ordinary ways of recognizing people . . . or not.

Attending to the talk about intersections of difference in our daily lives is a way to understand that we are active participants in making up the meaning of people. Differences are never merely noted since we always notice from a particular context and guided by interests. Noticing differences, we actually *produce* a depiction of storms and their aftermath; we note differences and make the story of what happened to and for other people. We perform the meaning of our embodied existence by the *way we narrate* the intersections of human diversity in the midst of which our bodies appear.

Disability is gendered, raced, and classed through everyday talk and disability also intersects with sexuality, ethnicity, age, family status, region and all other forms of difference. But disability has typically been left out of the politics and theorizing of gender, race, and class. Disability is not merely the Other to normalcy, but is rather an irreducible productive force, a kind of alterity to any interest we have developed to identity and difference. This means that everyday talk about disability can serve as a prime discursive field where the meaning of alterity under contemporary conditions can be considered. This is not just adding disability into the existing sense of legitimated differences. Instead, this is another way to think of new relations to alterity. In regards to feminist projects, Elizabeth Grosz (2003:22) puts the issue of alterity this way: " . . . how to think, write, or read *not* as a woman, but more complexly and less clearly, how to think, write and read otherwise . . . how to accommodate issues, qualities, concepts that have not had their time before."

How to notice, write or read disability otherwise than we ordinarily do will give new space to alterity and even rearrange the intersections through which we make embodiment appear. Interrogating the various appearances of disability with the critical concept of intersectionality allows for the possibility of pausing, noticing, reading and writing our selves otherwise. By analyzing how disability is made both present and absent in daily life, social theorists can begin to disrupt the seemingly natural conflation of disability with undesired vulnerability and ineptitude. In this way, perhaps embodied existence can be lived and imagined a little differently.

Reference

Grosz, Elizabeth, 2003. "Histories of the Present and Future: Feminism, Power, Bodies," in Jeffrey Jerome Cohen and Gail Weiss (eds). *Thinking the Limits of the Body.* New York: State University of New York Press. 13-24.

---

[1]For example, the inclusion of disability as the symbol of problem intersects with "normal expression," but it could be made to intersect with other identifications, other readings, other meanings.

UNDERSTANDING INTERSECTIONS: MEDICINE AS A CASE STUDY

Medicine is an excellent case study for exploring the ways that race, class, and gender intersect. Medicine historically has treated and continues to treat women and men differently. For example, nineteenth-century doctors routinely diagnosed women with "hysteria" and "treated" them by removing of their ovaries or clitoris, especially if those women appeared to be too educated or too sexual. In addition, women were robbed of their status as midwives when childbirth entered the realm of medicine. Midwifery became illegal, no longer a choice of women or practitioners, because the medicine of childbirth belonged to the male physician establishment. Moreover, in modern times, the medical establishment has designated far more boys than girls as ADHD and have used pharmaceuticals to "calm" them. Until very recently, people with mental or physical disabilities, primarily women, were sterilized to prevent them from reproducing. The medical literature also taught that people with disabilities were asexual and that gays and lesbians were "mentally ill," needing "treatment" in psychiatric wards.

Moreover, access to modern medicine has not been equal. In Canada, people of colour consistently receive poorer access to critical medical services than do whites, as do those from lower socio-economic classes, despite our universal healthcare system. As the social safety net is increasingly eroded in Canada, especially through the creation of a two-tiered medical system, this class- and colour-based disadvantage will be exacerbated.

Study 1: ADHD

Let's start with the example of **ADHD** (Attention Deficit Hyperactivity Disorder), which involves interesting intersections of notions about how children, especially male children, should behave. Often attached to the expectations about children are expectations about mothering and the ways mothers should respond to the ADHD child. This example considers a variety of facets of the ADHD phenomenon, the social construction of childhood, behavioural expectations for boys, the demands on women (particularly around the notion of the "good mother"), and the way these expectations intersect. Age, ability, gender, and class all play a role. When we think about behavioural expectations for boys—more aggressive, assertive, boisterous—and their socialization, it seems odd that we then drug them for those very behaviours.

Ilana Singh researches the intersection of the boy/mother relationship with ADHD. To contextualize, "seven percent of American children between ages six and eleven have been diagnosed with ADHD, [and] approximately 75 percent of these children are boys" (2004, p. 1193). Symptoms include hyperactivity, inattention, and impulsiveness, which we may argue are extremely vague for any sort of conclusive or accurate diagnosis. Moreover, by listing symptoms that are exhibited by the individual child, the social context in which he is situated is bypassed as a factor in his behaviour. In addition, interactional characteristics are framed in negative diagnostic terms situated within the child and not on his co-actors. Thus, family life and events, lack of challenge, new or difficult challenges at school, and reaction to life events all disappear or are muted by a medical/diagnostic approach.

In his critique of DSM IV-R (Diagnostic and Statistical Manual of Mental Disorders 4th Edition, Revised), Richard Mitchell (2003) argues that this widely used diagnostic tool is inadequate and indeed perhaps inappropriate for thinking about children's behaviours. He identifies its approach as *deficit labeling* and notes that it is based on wrong assumptions about children and young people and their development. This line of criticism argues against assigning ADHD diagnoses to young people (who, statistically, are primarily boys). Mitchell says "the whole notion that young people's most distressing behaviours may only be interpreted only as disordered seems untenable when examined critically. In fact, the DSM-IV R's 'common language' has been translated through use of deterministic theories that view young people as objects and not subjects, as non-competent rather than competent, and as adults-in-miniature rather than citizens in their own right" (2003, p. 284). Not only is diagnosis negative—a burden—and puts the young person into a rigid behavioural category, but it also fundamentally fails to see the child as a person with agency and rights. Mitchell points out that child development literature is developed by adults for adults for the purpose of ordering and controlling children's lives. The range of "normal" is not nearly inclusive enough. If we think about the architectural drabness of the average school classroom, combined with the relative rigidity of the one-size-fits-all programming of educational institutions, Mitchell's point becomes even clearer.

Moreover, Mitchell advocates an acceptance of the idea that "childhood" is a socially constructed phenomenon; and because it is such, we must think a bit more critically in our ideas about how children should or must act. With 20 years' experience as a psychiatric professional dealing with children, Mitchell states, "Through dialogue with young people regarding issues of poverty, gender, sexuality, ethnicity, power, and physical and sexual abuse, I came to look beyond ideas of pathology, beyond viewing children as adults-in-waiting or 'human becomings' rather than 'human beings'" (2003, p. 288). Mitchell doesn't deny the real pain endured by children (and their families) who are diagnosed with mental illness or mental disability, but advocates a more inclusive, less hierarchical approach to ADHD, as well as a healthy caution regarding its diagnosis. He proposes including young people themselves as collaborators in the diagnostic and treatment process. This is a point that bears repeating, because occasionally when we bring to the classroom a critical thinking approach to medicalization generally and ADHD specifically, there are inevitably students in the classroom who report that they have been diagnosed and treated for ADHD and who state that they are/were happy to be able to concentrate as a result of medication therapy. To be sure, ADHD can be real for some children; but its present overdiagnosis is a concern.

How does this process work in relation to the "good mother"? Dorothy Smith's work (1987, 1990, 2005) contributes to the foundation for our interpretive framework of this odd phenomenon. Smith explored the "mother work" of the educational system (1987), arguing that underlying the institution of school are many gendered assumptions about the sort of work women/mothers are doing and will do at home to support the educational process (for example, helping a child with homework and attending parent-teacher interviews). Schools play a key role in the diagnosis and monitoring of ADHD in boys, and mothers often (but not always) do the liaison work between school, child, and family. In research that supports Smith's arguments, Claudia Malacrida (2001) argues that ADHD is highly medicalized in Canada; but because teachers have few resources in terms of social control in the classroom, they are perhaps more willing to identify and encourage treatment than they might be if there existed alternative mechanisms for preserving the order necessary to create a good learning environment. She identifies the perceived root of the problem that is the starting point for change. "It is clear that, although the child's problems take place outside the home, the first assumption is that home life, rather than class-room practice or the child's capabilities, is at fault. The ADD/ADHD child's inability to rise to a standard of what is 'normal' in the classroom is seen by teachers as a reflection of a home life that is not 'normal'" (2001, p. 148).

Singh (2004) argues that the phenomenon of mother-blame means that women assume both blame for their sons' ADHD behaviour as well as responsibility for its treatment. In her research, which included in-depth interviews with mothers and fathers of ADHD-diagnosed sons, Singh found that women talked about being good mothers, which included self-blame as the inadequate mother. Fathers were largely absent from participation in the diagnostic process, as well as in the development of treatment strategies. This absence of fathers in the diagnostic process (and there were fathers in the households) exacerbated women's feelings of responsibility and self-blame. One of Singh's interviewees gives us an illustration of the co-parent and community intersection that reinforces women's tendency to self-blame. "I'd be in church with him and he just wouldn't sit still. He'd be fidgeting and I couldn't get him to stop at all, and people would just be turning around looking at me like why couldn't I do something about him. My husband is sitting right there too, but they're looking at me" (2004, p. 1200). Anna not only assumed blame, but also had to deal with the social pressure that fell on her as the mother, not on her husband as the father. Singh's findings mirror Smith's earlier research that shows that there is a gendered division of labour in the family. This division transcends the so-called private realm because women are expected to mediate between the family and the "public," according to institutional expectations that organize women's lives.

Smith's second contribution to understanding the ADHD phenomenon research comes from "K is Mentally Ill" (1990), in which she documents the ways in which K's behaviours are worked up by non-professionals to constitute or construct her mental illness. Teachers, parents (especially mothers), social workers, and eventually psychologists and physicians become part of the network of people who assess, diagnose, monitor, and medicate boys. As Leonard Green (2000) points out in his work, diagnostic decisions are often made in isolation, apart from context; but once identified, the case of the ADHD boy comes together in a seemingly seamless story that identifies him as deficient and in need of help.

The intersections in this example are complex. Youth and expectations of children combine with contradictory messages to boys about how they should be behave, which combine with expectations of mothers. Class divisions may exacerbate these disjunctures, and institutional demands also play a role in the working up of the ADHD child. As a result, the diagnostic process and critical intersections of the ADHD phenomenon become a pattern, one that reveals itself in other socio-medical phenomena.

Study 2: Eugenics

This second case study explores the intersection of gender, mental disability, class, ethnicity, and race in **eugenics**, or what we might term "unnatural selection." Mitchell and Snyder (2003) define eugenics as "the science of racial purification and the elimination of human 'defects'" (2003, p. 844). Eugenics policies can be large-scale and drastic (for example, the horrific strategies of the Nazis in Germany during the 1930s and 1940s, which had as their primary goal the murder of all Jews; and more recently, the ethnic "cleansing" in Rwanda). But the focus of this case study is the smaller-scale eugenics policies in Alberta between 1929 and 1972. Both large- and small-scale eugenics policies have in common the underlying notion of a binary division of human beings that posits one group as superior to the other. Also embedded in eugenics policies is the notion that human beings can control and enhance the dominant group by managing or eliminating "inferior" human beings.

Eugenics policies typically either directly or indirectly target marginalized groups in society—groups who are less able to resist or challenge institutional mechanisms. Women in particular have been targeted for involuntary sterilization in an attempt to keep them from reproducing. In the United States, the first systematic eugenics program targeted "feeble-minded" female paupers in the early 1900s. Other similar programs were almost inevitably based on class, gender, and racial stereotypes (Grekul, *et al.*, 2004). The logic of justification in eugenics policies was twofold. First, individuals assessed as inferior were told that the eugenics program was "for your own good," on the philosophy that these individuals might need to be offered at least a superficial explanation. Secondly, a broader project of societal engineering was seen as being sufficient reason to carry out the systematic involuntary sterilization of designated groups.

Grekul *et al.* have done an extensive examination of the Alberta eugenics program carried out by the Alberta Eugenics Board under the authority of the Sexual Sterilization Act. Only Alberta and British Columbia carried out such official programs.

Approximately 2800 people were sterilized on approval by the board between 1929 and 1972. Although consent to "treatment" was required, consent could be bypassed if the patient was deemed mentally incapable. Given that provincial mental hospitals referred the all of the candidates, it seems reasonable to infer that these institutions could "construct" mental incapacity as needed. Moreover, the Act provided that sterilization of inmates could occur if "the patient might safely be discharged if the danger of the procreation with its attendant risk of multiplication of evil by transmission of the disability to progeny were eliminated" (Grekul *et al.*, 2004, p. 363). Simply put, release could be possible only if the inmate were sterilized. Realistically, this must surely have opened the doors wide for coercive consent: that is, "give your consent to be sterilized and we'll authorize your release."

As Grekul *et al.* report, over its 44 years of sterilization decisions, the Alberta Eugenics Board approved or recommended the sterilization of 99 percent of the people whose files came before it. Moreover, because the Board heard an average of 13 cases per meeting, they spent a maximum of 13 minutes per file. Grekul *et al.* also found that women, First Nations people, teenagers, and young adults were more likely to be recommended for sterilization. They also found that "patient consent was required in only 17 percent of the Aboriginal cases, compared to 49 percent of Western European cases, [and] 38 percent of Anglo Saxon/Canadian patients" (2004, p. 367). In other words, the process was far more likely to discount Aboriginal agency and deem Aboriginals mentally incompetent and proceed with sterilization without even token consent.

You might ask what a historical example from Alberta has to do with our understanding of gender and intersectionality in today's society. Mitchell and Snyder have a rather pointed answer to this question. They argue that discrimination and eugenics regimes are linked, and that the latter are the root of policies related to the former, including "marriage restriction laws against people with cognitive disabilities, coerced sterilization, routine institutionalization, mandated segregation in schools, class-based communities of the homeless, sheltered workshops and farm colonies." People with disabilities are designated as "existing at the bottom rings of social ladders of being" (2003, p. 860).

The eugenics mentality of the last century is the foundation of the current idea that we can genetically "breed out" cancer and other potentially debilitating diseases. Genetic engineering is another version of eugenics. It raises the critical question: to what extent to we want to control human life? You might consider the ways that some reproductive technologies replicate ideas about eugenics, as well as the ways that genetic engineering and eugenics are different. There are not easy answers to this question, as is evidenced by the heated debate over stem cell research. The debates are also implicitly gendered, because women give birth; and thus their bodies are the locus of examination and intervention.

CONCLUSIONS

Intersectional thinking is challenging precisely because we must attend to several categories simultaneously. If we accept that those categories themselves are contingent, fluid, and socially constructed, then we can begin to see why such analyses are especially difficult. Ultimately, though, if we are to appreciate the complexity of gender, we must engage in analysis that leaves space for the messiness of social life and the ways that people participate in it. This approach does not advocate making one point of intersection more important or relevant than all others, but rather, it advocates exploring the ways in which intersections impact on gender and inequality.

CHAPTER SUMMARY: KEY POINTS

1. Considering the ways that gender intersects with other points of identity is critical to understanding the social construction of gender as well as understanding inequality.
2. Identity is fluid: we construct our identities in multiple ways at any given time, and they shift over our life course.
3. *Intersectional thinking* considers the ways in which gender is woven through other dimensions of domination.
4. Even those who think that they are not racist or sexist often employ those categories to frame their interactions with others.
5. Considering intersections means listening to the voices of those who experience these intersections.
6. Disability has often been left out of intersectional theorizing and politics.
7. Historical examples, such as the eugenics movement, help us to see more clearly contemporary intersections.
8. The medicalization of phenomena like ADHD impact on different intersectional points. For example, boys are affected differently than girls. But the addition of class and gender considerations adds a new dimension. Moreover, the work of mothers is different from the work of fathers in such situations.

DISCUSSION QUESTIONS

1. Think about all of the markers of your identity that you consider important. Then think about how they work in combination with gender. For example, does your religion prescribe gender-based roles?
2. How can we shift our thinking about equality from a *misery justice* model to a transformative model?
3. What is an important identity point in your community (for example, race or class)?
4. Can you think of times when intersectional thinking might not be effective or desirable?

KEY TERMS

ADHD	eugenics	misery justice
essentialism	intersectionality	race

Gender and Interaction

chapter eight

Doing Gender

Of the four dimensions of gender (individual, interactional, institutional, and socio-cultural), which one has the most significant impact on the shape of your experiences, choices, and relationships? This is a great examination question (in fact, one of the authors was asked this question at her PhD dissertation defence). The answer is *inter-action*. The socio-cultural macro structure is certainly important, influencing our beliefs and values as well as the parameters of our opportunities. But the shape of this gendered landscape becomes known to us through interaction. Similarly, while gender is an element of our identity, influencing our actions and expectations, we only learn to enact gender through interaction.

Section Two of this text explored the gendered experiences of individuals—the ways they learn about gender and the impact it has upon them. Everything from health to friendships to financial position is influenced by gender, not because gender is a per-manent facet of selfhood, but because it is an identity that influences all interactions with other people. This section discusses *doing gender* and considers interaction in relationships, sexualities, power, and conversation.

Our interaction patterns are shaped by our location in society. Think about the ways you communicate with someone who has more power than you (for example, a super-visor, employer, or professor). You are likely to be careful with your words, making an effort not to offend. When you are interacting with equals (for example, friends, a part-ner, or colleagues), you more likely feel freer to be casual, maybe even bluntly honest.

In a similar way, there is often an element of power implicit in communication patterns between women and men.

Virtually all interactions are influenced by gender—even when gender seems to be completely irrelevant to the exchange. Have you ever been in conversation with someone, either on the phone or in person, when you did not know whether that person was a woman or a man? Typically we find such situations problematic. We really want to know the gender of the other person, even when gender has no bearing on the interaction. I was once in a lengthy line-up at a post office, and the person helping the customers behind the counter was not easily identifiable as fitting into a particular gender category. The individual was wearing a uniform, had reasonably short, unstyled hair, wore no make-up and just a single earring, and had a moderate voice. Both the people in front and behind me in line began discussing the postal worker: man or woman? We were all wondering the same thing. But that person's sex is entirely unimportant to the selling of stamps and the mailing of parcels. Without even thinking about it, we take a person's gender into account when we communicate with them. When we don't know the gender of the person we are talking with, the interaction feels awkward and uncomfortable. This chapter explores the ways people do gender in social interaction.

DOING GENDER: DRAMATURGICAL ANALYSIS

One way to examine the connection between self and others is through **dramaturgical analysis**, a sociological tool developed by Erving Goffman (1959). Goffman used the analogy of the theatre to explore the ways people interact. Our status (in this case, gender) is like a part in a theatrical performance, and our role (in this case, gender role) is like a script. Goffman suggested that when we interact with others we are on **front stage**. We may be engaging in an activity called **impression management**: performing for those around us, showing them what we want them to see. When we are **backstage**, we no longer need to perform the public role. Thus, in my status as professor, I am on front stage when I am giving a lecture, or holding meetings during office hours. But I am backstage when I am not on campus. We all have many statuses (woman/man; queer/straight; young/old, as well as friend, co-worker, sister, or son) that have an impact on the roles we play and the impressions we strive to create.

As an illustrative example, think about what you look like when you roll out of bed in the morning. Now compare that to your appearance when you walk out the front door. In most cases, you will have spent some time grooming and clothing yourself to create the appropriate impression. If you didn't care about other people, you might not bother combing your hair, shaving, or applying make-up. In fact, if you lived in a warm climate, you might not even bother with clothes at all. But the opinions of others—both those in our immediate environment who may be shocked or disappointed by your ungroomed appearance, and those of the larger society, which has rules that you are compelled to follow (such as public nudity laws)—do matter. Some days, you spend more time on your appearance than on others. Why? Because you want others to gain a specific impression of you, so you work hard to present a particular image. When do you make an effort to "look your best"? When you are going to a job interview or out on the town with some of your friends? Very often, looking one's "best" involves following gendered expectations—shaving and wearing gender-specific clothes or carefully doing one's hair and make-up. We take care with our appearance because those around us expect it. Moreover, we may be trying to achieve a certain outcome—getting the job or meeting someone interesting. Backstage, we may wear comfortable clothes; but front stage, we wear clothing appropriate to the role we are trying to perform.

Yet dramaturgical analysis involves more than just appearance. Goffman outlines three components in the sociological drama we perform: one's setting (including props), one's appearance, and one's manner. He argues that we use props and mannerisms to enhance the impression we are trying to project. Because I am a professor, my props involve books, papers, and/or the remote control device for the projection equipment. The lecture hall setting is designed to support my performance as professor. Goffman uses the term **spoiled identity** to describe qualities that may be judged as disreputable or undesirable, sometimes referred to as a *social stigma*. A tactic of impression management, then, may involve hiding or minimizing a stigma. If I had a severe drug addiction, I might be identified as having a spoiled identity, which I would work to hide from my students, the department chair, and the university administration. Of course, there is wide variation in the appearance and manner of university professors. Some dress formally and others are more casual; some remain relatively aloof from their students while others are on a first name basis with them. But each professor is consciously or unconsciously adopting a style that works to create the desired impression.

In a similar manner, gender involves performance. People who wish to appear more feminine may wear make-up or high heels. Those choosing to "blend gender" may avoid any stereotypical signifiers (such as the person in the post office discussed above). In her study of Canadian female figure skaters, entitled "Passing as a Lady," Karen McGarry (2005) discusses the importance of image for success in this sport. McGarry's focus was on constructions of femininity and the intersections with race, class, and national identity, but she also outlined the elements involved in the creation of the "ladylike image." She notes that technical skating skill alone is not sufficient for success: these athletes must look the part. In Goffman's terms, they must engage in impression management. "One Canadian coach informed me that it was critical to ensure that her students 'pass as ladies'" (p. 1). Athletes who did not follow the ideal, even excellent skaters, were marginalized. A case in point is French skater Surya Bonaly, who had tremendous talent but did not receive high scores from the judges, who perceived her to be "aggressive" and "exotic." Impression management in skating involves all three of Goffman's elements. Female figure skaters need to present a non-aggressive, demure manner and pay great attention to appearance, including costume and make-up. The setting is managed via the music chosen to accompany the performance.

McGarry concluded that gender intersected with race to the advantage of some skaters and the disadvantage of others. As mentioned above, a skater's "exotic" appearance can harm her chance of winning (Bonaly is of African descent). But an ethnic appearance seems to be an advantage for Asian skaters. McGarry suggests that this is because Western society stereotypically associates Asian women with modesty and hyper-femininity, so it may be easier for them to create the ideal impression.

Of course, female figure skaters aren't the only athletes engaged in impression management. In her study of professional wrestling, Patrice Oppliger (2004) discusses the hyper-masculine image of many of these athletes and entertainers. She argues that wrestlers must carefully manage their "character," since their popularity and success are linked to image as much or more than their wrestling abilities. Male wrestlers must have bodies that are massive and chiseled; and they must wear costumes designed to enhance the impression they are trying to create. Costumes may involve boxing trunks with specific imagery (Val Venis has a suggestive phallic symbol on his shorts), capes, and masks. The manner of these athletes is especially important as they strive to retain audience support. Oppliger argues that there are specific wrestler character types, and wrestlers must maintain the mannerisms appropriate to their type whenever they are on front stage. The violent character type must appear to be brutal; the psychotic type must seem unpredictable and out of control; and the sexualized type is expected to engage in exaggerated sexual gestures (using "stripper" moves and "mooning" the audience). Interestingly, while the bulk of wrestlers are hyper-masculinized, there is a place for gender bending in this arena. Some wrestlers wear wigs or high heels or feather boas to create a "feminine" character type; however, they must be careful not to go too far:

> Feminization has what professional wrestling promoters crave: shock value. The trick is that while wrestlers are glamorous, they are careful not cross the line by playing their roles too feminine. These "glam" wrestlers do not act like stereotypical women . . . these characters have just enough feminine characteristics to get the crowd's attention and enough brutality so they will be accepted. (2004, p. 114)

Obviously, both the figure skaters and the wrestlers, as athletes and entertainers, undertake an exaggerated form of impression management in order to establish their statuses. They consciously strive to create impressions that will enhance their careers. And in each case, the desired and valued image is clearly gendered. Most people do not go to such extremes as they manage their impressions.

Canadian scholar Holly Devor (1989) studied people she identified as **gender blenders**. These included fifteen women who were regularly mistaken for men—some several times a month and others many times a day. Devor recognizes that most of us display *culturally defined insignia* indicating the gender category to which we belong. The people in her study rejected societal notions of femininity, though not their femaleness, and thus they presented themselves without these insignia. By refusing to adopt commonly recognized signifiers, they felt more comfortable with themselves, though regularly experienced frustration and the confusion of others during interaction with strangers. All three of Goffman's components contributed to their blending of gender. First, they avoided the "props" and appearance associated with femininity. They typically had very short hair and wore no make-up; they tended to dress in jeans and t-shirts or man-tailored shirts, with work boots, running shoes, or heel-less shoes; and they wore little jewelry. In addition, their mannerisms were also gender-neutral: they adopted ways of moving and sitting and nonverbal communication that were not feminine in style. In Devor's words, "My sense of them as a group was that their unfeminine mode of dress was only a small part of what made them appear more masculine than feminine. Their mannerisms, language, facial expressions, dress, and lack of feminine adornment all combined to convey a masculinity largely uncontradicted by any obvious femininity" (p. x).

The women in Devor's study could have chosen to manage their impressions and to work hard at employing more feminine signifiers, but they chose not to do so. When some of them tried to create a feminine impression, they found they were less comfortable. In fact, two women reported being mistaken for transvestites when they appeared in feminine clothing. To quote one of the women, "I'm not stupid. I could wear a skirt if I wanted to. I'd be uncomfortable, but I could force myself. I've done it for periods of my life . . . If you want to be part of a gang, you wear the appropriate costume. But the most important thing in my life is to be absolutely comfortable with myself" (p. 128). Devor describes the experiences of these women as they decided how to respond to being mistaken for men. Should they correct the error or let it pass? At times, this decision was quite painful, such as situations involving being asked for identification and then being challenged over its validity; or being challenged over their presence in women's public washrooms, occasionally experiencing rudeness and abuse from other women. In these situations, people treat them as though they have a spoiled identity. Not fitting in with expectations of femininity is considered a stigma by those who are uncomfortable with gender blenders. For this reason, the majority of these women chose rarely to correct wrong impressions, feeling that "passing for boys or men was the path of least resistance" (p. 123).

DOING GENDER: STATUS EXPECTATIONS THEORY

While we all engage in impression management, others interact with us based on their perception and assessment of our status and that impression. Status expectations theory furthers our understanding of this process.

As introduced in Chapter Three, **status expectations theory** maintains that society attributes statuses to individuals in a hierarchical manner. Some statuses are more highly valued than others. People judge those around them according to their perceived statuses. As Ridgeway and Bourg (2004) explain, "Status beliefs are widely shared cultural beliefs that inform people of the status relationships between one social group and another in their society . . . Status beliefs attach greater social significance and competence, as well as differing skills to persons in one category of social distinction" (p. 219). Previous chapters have already discussed how status expectations affect the assessment of job performance and career opportunities, as well as how these expectations can become self-fulfilling prophecies. However, our status as gendered beings is not limited simply to the two categories: *men* and *women*. We do gender in terms of several types of masculinities and femininities.

Hegemonic masculinity, by definition, is the version of masculinity which is afforded the highest status (see also Chapter Three). Thus, men are judged based on their compliance to this set of normative expectations. In his study of young men in western Canada, Kevin Davison (2000) found that gym classes were used by students to establish their status. His respondents, male adults who had participated in physical education programs during high school, all indicated that hegemonic masculinity was attributed to the "jocks." They felt that simply being a physically "normal" male wasn't enough: they had to actively *be* male, and this was typically accomplished through physical prowess. Davison says, "Boys and men must actively engage in hegemonic discourses of masculinities. One needs to both act masculine through speech and bodily gestures as well as physically embody masculinity through size, stature, and muscularity" (p. 258). Some of the boys did not feel that they had achieved hegemonic masculinity, but they were able to perform it in gym class by being "the fast guy" or the "extra competitive guy." Physical education enabled them to establish a desired status. Others who were measured and found wanting, though, were humiliated by both the other boys and the coaches. For example: "I used to dread every gym class because it acted to remind me continually that I did not fit into the masculine ideal. I was slim and unmuscular and was not good at sports. Along with the general competitive 'spirit' of PE, I remember gym class as an open struggle between boys" (p. 261). Gym class was described by some as a breeding ground for brutality and aggression, as boys struggled to "establish status" among the other boys. To avoid the humiliation of being labeled *geeks* or *gay*, they felt compelled to do gender in ways that were not comfortable. As Davison describes, "Learning to 'fit' into hegemonic masculinity, by definition, requires that young men accept and participate in homophobia, sexism, misogyny, and violence as everyday masculine practice"(p. 265). Davison concludes that the pressure to conform to the hegemonic ideal was an integral part of physical education, and his research suggests that it is harmful for many men.

In their review of the research in this area, Ridgeway and Bourg (2004) discuss the experiences of women who resist the status expectations. Certainly there are sound reasons for choosing to resist emphasized femininity, since it tends to focus attention on appearance and expressive relationships, rather than on economically productive activities. If women want to succeed in careers in the paid labour force, following expectations associated with emphasized femininity may be counterproductive: their skill and competence may not be recognized. At the same time, if they challenge these expectations and act knowledgeably and assertively, instead of deferentially, they might evoke a negative reaction. Competent, assertive women exhibit behaviour that "violates the essential hierarchical nature of status belief, and the competence assumptions that legitimate it. As a result, others react negatively and often dislike the assertive low-status person" (p. 231). Empirical research finds that assertive women are viewed as less trustworthy and less likeable than those who conform to status expectations. But there is a solution to this double bind: apparently women who act assertively but who also employ socio-emotional "softeners," so they appear co-operative and caring, can overcome the resistance of others. Ridgeway and Bourg conclude that while a woman can strive for success, she has to be sure to be perceived as both competent and nice in order to avoid resistance from others. This makes her challenge greater than that of an equally competent man; and, importantly, it confirms the original stereotype that women are more concerned with relationships and expressive activities than are men.

Men in "non-traditional" careers also experience challenges associated with status expectations. In their Nova Scotia study of men in nursing, Evans and Blye (2003) found that male nurses faced unique contradictions in gender status. On the one hand, they gained implicit advantages, sometimes called a **patriarchal dividend**, based on their status as men They were more likely to attain higher-prestige specialties and more administrative opportunities (the notion of the *glass escalator* is discussed in Chapter Twelve), as well as better treatment from the physicians than their female colleagues. On the other hand, because they performed "women's work," these nurses were also evaluated as less than masculine. They felt that their masculinity was always being questioned or challenged by other nurses, doctors, patients, and their friends and family because they were doing feminine work—caring for others. They reported having patients suggest they were nurses because they weren't smart enough to be doctors and having other men "laugh in their faces" when they revealed that their profession was nursing. In essence, some people considered a nursing career for a male as a spoiled identity. To address this concern, the men talked about ways in which they reaffirmed their masculinity. They engaged in impression management in a variety of ways to reinforce their status as men: for example, by intervening in situations with violent patients and doing "muscle work" when it was required. They also worked hard at avoiding other behaviours considered to be feminine. One of the men in their study stated, "There are things that I don't do—talk in a womanly manner, not too soft unless it's a person in a lot of distress who really needs reassurance. I conduct myself as a man. I talk to my male patients about manly things they do—manly things" (p. 281).

In addition to being challenged for failing to live up to the status expectations of men, these nurses faced an additional obstacle. Drawing on another study published by Evans (2002) that focused on the sexualization of nurses' touching, Evans and Blye state, "The problem of a 'spoiled identity' for men nurses is compounded by the stereotype that men are sexual aggressors, and in the case of gay men, sexual deviants" (p. 281). Nurses need to touch their patients, sometimes intimately, to provide professional care. This is seen as a logical extension of women's caring work, but it is judged differently when the nurse is a man. "Men's touch is surrounded with suspicion—suspicion that implies men's motives for touching are not comfort- or care-oriented, but sexual in nature" (2003, p. 281). The nurses describe how careful they are to engage in practices that reduce the likelihood of being accused of inappropriate touching, sometimes by moving into administrative roles. In essence, the suspicion associated with men who don't comply with status expectations reduced their ability to engage in caring work. The contradictions between their supposedly feminine profession and the status expectations associated with being men must be negotiated by each nurse. They know they are challenging status expectations when they choose this particular career. As one of the nurses explained, "You decide for yourself that you either don't care what people think or that you can live with it" (p. 289).

Obviously, the gender-blending women in Devor's study also challenge status expectations. By choosing not to present themselves as feminine women and not to manage their impressions according to cultural expectations, their actual status *as women* was not easily recognizable to strangers. While some of them felt that the problems they experienced were the result of other peoples' lack of observational skill and/or narrow perceptions of womanhood, other women took issue with societal notions of femininity. They felt that being feminine was defined much too rigidly and that they were responding rationally to its oppressive requirements. Most importantly, "All of these women found that their ambiguous gender status gave them certain privileges and freedoms which are normally available to men in their society. In the final analysis, each of them had decided that she was willing to pay a price to gain those freedoms and privileges" (p. 126).

Ridgeway and Bourg (2004) suggest that there are ways to counter the effects of status expectations. In the short term, disrupting the sex-based categories, as men who are nurses and gender-blending women are doing, challenges the legitimacy of these status expectations. Encountering people who don't fit our expectations may lead some of us to devalue the status resistor (as evidenced by the rudeness experienced by both the women and the men). But others reconsider their expectations and assessments when they interact with gender resistors. "Individuals carry status and expectation information gained in one interaction into subsequent ones . . . over time, such iterative pressures on people's performance expectations for individual men and women will put growing pressure on competence assumptions embedded in gender status beliefs and reduce the size of the implied gender difference" (pp. 235–36).

DOING GENDER: TWO WORLDS APPROACH

A third explanation of gender difference, currently known as the **two worlds approach**, suggests that the ways people do gender result from socialization and unchangeable biological difference. In essence, this approach revives the old argument that gender is a stable property of one's identity. As shown in earlier chapters, this position has been challenged and critiqued; but it still is worthy of review because so many people, both scholars and laypersons, accept it as legitimate.

The two worlds approach suggests that women and men do gender differently because we are, in fact, different. Difference is not simply a case of gender performance and/or living up to expectations; nor is it even a case of overwhelming physiological sex-based differences. Our ways of interacting differ because we have been socialized to fit into one of two gendered *worlds*. A popular version of this theory is espoused by John Gray (1992) in his bestselling book *Men Are from Mars, Women Are from Venus*:

> Men and women differ in all areas of their lives. Not only do women and men communicate differently but they think, feel, perceive, react, respond, love, need and appreciate differently. They almost seem to be from separate planets. (p. 5)

While the validity of a popularized self-help book is always questionable, media personalities aren't the only ones disseminating the two worlds argument. Scholarly studies have resulted in similar conclusions: "It is clear that men and women do come from different cultures, the crucial difference between those cultures is that men come from a culture that emphasizes status and power, whereas women come from a culture that emphasizes relative closeness" (Noller, 1993, p. 148). Moreover, in their review of research and teaching practices, Borisoff and Hahn (1995) found that, more and more, universities are teaching this two worlds approach as if it were a proven theory. A collection of essays edited by Daniel Canary and Kathryn Dindia (1998) explores and debates this issue of gender similarity and difference in interaction. The discussion that follows considers many of the arguments raised in Canary and Dindia's collection.

Certainly, there is ample evidence in the research literature that could support the conclusion that the genders are vastly different in the ways they interact. The following list briefly summarizes some of the findings:

- Among children and adolescents, boys interrupt more and make stronger assertions and judgments than do girls.
- Men prefer shared activities to express intimacy, while women are more likely to base friendships on communication and intimate disclosures.
- Men are less perceptive of non-verbal cues than are women.
- Women enjoy discussing the quality of relationships more than do men.
- Caring activities are more likely to be undertaken by women then men.

(summarized by Wood & Dindia, 1998, p. 20)

- Women tend to be more sensitive and emotionally expressive, while men are more instrumental.
- Women are more likely to ask about upsetting situations and provide emotional support.
- Men are less likely to seek support or to value support-giving skills.

(summarized by Kunkel & Burleson, 1998, p. 101)

This list, however, leaves unanswered the fundamental questions at the heart of this text and this area of study. 1) Are these gender differences real? Are most women and men polarized at the far ends of a spectrum as opposite sexes? Or do most fall within the central part of the normal curve with characteristics shared with the other sex? 2) Are most differences real or perceived? That is, are they inherent and immutable, or are they created?

Gender socialization (see Chapter Five) may have contributed to some of these patterns. Moreover, the social world is gendered through normative expectations, language, media, and culture (see Chapters Two, Three and Four), which could further contribute to these differences. However, not all researchers accept that such social conditions create separate gendered worlds. There is a significant difference between choosing to perform gender because of the constraints of social context and becoming the citizen of a planet or culture based on specific prescribed patterns. Many sociologists believe that the argument that gender socialization creates separate and complete cultures is problematic because it is as deterministic as the "biological differences" explanation. As far back as 1961, Wrong challenged the notion that socialization is all-powerful in determining behaviour in his now-classic argument "The Oversocialized Conception of Man in Modern Society" (written during a time when the masculine generic reigned). However, in addition to dismissing the contribution of socialization, the two worlds approach also ignores issues of power that recreate differential opportunities for women and men and influence their behaviours within situational contexts (see Chapter Ten). Moreover, it seems to confuse correlation and causality (see Chapter Two). If the sexes often act differently, does this prove that the sexes are intrinsically different? Or are there alternative explanations? Quite simply, "Human life does not simply divide into two realms, nor does human character divide into two types. Our images of gender are often dichotomous, but the reality is not" (Connell, 2002, p. 8).

Elizabeth Aries (1998) documents a series of concerns that cast doubt on the legitimacy of the two worlds approach. She focuses specifically on empirical research design issues to challenge the findings.

First, Aries considers the samples used to study these gender patterns. A preponderance of the people studied were white, middle-class Americans. In general, if one particular group exhibits a certain pattern of behaviour, this is not a sufficient reason to assume that other groups will behave the same way. Thus, one cannot conclude that poor, upper-class, or non-white people would behave like middle-class whites in similar situations. Aries notes that contrasting research has compared and assessed behaviour differences by gender and by minority group status. Those findings suggest that communication styles and behaviour patterns vary by race. She concludes that if similar gender research also considered class and sexual orientation, it would likely reveal still more different patterns. Thus, the two worlds research fails to examine a broad enough sample of people and then fails to consider the impact of non-gender factors on behaviour.

Second, Aries questions the magnitude of the measured differences in the two worlds research. As discussed in Chapter Two, statistical significance means only that findings about a sample are likely to be reflective of the larger population: it does not measure the *size* or *social importance* of a relationship. So while there are measured differences, the research does not assess the relevance of those differences. Aries points out that the two worlds research also tends to minimize or ignore the overlap between groups, instead treating the difference as the central finding. It then interprets any significant difference as an *explanatory* difference, even when the actual magnitude of the difference is minimal. Thus, their interpretation of the statistical findings is questionable.

Aries gives two examples that illustrate the problem. First, in one study of interruption patterns during conversation, the researchers found that men interrupted more than women—a fact often reported. But sex of speaker only accounted for 7 percent of the observed pattern in that study, while speaking time accounted for 63 percent. In other words, men may have tended to interrupt more because they tended to talk more. (Note that in statistical analyses, it is possible to partition the variance. That is, you can determine how influential each of a series of variables is for explaining a relationship, as well as the portion unexplained by the variables measured. In this example, gender differences explained less than 10 percent of the pattern.) Clearly, all the dynamics of the conversation need to be considered before attributing behaviour to the sex of the speaker.

Aries' second example examines a meta-analysis of self-disclosure studies (how much people are willing to tell about themselves) showing that women disclose more about themselves than men. But there was a large degree of overlap between the two groups (over 85 percent), and the variance explained by sex was only 1 percent! That means that about 99 percent of the differences in disclosure patterns were caused by something other than the individual's sex. However, because the findings of difference were usually statistically significant (albeit tiny), they were reported as evidence of gender difference. (The ways in which statistical significance can be used to create misimpressions is considered in Chapter Two.) Aries also notes that while many gender studies do find gender differences in behaviour, many don't. Perhaps not surprisingly, these latter studies are less likely to be published.

A third problem with the two worlds research is its lack of consideration of alternative explanations. Aries describes one study that illustrates the problem. While men are more likely than women to show dominance and leadership in mixed-sex groups, "when status is controlled for, sex differences are diminished" (p. 72). In essence, differences attributed to the sex of the people involved are actually a function of the people's status. If women are more likely to be in subordinate positions (such as lower-prestige jobs), their lack of dominance and leadership is related to their lack of power, rather than the fact that they are women. In addition, qualities associated with women, such as politeness and sensitivity, appear to be a function of power rather than sex. "In two studies of interaction in dyads in which one person was the leader and the other the follower, subordinates showed more sensitivity to the way the leader felt about them than the leader showed to the subordinate's feeling; but there were no gender differences" (p. 72). A study by Risman (1987) compared the behaviours of mothers and fathers. As Aries summarizes, "The behavior of men who were single fathers and had primary responsibility for the care of young children was more similar to the behavior of working or single mothers than it was to married fathers" (p. 73). Thus, perhaps status and power, rather than sex, places men and women in separate worlds.

For these reasons, Aries argues that the research community has overstated claims of gender difference, ignoring design flaws and other significant variables. They have reified notions of gender difference into the two worlds theory. Their approach also marks a return to the "stable identity" model that treats gender as a dichotomy and oversimplifies real behaviour. More importantly, Aries concludes, "[this] construction of polarized conceptions of men and women in interaction helps sustain current realities and keep inequalities in place" (p. 77).

DOING GENDER: FRIENDSHIPS

We all know what friendship is, but it can still be tricky to define. In part this is because many of us have a variety of friends and diverse relationships with them. Chances are that you have friends with whom you like to spend time simply having fun; other friends that you call upon when you need advice or assistance; and friends who rely on you for emotional or practical support. A formal definition of friendship might sound something like this:

> Voluntary interdependence between two persons over time, that is intended to facilitate socio-emotional goals of the participants, and may involve varying types and degrees of companion-ship, intimacy, affection, and mutual assistance. (Hays, 1988, p. 395)

Friendships differ from other relationships because they are entirely voluntary. If your friend lets you down, you have the option of ending the relationship relatively easily, certainly more readily than you could with a work colleague or a family member. Moreover, most friendships are reasonably egalitarian in the sense that the parties typically have similar degrees of power: one person doesn't always control the activities and the interactions. In contrast, relationships in families and workplaces are often more hierarchical, with people more frequently occupying either a dominant or subordinate position. While both friendships and romantic partnerships are likely to have the qualities listed in the definition above—companionship, intimacy, affection, and mutual assistance—romantic relationships differ from friendships because they involve passion and a higher degree of emotional and practical support (Fehr, 1996).

Certain qualities are normally absent in friendships, such as competitiveness, hostility, inequality, task-orientation, and formality. Friends serve a valuable purpose in life, each appearing to need to connect with the other. Those who study human relationships suggest that "human beings have a pervasive drive to form and maintain at least a minimum quantity of lasting, positive, and significant interpersonal relationships" (Beaumeister & Leary, 1995, p. 497). Whether we define friendship formation as a "drive" or not, a wide range of research supports the notion that friendship is important, in part because it provides love and esteem, as well as stimulation and support (see Fehr, 1996).

Friendships are also influenced by gender. People are likely to have more same-sex friends than cross-sex friends. In addition, a significant body of research suggests that friendships among men are qualitatively different from friendships among women. When we ask our students about this observation, many of them agree that it is true. Women may talk on the phone for hours while men may be more inclined to do something active when interacting with their friends. Women are more physically affectionate with their friends, and men are more likely to tease and joke. In her review of the research literature, Fehr (1996) highlights specific gendered patterns in friendship:

- Women spend more time interacting with friends than do men.
- Men are indeed more likely to engage in activities and women are more inclined to conversation.
- Men are more likely to talk about sports, work, and cars, while women are more likely to discuss relationships and problems.
- Women provide and receive more social support than men.

Wright (1982) coined the phrases **side-by-side** and **face-to-face** relationships to describe the different patterns noted above. Others have observed these patterns and described women as **relationship experts** and men as having **deficit relationships** (see Wood, 1999 for a detailed discussion of these terms). As relationship experts, women are perceived to have more intimate relationships with their friends, including discussions of the dynamics of the relationship itself. This perception of women reflects the basic normative expectations for femininity—that women are nurturing and empathetic. Certainly when we ask our students, they agree that women's friendships do reflect these qualities. Meanwhile, the deficit relationship concept suggests that men are less interested in or unable to disclose emotions or reveal personal information.

These notions warrant closer examination for two reasons. First, they represent an **agentic-communal dichotomy**, suggesting that men are more agentic (focused on action) while women are more communal (nurturing and expressive). If this dichotomy exists, we would see more male friendships at the agentic end of the spectrum and more female friendships at the communal end. But even Paul Wright, the scholar who initially coined the phrases *face-to-face* and *side-by-side* relationships, has since challenged this perception. He reviewed the existing literature and started to question the conclusions about strong sex differences in friendships, simply because the empirical research actually revealed a great deal of similarity.

Wright explored agentic-communal patterns using a new approach. Instead of measuring concepts on a single continuum, where a high agency score by definition necessarily resulted in a low communal score, Wright untied these two qualities and measured them separately. Instead of asking, "Are you more agentic *or* more communal?" he asked two questions: "How agentic are you?" *and "*How communal are you?" This reframing of the questions circumvented the either/or problem. In fact, Wright points out that assumptions about the either/or nature of agentic and communal traits has led researchers to measure only one set of variables. If that set scored highly (*i.e.,* the friendship was agentic), the researchers stopped asking questions (logically, if there is polarization, once the friendship is *one* thing, it cannot be the other) and did not even measure the "opposite" variable (Wright, 1998). However, when Wright measured the same traits using his non-polarized questions, he found an unexpected result. Women's friendships were no less agentic than men's friendships, though they did differ on communal values, That is, the sexes "did not differ in the degree to which they regarded their same-sex friends as providing concrete, practical forms of cooperation and assistance (utility value) or as being a source of new ideas, activities, and ways of doing things (stimulation value)" (p. 49). When actually asked how they valued different aspects of their friendships, both women and men rated *talk* as the most valuable form of interaction, and *working on a task* was ranked second (Duck & Wright, 1993). Thus, the agentic-communal dichotomy is not a dichotomy at all.

Second, the accepted notions of "expertise" and "deficiency" are inadequate for fully comprehending gender and friendship. One of the inherent problems with identifying women as relationship *experts* (beyond the basic question whether this notion is accurate) is that it can lead people to assume that women's relationships with one another are or should be expressive. But not all women's friendships are intimate or expressive. In fact, feminine norms contribute to communication problems between women when dealing with issues such as competition or envy (Eichenbaum & Orbach, 1987). Women certainly feel emotions related to competition and envy, but normative expectations prohibit their expression. In fact, patterns of relational aggression among girls may stem from their reluctance to express negative emotions. Direct disapproval, anger, and aggression are outside the normative expectations for girls and women; consequently, other tactics, such as gossip and ostracism, may be used to replace them (Whitesell & Harter, 1996). Moreover, these notions of feminine friendships might also stand in the way of honesty. Expectations of nurturing kindness may cause difficulties for a woman who wants to tell a friend that she is making a mistake or that she needs to stop complaining. As Fillion describes:

> Because friends reveal weaknesses and vulnerabilities to each other, and because women are expected to reassure, nurture, and agree with each other . . . sometimes we tell harmless lies to spare friends' feelings . . . this may make the friend feel better in the short term, but it doesn't help to extricate her from a bad situation or break a chronic pattern. (1996, p. 29)

In her thorough discussion of the research exploring women's lives and behaviours, Carol Tavris (1992) argues that there is a price to be paid for sharing deeply felt concerns with friends. "It leads many women to rehearse their problems and constantly brood about them, rather than learning to distract themselves or take action to solve them. Some women come to believe that talking *is* doing something, and that talking is enough" (1992, p. 268). So, while women's friendships have been characterized as face-to-face and emotionally supportive, they don't always reflect this idealization.

Men's friendships, on the other hand, are called *deficit* relationships. But alternative explanations suggest that male friendship patterns are not dysfunctional. Sattel (1976) suggests that masculine inexpressiveness does not necessarily indicate a *lack* of intimacy. Instead, he argues, it can be valuable tool for managing relationships. If you refuse to enter into a discussion about subjects you don't wish to talk about, you control the parameters of the relationship. In addition, you can use silence to put a friend in the position of having to exert greater effort to maintain the relationship. A further challenge to the deficit model is the non-objectivity of the measurement standards. How did we come to define intimacy and disclosure as the measure of a relationship? In her discussion of this issue, Francesca Cancian (1989) argues that the separation of home and work during the Industrial Revolution led to differential behaviours and expectations for women and men. Because women were home looking after the family, their emotional/caring work came to be understood as *love*, and men's practical labour to provide financially for the family was regarded as *work*. This **feminization of love** devalues the contributions of both men and women, since women's activities were not seen as work and men were not seen as loving. Cancian argues that this standard is still in place, misrepresenting masculine patterns and ultimately creating the notion of deficiency.

Scott Swain (1989) argues that the differential patterns of friendship are outcomes of socialization. He accepts the two worlds approach as he refers specifically to the "separate worlds of boys and girls" to explain the patterns. But he does not accept the notion that masculine styles are deficient. Rather than using the "feminized" measurement of self-disclosure to measure intimacy, he advocates focusing on "behaviour in the context of friendship that connotes a positive and mutual sense of meaning and importance to the participants" (p. 72). In other words, if men aren't interested in self-disclosure, we should measure intimacy by another standard. Swain's research involved two surveys measuring activities and their importance in same-sex friendships among men (samples of 232 and 104 respondents, respectively). Then he conducted in-depth interviews with 20 college students (15 men and 5 women) to further explore the relationships. Swain concluded that men have deeply meaningful relationships, but their intimacy is expressed through action rather than words. "Meaningful times involved the shared enjoyment of learning and mastering skills . . . the essential ingredients in these experiences seem to be comfort with a competitive challenge and a shared sense of accomplishment" (p. 76). Even joking and shared laughter are means for expressing closeness and acceptance. Swain describes the concept as **covert intimacy**. "Men implicitly demonstrate closeness without directly verbalizing the relationship" (p. 79). Because there are perceived restrictions on men expressing emotions such as sadness or fear, and because societal homophobia may keep them from physically demonstrating affection, men are less likely to engage in such discussions and actions. This physical distancing leads researchers to regard their friendship relationships as deficient. But Swain points out that "these limitations of male intimacy may distance men from all but their closest friends, and may also create a premium on privacy and trust in close relationships" (p. 84). Thus, men are not inexpressive; they just do intimacy differently.

These popular notions about friendship show that social researchers must always critically evaluate their definitions and assumptions. If something is defined as deficient, we may be more likely to notice its flaws than to challenge the definitions. Swain's research compels us to rethink our notions of intimacy among men. Conversely, by labeling women as relationship experts we may fail to consider the negative ramifications of feminine normative expectations for friendships.

What, then, do we know about men's and women's friendships? Walker (2004) found that the male/female-polarized stereotypes are "more accurately viewed as cultural ideologies than as observable gender differences" (p. 403). When she asked the people in her study to describe their friendships, the stereotypical patterns did emerge: women like to talk and share, while men like to do things together. But when she asked them specific questions about their actual friendships and their most recent contact with their friends, a different picture emerged: *men talked and women did things together.* In fact, 75 percent of the men had participated in *non-gendered behaviours* (a term Walker uses to describe activities associated with the other sex) with their friends: for example, shopping and disclosing feelings. To illustrate, Walker provides detail about one man's experience. He talked about friends going through divorce and the way he listened to their concerns and feelings. He also talked about "friends who helped him through his divorce, men who allowed him to 'ventilate.' This man repeatedly told me that he was very emotive and expressive and that he complained a lot to his friends" (p. 406). But later in the interview, this same man stressed that he and his friends usually discussed sports and that he wished he could be more open. The contradiction was obvious: he knew how men were "supposed to be" and worked to create the impression that he followed that ideal. (Still later in the interview he mentioned that he didn't much care for sports.) The same contradiction was evident in the women's friendships. While the women spoke of their emotional connection to their friends, Walker found that 65 percent of the women reported engaging in non-gendered behaviours: for example, playing sports or exercising together. Twenty-five percent of these women "reported that they considered certain information private and would not discuss it with friends" (p. 408). For example, they would not discuss relationships. She found that women in professional occupations were less likely to have intimate relationships: they were more mobile and had less time, and they faced competition among their colleagues at work. These findings suggest a structural component to the male/female patterns of friendship, rather than a gendered explanation. In other words, professional men face friendship challenges similar to those of professional women. In contrast, Walker found that working-class men were less mobile and more likely to have "old friends" from school or from their neighbourhood, with whom they shared intimate discussions. These findings suggest that gender is not the most salient variable for explaining friendship patterns.

In their research on gender patterns in friendship, Kunkel and Burleson (1998) assessed several hypotheses designed to measure intimacy through social support and comforting behaviour (effectively helping someone in distress). Their research revealed strong similarities between women and men, who are

> quite similar in the criteria, preferences, values, and patterns of interpersonal liking. Both men and women view highly person-centered comforting messages as most sensitive and effective . . . Both sexes viewed comforting skills as important in the context of various personal relationships and as substantially more important than instrumentally focused communication skills. (p. 116)

While Kunkel and Burleson did find some statistically significant differences between women and men, these differences accounted for less than 5 percent of the overall pattern, meaning that 95 percent of the patterns they measured were not explained by gender.

Wright (1998) also looks more deeply into this social context for an explanation of the measured differences. His research reveals that some differences in same-sex friendships do exist, but that in general, very similar interactions and experiences occur. The *embedded differences* indicate that on average women do tend to be more expressive than men in their relationships. But he raises the possibility that structural variables, rather than an inherent lack of desire to achieve them, make it more difficult for men to maintain such friendships. Because friendships are not obligatory, because they require ongoing contact, and because we can limit our interactions when other activities demand our attention, it may be harder for some people to maintain those relationships. "The greater number of roles one adopts and the more effort one expends on them, the less time and energy one has to devote to any friendships" (p. 59). Because adolescents and older adults have fewer demands from competing roles than adults in the midst of careers and child-rearing years, they typically have more time to devote to friendship interaction. Those with demanding careers (historically, a pattern more often associated with men than women) have less opportunity to invest time into friendships. While those whose primary focus is home and children (more often women) are certainly busy, there is a degree of flexibility to their work that may allow more opportunity for friendships. Those who juggle both work and family commitments (see Chapter Eleven) may have very little opportunity at all for friendships. Thus, structural variables can influence the quantity and type of friendships one has.

The work of Walker, Kunkel and Burleson, and Wright does not prove that gender differences in friendship patterns don't exist; in fact, they did find gendered patterns. But it supports the position that such differences are not pervasive, nor even sufficient for explaining the measured patterns. Other factors, such as social class, mobility, age, occupation and other social roles, also shape friendships.

CONCLUSION

This chapter considered both gender at the individual level and *doing gender* through interactions with others, set against the socio-cultural backdrop discussed in Section One. The primary theories and explanations for why we *do gender* in our interactions with others show wide variation. Research into friendships among those of the same sex shows that people know how they are "supposed" to act in a way appropriate to their gender and that these gender expectations can limit and define the nature of friendships. However, preconceived notions of femininity and masculinity can bias researchers and the general public toward seeing gendered patterns in friendships when they are not there or when they are not significant factors.

CHAPTER SUMMARY: KEY POINTS

1. Interaction plays an influential role in the gendering of society. Our socio-cultural landscape evolves through the interaction between individuals. Individuals also gain a sense of themselves as gendered beings through interaction.

2. *Dramaturgical analysis* uses a theatrical analogy to help explain how people *do gender*. People seek to manage the impression they create while on front stage, before the audience; and they may behave quite differently when they are backstage, where they are unobserved.

3. Both female figure skaters and male wrestlers carefully manage the impressions they create for the audience to enhance their careers. In both cases, these athletes/entertainers highlight gender-based qualities (beauty and brute strength, for example) using appearance, mannerisms, and props.

4. *Gender blenders* choose not to manage their impressions according to societal expectations. Rather than adopting a more feminine appearance of mannerisms, female gender blenders forgo gender signifiers and are frequently mistaken for men.

5. *Status expectations theory* suggests that people judge the behaviours of others according to gender-based normative expectations. These expectations also influence self-assessments.

6. People who challenge or resist status expectations—for example, assertive women, men who are nurses, or gender blenders—are often judged harshly by society. But their actions contribute the gradual breakdown of polarized expectations.

7. The *two worlds approach* to explaining gender patterns suggests that gender-based socialization is so polarizing that the sexes are actually members of different cultures. This notion and the research upon which it is based have been challenged as overly deterministic and flawed.

8. Same-sex friendships between women have been described as more intimate and supportive than those between men. In fact, women have been called *relationship experts* while men's friendships have been characterized as deficient.

9. Conceptions, definitions, and measurements of intimacy have tended to valorize one kind of interaction, blinding researchers to the merits of other patterns. The *feminization of love* and patterns of *covert intimacy* have supported notions of male inexpressiveness.

10. Empirical research suggests that while some differences exist, women's and men's friendships are much more similar than different. Both women and men engage in friendships based on activity and emotional and practical support.

DISCUSSION QUESTIONS

1. How do you manage your impression? Do you conform to gender-based status expectations or challenge them? Under what circumstances? How do your friends and family react if/when you present an image that does not reflect hegemonic/emphasized patterns? Think about how much flexibility or rigidity there is in your social milieu. Are the expectations at work different from school and family?

2. This chapter uses the gender performances of people from sports and entertainment fields to illustrate dramaturgical analysis. Use an example from your own social world and identify examples of all the key concepts (appearance, props, setting, mannerisms, front stage, backstage).

3. Assess the evidence of the two worlds approach to explaining gendered interaction patterns. Do you find it compelling or do you think other explanations provide more insight?

4. Many students, both male and female, believe that it's easier to be friends with males than with females. And yet the research suggests that women are the relationship experts. Can you explain what factors might contribute to this impression? Assess your own friendships. Do they follow the typical gender pattern described in the two worlds approach or not? Does the dynamic of the relationship depend on the qualities of the friend?

5. Do you think covert intimacy is equivalent to expressive intimacy? Which type of intimacy do you prefer? What do you think shapes your preference?

KEY TERMS

covert intimacy	front stage/backstage	side-by-side relationships
deficit relationships	gender blenders	spoiled identity
dramaturgical analysis	impression management	status expectations theory
face-to-face relationships	patriarchal dividend	two worlds approach
feminization of love	relationship experts	

Sexualities

What are the sexual scripts we adhere to? You might be thinking, "None, I do what I want." Yet our culture is imbued with notions, values, and mores about **sex**, **sexuality**, and sexual activity. *Sex* refers to biological characteristics of males and females, including the presence of ovaries or testes and external genitalia; whereas *sexuality* refers to sexual expression, including norms, identity, and performance. These ideas interact with race, age, gender, and ethnicity. Premarital sex, sex during menstruation, sexual positions, and sexual stamina are all subject to *scripts*; so is the purpose of sex (procreation, recreation, within a relationship, or casual) and the type of person one has sex with. Sadomasochism (S&M), swinging, and transvestite behaviours are also part of the sexuality scripts.

Our guess is that no matter how freely you think you are choosing, you are bound by some social scripts about sex and sexuality. Scripts include definitions of appropriate sexuality as well as roles within sexual encounters or sexual interaction. While we may think that sexual desire is somehow inherent or natural, it too is socially constructed and scripted to be simply biological. For example, in some cultures, the sight of women's ankles is considered erotically stimulating, whereas in North America, breasts are a popular object of erotic fixation, especially for heterosexual men. But there is nothing inherently sexual or erotic about particular body parts. These triggers of desire are socially constructed.

What is the relationship between sexuality and gender? So far, most of the emphasis in this book has been placed on *gender*, with only some consideration of issues of sexuality. In short, the two are related, yet distinct—intertwined, yet different. Arlene Stein (2004) talks about how she has shifted from "lumping" gender and sexuality together in her teaching practices to separating them, then back to lumping them again. She describes the challenges posed by such categories, which (citing Jeffrey Weeks) she describes as *necessary fiction*. Stein argues that although gender and sexuality are arbitrary categories, they are also cognitive categories that define and shape the world and the way we see it. "As categories, they are fundamentally limiting, but we cannot live without them. As queer educators, we have been marginalized on the basis of these categories, we have a particular investment in challenging hegemonic conceptions. Yet our perspectives, much like the ones we imagine ourselves opposed to, are always partial and incomplete, embedded in our own time, place and biographies. Our challenge is to recognize how these categories shape our understandings of the world, while doing our utmost to seize control of the means of reproduction" (2004, p. 257).

Definitions of *sex*, *sexuality*, and *gender* are not as straightforward as we might think (or hope). Stein believes that the delineation of these categories shifts as we continue to think about them and problematize them. Judith Butler considers these terms to be *performative*, meaning that they are transitory and socially constructed. She says, "Gender is not exactly what one 'is' nor is it precisely what one 'has.' Gender is the apparatus by which the production and normalization of masculine and feminine takes place along with the interstitial forms of hormonal, chromosomal, psychic and performative that gender assumes" (2004, p. 42). Definitions are further complicated by the notion of *sex*, which has often been simply assumed to relate to the biological and physiological body. However, if we consider **transexuality** and **intersexuality** as sexes, then there are more than two sexes.

Moreover, what is *sexuality*? This term is perhaps even more ambiguous and is, indeed, a socially constructed set of social *norms* about what is "proper" sexual expression. **Heteronormativity**, or the assumption and requirement that one engage in sexual relations only with opposite sex partners, is part of this normative package. Moreover, sexuality is practice: an individual may think of himself as gay, bisexual, or straight, for example, but engage in sexual activities that might be thought of to be outside of those categories. So, a man may say, "I'm not gay, but I do occasionally visit a bathhouse and have sex with men." Further, sexuality is also *identity*: gay, lesbian, bisexual, heterosexual, or transsexual. Adding to the complexity is the use of the word *sex* to delineate (most often) *male* or *female* (as on personal information forms) and to describe sexual activity (*i.e.*, having *sex* with someone). Further, the meanings behind all three concepts—sex, gender, and sexuality— are neither essential nor fixed. Time, place, circumstance, structural and individual forces, and choices contribute to the fluidity of these categories. Think for a moment about the same-sex marriage question that came before the Supreme Court of Canada in 2004. Subsequent legislation has opened the institution of marriage as a legitimate space for gays and lesbians.

CURRENT VIEWS ON SEXUALITY

In his three-volume *History of Sexuality* (1978, 1985, 1986), Michel Foucault makes some intriguing observations about contemporary attitudes toward sexuality. Foucault argues that never before has society been so obsessed with describing, analyzing, and reacting to its own sexual activity. We have problematized sex and sexuality such that it is in constant need of monitoring, adjusting, and controlling. We talk, for example, about people who are "addicted" to sex. We call on those who engage in "abnormal" sexual practices to identify or self-diagnose, with a view to seeking out a cure or to getting "help." The proliferation of "cures" helps the sexually dysfunctional person. Too much sex? Too little? Help is available.

Concomitant with this confessional imperative about sex and sexuality is the medicalization of sexuality—the framing of sexual behaviours in medical terms, which then allows for diagnosis and cure. Thus, men's *erectile dysfunction* can be cured with a pill, and women's lack of sexual desire can be too. Between 1968 and 1973, *homosexuality* was identified in the DSM–II as a mental illness which could be treated (Mitchell, 2003). The DSM–IV currently reflects the latest "expert" opinion that homosexuality is *not* a mental illness. *Hysteria* was once considered a result of too much sexual stimulation for women. *Masturbation* had its own set of medical consequences, perpetuated as truth primarily to enforce (or attempt to) moral codes about sexuality among youth.

In addition, sex-related scripts are gendered, with men being characterized as the ready, willing, and able initiators and women being portrayed as reluctant, caring, nurturing gate-keepers. Women who express sexual desire too frequently are considered "sluts"; too little sexual desire, "frigid" or merely playing hard to get. Behind these concepts, a hegemonic heteronormativity provides the context in which scripts about sexuality and sex are played out. Moreover, scripts are also raced and classed, a point graphically illustrated by the case of Pamela George (see Chapter Seven), where middle-class white men laid claim to "normal" sexual activities that ended with the murder of Pamela George.

SOURCES OF SEXUAL NOTIONS

Notions about how women and men should behave in terms of their sexuality are embedded in social institutions, such as law and religion. In law, we see judges reproducing notions of women's sexuality in their adjudication of sexual assault cases. These judgments often reflect notions about men's sexuality as well (he was out of control, wanting what any normal man would want; she was dressed in tight clothes, therefore not virginal, wanting it). Think for a minute about the social and sexual meaning of a bare-breasted man as opposed to a bare-breasted woman. Does a bare-breasted man "want it"? Is he being sexually provocative? The socially constructed meaning of baring one's chest is different for men and for women. Moreover, judgments about men's and women's sexuality affect rulings in custody cases. Law is one institutional forum in which sexual notions have been debated. We can see the extent of these beliefs when we examine how the law (and society) deals with sexual assault of prostitutes, most of whom are unwilling to report such incidents. Women and men who receive pay for sex are often seen as inviting whatever ill might befall them, thus positioning themselves outside of or unworthy of legal protection. Thus, sex-related behaviour determines one's position in the eyes of the law.

In a similar manner, religion reinforces the submission of women and headship of men in doctrine, even in so-called liberal religions. This teaching centres around the idea that there is a god-ordained hierarchical order in the world, which places men at the top. Most versions of this script state that women receive their fulfillment through mothering. Some versions of this script divide women into "virgins" and "whores": women who live according to divine plan fall into the former category, and those who live outside of the mothering/servant role fall into the latter. Religion also contains scripts about the purpose of sex (for procreation only, for example) and can go so far as to prohibit sexual relations except during ovulation. Same-sex relations are also problematized or condemned by some religious teachings. Chapter Fourteen discusses the role of religion in gender in more detail.

Does this mean that sexuality and gender are fixed? Absolutely not. We negotiate sexuality, gender, and sexual roles throughout our lives in a dynamic process. For some people, negotiation may involve fulfilling socially prescribed roles by marrying people of the opposite sex, having children, and then in mid-life, divorcing and choosing a same-sex partner. Or it may mean engaging in sexual relations with people of the same sex while in a traditional marriage or relationship. For others, resistance may mean straddling sex roles or identity.

Moreover, not only is sexuality negotiated at the micro (interpersonal) level, but scripts in the larger society (the macro level) undergo negotiations and changes as well. These two processes—individual and societal—are related, because the agency-structure dynamic (power/resistance relation) constantly shifts. Since the inclusion of sexual orientation in the Canadian Charter of Rights and Freedoms and the passage of same-sex marriage legislation, scripts in Canada have been shifting in profound ways. Scripts in other countries change at different rates. For example, Canada is north of a superpower that is much more hostile towards state recognition of same-sex relationships. In addition, other countries often have scripts that English North Americans are not even aware of. As we were writing this book, we spent a month in a small community in Mexico. We had a number of discussions with out Mexican landlord about gender, particularly after he learned that we were writing a book on the subject. He was well educated, and although his area of expertise was history, he had studied sociology during his undergraduate years at a state university in Mexico. He explained to us that in Mexico, a woman's smile or enthusiastic greeting to a Mexican man might be interpreted differently than it would be in other parts of North America. In the Canadian small communities in which we have each lived, passing someone on the street, male or female, without offering a greeting would be considered odd. But we would not expect a simple smile and greeting to be interpreted as "I would like to have sex with you." Yet in Mexico, particularly coming from a woman who was obviously a foreigner, a too-warm gesture could be interpreted this way. While our landlord may have been overstating the case somewhat, it was clear that male-female interaction had different rules and meaning than it does in other places in North America.

A BRIEF HISTORICAL SNAPSHOT OF SEX

Expectations about sexual behaviour and their connection to sex and social class need to be understood in a historical context. For example, in pre-industrial England, sexual scripts for aristocratic women were highly restrictive. It was essential that these women be virginal upon their marriage to ensure that their offspring had a right to inheirit their husband's wealth and land. If the bride was not sexually pure, then her child might actually be someone else's rather than her husband's, thus destroying the family lineage. To prove her purity, it was not uncommon for the sheets from the bridal bed to be put on public display, with blood from her broken hymen on the linens providing evidence that she had been chaste. In fact, in some cases where there were issues of royalty and succession to the throne, there would actually be observers in the bridal chamber, ensuring that the consummation did indeed take place. Meanwhile, aristocratic men had no such restrictions: it was expected that they would be sexually active, just not with unmarried aristocratic women. They were more likely to have had intercourse with servants and serfs. When we take into consideration the power dynamics of these sexual acts, we might more accurately describe them as sexual assaults. Illegitimate children of these men, who had no rights or legal protections and frequently lived in poverty, were commonplace. By the Victorian age, this sex- and class-based double standard was carried to extremes. In London, aristocratic unmarried women were carefully monitored until they "came out" (when they were introduced to society and expected to find a husband), and chastity was still required. The men, however, had great sexual freedom. Some estimates suggest as many as 50 000 working-class people, both women/girls and men/boys, were working at least part-time in the sex trade for wealthy men. Poverty was widespread, and prostitution was a means for supplementing an income and putting food on the table. Sexually transmitted infections were common, not just among the sex trade workers, but among their aristocratic "johns," who then passed them on to their chaste brides.

Sexual scripts, then, shift not only from culture to culture, but also through time and between classes. Perhaps the most profound shift in recent history were the changes brought about by the second wave of feminism. As women struggled to achieve equality, they sought reproductive and sexual freedom and control. Although it is debatable whether the "free love" of the 1960s "sexual revolution" was really emancipatory for women, the idea that women could make choices about their bodies and sexuality that did not involve reproduction (*i.e.*, they could choose to have sex and not become pregnant) became popular. Further, it became a reality with the arrival of the contraceptive pill, which became widely available in Canada in the 1970s.

However, increased availability of contraception has not completely shifted gender relations. In her 2005 study of heterosexual women's decisions about contraception, Pam Lowe found that condoms and other "coital-dependent" methods of contraception were less preferred by women because they were aware of men's preferences and assumptions and made choices accordingly. Lowe found that "[t]he women made specific contraceptive choices in the expectation of sexual activity within a particular form of heterosexual encounter" (2005, p. 90). Notions of proper sex (performance) were embedded in their contraceptive choices.

Second-wave feminism also contributed to the increased availability of abortion services. Henry Morgentaler was instrumental in securing the right to abortion for women in Canada. His Supreme Court case, *R. v. Morgentaler,* resulted in the striking down of the Criminal Code provisions that had criminalized abortion. Despite this change, some provinces, such as New Brunswick, are extremely restrictive in their provision of abortions to women. In the United States, abortion remains a contested issue. At the time of the writing of this text, the governor of South Dakota had just made all abortion illegal anywhere in the state. This law means that even in cases of rape and incest, an abortion is still a felony. A doctor can only perform one when the mother's life is in danger (Davey, 2006).

The ramifications of the sexual revolution are still not entirely clear, in part because the changes are still too close in history and in part because they are still unfolding. Like a rock thrown into a pond, the ripples are still happening.

But have the ripples started to reverse direction? Jacqueline Scott (1998) argues that the sexual revolution may not have brought about as many changes as we might think. She reminds us that the term *sexual revolution* was actually used to describe shifts in sexual norms in the 1920s, meaning that the 1960s revolution was a second or follow-up revolution. Scott's research, based on data from the United States and Britain, concludes that although the language of sexual revolution is pervasive, there has not been as much change in attitudes as the language would suggest. . . . Scott notes that even though there has been a relaxing of attitudes (and behaviours) about premarital sex, other behaviours have remained static.

Scott draws on some interesting statistics to contrast the shift in attitudes about premarital sex with those about other aspects of sexuality. She points out that cohabitation prior to marriage is now the norm. In Britain, fewer than 1 percent of those surveyed between the ages of 16 and 24 were married at the time of their first experience of sexual intercourse. Similarly, in the United States, half of the survey respondents had their first experience of sexual intercourse between the ages of 15 and 17 years and outside of marriage (1998, p. 810). However, these same surveys found that attitudes toward sexual fidelity and adultery have remained largely unchanged over the past few decades. Moreover, attitudes toward homosexuality are still complicated. Canada seems to be experiencing a shift toward a gay-positive institutional structure. But in the United States, attitudes seem to be regressing, with only women reporting greater acceptance of gays and lesbians.

Scott's second major finding is that religious institutions continue to have an influence over attitudes toward sex and sexuality. This would come as no surprise to sociologists of religion; however, we must be careful in interpreting Scott's observation. The transmission and practice of religious beliefs is always a *lived phenomenon*, meaning that religious believers can translate beliefs in their day-to-day lives in unexpected ways. For example, research has shown that despite the prohibition of birth control in Roman Catholic teachings, the use of birth control among Roman Catholics is widespread. Thus, while Scott's observation is correct at one level, the causal impact of religious teachings is a subject that must be treated with an appreciation of the complexity of religion as lived.

Historical Categories of Sexuality

Historically, creating categories of sexuality has limited the ways in which we can think about human beings and plays into the fetishization of sex and sexuality as identified by Foucault. "Gay, lesbian, transsexual, bisexual," often seen shortened to *GLTB* in academic literature, essentializes one wide set of sexual behaviours and identities, much like the category *woman*, which obscures the rich diversity of women's lives. How do the experts define *sexuality*? Sexuality covers a wide range of issues, from sexual orientations, preferences, behaviours, and fantasies. But Herdt (1990) argues that sexuality cannot be defined or studied outside of social context because it is interactive or relational as well as contextual. In other words, sexuality is socially constructed, requiring the active participation of the human agent and structure—or scripts—from which we draw. Remember that scripts are culturally specific, a fact that is illustrated by acceptance same-sex sexual relations between (especially) boys and men in other cultures. Some cultures in the Pacific and in Papua New Guinia see same-sex relations as part of the cycle of human life. They do not name same-sex sex in the same ways that we do (Herdt, 1990). Ultimately, "Truths about human sexuality created by scholars in general and by biologists in particular are one component of political, social, and moral struggles about our cultures and economies" (Fausto-Sterling, 2000, p. 5).

Throughout the past century, researchers have studied and attempted to categorize sexuality. One of the most influential researchers of human sexuality was Alfred C. Kinsey. He and his colleagues developed a six-point scale of sexuality, which was a linear scale measuring individual sexuality. The major contribution of Kinsey and colleagues was their conceptualization of sexuality on a continuum, on which most people fall somewhere in the middle. The disadvantage of Kinsey's continuum was that it was somewhat static and decontextualized. Sexuality does not just happen in isolation from society and culture. More sophisticated scales developed since Kinsey's time consider attraction, behaviour, and fantasies, for example, as well as behaviours over the life course. But despite its limitations, the Kinsey scale is still used to measure sexuality.

A controversial study by Simon LeVay (1991) reported that the brain structures of gay men and straight men are different. Such a finding was powerful ammunition for those who argue on the nature side of the nature/nurture debate (*i.e.*, that biology is destiny, or, more specifically, that being gay is not something that can be changed or "cured"). LeVay's research concluded that sexual orientation is not a desire or a choice, but an immutable characteristic that is non-negotiable. At one level, this was an important counter-argument to those who argued that "homosexuality" was "unnatural lifestyle choice." On the other hand, LeVay's finding could be used to decontextualize the social and cultural context in which sexuality exists and is constructed. If being gay is immutable, then so could many other aspects of sexuality, including popular ideas about gender. The changeable/immutable debate has important political repercussions that shape the way such data is used. Research that supports a biological imperative approach tends to subvert human agency and choice. If your genes determine everything, you have no choice or agency. Thus, LeVay's research poses new problems for sociologists of sexuality. The nature/nurture debate has dominated recent sociological and political discussion about sexuality, and there are no easy answers.

Anne Fausto-Sterling (2000) gives insights into ways of defining and understanding sexuality without discounting either nature or nurture. She demonstrates that nature and nurture are intertwined in important ways, and that neither is wholly determinative of sex or sexuality. Fausto-Sterling uses the example of intersexed Olympian Maria Patino to challenge notions of gender and sexuality and how we measure and assess them. Patino was competing as a hurdler for Spain in the 1988 Olympics. She had forgotten her doctor's statement identifying her as female (a requirement of the International Olympic Committee). On site, she was re-checked with a simple test involving a swab of cells from inside her mouth. After the first test, she was recalled for a further examination. She assumed the entire procedure was routine until she was banned from competing. The tests had revealed that her cells contained Y chromosomes and that there were testes within her labia. Despite the fact that she had lived her entire life as a female, Patino was excluded from the IOC's definition of *woman*. The consequences for Patino were profound and devastating at many levels. But two-and-a-half years later, Patino successfully fought the IOC ruling and was able to compete as a woman in the next Olympics. Fausto-Sterling uses this example to show that our culture is devoted to the notion that there are two sexes. Yet the existence of intesexed humans such as Patino challenges this two-sex dichotomy. "If nature really offers us more than two sexes, then it follows that our current notions of masculinity and femininity are cultural conceits" (2000, p. 31).

Fausto-Sterling's research is cutting-edge, innovative, and multi-disciplinary. She argues that the social and the material must be considered in concert if we wish to understand human sexuality. In other words, we cannot simply talk about social construction or biology: we must talk about both. Few social scientists or biologists are currently able (or willing) to do this. As social scientists, it is important for us to realize that we aren't "there" yet—that sexuality is one facet of gender studies about which we remain woefully ignorant and theoretically unsophisticated and inadequate. But Fausto-Sterling lays out a broad framework for future research. She proposes three principles for understanding the process of gender embodiment. "First, nature/nurture is indivisible. Second, organisms—human and otherwise—are active processes, moving targets, from fertilization until death. Third, no single academic or clinical discipline provides us with the true or best way to understand human sexuality" (2000, p. 235). Fausto-Sterling advocates an approach which should be second nature (pardon the pun) to social scientists. Yet we are quick to create categories that take on a life apart from the social life they are intended to describe.

HOW DO PEOPLE BECOME SEXUAL?

Explaining how we become sexual is not straightforward. As discussed above, perhaps most controversial question is the degree to which genetics contribute to sexual orientation. Most researchers agree that a combination of biology and socialization are the most likely explanatory variables; however, perhaps a more interesting approach is to examine the processes involved in the construction of sexuality, rather than seeking causal explanations. Biological and genetic information tends to be transformed into sweeping explanations that ignore cultural and social context. The relational aspects of gender thus become obscured by individual factors that have no connection to social life. What are some of these "social" contexts? Let's take a closer look at some of the issues around sexual performance in heterosexual relationships.

In their discussion of ways of counselling men about sexuality, Fracher and Kimmel (1995) note: "*That* we are sexual is determined by a biological imperative toward reproduction, but *how* we are sexual—where, when, how often, with whom, and why—has to do with cultural learning, with meanings transmitted in a cultural setting" (p. 367). We would add to this that an important part of this cultural context are power relations, which also shape how and how often we act sexually at an interactive and local level. Fracher and Kimmel also point out that "[f]or men, the notion of masculinity, the cultural definition of manhood, serves as the primary building block of sexuality. It is through understanding of masculinity that we construct a sexuality, and it is through our sexualities that we confirm the successful construction of our gender identity. Gender informs sexuality; sexuality confirms gender" (1995, p. 367).

Male sex scripts are narrowly defined and, we might argue, are highly likely to facilitate "failure." In other words, men are often in a no-win situation in relation to their sexuality and sexual expression. "The script contains dicta for sexual distancing, objectification, phallocentrism, and a pressure to become and remain erect without ejaculation for as long as possible, all of which serve as indicators of masculinity, so sexual problems will inevitably damage male gender identity" (1995, p. 370). Given the relatively high percentage of women who are unable to reach orgasm through intercourse alone, we might wonder why the myth of the need for perpetual erection is perpetuated. Suffice it to say that, like most areas of life, the social constructions of expectations and scripts and the needs of women and men are often very different. Thus, an inability or failure to sustain an erection is problematized, medicalized, and treated.

Women too suffer from the imposition of sex scripts that have little or nothing to do with their experiences and desires. But keep in mind that discussing the imposition of scripts is not meant to disempower men or women or to assume victimhood or lack of agency; it merely acknowledges that scripts are powerful. Tiefer (2002) argues that "[t]he medical model pays only lip service to women's self-determination" (p. 90); and for women, "[t]he necessary and sufficient ingredients for successful sexual experience are desire (vaguely indicated as being 'for sex'), genital arousal, a timely orgasm, and the ability to enjoy vaginal penetration" (2002, p. 90). In addition, women's sexuality is set in the context of social scripts that discourage recreational sex—that is, sex outside of a relationship and outside of love. In this script, women are the sexual gatekeepers, holding out until they have been properly wooed; and then when they are wooed and "give in," they should not enjoy sex too much (within the normative assumption that the partner is male). As Tiefer bluntly puts it, "In sexuomedicine, the amount of time devoted to getting the penis hard and the vagina wet vastly outweighs the attention devoted to assessment or education about sexual motives, scripts, pleasure, power, emotionality, sensuality, communication, or connectedness" (2002, p. 90). Tiefer critiques the medical model and its medical solutions, noting the lack of research around the interrelationship between sexuality and class, education and the media. She concludes, "The consequence of this imbalanced research is a perpetually gullible, anxious, and exploitable public, the perfect market for selling magical drugs" (2002, p. 90).

So, where do these scripts about sexuality come from? Certainly, law and religion are influences. But let's examine this issue a bit more closely. Think for a moment about some of the expectations around sexuality and sex that you have been exposed to. What sort of sexual expression is expected or accepted in your community? What model of sexuality have you grown up with? Are your parents of the same or opposite sex? Have you been raised by a single parent? Did she/he date? What are the norms in your family about premarital sex? Or does your family regard marriage and sex as linked? Have you had discussions about birth control and sexually transmitted diseases with family members? Family is an important source of scripts about sexual expression. These scripts can be reacted against or internalized, they can be resisted or embraced. Family scripts are tied with expectations about what kind of person one partners with in an intimate relationship, reproduction, and communication about sex.

School is another source of the information, expectations, and pressure that form scripts. In the same way that the education system shapes general ideas about gender, it can provide a forum for intense peer pressure—to engage in sexual activity or not, to express one's sexual orientation or not. For example, in 2002, high school student Marc Hall fought for a court declaration that his Catholic school's prohibition against same-sex dates for prom night violated human rights principles and laws. Hall won, and he was able to take his male date to the prom. (The school board argued that the prom was an important part of the mating ritual.) While his school was unsupportive of his open expressions of his sexuality, Marc's peers treated his orientation as normal. Thus, Marc received different messages about sexuality from the institution and from his friends.

Reflect also on how your school approached issues of reproductive health and sexuality. There is an intense debate about how sexual activity and sexuality should be taught in school. One position is that abstinence should be the baseline assumption in any educational program in public schools. If abstinence is the assumed behaviour of teenagers, there is no need to teach about birth control, abortion, or sexually transmitted diseases. Levy reports that the United States government has spent billions of dollars on educational programs based on an assumption of abstinence, despite the fact that many teenagers are sexually active and there is no evidence that abstinence programs convince teens that they should abstain from sexual intercourse (Levy, 2005). However, abstinence advocates argue that to teach teens about birth control is equivalent to promoting sexual activity. Moreover, as Cavanagh (2003) points out, "It is not a coincidence that such a moral panic unfolds in relation to teenage adolescent bodies. Bodies developing into 'natural' men and women are often thought to be especially vulnerable to 'deviant' role models, sexual transgressions, and temptations of the flesh" (2003, p. 263). In Canada, there is not quite the same aversion to teaching teens about birth control, abortion, and STDs (sexually transmitted diseases); however, there is nonetheless an abstinence lobby that follows the reasoning and beliefs of its counterpart in the United States. Thus, schools provide a forum in which a variety of scripts about sex and sexuality are conveyed.

The media is another powerful influence on the shapes and forms of sexuality and sexual expectations. Through television, movies, and magazines, people learn to look at human bodies in particular ways. This is one of the major objections to pornography, which objectifies bodies, especially women's bodies, and creates unrealistic images of how women's bodies look and what women's sexual desires are. It also creates unrealistic expectations about men's sexual prowess, often portraying men who stay erect for long periods of time. Through such images, phallocentric sex is defined as the norm. Sexual desire and pleasure are defined in relation to the penis and the man's needs, rather than around mutuality. The realities of desire often stand in sharp contrast to the fantasies created by media.

In her guest essay, Gayle MacDonald looks at sexuality as fashion—what is "in" and how that is negotiated. She argues that both sexuality and fashion act as mirrors of society.

BOX 9-1	**Sexuality as Fashion**

by Gayle MacDonald

It's hard to think of sexuality as fashion. After all, fashion is a commodity which relies on trends in marketing and which responds to the "gurus" of how we should look, feel, or act in name-brand clothing, or 'the latest' in make-up or hairstyle. Sexuality relies on inner feelings, connection with one's body or someone else's, or as some would argue, biological drive. What can sexuality possibly have to do with fashion? The interesting thing is that these two creatures of culture might have more to do with one another than one might think. Here's how.

Fashion is all about trends. Trends are expressions of social culture[1]—in what's "hot" or what's "not,"—in clothing, body products and the presentation of self in the public world: in other words, what's popular, and what isn't. Fashion is a billion dollar business, and far more about creating desire around a product than it is about need. A preoccupation with how others see you, as well as potentially obsessive behaviour around how you see yourself, is the premise on which fashion is built. "To see and be seen" is how many products are marketed.

| BOX 9-1 | *(Continued)* |

Fashion hinges on the idea that you will buy something to wear based on what you think you want, and you will wear it regardless of whether or not it really is "you." People will wear clothing or hairstyles or makeup to fit into certain social groups, regardless of whether or not this is actually a healthy decision. And much of this "fashion sense" is targeted towards people who are very, very thin, as if that is the standard for us all. Why else would people starve themselves to fit into a size zero? How else could a manufacturer get women to wear thin, filmy shirts in the dead of a Canadian winter?

Sexuality, we think, is all about feelings. Feeling sexual, acting on one's sexuality, and concerns about how others will relate to your sexuality when you express it are all about one's innermost dialogues with the self. Many think that sexuality and sexual expression is really "theirs," and does not come from anywhere or anyone else, and is private, rather than public. People can express their sexuality in various ways: a movement, a look, a word, a song or a piece of art. Sexuality is as "natural" as hunger and as "learned" as a script. As a basic human need, sexuality manifests as desire when it is healthy. When it is healthy, it is does not hurt one's self or others. When it is healthy, is can be one of the loveliest aspects of a social being. When is it unhealthy, or thwarted, when people get messages about expressions of sexuality as wrong or "dirty," then sexuality can manifest as aggression, or come out when people are in altered states (such as inebriation). If sexuality is repressed, people don't learn appropriate boundaries, and can't control it properly.

They may meet sexual needs in other ways that may not seem inappropriate at first, such excessive forms of social touching or a drive to elite athleticism.

So what's the connection you might be asking. What's the connection between sexuality and fashion? It is this. It can be argued that both sexuality and fashion act as social mirrors. Both are widely present in the social arena. One can see reflected in sexuality and in fashion what is popular, what is not. In the social world generally, to "act" sexually is quite popular. And it is getting popular at any age. Older people in nursing homes are now permitted "social time" with sexual partners. And although children *stay* children emotionally much longer than in any previous generation, they're getting sexual sooner. And fashion reflects that. Clothing for young girls, even infants, reflect fashion trends around a sexuality that is not yet understood by those who might wear it. The marketed message is that clothing and fashion reflect sexuality at a time when the social messages are all about repression, discouraging young people from exploring their sexuality based on fears of unwanted pregnancy or disease, or, from the religious right, before marriage.

What these mixed messages result in is a separation of sexuality from the self. Current sexual practices in high schools, for example, have resulted in either shame around sexuality (which represses sexual expression) or in braceleting behaviour, signaling sexual performance (which results in indiscriminate sexual expression). The "fashion" trend, the wearing of coloured bracelets to indicate sexual achievement, although a new phenomena,

(Continued)

BOX 9-1	Sexuality as Fashion (*Continued*)

seems to reflect "old wine in new bottles" as young men benefit far more from having their sexual needs satisfied, whereas young women appear to gain status, which can also be reflected in fashion. Sexual acts that are just about sexuality are fine if both parties are playing equal roles or are in the same script. Neither behaviour, shame nor braceleting, really prepare a person for the type of negotiation that can be involved in healthy sexuality. A sexuality that is integrated with the self does not respond to social trends as a matter of course, but can as a matter of choice.

At another point in the sexual landscape lies the sex trade. As the most commodified form of the separation of sexuality from the self, the sex trade, not unlike many current-day forms of sexual expression, is simply a mirror of the social world.[2] Sexual services for sale mimic fashion trends—what's popular, what's not. The clients (usually men) can "buy" a sexual service, a sexual fantasy, or simply company from the sellers (usually women). The seller of sex services is a powerful negotiator,[3] making sure she gets what she needs from the interaction in terms of financial gain, and making sure that her client is "satisfied" with the product. The selling of sex services fits with a marketplace sensibility around

sexuality, and it also fits with an empowering of women's sexuality. For the clients, this is "sex" they buy. For the sellers, this is a "service" they offer. Both are reflected as trends of buying and selling. And both represent the separation of sex from the self. Sex becomes a commodity in this social setting, a service to be bought and sold, a means to "scratch an itch" for some and a means of financial survival for others.

In other words, there are many, many messages in our social world about sexuality. How they are presented, which sexual "scripts" we choose, can be like fashion. Fashion can be a reflection of social trends, as can our sexuality. Our presentation of self[4] can have more to do with who we are and the social messages we receive about sexuality than we might think. How we act out our sexuality, or how we do not, can be as fickle as fashion. And just as much of a commodity.

1. F. Davis. *Fashion, Culture and Identity.* Chicago: University of Chicago Press, 1992.

2. Cf S Bell *Reading, Writing, and Rewriting the Prostitute Body.* Bloomington: Indiana University Press, 1994, for an explanation of how sex workers 'mirror' the social world.

3. L. Jeffrey and G. MacDonald *Sex Workers in the Maritimes Talk Back.* Toronto: UBC Press, 2006.

4. E. Goffman *The Presentation of Self in Everyday Life.* New York: Anchor Books, 1959.

ACTING OUTSIDE OF THE SCRIPTS

As we mentioned earlier, sexual scripts undergo change, both at the societal and cultural level, as well as in the ways individuals internalize or appropriate them. One of the major disadvantages of thinking about sex and sexuality as scripts is that this can reify the idea that there are "normal" and "abnormal" expressions of sexuality. This is not our intention. The problems faced by women and men we discussed above are even more exaggerated for gays and lesbians, who are often on the margins of sexual scripts, a marginality that is hopefully changing. One of the positive effects of being on the margins of (or outside of) sexuality scripts is that to some extent one has an opportunity to write one's own script, acting out sexuality in inventive ways. However, while this may be the case in theory, the day-to-day working out of resistance or radical sexual identities comes with its own sets of rules.

Until recently, gay and lesbian sexual scripts have not been highly visible in mainstream society. This meant that few scripts were available to guide those who are not heterosexual. Many argue this is advantageous because it frees people from larger cultural expectations, many of which were negative and uninformed. Usually gay and lesbian sexual scripts are learned after the individual comes into contact with gay and lesbian communities. Blumstein and Schwartz (1983) have researched three types of couples (single-sex male, both sexes, single-sex female) and found that men and women are likely to follow the social script for their gender regardless of the sex of their partner. Their data reflected these patterns in terms of both monogamy and sexual frequency.

In her study of college women's sexuality, Carla Golden (1997) identified two basic types of lesbian identity. *Primary lesbianism* was experienced as deterministic and determined, essential and central to women's identities. *Elective lesbians* had self-consciously chosen their identities and were more likely to have experienced their sexuality as fluid and dynamic in nature. Golden observed that "some women whom I have characterized as primary lesbians referred to themselves as 'born' or 'real' lesbians, with the implicit designation of elective lesbians as 'fake'" (1997, p. 157). Golden's research revealed that like the scripts around heterosexuals, there is some rigidity in sexual identities outside of heteronormative hegemony.

Re-scripting or resisting can also take the shape of sexual and intimate relationships that challenge the "two person" orthodoxy. Polygamy is one way this happens, although polygamy is often complicated by religious scripts that are rigidly patriarchal (see Chapter Fourteen). Some researchers have challenged such a superficial description of polygamous relationships after conducting research with women who describe this form of relationship as freeing rather than constraining (see, for example, the work of Janet Bennion, 1998). It is important to remember that polygamy is not about sex as much as it is about family forms.

Perhaps more interesting in terms of re-scripting sex and sexuality are **polyamorous relationships**, defined by Sheff as "a form of relationship in which people have multiple romantic, sexual, and/or affective partners. It differs from swinging in its emphasis on long-term, emotionally intimate relationships and from adultery with its focus on honesty and (ideally) full disclosure of the network of sexual relationships to all who participate in or are affected by them" (2005, p. 253). What is of note is that in this type of relationship, women have equal access to additional partners. However, Sheff's research has found that women who desire two male partners have a difficult time finding willing partners. Women complained that most polyamorous relationships fulfill men's "hot bi babe fantasy." Most of the women in Sheff's study described themselves as bisexual, and it was their bisexual subjectivities that provided the entry point for subverting scripts. Women were able to "have their Jake and Edith too" (2005, p. 266). They were attempting to resist the sex and gender scripts that overemphasize differences between men and women.

Many of the polyamourous women Sheff interviewed "embraced forms of sexual subjectivity that allowed them to redefine mores and social institutions, such as sexuality and monogamy, to better fit their own needs" (2005, p. 262). However, this subjectivity does not mean that women involved in polyamourous relationships are completely able to escape conventions about intimate relationships and gender. For example, one woman reported being hurt when her husband told her that while she met his physical needs, one of his girlfriends was the person he could "talk to." She said, "And that's the worst thing you can tell a woman. That some other woman has your emotional connection and you're just the physical" (2005, p. 264). This woman's feelings draw on the idea that for women, sex and emotional intimacy go together; and that for some women, emotional intimacy is more important than sex, an idea that this woman had clearly internalized as part of the gender script around sex. Thus, as Sheff notes, "While many respondents reported exhilaration at the liberation from confining traditional roles, they also reported terror that accompanied psychic freefall with no roles to emulate" (2005, p. 262). Scripts are not as easily escaped as we might wish they could be.

Carol Queen (1997) came to similar conclusions in her research on bisexuals. She tells the story of her own experiences as an adolescent trying to identify as bisexual in the gay community, a position which was criticized. "Patiently it was explained to me that almost every young gay person eases into her or his rightful homosexual identity by leaning on a 'safer' and 'more socially acceptable' bisexual indentification, which proves the person just coming out with a cushion of 'heterosexual privilege' until s/he acquires enough gay pride to drop the charade" (1997, p. 258). Although she eventually found a home in the gay community, Queen had to closet her bisexuality. Accused of being "confused" by both heterosexual and gay communities, bisexuals are often marginalized in both. Queen is critical of bisexual marginalization in the gay community, stating, "We expect more of others who have faced homophobia" (1997, p. 262). Scripts and expectations can, then, transcend heterosexual communities. Moreover, those scripts may not be so far from those we know well.

Avril Levy (2004) interviewed a number of "**bois**" in her exploration of gender and sexuality among young women. Bois are androgynous biological females whose gender identity is fluid. As described by Levy, they are part of a genderqueer movement whose project is to slip between the gender binary (2004, p. 126). Bois sometimes make a transition from female look to male look by taking testosterone and having their breasts removed. On a superficial analysis, boi-hood exemplifies resistances and subversion of scripted sexuality: bois are not bound by gender rules in the same way that the rest of society might be. But closer examination reveals that bois too reuse gender scripts. Levy reports, "There is another camp of bois who date femmes exclusively and follow a locker-room code of ethics referred to by the phrase 'bois before hos' or 'bros before bitches,' which means they put the similarly masculine-identified women they hang out with in a different, higher category than the feminine women they have sex with" (2004, p. 130). Does this sound like a new gender script? One young woman interviewed by Levy was anxious about seeing her current boi "friend". "I'm nervous to see her now because I'm not dressed up. And then all of a sudden it's like I'm trying to please a guy. It's like I've come full circle" (2004, p. 135). Does this mean that we should understand what at first might seem to be innovative or transgressive breaks with sexual scripts as really nothing new at all?

Alison Eves (2004) cautions that we should not be too quick to dismiss such expressions of sexualities as simply replays of heterosexual scripts. She argues that even though they may seem to imitate, they are innovative and not simply derivatives of heterosexuality. In this instance, context is everything, "Subversive and transgressive gender performances, although framed by the dominant discursive formation, may have some transformative impact, establishing new subject positions and [sub] cultural spaces" (2004, p. 495). The context in which "butch" and "femme" lesbians are socially constructed, for example, positions them as such; but Eves argues that they are not just re-enacting heteronormative roles. They are not "new," but nor are they simply copies.

CONCLUSION

Does the existence of sexual scripts or the difficulty in breaking free of them mean that we are bound to the narrow confines of present day sexuality? Must we continue the confessional identified by Foucault (1978) and the continuous monitoring of sexual activities and proclivities so that we may confess them and thus reform our sexual selves into the ordinary? Old scripts are replaced by new scripts. What was formerly a violation of religious codes becomes now a violation of the state and media-disseminated medical codes—of the sexually healthy individual, who must self-assess and monitor, seeking treatment or help for too much sex drive, too little sex drive, or inappropriate sex drive. Must women continue to play the role of gatekeeper, repressing sexual desire or enthusiasm? Are men forever caught in the expectation of sexual knowledge and endless capacity?

Section Two explains how even those who seem to subvert gender scripts often remain caught up to some extent in familiar patterns of gender relations. Critical examination of patterns of sexual interaction and expectations about sexuality at both the individual and institutional levels is one way to subvert and to rewrite scripts. This approach would move past subversion for its own sake, which tends simply to reply another version of gendered relations with which we are already far too familiar.

CHAPTER SUMMARY: KEY POINTS

1. Gender, sex, and sexuality are socially constructed, interrelated, and complex in their definitions.
2. Sexuality is an issue of norms, identity, and performance.
3. Sexual behaviours that fall outside of normative expectations are often medicalized.
4. Messages about sex and sexuality come from a variety of sources including the media, religion, laws, and the education system.
5. Definitions of appropriate sexual behaviour are culturally and historically specific.
6. The second wave of feminism resulted in important shifts in women's and men's sexual expression.
7. Nature and nurture both contribute to the way in which sexuality is experienced and expressed.
8. Social scripts around sexuality are sometimes difficult to reshape or to resist.

DISCUSSION QUESTIONS

1. How repressive is our culture when it comes to the expression of sexuality?
2. Judith Butler, a well-known postmodern theorist, describes gender as "performative." What do you think she means by this?
3. Do you agree with Fausto-Sterling that gender is a combination of biology and socialization?

4. Are we far too preoccupied with analysing, discussing, and confessing our sexual behaviour? (Think about some talk shows you might have seen.)

5. Imagine a society in which sexual orientation simply didn't matter. How might such a society look?

KEY TERMS

ambiguous genitalia	heteronormativity	sex
bois	intersexuality	sexuality
gender	polyamorous relationships	transsexual

chapter ten

Negotiating Power

Problems of gender are less a matter of discrimination and equality than of power. (Winter, 1996, p. 723)

Why is this textbook devoting an entire chapter to discussing power? The concept of power is an elusive one. Sociologists, political scientists, and philosophers have devoted a great deal of energy to exploring the forms and qualities of power. Some have reduced power to force, although few adhere to such a simplistic view. Other theorists have examined the differences between individual and structural power. Power has been recast both as social and cultural capital and as a resource.

The way people think about power has profound implications for the way they analyze gender. Each of the authors of this book thinks about power differently; and in our discussions about power, we have realized that the perspectives we use bring different insights to our conclusions about gender relations and the social construction of gender in society. Thus, this chapter presents two major strands of power theories, and then explores three topics that highlight the similarities and differences between the two strands. The first application examines conversation and language; the second looks at violence against women; and the third considers the ways that the creation and presentation of art is implicated in power relations and power hierarchies.

Our choice of topics might seem like a bit of an odd assortment. And we might say, modelling Michel Foucault's version of power, that power is everywhere! But our examples are intended to illustrate the complex dynamics of power in a variety of areas of social life.

Moreover, you might ask: What does power have to do with gender? We would answer: everything! In fact, as stated by Steven Winter at the very beginning of this chapter, gender is subsumed by problems of power. While the authors perhaps don't want to go that far, we certainly think power is important enough to devote a chapter to its exploration.

TRADITIONAL VIEW ABOUT HOLDING POWER

Defining power is not an easy task. Sociology has traditionally conceptualized power as being *hierarchical,* in which one person or group is seen to "hold" power, and the other individual or group being "powerless." For example, Marx held that in society, the bourgeoisie held the power, while the proletariat or workers were the exploited, powerless class. Nonetheless, Marxist theory leaves open the possibility of a shift in power relations: Marx called on workers to rise up and revolt, and to restructure the power relationship through socialism and communism. In this way, Marx acknowledged the power of ideas, not just force, to shape human relations.

If we apply the hierarchical view of power to gender, then we believe that one group holds power over another. Most often, men are seen to hold power over women. A slightly more nuanced version sees women and men as having separate *spheres of power*, with the women's sphere situated in home and family (the "private" sphere), and the men's sphere being the "public" realm. For this reason, even as women have moved into the "public" sphere, they are still paid less on average than are men, they hold fewer positions of "authority," and they are likely to be disadvantaged should they bear children. Meanwhile, even though many men now share in household responsibilities and caregiving, most of these tasks are still largely the domain of women. But the two-spheres notion of power still places women in the lesser-power position. Women are much less likely than men to hold positions of political power: only 21 percent of members of Parliament are women, and only 32 percent of Senate members are women. Moreover, these women are likely to have their actions assessed in stereotypical and negative ways when they do hold public office. Belinda Stronach was vilified when she switched political parties in the spring of 2005, "painted as a spoiled, callous, deceitful woman of ambition—a latter-day Jezebel" (George et al, 2005, pp. 26). The hierarchical view of power posits that the patterns cited above are as a result of a gendered hierarchy of power: men having power and women remaining largely powerless.

Moreover, historically, men have been dominant in both the so-called public and private spheres. They have held the vast majority of public offices in Western societies; they have been economically advantaged; and indeed, until relatively recently, women were viewed not only culturally but legally as men's property. The treatment of women as property had profound implications for women in the private sphere. Without their own assets, women had very few options if they found themselves in abusive relationships. Many students will often respond, "Yes, but that was then, and this is now." Yet have these power inequalities disappeared? We still see vestiges of this pattern of domination and power inequities in today's societies. Unequal pay for similar or same work, and the existence of the double shift for women (*i.e.*, women work at home, go out to work in the paid labour force, and come home and work again) are but two examples of the ways in which the power structure of the past continues to this day.

The hierarchical view of power sees power as something that is held by one person or group over another. Thus, power means the ability to control materials, resources, or people.

A hierarchical view divides the world into the powerful and the less powerful, and sees the powerful as holding and using power as a tool or weapon with which it manipulates social institutions (such as law, social policy, and the military) to its advantage, ensuring its will and maintaining its rule. Less powerful groups are not completely without power; but they use power at an interpersonal level through intelligence, intuition, and avoidance of the power deployments of the more powerful. The hierarchical power division plays out in a gendered way in that men, who are characterized as the powerful, control the macro or structural use of power, and women use micro techniques to subvert men's power or to use power themselves.

What does hierarchical control look like? It can take the form of *coercive power*, in which the person who holds the power uses threats or punishments to force another person to do what the power-holder wishes. Sexual assault in the workplace often falls under this model of power, or under a similar model that focuses on rewards—*i.e.*, "If you submit to this, you'll get a raise or promotion." Power can also emanate from the office or position held by a person of power, often referred to as *legitimate power*. It can result from expertise or knowledge (*i.e.,* a physician's power). These types of power often exist in combination. In this way, hierarchical power is about power held by individuals or groups.

For our purposes, the links between gender and types of power are most important. For example, *who* is likely to use coercive power, to have the resources to use reward power, to be accorded legitimate power, or to be perceived as an expert? The answers to these questions show that men hold and use a disproportionate amount of power compared to women. However, traditional views of mothering might regard women as being more likely to hold power in the home, although some theorists would argue that even that power has always been overseen by men. But before we can explore *who* holds power, we have to examine what kinds of power there are to hold.

Informational power (or intellectual power) is the management of knowledge as a type of power. Historically, men's knowledge has usually been valued over women's knowledge. Women have challenged this dominance, such as writers like Virginia Woolf or Sylvia Plath. Woolf (1882–1949) was a prolific British writer whose works included explicitly feminist insights, including the idea that women needed their own money and their own space. She recognized that men's voices were often valued over women's. Woolf drowned herself in 1941. Plath (1932–1963) was an American writer whose work also focused on the restricted role of women. She too killed herself. Both Plath and Woolf are better known now then they were during their own lifetimes. Women who have managed to break or challenge the male dominance on knowledge have often lived in a state of existential angst that was quite likely produced by living in tension with the gender expectations of their time. The work of both Plath and Woolf reflects these tensions, although it would be too simplistic and somewhat overstated to reduce their work and lives to being solely about this tension.

Sexual power refers to the use of sexual favours to control situations. As such, sexual power has often been regarded the territory of women, who have the power to "give" sex when they want to and to withhold it in order to control or gain power. This version of power is a fairly narrow representation of the sexual lives of men and women. Not only is it heterosexist, but it also reinforces the view that women have no sexual desire other than to control men and that men are constantly in search of sex. Moreover, sexual assault, or rape, has been to some extent successfully recast as a power issue rather than an issue of desire or sex. In other words, when men sexually assault women, the motivation is not to fulfill sexual desire, but to wield power over woman/women.

But hierarchical, all-or-nothing views of power are problematic. One clear illustration of these problems is found in Catherine MacKinnon's argument (1987; 1989) about heterosexual relationships. Because gender relations are a system of power, MacKinnon argues that heterosexual sex must be understood as rape. Why? Women are so immersed in male patriarchal structure that they cannot possibly willingly consent to sexual relations; therefore, sexual interaction between women and men is never truly consensual. Students are often quick to criticize MacKinnon's work as extremist and absurd, but her work is important in pushing us to think about the boundaries of power and the possibilities for resistance. Can social structure bind us to the point that we really don't have a choice? Can we think we are making a choice, when we really, as Marx suggested, possess just a "false consciousness"? Who gets to decide whether we are *really* happy or whether we just think we are? The questions about choice go to broader debates in sociology about *agency*, or how and when people make choices. Whether we agree with MacKinnon's argument or not, she has made a valuable contribution to the dialogue on power, agency, and gender.

Anthony Giddens (1986) develops an equally hierarchical, although more subtle conceptualization of power, which he equates with *transformative capacity*—the power to change things. Although he acknowledges a relationship between power and the role of individual actors in power's transmission, he believes that power remains something that is *held* and *wielded*. "Power in this relational sense concerns the capability of actors to secure outcomes where the realisation of these outcomes depends upon the agency of others" (1986, p. 93).

However, hierarchical power has to be considered in terms of *level* of power, in addition to type of power. The old adage "the hand that rocks the cradle rules the world" illustrates levels of power. This saying suggests that women have *micro, behind-the-scenes,* or *private power* that transcends their behind-the-scenes role. Moreover, this indirect power is as important as the power men hold at the macro level and in fact shapes the macro level. In part, the first wave of feminism used this argument to gain women's suffrage: women as mothers were seen to have a moral superiority and thus needed to more directly shape public affairs.

The second wave of feminism also renegotiated the space between the public and the private, with the slogan "**The personal is political**." Women wished to move "private" issues into the public sphere, repudiating the notion that some aspects of life should be beyond the purview of political and legal action. For example, consider the Criminal Code provisions which exempted husbands from being charged with the rape of a wife, on the assumption that his wife was his property and he could do what he liked with her. Underlying this was a belief that what happened between a couple should be beyond the state's intervention. This is not ancient history either; these provisions were not repealed until 1983. When the second wave of feminism began moving the personal into the same level as the political, they began confronting these invisible power structures.

How do we "solve" the problem of power inequities between the genders? Institutional changes can shift inequities, such as equal pay and equal access to employment opportunities, but such structural changes do not necessarily result in *equality*. How do we explain the fact that women continue to do the vast majority of home labour, even when they are employed full-time in the paid labour force?

The second wave of feminism also addressed levels of power by confronting the "separate spaces" argument. The "separate spaces" argument states that women have advantages by having their own spaces to share exclusively with other women. Of course, women have always had their own organizations and spaces. Consider, for example, community organizations and church groups that have been the traditional territory of women. However, these spaces have often reflected women's domestic domain, reified the domestic role of women, and gendered the power relations. Moreover, the second wave of feminism shifted the use of these separate spaces, as women used the presence of other women to develop "consciousness raising" strategies, exploring their roles and their oppression. Today, some people would argue that the time for woman-only space has passed, and that women no longer need to raise their consciousness about women's issues. Others would argue that by creating and maintaining women-only spaces and organizations, we continue the ghettoization of women, rather than contributing to their empowerment. Moreover, the maintenance of separate spaces for women facilitates the argument for separate spaces for men, thus reinforcing the power base among men. For example, some people argue that if girls can have access to groups like Scouts, then so too should boys have access to Guides. Or if girls can play on boys' hockey teams, then boys should be able to play on girls' hockey teams. But this version of equality—treating everyone the same—fails to recognize the long-term structural disadvantages under which women have struggled. Thus, the "separate spaces" argument is being confronted from all sides.

Certainly, there are some strengths to a hierarchical view of power which presents a seemingly clear-cut view of power. It allows us to identify the "oppressed" and the "oppressor" with apparent ease and to take action that might alleviate inequality and eliminate the hierarchy. But there are problems hierarchical notions about power. First, not all men are "powerful" or hold power. For example, men of colour, men who are impoverished, and men who are physically or mentally challenged are not at the apex of the power hierarchy. Certainly, one could argue that even these men hold power over women in the same class. However, in general, intersections of particular groups of people affect their position on the power hierarchy. Secondly, hierarchical views of power can obscure *agency*—the ways that individuals and groups resist or fight power hierarchies. Women have gained the right to vote, secured equal pay legislation, and gained entry to professions such as law and medicine. In other words, if power existed only in an all-or-nothing form—in other words, you either have it or you don't—then these types of change would be difficult if not impossible.

POWER RELATIONS

Recently, postmodern challenges to the hierarchical view of power have resulted in a more nuanced conceptualization of power. From a postmodern view, power is relational: it is worked out between people, it is productive rather than repressive, and it is not an all-or-nothing proposition. Despite challenges, the **relational view of power** has added an interesting dimension to current theory. The French theorist Michel Foucault is perhaps primarily responsible for setting off this postmodern approach to understanding power (although Foucault did not define himself as a postmodernist, and there are clear influences of modernist thinkers in his work such as Karl Marx).

Following Foucault, Steven Winter has written an extensive critique of hierarchical power conceptualizations. He embraces a relational view of power and summarizes its important features:

> For Foucault, socio-cultural construction is an all-pervasive process from which no one escapes and in which everyone participates. This dynamic view of power underpins Foucault's claim that power is always vulnerable to disruption . . . Power as such is neither a 'thing' nor a quality, capacity, or possession of particular people. Rather, power is an emergent quality that can only take shape through the joint agency of all those who participate in a given set of social relations. (1996, p. 728)

The relational view of power has some key features. First, power is intimately linked to knowledge. Foucault succinctly stated this in the phrase "another power, another knowledge." Sociologists sometimes express this idea as *power/knowledge*. Be careful not to reduce this idea to "knowledge equals power," for in Foucault's way of thinking, power is *exercised*, not held. Second, power is a productive rather than a repressive force. If you think about the production of a social work or psychological file, for example, it may help you to think about what this means. Recall the work-up of the ADHD child described in Chapter Eight. The working up of the file was a productive process in which a multitude of people (including the child) participated. The creation, or production, of the file is intimately linked to knowledge—that of the parent, the teacher, and the expert. This example does not show that "they have the knowledge and therefore the power"; rather, if power is relational, then knowledge is part of the process. Hence, power is not held or filtered from the top down but is enacted from the bottom up. All persons involved participate in its working, such that the power is diffuse, like a net. In this respect, power is not hierarchical.

This non-hierarchical feature of the Foucault model is perhaps the most difficult part to understand, for we are so embedded in a culture that sees power as hierarchical and reproduces that view through language. As a result, it is sometimes difficult to grasp a model that does not start with a top-down vision of power. But consider the widespread, netlike nature of power. Power is everywhere and is produced at all micro-levels of society. Social relations are power relations, and thus power exists in the ways in which we speak, frame problems, and find solutions. Language is another vehicle through which power is reproduced on a day-to-day basis. As well, resistance is always a part of power relations. When we introduce this relational model in our classes, we ask students to think about the language we use to describe power: "they have the power . . . ," "if I had more power . . . ," "how can we get more power . . ." These expressions show the centrality of the hierarchical model. They also exclude the relational dimension of power and its enactment in everyday life.

An important focus of power as a relational process is the issue of *agency*. How and under what circumstances do people act or make decisions? Think back to MacKinnon's position that women are so oppressed that their agency is essentially eviscerated. MacKinnon's conceptualization of agency is integrally linked to power. In contrast, in a relational view of power, agency is exercised by both men and women. Women aren't simply "victims", they participate in the process of power relations. They are not acted upon; they act as well.

Robin West (1988) provides insight about gender and agency in her examinations of the notion of agency in the context of law. She argues that our society privileges autonomy and separation because it is rooted in classical liberal theory about personhood and state. In classical liberalism, individuals are free to make decisions about their own destiny. Thus, West argues, the context in which a person exercises agency is bounded by the idea that we are autonomous beings. But she challenges the idea that people within our society are freely choosing agents, autonomous and disconnected from social relations. Rebecca Johnson supports West's ideas. "The rhetoric of choice provides a simple model for locating power and fixing responsibility for consequences. If a given situation is the result of a person's own choosing, it would be inappropriate to intervene: the person suffering made choices—made their own bed, so to speak. If, on the other hand, the situation is the result of force or coercion, intervention may well be called for: where power obviously lies in the hands of a second party, the first person cannot be said to have meaningfully chosen" (2002, p. 125). Both West and Johnson emphasize the connectedness of human beings, one to another, through social relations; and they both argue that this connectedness must be considered in theories about power and agency. Although West's language uses hierarchical notions of power, her point about the relational nature of agency is important for this discussion.

However, feminist literature challenges the relational view of power such as that followed by Foucault and Winter, because relational power denies the very real oppression of some groups by others. Moreover, it shifts the focus away from the structural elements of power, which are critical ideas for social change movements. Alan Hunt (1993) proposed a compromise position: that power theories must recognize these structural elements, which he calls *condensation*. This compromise means that power can be recognized as not wholly transitory, but as having patterns in which it is reproduced. This does not mean patterns cannot be shifted or contested, but that they must be recognized as existing over time and place.

WOMEN AND MEN IN CONVERSATION

Hunt's notion of condensation of power through patterns is evident in patterns of conversation. Communication is central to the social construction of gender. Human beings communicate through the spoken word, texts, and gestures. Often as important as what is stated or written is what is *left out*. **Discursive frameworks**—ways of organizing knowledge that produce "truths" or "facts"—remain invisible and unchallenged. A significant body of research has been done on the topic of conversation interaction patterns between women and men. Moreover, some researchers have focused on gendered discourse in specific situations, such as classrooms and courtrooms, focusing on ways that people in positions of authority talk about women or men.

Consider all of the non-verbal signals you use in day-to-day life. Frowning, smiling, and nodding are all non-verbal methods of communicating that work to affirm or complement the speaker. Sometimes you use those signals to supplement verbal communication, but sometimes the signal is all that is expressed. Instructors are used to looking for non-verbal signals from students: for example, frowns means either disagreement or lack of understanding. Gestures can act as a signal to others to join in a conversation or to stay out of it. Non-verbal language can convey respect or lack thereof, not only to the conversation partner but also to others around her or him. For example, consider the message conveyed to a woman's co-workers if her male boss lets his eyes keep drifting to her breasts while she is trying to communicate a concern or an idea. Non-verbal language can reproduce power or resist power condensations.

The power of even very subtle gestures cannot be understated. In "Blink," Malcolm Gladwell (2005) reviews the research of Ekman and Friesen, who have developed a typology of facial movements they call *action units*. These action units convey subtle meaning beyond the spoken word. Gladwell introduces his discussion this way: "If you were to see me grinning, for example, with my eyes twinkling, you'd say I was amused. But if you were to see me nod and smile exaggeratedly, with the corners of my lips tightened, you would take it that I had been teased and was responding sarcastically. If I were to make eye contact with someone, give a small smile, and then look down and avert my gaze, you would think I was flirting. If I were to follow a remark with a quick smile and then nod or tilt my head sideways, you might conclude that I had just said something a little harsh and wanted to take the edge off it. You wouldn't need to hear anything I was saying in order to reach these conclusions"(2005, p. 195).

However, there is some evidence that the two sexes have different ways of working with non-verbal language. Men tend to use gesture and space to command and retain attention, while they use volume and inflection to emphasize ideas. Women are generally better at reading non-verbal communication accurately, and a variety of explanations explain why. Some attribute this skill to differences in brain "wiring" in men and women; others argue that women are socialized to be more attentive to feelings and their expression; and some people argue that women's subordinate position has trained them to be able to interpret non-verbal cues more readily.

In the classic Fishman study (1978), conversations between three couples were recorded over the course of several days, resulting in 50 hours of tape. The couples were all graduate students who were sympathetic to the women's movement. But the tapes revealed distinctly gendered patterns in the conversation that exposed an inequality between the men and women. First, women had to work harder to finish interaction; that is, they had to struggle to finish their sentences or to recover from interruption. In addition, men had more control over the direction of the conversation. For example, when women introduced topics (over the course of the experiment, they introduced 47 topics), only 36 percent (17 topics) got responses. But when the men introduced topics (they introduced 29 topics), fully 96 percent (28 topics) got responses. As well, during the course of their conversations, women asked questions two-and-a-half times more often than did men. Women always responded to men's statements, but men didn't always respond to women's statements. The conclusion of the study was that the work of doing conversation is gendered.

Similarly, the Tannen (1990) study found that there is a difference in type and style of talk between men and women. Tannen divided the types of talk (or communication) into two categories: *rapport talk,* which builds relationships by showing support for the conversational partner, and *report talk*, which communicates information. Women were more likely to engage in rapport talk, responding to and building upon the ideas of the other. Tannen notes that rapport talk has a certain tentativeness and uses qualifiers and questions to maintain openness. Men, on the other hand, are more likely to use report talk. Report talk exerts control, is directive, and uses forceful language. Moreover, it leaves out personal information and is not responsive to the conversation cues (in other words, it doesn't build upon the ideas of the other). Tannen also found that men tend to talk more in public, and women more in private, following the public-private sphere divisions discussed earlier.

What conclusions can we draw about conversation, power, and gender? James and Drakich (1993) assessed the findings of 63 studies about gender and conversation. They conclude that men and women tend to talk more in areas in which they are socially constructed to have expertise. In other words, men and their report-talk style of conversation do not dominate in all conversation situations. As a result, the hierarchical power model needs to be augmented with a more nuanced understanding of power. "Our work complements and extends the power explanation by moving the discourse from gender dispositions of power to the shared set of performance expectations which differentiate individuals, and as a consequence both give rise to power differences and maintain and perpetuate status hierarchies in social interaction" (1993, p. 301). While men and women do deploy conversation in different ways, there is a relational aspect to this playing out of power that needs to be more fully explored.

What about conversation between women? How is it gendered? Research by Guendouzi (2001) focusing on "gossip" found that while women's conversation does contain elements of co-operation and collaboration, there are some important gendered patterns that suggest our society is not yet in a post-feminist era. Guendouzi concluded that women's conversation is both co-operative and competitive; and this latter aspect "reproduces and recycles hegemonic versions of femininity that ultimately constrict the options of gender identity available to women" (2001, p. 48). In other words, women still reproduce condensations of patriarchal power in their conversations.

But conversation is not merely about two people in verbal interaction. Conversation also uses cultural tools, such as language, that are imbued with gendered meaning. As such, these cultural tools structure gender relations and reproduce power relations. Sociologist Dorothy Smith (1987) is well known for her use of textual analysis in a variety of settings. Using a methodology she calls **institutional ethnography** (which begins from the standpoint of the oppressed and then considers the organizing mechanisms of social structure that shape their experiences), Smith's work reveals the gendered patterns in everyday life and links them to social structure. It is important that we understand the links between conversation patterns and the creation of texts and power beyond an individual level. Smith's work highlights the links between conversation patterns and broader-level texts and power and then explores the importance and relationship of these patterns to gender. Like Foucault, Smith is interested not only in what is said, but also in what is left out of the discursive framework. She argues that all too often, women's experiences are not reflected in the working up of official narratives or stories; and when women's experiences or voices do make it into the framework, they are minimized.

Smith's institutional ethnography begins from the standpoint of people who are marginalized (2005). The stories of marginalized peoples are un-tellable in the discursive framework. In other words, they remain outside of the story that emerges as the official version. Smith reflects on the ways in which some versions of "the facts" are privileged over others, often because of race or gender. The following simple example illustrates what she is arguing:

> Riding a train not long ago in Ontario I saw a family of Indians: woman, man, and three children standing together on a spur above a river watching the train go by. There was (for me) that moment—the train, those five people seen on the other side of the glass. I saw first that I could tell this incident as it was, but that telling as a description built in my position and my interpretations. I have called them a family; I have said they were watching the train. My understanding has already subsumed theirs. Everything may have been quite other for them. My description is privileged to stand as what actually happened, because theirs is not heard in the contexts in which I may speak. (1987, p. 112)

Smith challenges us to think about whose voice is privileged in the working-up of the "facts" and to raise questions about the race, class, and gender of those whose voices "count". Jo-Anne Fiske gives us an example of how the "facts" are worked up in the following discussion.

BOX 10-1	ASD and FASD: The Ambiguity of Power and the Power of Ambiguity

by Jo-Anne Fiske

Feminist scholars share a common interest in exposing, explicating, and often altering processes of power. In so doing, many will turn their analytical gaze to social movements and advocacy campaigns to analyse the origins, manifestations and consequences of power. A recurring object of study is the construct of social identities that stigmatize women, their bodies, and their children. Thus we ask: How do identifying categories emerge and what are the individual and social consequences of these social constructs? Who holds the power to construct identities and who wields powers that sustain constructs that marginalize groups of women and render them suspect in the public eye?

Recognition of production of women as marginal and suspect is by no means new; the issue is as old as the social sciences themselves. In the last half century in particular, numerous theories offered insights into how this production takes place. The path-breaking work of Erving Goffman (1963) on stigma and "spoiled identity" was rapidly followed by numerous threads of theory and diverse case studies. In 1984, Schur illustrated the approach of "labelling theory" or "social reactions theory" to study the construction of deviance. Others turned to social and construction theories to study pre-menstrual syndrome, menopause, and other constructs that pathologize women's bodies and behaviours (see, for example, Weitz 1998). At the same time, social scientists engaged in what is now called the " linguistic turn" from empirical studies of observed behaviour to consideration of discursive culture as they followed the lead of post-structuralist, postmodernist and post-colonial theorists, most notably Michael Foucault (DiQuinzio, 1999). These theoretical frameworks posited new concepts that seek to expose the power inherent in us all to assert control over others and the role discourses play in defining our subjectivity and placing in relations of power.

These theorists have advanced our understanding of how power works within the context of ambiguity as social members take up social constructs and append new and shifting meanings to them (Groz, 1994). One process that is of particular interest to feminist scholars is the emergence of ersatz medical constructs as social categories of identity and being: that is, the medicalization of individuals who, so marked, become popularly understood as problematic and even dangerous. Medicalization occurs when behaviours or conditions are given medical meanings, and in consequence medical practices become a vehicle for exerting power to control problematic behaviours that are deemed deviant or abnormal. Of equal interest is the rise of social movements that contend doctors lack competency to diagnose putative medical conditions and need direction from the pubic. In these instances, medicalization emerges from a public consciousness that a major problem exists and must be remedied for the benefit not only of the afflicted but also of society at large. In these instances, power lies within a social movement that is successful in its appeals for mass support and for legislative

BOX 10-1	*(Continued)*

changes. In the process, ersatz medical discourses take on new meanings as diagnosis becomes politicized and contested. Power resides in what we already know; what we bring to potentially novel encounters determines to large degree how we react and what we produce in our social interactions in consequence

Illustrations of these power relations can be found in rising attribution of two medicalized categories popularly used to label children and in consequence their mothers: autism spectrum disorder (ASD) and fetal alcohol spectrum disorder (FASD). By critically analyzing representations of these conditions by support groups and social movements on the World Wide Web, we can locate some processes of power that underlie their social construction and popular responses to them.[1]

Their discursive appeal lies in emotional resonance they construct for innocent victims of alleged negligence and or accidental misfortune. Representations of these two conditions have a number of facets in common: they lack certainty and clarity of diagnosis; diagnosis is relatively recent and relies on defining characteristics listed in the psychiatric diagnostic and statistical manual of mental disorders; international networks have emerged to guide parents, teachers and the public in the identification of individuals afflicted by the applied diagnosis; the numbers of children so diagnosed is increasing; and identification has spread beyond medical diagnosis to "social" diagnosis undertaken by educators, social workers, counsellors and other "helping" professionals, and even by non-credentialed members of support groups and electronic networks. Significantly, the symptoms used

to diagnose each of the three are so unclear that confusion of diagnosis within and between the conditions is common and as more children are presented for testing the spectrum of these disorders increases. FASD, for example, now contains six diagnostic categories where twenty years ago there was but one. Similarly in current discourses autism has gone from a singular category ("autism", that once was defined only as a neuro-developmental disorder of communication) to a spectrum of a communication and social problems through to the anomalous PDD-NOS, pervasive developmental disorder not otherwise specified.

Competition between advocacy groups highlights the conundrum of diagnosis and identity construction. Their debates are voiced in a moralist discourse marked by urgency and unequivocal assertions that there can be no doubt as to the truth they proclaim. The International Fetal Alcohol Disorders Society asseverates,"FASD is so grossly under-reported that the FASD statistics are almost meaningless. There are very few doctors who have received any training in diagnosing FASD, and most prefer to use "non-judgmental" diagnoses such as ADD, ADHD, LD, MR, RAD, ODD, Bi-Polar, Autism, Tourette's, etc.. These 'diagnoses' don't imply the mother has done something that could have affected her baby during her pregnancy." Complexity is elided and ambiguity of developmental disorders denied in statements such as this; by appealing in simplistic terms, the advocacy group frames its appeal in simple terms that impute lack of medical competence and a politic that refuses to hold mothers accountable for their actions. Centuries of censoring women's

(Continued)

BOX 10-1	ASD and FASD: The Ambiguity of Power and the Power of Ambiguity (*Continued*)

use of alcohol in conjunction with centuries of pathologizing the expectant mother conjoin in FASD discourse. In a similar vein, autism advocacy groups claim underreporting of autistic disorders and cite rising numbers in estimates ranging up to 1 in 150 births from 1 in 1000 a decade ago.

Medicalization of conditions that carry notions of deviance and abnormality carries with it discourses of identity. Through the Internet and support groups, FASD and ASD "communities" emerge. Frequently, parents, professional experts, and the general public speak of children who *are* FASD, ADHD, and autistic, as opposed to children having any of the conditions. Identity formation is taken up by individuals so categorized that in common conversation one hears such personal representations as "I am FASD." The assignment of subject positions through these discourses stands in sharp contrast to discourses of medical illnesses. (Thus one does not hear mothers describing their children as *being cancer,* for example, but as having cancer.)

Identity of children through medicalization of development delays and undesired behaviours extends to and is taken up by parents, most notably mothers. This is most evident in ASD and FASD advocacy groups, the former meets in April, the latter in September. Mothers organizing these events are positioned as heroic indefatigable women struggling not only for their own child but fighting to change the consciousness of the public. These heroic mothers, in the case of FASD, usually adoptive mothers, stand as foil to mothers who have failed their children by drinking during pregnancy.

Power of definition carries with it power to alarm. Advocacy actions such as international FASD day (September 9 marked at 9 a.m. by ringing 9 bells) constitute an emotive appeal that constructs not only claimed reality of affliction but the alarm of ballooning costs to care for the afflicted, fears of rising criminal behaviours and prison costs, and dependency on welfare.

Thus, FASD children are positioned as marginal social subjects who in infancy and youth are an economic burden and who in adulthood emerge as a social threat, as retroactive attribution of FASD is applied to incarcerated individuals. ASD discourses carry similar alarms, as advocacy groups claim each child will costs tens of millions through their lifetime. It is the all-encompassing nature of these identity constructs that sets disempowered individuals apart and creates them both as burden and threat—burden on taxpayers and a threat to social order. As these two cases illustrate, those who are marginalized by markers of difference are associated with danger and vulnerability.

As the alarm spreads and advocates make even more impassioned claims as to the social consequences of developmental disorders, the medical community continues to struggle with conflicting and contradictory evidence as to aetiology of abnormal development. The power to define the diagnosis no longer lies solely in their hands but is increasingly in the hands of moral crusaders ever anxious to find a cure and a means to impose moral regulation on mothers and the medical community.

BOX 10-1 | *(Continued)*

References Cited

DiQuinzio, Patrice. (1999.) *The Impossibility of Motherhood: Feminism, Individualism and the Problem of Mothering*. New York: Routledge.

Foucault, Michel. (1977.) *Discipline and Punish: The Birth of the Prison*. Translated by Alan Sheridan. London: Allan Lane.

Goffman, Erving. (1963) *Stigma*. Englewood Cliffs: Prentice Hall.

Groz, Elizabeth. (1994.) *Volatile Bodies: Towards a Corporeal Feminism*. Bloomington: Indiana University Press.

Schur, Edwin M. (1984.) *Labeling Women Deviant: Gender, Stigma and Social Control*. Philadelphia: Temple University Press.

Sample of Websites Consulted

Alberta Region 3 FAS Partnership (www.fas-region3.com)

Alcohol Related Birth Injury (FAS/FAE) Resource Site (www.arbi.org)

ASA: The Voice of Autism, The Autism Society of America (http://www.autism-society.org/site/PageServer)

Autism and PDD Support Network (http://www.autism-pdd.net/)

Canadian Centre on Substance Abuse (www.ccsa.ca)

Crime Times: Linking Brain Dysfunction to Disordered/Criminal/Psychopathic Behaviour (www.crime-times.org)

Facts about FAS/FAE (www.taconic.net/seminars/fas-a.html)

FAS Community Resource Centre (http://www.come-over.to/FASCRC)

FAS Family Resource Institute (http://fetal-alcoholsyndrome.org)

FAS/E Support Network of BC (http://www.fetalalcohol.com/)

FASlink: Fetal Alcohol Syndrome Information Support and Communications Link (www.acbr.com/fas/)

FASSTAR Enterprises: Fetal Alcohol Syndrome: Support, Training, Advocacy, and Resources (www.fasstar.com)

Fetal Alcohol Syndrome Diagnostic and Prevention Network (FAS DPN) (http://depts.washington.edu/fasdpn/screening.html)

Generation Rescue (http://www.generationrescue.org/)

League for the Prevention of Alcohol Related Fetal Brain Injury (www.Worldprofit.com/ma.fas.htm).

National Organization on Fetal Alcohol Syndrome (www.nofas.org)

Screening for Mental Health, Inc. (www.nationalalcoholscreeningday.org)

Substance Abuse Mental Health Services Association (SAMHSA), US Department of Health and Human Services FASD Center for Excellence (www.fascenter.samhsa.gov/indexcfm)

1. Scans of websites for each of the three medicalized categories constituted a portion of research I conducted over the past two years. This work in part was funded by the Centre of Excellence for Children with Special Needs (University of Northern British Columbia) and CHILD Project of University of British Columbia through SSHRC. A sample of websites studied is given in the reference list.

VIOLENCE AGAINST WOMEN

Violence is often equated with hierarchical power, and the case study of male violence against women illustrates the need for a complex model of power. This section focuses on violence against women, especially (but not exclusively) in the context of intimate family relations. It is interesting that even the term *violence against women* has been the source of great contention. Terms such as *domestic violence* and *family violence* are linguistic representations of power relations and are an attempt to displace "blame" for violence and to situate responsibility with both men and women. This struggle to name the behaviour is based on a relational model of power, which accepts the negotiated and contested aspects of any label or terminology.

Why focus on violence against women? While violence against women is about coercive and physical expressions of power, it also raises the question of the equation of force and power. Despite two decades of research on violence against women, there are no easy answers to the question *why*. Some researchers argue that it is as a result of male power, while others argue that men who abuse are acting on feelings of powerlessness. Other theories incorporate structural expectations about masculinity and the exercise of force. Moreover, when the authors raise this issue with students, they frequently hear the response, "Yes, but what about women abusing men?" This question is often followed by a story connected to that student's own experience. This discussion is not a denial of female-to-male violence, but the evidence is overwhelming that patterns of violence in North American society are male-to-female.

Statistics from the "Fact Sheet: Statistics On Violence Against Women In Canada" (December 6, 2004) on the *Status of Women Canada* website show that male-to-female violence, both physical and sexual, is pervasive:

- Over three-quarters (77 percent) of reported victims of criminal harassment in 2000 were women.
- Half of Canadian women (51 percent) have been victims of at least one act of physical or sexual violence since the age of 16.
- Of all victims of crimes against the person in 2000, females made up the vast majority of victims of sexual assaults (86 percent), criminal harassment (78 percent), and kidnapping/hostage-taking or abduction (67 percent).
- Of the almost 34 000 victims of spousal violence reported in 2000, women accounted for the majority of victims (85 percent), a total of 28 633 victims.
- Female victims of spousal violence tend to experience more severe consequences than male victims. Of all victims of spousal violence in the five years prior to the 1999 General Social Survey, female victims aged 15 years and over were almost seven times more likely to be sexually assaulted than male victims (20 percent versus 3 percent), five times more likely to report being choked (20 percent versus 4 percent), more than twice as likely to report being beaten (25 percent versus 10 percent), and almost twice as likely to report being threatened with a gun or a knife or had one used against them (13 percent versus 7 percent). Female victims were also pushed, grabbed or shoved almost twice more than male victims (81 percent versus 43 percent). (http://www. swc-cfc. gc.ca/dates/dec6/facts_e.html)

Is there something about being male that is linked to the use of violence? Certainly, if the statistics above were reversed—if female-to-male violence showed the sort of systematic use of violence outlined above—we would probably conclude that there was something about being a woman that included an inherent tendency toward violence. Sometimes in our classes we've asked students to imagine what the world would look like if women were, on average, physically larger than men. Often, the students conclude that women might use their physical might in violent ways; but they also conclude that how the use of violence is socially specific and the circumstances in which it is used are the more important considerations.

Some researchers have tried to link male aggression to testosterone. But the causal link is not as clear as popular reports would have us believe. For example, non-violent men do not become violent when their testosterone levels are increased. In general, purely biological explanations do not account for the manner in which we encourage or discourage aggression or violence in society. Considerable evidence suggests that the way men are socialized is key to understanding male violence and its use.

Unfortunately, we live in a culture that seems to have the structural support for male use of violence. North American men are the most violent people in the industrialized world (homicide, assault, sexual assault). But what about North American women? Aren't they violent too?

Initial research on violence against women by their intimate partners was highly contentious. Some measures purported to show women as aggressors too, thus leading some researchers to minimize the male-to-female aspect of such assaults (see Straus, 1979; Straus & Gelles, 1986). But subsequent research showed that when women did use violence, it tended to be defensive in response to male aggression. Moreover, when women used force, they tended to do less damage (*i.e.*, injury was much less serious or less likely). Further, motivations for violence seem to be different between men and women. Men use violence instrumentally to achieve a goal, whereas fear and feelings of helplessness motivate women to use physical force. Statistics Canada (2000) data showed that women were three times more likely than men to be injured by spousal violence. Homicide in such circumstances is much more likely to be perpetrated by men than by women.

Despite nearly 30 years of research on violence against women, we seem to be making minimal headway in resolving this issue. Joseph Michalski (2004) argues that there needs to be clearer sociological discussions of those features of social life that facilitate violence. In other words, we need to focus away from the interpersonal factors discussed above. He argues that there are six structural factors that need to be more fully researched:

1. The degree of social isolation (how much contact does the couple have with others in the community?);

2. The interdependence of the couple's support networks (how linked is the community and how integrated is the couple in that community?);

3. Inequality in the couple (does the woman have as much decision-making authority as the man? Who controls the finances?);

4. Relational distance of the couple (how close is the couple? Are they distant but "stuck together" because of lack of geographic mobility?);

5. The centralization of authority (is it a patriarchal family structure or an egalitarian one?);

6. Exposure to violent networks (did either person grow up in a violent family, or has either been in a violent relationship before?).

However, even these structural factors cannot be considered in isolation from interactional aspects. For example, research has found that domestic violence varies according to the balance of power in the household. Spousal abuse is most common when power is concentrated in the hands of the husband. Increased equality between spouses can equal decreased violence (Yllo & Straus, 1990).

Certainly, the reasons why a woman stays in an abusive relationship are often closely linked to resources and their perceived availability by women. Dependence, in other words, produces a power imbalance, which in turn may facilitate violence. If the abused woman feels isolated, without economic or social resources, she will perceive herself as having no choice but to stay in the relationship (Yllo & Straus, 1990).

A. Violence in Same-Sex Relationships

The discussion thus far has assumed a heteronormative order. Much less is known about violence within same-sex relationships. But certainly we can argue that power inequities play a key role.

In their research on sexual identity, Miller *et al.* (2000) point out that research on violence in same-sex relationships is extremely limited. What they have noted is that power relations in same-sex couples exist in the context of "cultural oppression and internalized homophobia" (2000, p. 190). Thus, since responses to intimate partner violence are primarily directed at heterosexual couples, gays and lesbians in violent relationships find themselves isolated.

Janice Ristock has challenged the denial of abuse in lesbian relationships in her book *No More Secrets* (2002). She acknowledges the potential political costs of focusing on such violence, including deflection of attention from male violence and the possibility of a backlash against feminism and lesbians (2002, p. 3). But denial of violence in lesbian relationships has the effect of closeting such violence, rendering its victims even more vulnerable.

Ristock seeks to set violence in context, which includes homophobia, fear of discovery, need for secrecy, lack of same-sex relationship experience, immigration issues, previous relationship abuse, drug and alcohol abuse, poverty, and racism. She cautions against using a simplified version of power theory to analyze violence in this context. "It is not that power and control are not features of abusive relationships, but that we rely on a simplified version with a corresponding set of assumptions to distinguish a victim and a perpetrator rather than exploring contextualized relations of power" (2002, pp. 113–114). Ristock calls for a more complex theory of power to understand the intersection of violence, gender, and sexuality.

B. Power Structures and Violence Against Women

How does abuse in relationships relate to power? We might be tempted to return to a hierarchical vision of power to conceptualize the abusive male (or other more powerful partner) as holding all the power and the abused female as having no power. However, some important feminist research has highlighted the fact that abused women are not simply victims but also agents in their own abuse. This does not mean that they *cause* the violence or abuse or that they are in any manner responsible for it; it simply means that women can and do exercise agency in such situations. For example, some women successfully bring together their resources to end violence in their relationships, while others return to abusive relationships after escaping. Martha Mahoney argues that "neither concepts of agency nor of victimization fully take account of women's experiences of oppression and resistance in relationships"

(1994, p. 63). She is critical of the all-or-nothing approach to agency that "treats agency in women as synonymous with exit from violence relationship" (1994, p. 73); and she calls for a more nuanced understanding of how agency is conceptualized and exercised. This is difficult terrain to walk, for a simpler model that conceptualizes such violence hierarchically makes violence against women easier to deal with. One of the problems with the hierarchical model has also been a tendency to focus on women's perceptions of violent interaction. These perceptions are certainly important; but if we are to understand the dynamics of abuse at both the interpersonal level and the structural level, we need to understand how men think about violence as well. To be blunt, if men do not conceptualize their use of force as a problem, strategies to deal with their "problem" by women will be unlikely to succeed. The key is to problematize the use of violence at both structural and interpersonal levels.

Moreover, Boonzaier and de La Rey (2003) argue that focusing on the experiences of women in abusive relationships has resulted in a characterization of woman abuse as a "woman's problem," deflecting responsibility for the problem from men, both interpersonally and structurally, despite the preponderance of male-to-female violence. Boonzaier and de La Rey focus on both men's and women's accounts of violence and attempt to assess both the differences and similarities in those accounts. Especially important for our discussion of gender and power, they found that the participants had constructed forms of gendered identities that were both ambiguous and contradictory: that is, they perform gender and reify hegemonic constructions of femininity and masculinity. Wood's (2004) findings are similar. Her interviews with abusive men revealed a commitment to both the idea that men are dominant and superior and need to be in control of a relationship and the idea that men are protectors of women and as such should not hit them. This research reveals the centrality of gender in violent relationships and its link to power relations.

ART: CULTURAL ICONS AND THE NEGOTIATION OF POWER

The link between violence, power, and gender is fairly straightforward. But some aspects of power in gendered situations may not be quite as obvious. The creation and content of works of art illustrates the net-like qualities of power. Historically, the social construction of art is of a male project and often takes as its beginning point the female nude. But this social construction is not easily identifiable as a place in a hierarchical order. Rather, what is valued as art and the power relations implicit in that process is produced from the ground up, not the top down. The following case study illustrates the subtle workings of power.

How does the production and content of works of art relate to gender and power? Take the time to go to your local art museum and head for the permanent collection, paying particular attention to the art of the last 500 years. (We focus in this section on the visual arts, specifically on painting. We encourage you to think about other forms of art and the gender divisions within them.) How many women artists are represented in the collection? Likely not many. Is this because there were no women artists during that time period?

Now, go to the contemporary section of the museum. Even there, you are unlikely to see as many works by women as there are by men. Look at the websites of a sample of contemporary museums—what are their current exhibits? What percentage feature women? Is this because there are no contemporary women artists?

In her article "Why Have There Been No Great Women Artists" (1988), Linda Nochlin responds to this question by sorting through the "locker room" of the great male artist. She argues that the question subverts attention from the conditions under which the great male artist is produced. She asks provocatively, "What if Picasso had been born a girl? Would Senor Ruiz have paid as much attention or stimulated as much ambition for achievement in a little Pablita?" (1988, p. 155). Nochlin's question raises both the structural conditions of the production (and definition) of "greatness," but also highlights the interactive components of that process. Power is implicated at both production and interaction levels, and it is gendered in the process. Nochlin concludes that "art is not a free, autonomous activity of a super-endowed individual, 'influenced' by previous artists, and, more vaguely and superficially, by 'social forces,' but rather, that the total situation of art making, both in terms of the development of the art maker and in the nature and quality of the work of art itself, occur in a social situation, are integral elements of this social structure, and are mediated and determined by specific and definable social institutions, be they art academies, systems of patronage, mythologies of the divine creator, artist as he-man or social outcast" (p. 158). In other words, what art museums consider "great art" has been collected not just as works of *art*, but as expressions of "greatness" as defined by human interaction embedded in power relations.

Now, look again at the art in the museum. What is the subject matter of the works? Do male artists focus on the same subject matter as female artists? To challenge the dominance of the male perspective in art, some women artists have appropriated traditional women's crafts as media through which contemporary messages can be conveyed. For example, quilts may be used to portray women's fear, agony, or pain, rather than the traditional pretty patterns. Moreover, some women's art is overtly feminist, challenging the gender divide and the relations of power that are supported by and through that divide. Judy Chicago's famous installation *The Dinner Party* premiered in 1979. Using a triangular table set with elaborate place settings, whose "butterfly designs" were obviously meant to represent female genitalia, Chicago constructed a simultaneously complex yet simple commentary on gender and the social construction of "importance" in art as well as in life (Jones & Cottingham, 1996). The installation was both a celebration of notable women from history as well as a challenge to the gendered order of the art world. In addition, beginning in 1985, the Guerilla Girls continued to challenge the art order. The Guerilla Girls (http://www.guerillagirls.com/index.shtml) were a group of women artists who wore gorilla masks to both disguise their identities to avoid retaliation as well as to retain a focus on the issue of male dominance of the art world: "For the next fifteen years or so, the Guerilla Girls became famous for their sly posters and inspired street theatre. 'Do women have to be naked to get into the Met Museum?' one poster asked, noting that less than five percent of the modern artists shown there were women but more than eighty-five percent of the museum's nudes were female" (Toobin, pp. 34–35, 2005).

Let's also examine the role of the nude in art. In his classic book, *Ways of Seeing* (1972), John Berger analyzes the use of the nude and implications of its use, as well as its portrayal of women. Berger argues that in art, men act and women appear. Thus, the woman is always surveyed and available to the spectator-owner. Women are passive, nude, and available for the viewing (and the taking). Berger argues that of the hundreds of thousands of nudes in the European tradition, only about 100 do not leave room in the picture for the male spectator. Berger goes further, though, and argues that "today the attitudes and values which informed that tradition are expressed through other more widely diffused media—advertising, journalism, television. But the essential way of seeing women, the essential use to which their images are put, has not changed. Women are depicted in a quite different way from men—not because the feminine is different from the masculine—but because the 'ideal' spectator is always assumed to be male and the image of the woman is designed to flatter him" (1972, p. 64).

One of the major impediments to women's artistic training was the use of the nude in art schools and studios. Because it was thought to be unseemly for women to see a nude body, particularly in the company of men, women were excluded from such "scenes." Griselda Pollock (1988) notes that educational institutions that trained artists resisted women's participation. Women did sometimes resist their exclusion by studying privately and hiring their own models or soliciting the help of friends or family. But Pollock notes that this did not really resolve the problem. "It was the men of the academy and the ideologues who determined what images were produced in the most prestigious and ideologically significant arenas of cultural production. Control over access to the nude was instrumental in the exercise of power over what meanings were constructed by an art based upon an ideal of the human body. Official exclusion from the nude model ensured that women had no means to determine the language of high art or to make their own representations of the world, from their point of view, and thus to resist and contest the hegemony of the dominant class or gender" (1988, p. 45). The complex power relations involved in the process of training in art, the production of art, the display of paintings, and their critical review were inherently gendered.

Whitney Chadwick (1990) makes a similar point, arguing that the gendered norms for women dictated against their training as artists. Her historical research includes a letter that captures the difficulties women who wished to be artists faced. "'Does it pay,' wrote an irate member of the public to the Board of Directors of the Pennsylvania Academy in 1883, 'for a young lady of a refined, godly household to be urged as the only way of obtaining a knowledge of true art, to enter a class where every feeling of maidenly delicacy is violated, where she becomes so hardened to indelicate sights and words, so familiar with the persons of degraded women and the sight of nude males, that no possible art can restore her lost treasure of chaste and delicate thoughts . . . ?" (1990, pp. 165–66).

A recent article in the *New York Times* (Allen, 2005) compared the selling prices of contemporary works of art by well-known female and male artists. Although admittedly difficult to compare, the article points out that the top auction prices for works of art for male and female artists differ significantly. In comparing two similarly situated British artists, the auction price suggested for the female artist is $400 000–$600 000, and the piece by the male artists sold for $13.3 million. Although this comparison is obviously not a scientific measure, experts in the arts field admit that the work of male artists is valued significantly higher than that of female artists.

So what does all of this tell us about power? With a hierarchical view of power, we could argue that patriarchy and men have structurally prevented women from entering into the world of the visual arts. Yet, although both views are true to some extent, there is evidence of women's success in the realm of the arts without official recognition. Women have created their own definitions of art and have used what has been available to them—leftovers, scraps, hand-me-downs—to create works of art. But these "resistances"—quilts, embroidery, tatting, needlepoint, rug hooking—have been designated as "craft," effectively removed from the realm of "high art" and as such devalued both monetarily and culturally.

CONCLUSIONS

How you think about power, as a student and as a scholar, is ultimately your decision. When you look at the world around you, think about the different ways models of power make sense of what you see. Different perspectives lend different insights, all of which help us to think about gender and the way it is constructed and reproduced. Perhaps most important is to see gender and power as an ongoing relationship that is not static in nature.

Yet no matter which model of power we, gender inequality remains a problem. The research of Diekman *et al.* (2004) does not support optimism: they conclude that despite gains in political, economic, occupational, individual, and relational power, women will not reach power parity with men even by 2050! They point out that "much empirical evidence documents that people react more negatively to women than to men in powerful positions—in part because women in traditional roles are especially valued (*e.g.*, benevolent sexism) and in part because women in non-traditional roles are especially devalued (*e.g.*, hostile sexism)" (2004, p. 202). It may be that if we come to better understand the circuitous, complex nature of power and its everyday workings, we can unravel the power relations that reproduce gender sedimentations (repeated patterns of gender relations) and inequalities. It may be, as Steven Winter argues, that power lies at the heart of problems of gender.

CHAPTER SUMMARY: KEY POINTS

1. Gender and power are inextricably linked.
2. How we theorize power has important implications for how we theorize and respond to gender inequality.
3. Modernist views of power employ a hierarchical or top-down view of how power works.
4. Postmodern views of power shift the focus to the relational and diffuse ways in which power works.
5. How we think about power is critical to how we conceptualize agency.
6. Discursive frameworks shape the way knowledge is created.
7. Conversation and gesture form part of how power is enacted.
8. Violent intimate relationships illuminate the complexities of power, and raise questions about how power is defined.
9. The production of cultural artifacts, such as paintings, is gendered.
10. The relationship between gender and power is dynamic and must be analyzed as such.

DISCUSSION QUESTIONS

1. Is violence against women simply about men "having" more power than women?
2. What are the factors that create a "work of art"? Think about some of the pieces of art that make the news. Who creates them? Why are they in the news?
3. Have you experienced conversation in gendered ways?
4. Do you think it is useful to talk about shifting the balance of power when dealing with gender inequality?

KEY WORDS

agency	hierarchical power	relational power
discursive frameworks	informational power	sexual power
gender sedimentations	institutional ethnography	the personal is political

Gender and Institutions

chapter eleven

Families

Gender relations and family arrangements have always been fully entwined in human societies. Throughout history, people have created family units to feed and nurture themselves and each other. Earlier chapters have discussed some of the relationships people choose and the decisions they face (Chapter Six, for example). Now it is time to consider family as a **social institution**—that is, a social practice that has evolved over time to meet specific needs.

Like other social institutions, family arrangements vary according to the physical environment, shared history, and culture. Their evolution depends on the circumstances of the population. For example, in Canada, family patterns are changing rapidly. Arrangements that were considered inappropriate just decades ago (most notably common-law unions and same-sex relationships) are now protected by law. The goal of this chapter is to explore the shifts in family patterns from a two-sphered, gender-polarizing arrangement to a much more diversified range of possibilities. And, importantly, it will consider the connection between gender and family.

While people are most familiar with the family arrangements common in their own society, many different family patterns have existed through time and across cultures. Students who have studied anthropology or have traveled to communities with cultures different from their own likely have observed that the nuclear family, popular in North America, is just one of many workable arrangements for meeting the economic and emotional needs of individuals and families. Some cultures, for example, encourage men to have several wives. Others make room for same-sex relationships, which have only recently been legally recognized here in Canada. Despite the variety of possible family forms, in virtually every known culture there is a normative structure that reinforces specific expectations for people's family activities based on their age and gender and social standing: a critical nexus exists between gender and family.

In some societies, the normative expectations for family activities are fairly flexible, while in others they are very rigid. Mainstream Canadian society has accepted that women stay home with their newborn infants: the right to **maternity leave** is entrenched in our social policy. But this principle also has flexibility. Recent laws have made paid **paternity leave** available in addition to paid maternity leave, so that fathers, as well as mothers, have the opportunity to care for their young children. In contrast, the United States does not even have a national maternity leave policy, let alone paternity leaves—demonstrating a lack of support, at least on the national level, for parents of either sex to combine paid work with caring for their newborns. Moreover, as Canadian parents change their child-rearing activities (such as fathers taking paid paternity leave), there is a ripple effect on other gendered arrangements. For example, the workplace must adapt to each new behaviour, such as providing benefits for same-sex couples or providing time off for new fathers. Clearly, gender expectations within the culture influence activities within families, just as choices made within families influence non-family gender arrangements in an ongoing recursive relationship between gender, families, and other institutions.

Another critical role families play in recreating gender is the gender socialization of children. As Chapter Five explained, families are the primary environment in which young children are nurtured. Through the choices and actions of parents and families, children learn about gender—how to be a boy or girl, woman or man—in their own particular culture. When we consider the roles of adults in families, we must recognize that the division of roles recreates a gendered environment in which children are socialized. If children are primarily raised by mothers, then they learn specific notions about appropriate roles for women and for men. However, even though families recreate gender patterns, they are also significant sites for resistance: that is, families also challenge and change existing gender arrangements. Recent trends in families reflect these changes.

To illustrate the connections between age, sex, social standing, and family patterns, let's briefly consider upper-class families in Victorian England. Aristocratic men had the duty of attending to political, military, religious, and economic matters. Eldest sons were expected to ensure the continuance of the family line by marrying a suitable wife to produce an heir who, in turn, would inherit the family title, property, and wealth. Aristocratic women were primarily responsible for overseeing the running of households (which frequently included dozens of servants and sometimes multiple residences). One key task of the aristocratic young woman was to find a suitable husband and produce the next generation of nobility. Their children were typically reared by a series of paid employees, beginning with wet nurses to breastfeed the infants, and then later, nannies, governesses, and tutors to prepare children for their adult roles. Daughters were taught fine arts and household management, while sons were taught academic subjects as well as physical skills. Children of neither sex were expected to make an economic contribution within these aristocratic households. Thus, these arrangements were highly gender-polarized: women were excluded from activities outside of the household, except for social engagements, and men were far removed from daily household concerns. Children were raised to follow in these gender footsteps.

At the same time, the vast majority of people in Victorian society were *not* members of the aristocracy. Women, men, and children in the working classes were all actively involved in the labour force, trying to earn a living. Some participated in specifically gendered occupations (*e.g.*, as domestic servants or soldiers), while others worked in occupations that were not segregated by sex (*e.g.,* in factories). In the working class, there was no notion that women's activities should be limited to caring for their children—their economic position was such that earning an income was essential. Children in working class families were also active participants in the labour force. From a very young age, they were expected to contribute economically to their families, by either doing unpaid labour within the household or earning money through employment.

Because gender polarization in the aristocracy kept upper-class women from engaging in intensive physical activity, the notion that women were frail and helpless became widespread. At the time, "scientists" were claiming that humans had only a limited amount of energy; if women used their energy unwisely (studying academic subjects or engaging in demanding physical activity, for example), their actions would damage their capacity to reproduce. As discussed in Chapter Two, the experts of the day noted that upper-class women who were highly educated had fewer children than their peers who were not. They concluded that energy spent on learning lowered women's ability to reproduce. They ignored the whole issue of choice: women with more opportunities to learn might also have more agency within their relationships and thus more freedom to manage their childbearing activities. Another piece of evidence used to prove women's frailty was their myriad health problems and their likelihood of fainting when called upon to physically exert themselves. They concluded that female bodies are fragile, not equipped for physical exertion. Again, the experts ignored obvious counter-evidence. Working-class women (including servants in the experts' own households) worked incredibly hard for long hours and were not considered frail. Moreover, working-class women frequently had many children, despite the physical exertions. Upper-class women often did have mysterious ailments, but scientists at the time failed to consider alternative explanations than innate weakness. Upper-class women typically dressed in tight corsets that compacted their lungs, digestive tracts, and reproductive organs. Add 30 pounds of clothing on top of their squeezed bodies, and it is easy to see how fashion undermined their health and activities.

Of course, not everyone in the aristocracy followed these culturally based gender expectations, any more than everyone follows norms today (though there was a social price to be paid for flouting the norms). Victorian women in aristocratic families who remained unmarried typically spent a lifetime under their father's guardianship. They had limited autonomy and were frequently treated by others in society as undesirable "spinsters." Aristocratic women who sought to work outside their homes were considered to be engaging in activities "beneath their station" and viewed unfavourably. Social exclusion was often the punishment exacted upon those who failed to conform to expectation.

This historical example illustrates the gender polarizing nature of family in a particular era and shows the variations due to social class. But, of course, it would be shortsighted to conclude that there is a unidirectional flow from families to gender. Just because a family arrangement in a particular time and place influenced the activities of the women and men within those families, it is not a deterministic situation. Individuals have a degree of autonomy and can work to develop arrangements that best suit their individual needs. Over time, the choices of individuals shape the institution itself. For example, upper-class women of the mid and late Victorian period became politically active despite opposition, eventually gaining the right to vote and to run for political office. But this was not without personal sacrifice. When the economic conditions among working-class families improved, it was not uncommon for the women to leave paid employment and focus on managing their households. Choices made within individual families eventually led to a wide-scale change in family arrangements, which we will discuss in later sections of this chapter. But first we will consider some of the demographic changes in Canadian families and the links between these patterns and gender arrangements.

DEMOGRAPHIC PATTERNS

The three biggest demographic changes in the twentieth century and continuing into twenty-first century in Canada are a decrease in family size, an increase in divorce rates, and the emergence of an increasing variety of family arrangements: single-person households, common-law unions, step and blended families, lone-parent households, and same-sex households.

Family size has declined significantly. Consider the number of children in your great-grandparents' families (mine had six each) and the number of siblings you have. How many children do you expect to have? When we ask our students these questions, we find that most expect to have only one or two—with far more expecting to have no children than the number expecting to have four or more. Our students' choices are reflected on the national level. All Western countries experienced a long-term decline in fertility during the twentieth century, and many non-Western countries are also showing a similar trend. In Canada, the **total fertility rate** (the measurement of the average number of children born to women when they are between the ages of 15 and 49) declined from 6.8 children per woman in 1851 to 3.53 children in 1921 (see Figure 11.1). In 2003, the rate sat at 1.53

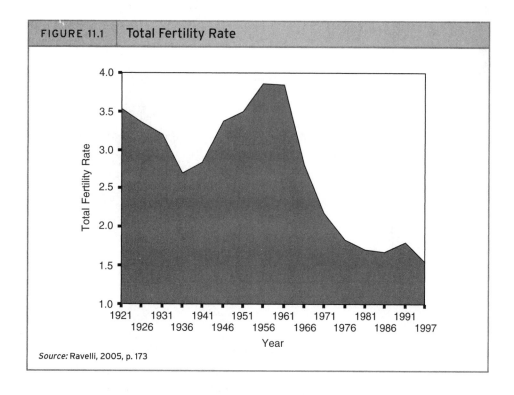

| FIGURE 11.1 | Total Fertility Rate |

Source: Ravelli, 2005, p. 173

children per woman. Obviously, some women have more children and others have fewer, but at current rates, the adult population is not even replacing itself. Without immigration, the Canadian population will begin to decline. Figure 11.1 shows that this rate has changed significantly. The sharp peak in the late 1950s and early 1960s indicates the "baby boom," a time when there was a brief return to a particular two-sphered family arrangement.

Just as the patterns in family size have changed dramatically, so too have divorce rates. For the most part, there has been a significant upward trend, rising abruptly during years when divorce laws changed (1968 and 1985). In 1921, there were only 6.4 divorces for every 100 000 Canadians (Statistics Canada, 2002a), but in the year 2000, there were 231 divorces for every 100 000 Canadians, a total of 71 144 divorces (Statistics Canada, 2002b). Gone are the days when people marrying are assured that they really will be together until death. This change has had an impact on the choices of women and men and the gender arrangements within their families. Figure 11.2 shows divorce trends.

Patterns in divorce are closely linked to gender issues in a variety of ways. Most obviously, the increase in women's labour force participation has made them less dependent on their spouse's income and therefore more financially able to leave an unworkable marriage. However, this should not be interpreted to mean that women who believe in equality are more likely to divorce. Research indicates that attitudes about gender roles among young women do not predict the occurrence of divorce in their future (Thornton, Alwin, & Camburn, 1983).

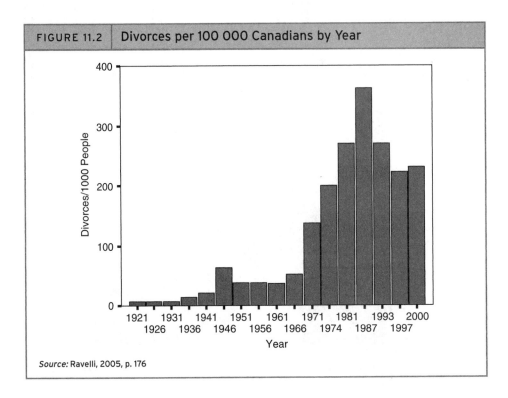

| FIGURE 11.2 | Divorces per 100 000 Canadians by Year |

Source: Ravelli, 2005, p. 176

A second link between gender and divorce has to do with the gender division of labour within families. Changing expectations about who should do domestic work has led to strife in many households. Some of the research discussed later in this chapter indicates that tension around gendered work leads to conflict and can contribute to marital break-down (Hochschild, 1989).

And a third issue related to gender is post-divorce parenting. Because mothers are often the primary child caregivers, they typically receive custody of the children upon divorce. This means there are more mother-led lone-parent families and more children living with stepfathers than stepmothers. And certainly, there is concern about women and children living in poverty, because women typically don't earn as much as men (a subject we'll return to in Chapter Twelve). Just as gender and family are intricately entwined, so too are gender and divorce.

The most obvious change in family arrangements during the late twentieth century was the emergence of new kinds of households. More than ever before, Canadians have options about how we live and who we live with. While almost 45 percent of family households are married couples with their children (this includes step/blended families as well as "intact" families), the majority of Canadians do not live in households with two parents and their children. The 2001 census found that 25 percent of households were single-person households. That is, people live alone in one out of four dwellings in Canada. Ten percent of Canadians live alone. Many of the women who today live on their own would not have had this option in previous generations. Changing gender arrangements have provided younger women the opportunity to earn enough income to support themselves independently, giving them more choices about their lives. In addition, older women, either post-divorce or widowed, also have more options, many choosing to live alone rather than with their grown children or other family members. This would have been unthinkable in the past; it reflects changes in our gender beliefs about women's abilities and their desire for autonomy.

Even people who choose to live in long-term relationships rather than on their own have more options than in the past. The number of people living in **common-law unions** (CLU) (legally recognized unions by which two adults form a long-term, intimate relationship without participating in a legal or religious ceremony) is rapidly increasing and CLUs are now recognized by law (for tax purposes, for example). As Figure 11.3 shows, when common-law unions were first counted in the 1981 census, they accounted for less than 6 percent of all family households. Only 20 years later, they accounted for almost 14 percent of Canadian families. Moreover, the number of CLU families with children has tripled, from less than 2 percent to 6.3 percent of families during that time span. This increase in non-marital relationships shows a shift in thinking about sexuality, particularly for women. While there has long been an expectation that men may be in sexually intimate relationships outside of marriage, this has not been considered acceptable for women in Western cultures. But during the twentieth century, cultural scripts regarding women's sexual activities underwent a profound change. The double standard gradually eroded, and women were much less likely to be sanctioned for non-marital relationships. However, even in the early twenty-first century, significant remnants of the old sexual scripts for men and women still remain.

In addition, in 2001, for the first time, the Canadian Census attempted to measure the number of same-sex households. Although this new question has generated information

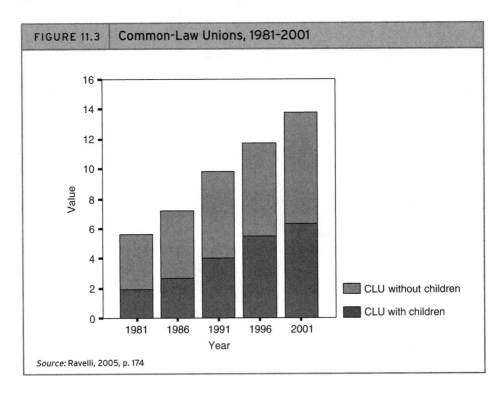

FIGURE 11.3 | Common-Law Unions, 1981–2001

Source: Ravelli, 2005, p. 174

about the current number of households where the adults identify as same-sex partners, it will not be possible to effectively assess whether this is a growing trend until the number has been measured several times (and even then, growing numbers might only indicate a change in people's willingness to make public their living arrangements). It is important to realize that the question was *not* designed to measure sexual orientation. So the findings do not tell us the number of gay and lesbian Canadians, only how many people self-identify as living in a same-sex union. Of the 34 200 same-sex couples who self-identified in the 2001 census, 19 000 were males and 15 200 were female. Table 11.1 shows the breakdown of types of two-adult family households.

While rates of divorces and common-law unions have risen fairly steadily, the trend in lone-parent families has been more complex. As previously noted, the number of lone-parent families is increasing. However, this trend has not been uniform. Early in the twentieth century, approximately 13.6 percent of family households contained a single parent. This percentage dropped to a low of 8.2 percent by 1966 and has now risen to 15.7 percent.

TABLE 11.1 | Type of Union, 2001

Married with 2 Sexes	CLU with 2 Sexes	Same Sex
83.5%	15.9%	0.5%

Source: Ravelli, 2005, p. 175

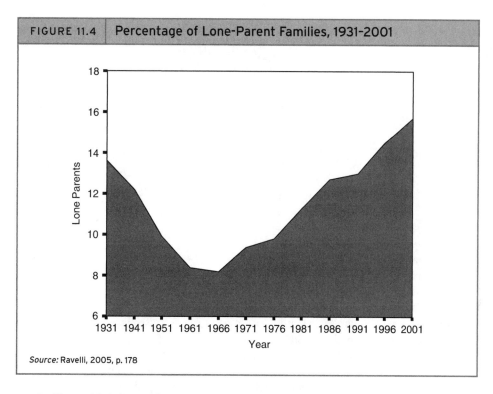

FIGURE 11.4 | Percentage of Lone-Parent Families, 1931-2001

Source: Ravelli, 2005, p. 178

As Figure 11.4 shows, the number of lone-parent families is not that much higher now than it was in the 1930s. The difference is that the origin of these family arrangements has changed. Prior to the decline of such households during the 1950s, the main cause of single-parent households was death of one spouse. Life expectancy was shorter, and it was not uncommon for a parent to die before the children were fully grown. But the new rise in single-parent households is a reflection of higher divorce rates and of single women raising children. Children in these families typically do have two living parents, but one resides elsewhere. "In the 1950s and 1960s, more than 60 percent of lone parents were widowed. This proportion fell to 20 percent in the 1990s, as a result of the growing incidence of divorce, separation, and birth outside marriage" (Statistics Canada, 2003). Table 11.2 shows the parental status of families with children.

TABLE 11.2	Percentage of Families by Parental Status, 2001
Parental Status	**Percent**
Married	70%
CLU	14%
Lone Mothers	13%
Lone Fathers	3%
Source: Ravelli, 2005, p. 176	

TABLE 11.3	Types of Step Families
Types of Step Families	**Percent**
His Children	10%
Her Children	50%
Blended Family (Children in common)	32%
Blended Family (No children in common)	8%

Source: Ravelli, 2005, p. 177

Note that not all two-parent households enumerated here consist of the children's biological parents: this number also includes step and blended families (see Table 11.3). According to Statistics Canada's definition, "**step family** refers to a family in which at least one of the children in the household is from a previous relationship of one of the parents. In a 'simple' step family, the child(ren) of one of the spouses lives in the household. A '**blended' family** contains children from both spouses from one or more previous unions or one or more children from the current union and one or more children from previous unions" (Statistics Canada, 2002c). In 2001, 12 percent of all families with children were step families. "The total number of step families is split equally between married and common-law couples, just over 250 000 of each" (Statistics Canada, 2002a).

THE RISE AND FALL OF THE HOMEMAKER/ BREADWINNER FAMILY ARRANGEMENT

As the figures and tables above reveal, Canadian family patterns have changed dramatically over the past century. There are many causes underlying these patterns, including changes in technology, values, and economic patterns (see Chapter Twelve). Especially important for this text are the changes influenced by shifting cultural expectations of gender.

A study of gender and family must begin by examining the notion of the "**traditional family**." We place this term in quotation marks because this notion of family must be considered carefully. Much of what we believe to be true about the "traditional family" is based on misconceptions. The *myth* of happy families where dad worked for pay outside the home and mom cared for her family without being paid lasted much longer than the reality. Many people did not aspire to or did not live in this kind of household. However, because it has come to reflect our ideas about past family arrangements—the institution of family—it needs to be studied and analyzed.

The "traditional family" is a significant family form for several reasons. First, it was the dominant pattern in middle-class North America both early in the twentieth century and again briefly during the 1950s (when lone-parent families were few, divorce rare, and fertility rates high). But second and more importantly, the general population and many scholars regarded the "traditional family" as the ideal family form. It seemed to be the best arrangement for societies at large and for individual families as well. But it was entirely based on gender polarization. Like the Victorian aristocrats, early-twentieth-century men and women were expected to fulfill entirely different tasks in different locations. It was a two-sphered arrangement, where men worked outside the home as paid-income earners for their families and women worked inside the home, unpaid, nurturing and maintaining the children and their husbands. In some of the literature, this "traditional family" model is a referred to as the *homemaker/breadwinner family.*

Advocates of the "traditional family" work to promote this model as the best possible arrangement for children and communities. For example, the organization REAL Women (discussed in Chapter Two) extols the virtues of families where moms can be homemakers. Frequently, socially conservative organizations describe "the family" in nostalgic terms: they long for the good old days of polarized gender arrangements. Some also suggest that young people get involved in drugs, bullying, and violence because of a lack of supervision, since their mothers work outside the home. Moreover, the erosion of the "traditional family" has been identified as the cause of many crises. What many people fail to understand, however, is that the "traditional family" was a relatively short-lived middle-class phenomenon. It had many advantages but also many disadvantages.

More importantly, the "traditional family" is not a sustainable family form for the vast majority of humans on this earth. It has not existed throughout history: economic demands made that impossible. Prior to the Industrial Revolution, in all but the most privileged classes, everybody worked in order to survive. Women, men, and children had economic roles to play. While work was often divided along gender lines, everyone participated, and there was frequent crossover. For example, in farming families, women and children worked alongside men during planting and harvest; and men and children worked alongside women when it was time to undertake major household chores, such as making candles. There was no conception that men "worked" and women "reared children." Work, both producing goods and rearing children, was shared by both sexes.

When the Industrial Revolution expanded throughout Europe in the early nineteenth century, historical records show that men, women, and children continued to work; but instead of working on the land, close to home, they were often in urban centres, working in organized jobs (possibly in factories or as servants in aristocratic households) or in irregular activities on the street (selling goods or services). Demographic data shows that this new separation of home and workplace was a difficult time for most working-class people. Child and infant mortality rates were very high, life expectancy low, and sickness and poverty rampant (as were crime and suicide). However, as the Industrial Revolution grew in strength, there was an increase in the standard of living for many people—better diets, better public health, and better housing. A "middle class" emerged as the economy shifted and as families became less poor. By the early twentieth century, children and women gradually withdrew from the paid labour force. At that time, this change was seen as a tremendous benefit for families. Instead of everyone working long hours and coming home to a cold, dark house, needing to complete all the tasks required, someone could remain home throughout the day and look after the family's needs. As historian Carl Degler (1980) explains, the new middle class sought to emulate the upper class by creating separate spheres for women and men. This new family form was perceived to be in everyone's best interest. Thus, not only were home and paid work separated, but men and women were also separated into these two spheres. It was a sign of success when women did not need to work outside the home.

Over time, some of these patterns became entrenched in law, first through legislation that shortened working hours for children and women. This change did women the great favour of limiting their exploitation by employers but also the great disservice of guaranteeing that they earned less than adult men and thus were in perpetual poverty unless they were attached to a working man. Later, laws required that children attend school for a specific number of years. Again, mandatory schooling was an incredible opportunity for children of all social classes to become literate and potentially to improve their lot in life, but it also meant a loss of economic activity that put people without a working adult male in their family in financial jeopardy.

Note that in the separate-sphered households, women did continue to work. The life of leisure of the aristocratic class did not occur for the majority of middle-class women. In those years before households had access to refrigeration, vacuum cleaners, washers and dryers, *and* before disposable diapers, it was physically hard work to feed and clothe a growing family. Moreover, these women also frequently contributed financially to the household by taking in boarders (for whom they typically provided meals and laundry service), laundry, or sewing—any work that was compatible with running a household that could enhance the family's economic position.

While it was possible for some families to achieve this two-sphered arrangement, it was impossible for many others. Women and mothers needed to earn money to support themselves and their dependents, especially if there was no male family member able to earn a sufficient income. Most working-class families could not get by on just one income. In Canada, there has been a long history of women in many walks of life working for pay outside the home. In fact, the "traditional family" was never universal. It was a short-lived, middle-class phenomenon.

Jesse Bernard's work (1981) on breadwinners in the "traditional family" discusses the development of the "good provider role" for men. She argues that a specialized male role evolved with separation of home and work. This separation limited women's power as they made a smaller financial contribution to the household. It also linked gender to worksite. Women worked at home; thus, their domestic activities came to be seen as a measure of their womanhood. Men worked outside the home; thus, the paid workplace was understood to be male **sexual territory**, and manhood came to be measured by the ability to provide. This separation contributed to the devaluing of unpaid work and reinforced the position of men as the heads of their families. This creation of sexual territory polarized gender and had a profound impact on both sexes, particularly on men who were unable or chose not to participate fully in the paid labour force and on women who actively worked for pay (see Chapter Twelve).

Parsons and Bales (1955), predominant sociologists writing in the 1950s, argued that this two-sphered arrangement was the most efficient, ideal type of family. The specialization of men and women into what they called **instrumental roles** and **expressive roles** meant that all the family's needs could be met. Men focusing on earning an income (instrumental activities) would not be distracted by issues at home, and women, not needing to contribute to the family income, could devote all their time and energy to the nurturing their husbands and their children (expressive activities). Thus, "sociology of the family" texts published in the 1950s and 1960s described this homemaker/breadwinner "traditional" arrangement as an ideal towards which all families should strive. They regarded families that did not follow this pattern as problematic. (For example, it was not uncommon for chapters on family problems to include a section on families with working mothers.) And they failed to see the problems inherent within this model (for example, the imbalance of power between the sexes that led to the economic and physical vulnerability of women).

Another myth about the "traditional family" is the notion that it was an ideal arrangement that benefited all but that was undermined by feminists who are *anti-family*. In fact, the two-sphered family was already starting to disappear long before the "women's liberation" movement began to challenge it in the 1960s. Even prior to the Depression, a significant proportion of women worked in the paid labour force, though they often left their jobs when they married, if they could afford to do so. But with the advent of the Great Depression and then World War II, there was a large-scale movement of married women and mothers into the world of paid work. It was not necessarily a choice based on a desire to improve their positions within the family: it was a necessity. During the Depression and prairie drought in the 1930s, men from all walks of life were unemployed and searching for work. In many cases, this search took them away from their families and communities, so women earned the money necessary to feed their families.

World War II furthered the trend of women working for pay. During the war, the economy was growing, and the industrial requirements of war meant there were far more jobs than men to fill them. As most able-bodied men were active in the military, governments promoted work outside the home as women's patriotic contribution to the war effort. Ask your great-grandmothers what life was like (if they were in Canada during this time period). While they are unlikely to call themselves feminists, these women shared much in common with working women today—balancing work and family demands. Married women and mothers worked in factories and offices in greater numbers than ever before. Their contribution was acknowledged as vital and was fully supported. The Canadian government opened daycare centres where young children played and learned as their mothers worked. Women who used daycare were not disparaged as inadequate mothers, nor was there discussion about the harm being done to children spending their days with paid caregivers. Instead, daycare was regarded as a wonderful way to keep children safe and keep women in the paid labour force.

Once the war ended, there was a resurgence of the "traditional family" pattern: more couples married young and had large families. Younger mothers were more likely to stay home with their children than in the previous decade. However, this pattern was short-lived and largely limited to middle-class, non-immigrant, young families (see Figure 11.5). Even in the 1950s, older married women were active in the paid labour force. And a large proportion of working-class mothers remained in the paid labour force as well (see Wilson, 1991 for a detailed overview).

This resurgence of young families in the 1950s created the *baby boom*—a large cohort of children born between the late 1940s and the early 1960s. This generation has had a profound impact on social patterns in the second half of the twentieth century and into the twenty-first century. One of the most significant changes is in gender roles and family patterns. The baby boomers effectively transformed families into a variety of new forms.

In part, social changes were due to the second wave of the women's movement that began challenging ideas about women's place and patriarchal family arrangements. Betty

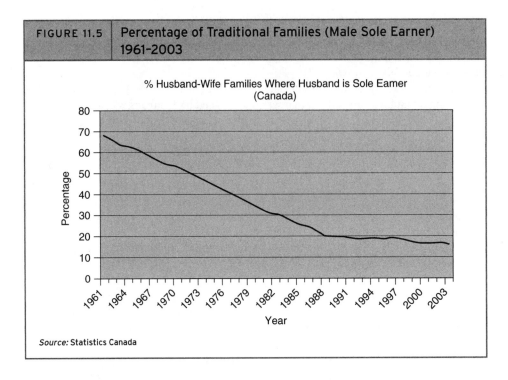

FIGURE 11.5 **Percentage of Traditional Families (Male Sole Earner) 1961-2003**

Source: Statistics Canada

Friedan's classic work *The Feminine Mystique,* published in 1963, was a compelling treatise on "the problem that has no name." She examined the lives of middle-class women who were, she argued, suffering silently in their homes: doing an admirable job raising their children but feeling unfulfilled, wondering if this was all their lives were meant to be. Friedan argued that these women had vast untapped potential that was stifled under their domestic responsibilities. Her solution was for women to become more active outside their homes: to use their educations, to work for pay, to develop their abilities, and to end their economic dependence on their husbands. She argued that the two-sphered arrangement was not problem-free for homemakers.

As Bernard (1981) points out, the "traditional family" was not a problem-free arrangement for the breadwinners, either. While acknowledging the obvious rewards—freedom from mundane domestic chores while being granted the decision-making authority within the household—the position also had inherent costs. As work and the ability to provide financially became associated with masculinity, men were locked into a competition to earn as much as possible. Not only were those who failed to adequately provide for their families poor, but their masculinity was also called into question. This was a cruel standard, given that a worker's earnings are not simply based on effort and ability. Changing economic conditions, the management decisions of any particular business, as well as trends in the market place, all play a part in determining the availability of work and promotions for any individual worker. Defining gender identity in terms of a work role when so many factors lie outside of individual control creates impossible standards. Moreover, in living up to the masculine expectations, by putting almost all their energies into providing for their families, many men had little time to actually enjoy family life. They often ended up working hard to financially support a family with which they had a limited emotional connection.

So despite the fact that some sociologists in the 1950s and 1960s argued that the homemaker/breadwinner family was the ideal arrangement for modern societies, the problems for its members were already apparent. Women were not fulfilling their potential and were economically vulnerable, and men's efforts to support their family financially often left them isolated from their spouses and children.

Other factors also played a part in changing family gender relations. Better birth control methods developed in the 1960s effectively separated sexual relations from childbearing. People could engage in intimate heterosexual relations without beginning families. A pattern of delayed and limited childbearing began in the 1960s: people were having smaller families later in life. This trend continues. Right now, the average age of women when their first child is born is 28 years (in 2003, 48 percent of first-time mothers in Canada were over age 30). These women also normally have fewer than two children (Statistics Canada, 2005). Today, women are much more likely to have paid employment before they have children, and they are likely to return to it after their children are born. Longer lives, lower fertility rates, and later first births all tend to diminish the proportion of one's lifetime spent raising a family. If you lived a century ago, chances are you would have had at least four children, and the youngest would still be at home when you or your spouse died. Thus, your entire adult life would be spent child-rearing—quite different from today, when people often have one or two children, relatively close together, so they spend less than 10 years with young children. For example, one of the authors had her two children when she was 24 and 26. They will both be finished high-school by the time she is 44 years old, leaving her, potentially, with 20 years of post-child-rearing, pre-retirement adult life. With childbearing patterns like this, having one spouse dedicate herself to being a full-time, permanent homemaker is often not a rational choice. Children are young for only a short time span, while other economic demands and opportunities continue much longer.

As sociologist Kingsley Davis (1984) points out in his study of family patterns, many factors contributed to the decline of the "traditional family." The changing economy after the Second World War that resulted in more jobs in the service sector and fewer in the industrial sector meant that women were excluded from fewer jobs than they had been in the past. The growing economy meant there were more positions available in the paid labour force, and thus there were more opportunities for women. Women reaching "marriage age" in the later 1960s, the 1970s, and beyond were all born after World War II. They had not experienced the Depression or the War. Thus, they were not necessarily as eager to form families as those in previous generations who had experienced widespread insecurity. Many women attended college or university, meaning that more attained the credentials necessary to pursue professional careers. Increased opportunities for women pulled them into the labour force. In addition, the rising standard of living across the developed world led to an increase in demand for consumer goods, from TVs and washing machines in the 1950s to second cars, televisions, and computers, The desire for these items makes family life more expensive, making a second income seem increasingly necessary.

While all these factors contribute, Davis argued that the key factor that led to the downfall of the homemaker/breadwinner arrangement was the rise in divorce rates. The "traditional" arrangement worked, after a fashion, as long as both parties were committed to it for life. As long as the breadwinner financially supported the homemaker until the end of her life, she did not need to develop her own income-earning potential. But when the divorce rate rose, and women saw more and more of their peers without husbands, without recognized means for financially supporting themselves, they perceived themselves to be vulnerable. If a homemaker can't count on a lifetime of economic support, she simply can't afford to focus all her attention on domestic tasks and ignore the need to develop her own marketable skills. Davis argues that the upward trend in divorce, combined with changing economic patterns, caused a decline in the "traditional family."

As a result of all these changes, today a relatively low percentage of families can be characterized as "traditional." Many families are led by lone parents (16 percent), and others are same-sex households. In two-sex couples, less than 20 percent depend solely on the husband's income. And the increasing participation of women in the paid labour force has resulted in shifts in power and labour both within the home and in the workplace.

GENDERED DIVISION OF LABOUR IN FAMILIES

The demographic trends in the last two decades show that more and more couples are both working full-time outside the home. Nonetheless, research on income shows that women still earn less than men, even when the work is considered to be of equal value (see Chapter Twelve). Consequently, there is more often than not an imbalance in families, with men earning more than women even if they are both working 40 hours per week. Does this make them equal partners? Meg Luxton (1980), a Canadian sociologist, examined the division of labour within these households during the 1970s, in an attempt to understand the gender relations within families. Her qualitative study was an in-depth examination of family patterns. From a sample of 49 couples, all of whom had at least one child under twelve years of age, and in which all of the women and men worked outside the home for pay, Luxton found that women's participation in the paid labour was not always a reflection of beliefs about gender equality.

Almost 15 percent of the couples had created what Luxton calls **hierarchical relations**, even though both adults worked outside the home. In these families, both partners agreed that women should not work for pay—that everyone was better off if mom could be at home and dad was the head of the household. But for financial reasons, women in these households needed to have paying jobs. In these families, women did double duty. They earned an income but also were entirely responsible for household work. They did not ask for or receive assistance from their husbands, and they did not relax their domestic standards. Luxton found that most of these women were exhausted and unhappy. Moreover, the unhappiness of such women was taken as proof that everyone—children, men, and women—suffers when wives work outside the home. Instead of finding that paid work gave them more opportunities and independence, this 15 percent of the women in her study saw it as the cause of a significant decline in the quality of their lives.

Luxton described another 35 percent of the couples as **separate spheres/co-operative relations**. Like the previous 15 percent, these couples believed that men and women should have separate priorities both within and outside the family. But they also believed that it is appropriate to help each other out, when necessary. While they still raised their daughters and sons following traditional gender divisions, they accepted the notion that moms often need to work outside the home for the income, and dads often need to help out at home while mom works. When Luxton measured the division of labour within the home, she found that most of these women still did most of the housework; but they relaxed the standards somewhat. It was okay to live with a little mess, to let the laundry pile up, and to eat fast food sometimes instead of home-cooked meals.

The 51 percent majority of the families in Luxton's study had **shared spheres/ changing relations**. These couples agreed that women have the *right* to work if they want to. They also believed that husbands and wives should be equal partners. They agreed that the division of labour at home should be changed, with husbands shouldering a more equitable share of the load. However, Luxton found a great deal of tension in many of these households. Even though they said that both partners should be responsible, the reality did not reflect this. She found that many women had to pressure their husbands to do domestic chores, and many husbands, not surprisingly, resented this pressure. Luxton documented the many strategies husbands and wives devised to address this problem. Unfortunately, these strategies were often not successful. "In the majority of cases negotiations appeared to be out of the question. Instead, the couples seemed locked into tension-generating, manipulative power struggles" (Luxton, 1980, p. x). The result was frustration and resentment. Thus, Luxton found that economic demands certainly influence the choices that families made, but that their expectations about unpaid "gendered" work (who cooks and who washes the car) had profound implications for their relationships.

Hochschild (1989) undertook a larger, longer-term study exploring the same issues that Luxton addressed a decade earlier. This study focused on interviewing and observing families as they coped with the competing demands of paid and unpaid work. Hochschild's study followed these families over a period of years to gain insight into the long-term results of these arrangements. She found that women shouldered a much larger share of the domestic chores, even when they worked longer hours or earned higher pay than their husbands. Hochschild called this extra domestic work the *second shift*: after working all day, mom comes home to start the second shift—the household work that is required to keep a family thriving. (Other scholars, such as guest essayist Muriel Mellow in Chapter Twelve, envision a *third shift*, where women work as volunteers in their communities.) Like Luxton, Hochschild found that juggling these competing demands was a source of tension in many homes.

Hochschild argued that every person develops a **gender strategy**, "a plan of action through which a person tries to solve problems at hand given the cultural notions of gender at play" (p. 15). For example, in a two-sphered arrangement, the gender strategy involves finding your own identity when the culture supports a gender-polarized division of labour. The struggle, when it exists, involves finding ways to live up to or resist this polarized arrangement. With the large-scale movement of women into the paid labour force, current gender strategies involve juggling the demands of work and home life, at a time when cultural expectations are also shifting. Hochschild also believed that in the late 1980s, Western culture was in a **stalled revolution**. That is, the activities of women and men had changed, but the institutions within the society had not kept pace. For example, Canadian women did not have easily accessible, affordable childcare. Many work places still don't accommodate family responsibilities.

Fortunately, Canada has taken many steps to address the problems of the stalled revolution. For example, Canadians now have access to maternity and paternity leaves for parents. At the time of writing this chapter, the government has just announced plans for improvements to parental leave, so that new parents will be able to earn between 70 and 75 percent of their pay if they stay home during the first 50 weeks of their child's life. Federal and provincial governments have begun instituting family leave policies for those who are responsible for the care of sick and dying family members. As another example, the Martin federal government attempted to institute a national childcare policy. But because the provinces did not all accept this policy, Canada has a piecemeal provincial approach—its efficacy is yet untested. These policies are signs, however, that the revolution is gaining strength. But there are significant opponents within Canadian society who actively work against these changes. Political activists have fought against funding national childcare because they think this will harm families in which one parent stays home to raise the children. Other lobbyists have argued against extended parental leave benefits because guaranteeing a parent's right to her or his job after they take an extended leave will harm business. Businesses need a stable workforce, this argument suggests, not one that is frequently disrupted by the comings and goings of new parents.

Both families and workplaces have yet to adjust to changes in the parenting activities of women and men. As both Luxton and Hochschild found, individuals within families are also struggling with the same issues: conflict over who does what and assumptions based on gender stereotypes cause strife in many households. Changes have not come easily.

Why do so many people, men and women, agree that domestic work should be equitably shared but then find it difficult to actually put this into practice? And, if Luxton and Hochschild are correct, why do so many men resist this change? LaRossa (1988) explored this question of resistance. He says that change in the gender system is not uniform: there is a gap between *culture* and *conduct*. Our **culture** (ideas, norms, values, and beliefs) change at a different pace than our **conduct** (our actions, institutions, and expectations). Not surprisingly, women's conduct changed first. For women, entering the labour force was seen to have many advantages: earning their own income, developing their potential outside the home, and feeling more fulfilled. But during the 1960s, when women began entering the paid labour force in large numbers, they experienced conflict on many fronts. The world of work was not ready for women managers, professionals, and heavy labourers, so women frequently had to battle to get jobs and promotions in fields that had previously been all male (*sexual territory,* according to Bernard, 1981). They also had to face social criticism from many who felt that women who worked were neglecting their families and emasculating their husbands. Bernard also mentions the difficulty men faced when their wives wanted to work, because so much of their identity and masculinity was tied up in the "good provider" role. But the advantages were seen to outweigh the problems; that factor, combined with other advantages discussed earlier, resulted in a marked increase in women's labour force participation. Gradually, the culture changed to reflect this change in conduct. It is now accepted that women have a right to work for pay and that women's incomes keep many families from poverty.

However, for men facing this revolution of gender roles, LaRossa argues that the *culture* changed *first,* and conduct has lagged behind. Men are expected to acknowledge women's right and need to work and the equity of participating fully in the domestic labour, but their conduct hasn't caught up with the cultural expectations. This is not surprising: while women were seen to be gaining independence by moving outside the home, for men there is no real freedom or independence associated with getting to do the laundry and vacuuming. This work had been devalued by the society at large, so engaging in it is more likely to be seen as a loss than a gain. Moreover, changing their conduct feels like a loss of status. Thus, when it comes to men's family obligations, culture changed more quickly than conduct, leaving individual couples to negotiate a workable arrangement for completing unpaid domestic chores. As a result of the conduct-culture gap, frequently these negotiations are a source of conflict.

One element of *conduct* related to family life that has changed rapidly is the expansion of new family forms. As more and more people choose to live in arrangements that were largely invisible prior to the 1960s (same-sex relationships, common-law unions, lone-parent/ step/blended families), the culture is still catching up to this conduct. New laws are being enacted to protect the right to live in and have official recognition of such arrangements. But whatever their particular structure, all families face similar issues—how to accomplish all the work necessary to run a household. While individuals may enter these arrangements with particular gender strategies about division of labour, they are already challenging the *culture* of family through their *conduct*, by choosing to resist long-standing notions about so called "ideal" family arrangements.

As noted earlier, Canada is currently instituting policies that should make it easier for parents to provide safe and caring environments for their children as well as to work productively in the paid labour force. More recent empirical research has been undertaken to measure the actual amounts of work that women and men in families complete on a daily and weekly basis. The goal is to find out if the second shift is being shared more equitably, or if the gender strategies still result in women carrying the bulk of the load. Canadian scholar Rod Beaujot has studied these patterns and discusses them in the following guest essay. Beaujot concludes that family work appears to be shared more equitably in many households than it had been in previous research. There is also demographic data showing that family arrangements are more diverse than ever before. Thus, the polarization that people experienced in the past appears to be diminishing. More people are able to create workable arrangements based on their personal needs and goals, rather than be having their choices circumscribed by narrowly defined gender expectations.

| BOX 11-1 | Gender Models for Family and Work |

by Roderic Beaujot

In *The Gender Factory*, Sarah Berk (1985) proposes that through the allocations of domestic work, households and families are gender factories. Arlie Hochschild (1989) also proposes that families play significant roles in maintaining gender differences. In most of the households that she studied, Hochschild found that the double burden belonged to women. Yet 10 percent of her households were making deliberate attempts to divide unpaid work more equally. If the gender revolution involves women achieving equal opportunity, we could say that this has been achieved much more outside of the household than in families. The feminist agenda has been to complete the gender revolution.

Changing Norms

In surveys that I take with my undergraduate students, there is almost unanimity to say "both equally" in response to questions on how domestic work and childcare should be shared in couples. For many, the norms have changed in the direction of sharing paid and unpaid work as a form of mutuality.

In *Gender in Families*, Scott Coltrane (1998) proposes that several factors are pushing in the direction of men doing more domestic work. First, there is the rising women's incomes and share of family income. Second, there are normative changes in the direction of equality and sharing, in contrast to family models based on dividing earning and caring

(Continued)

BOX 11-1	**Gender Models for Family and Work** *(Continued)*

along gender lines. Third, the family changes themselves, including later marriages, more cohabitation and more remarriages, prompt alternate models of the division of work. By now, young men know that they need to share the burden if they want to enter a relationship, and it is not uncommon for women to abandon relationships that are not based on a sense of fairness in the division of work.

The models of marriage have changed. Gary Becker (1981) proposed that it was efficient for households to divide paid and unpaid work, and that at most one person would spend time doing both market work and domestic work. Many have since seen this complementary-roles approach as a man's view of efficiency, or they see more important goals in relationships, like mutuality and equality rather than efficiency. Valerie Oppenheimer (1988) proposes a "career entry" theory of marriage, where enduring relationships are formed once jobs are established. Once couples start out with two jobs, they are more likely to be oriented to also share the domestic work. Christiane Bernier and her colleagues (1996) saw women's paid work was a "trump card" against their exploitation through domestic work.

Co-existing Models

In an American study, Shelly Lundberg and Elaine Rose (1998) found that, on average, women's work time is reduced after the birth of a first child, and men's average wage increases. Couples in which wives interrupted their careers for child-rearing showed increased task specialization associated with child-

birth, including a reallocation of time of both husband and wife, and declines in wages of wives. However, there was also evidence of the emergence of other patterns. Lundberg and Rose found significantly different patterns for couples in which the wife participated continuously in the labour market. In those cases, the mothers' wage rates did not decline while the hours worked by fathers declined after the birth of the first child. Furthermore, the wage differentiation on the birth of a first child was not as significant for younger cohorts. Thus, the increase in task specialization associated with childbirth was less applicable to younger cohorts and to the sub-sample of couples in which wives continuously participated in the labour force. As the model of continuous participation in the labour force becomes dominant, the authors see converging time-use patterns for husbands and wives and a declining wage differentiation associated with parenthood.

Converging Employment Patterns but Parenthood Brings Divergence

The Canadian employment/population ratios have converged considerably between women and men. Men's employment ratios have declined since 1981, and women's have increased since 1971. Among the OECD countries, Canada is exceptional for the amount of change between 1960 and 1990 (Engelhardt and Prskawetz, 2004, 38). In 1960, with 32 percent of women in the labour force, Canada was among the countries with the lowest participation; in 2000, the rate of 71 percent puts

| BOX 11-1 | *(Continued)* |

Canada in the group with the highest participation. At age group 15–24 in 2001, the employment/population ratio is identical for males and females, at 55 percent; however, at age groups 25–54, there remains a 10–11 percentage point difference.

While the trends for women and men are converging, parenthood still has the opposite average effects, leading to divergent employment patterns for women and men. When they are living with children under six years of age, 90.5 percent of men in 2001 are working full-time compared to 49.7 percent of women (Beaujot and Ravanera, 2005).

Similar results are shown in time use patterns. Compared to persons who are single, being in a relationship increases the unpaid work of women, but also of men, and the paid work of men (Beaujot and Liu, 2005). The presence of children especially differentiates women and men in terms of the proportion of total productive activity that occurs in the categories of paid and unpaid work. For instance, in 1998, married men under age 45 with children spent an average of 66 percent of their productive time in the market, compared to 35 percent for women in this category.

What Would It Take to Achieve Convergence in Paid Work Patterns of Women and Men?

Much change has occurred outside of families, but there remain important differences in the division of family work. The norms appear to be changing in the right direction, but on average parenthood still brings differentiation in the division of work. It is useful to reflect on the kinds of policy initiatives that could prompt further convergence.

Parental Leave

One might start with equal parental leave, or at least men taking a substantial part of the leave. Extending the leave from six months to a year has increased the leave time taken by women and it has increased the proportion of men taking leave. It seems that fathers are more likely to take leave if the mother takes eight months, and the father has benefits that top up the EI benefits. To push this further, one might consider increasing the replacement rate on parental leaves, and having a maximum of eight months leave per parent.

Benefits for Part-time Work

Especially when children are under three years of age, there is considerable interest to work fewer hours. This could be supported by policies that would treat part-time workers the same as full-time workers, as currently occurs for EI and CPP benefits. That is, regulations could prohibit discrimination against part-time work in terms of wage rates and benefits. One could even adopt policies like in Sweden to give parents the right to work part-time when children are young, along with the right to go back to full-time work at any point. Further, one could subsidize part-time work when it involves a parent of a child under three years of age. To make this symmetrical, how about allowing each parent one year of such subsidy per child?

(Continued)

BOX 11-1	**Gender Models for Family and Work** (*Continued*)

Removing Assumptions of the Breadwinner Model

As we opt for a society where there are fewer dependencies, and more equality between men and women, it is useful to take note of legal provisions that remain based on a traditional breadwinner model. This may apply to widowhood benefits, spousal allowance, pension splitting, and tax deductions for a dependent spouse. While these provisions are a means of accommodating dependency in couples, they can also discourage rather than promote the economic independence of women and men.

In Sweden, they have never had pension splitting, and they eliminated widowhood benefits for persons who married after 1989. Such changes would need to be grand-parented to accommodate those who lived their lives under the assumptions of the breadwinner model.

The income tax deduction for a dependent spouse makes sense when one spouse is not in the labour force because of young children at home. But in other circumstances, why do we encourage dependency through this tax provision? For lone parents, we already have an "equivalent to married" deduction for the first child. How about using this for all parents, giving them a deduction for the first dependent child rather than for a dependent spouse? Of course, this change would only benefit two-parent families, and thus I would propose that the benefit be doubled for lone-parent families.

Conclusion

The difficulties of work-life balance originate in the fact that changes in some

areas of life have not been matched by changes in other areas. Peter McDonald (2000) proposes that fertility is particularly low in societies where women have equal opportunities in education and work, but where they carry an undue proportion of family work. For instance, Livia Olah (2003) finds for Sweden that women are more likely to have a second child when their husband has taken parental leave after the first birth. Eva Bernhardt (2005) proposes that low fertility is due in part to the unfinished gender revolution. The norms are changing in the direction of more symmetry in the division of work, we need to make other changes that would encourage a better sharing of family work.

References

Beaujot, Roderic and Jianye Liu. 2005. "Models of Time Use in Paid and Unpaid Work." *Journal of Family Issues* 26, 7: 924–946.

Beaujot, Roderic and Zenaida Ravanera. 2005. "Family Models for Earning and Caring: Implications for Child Care. University of Western Ontario, Population Studies Centre, Discussion Paper 05–01. Available at: http:// www. ssc.uwo.ca/sociology/popstudies/dp/ dp05_01.pdf

Becker, Gary S. 1981. *A Treatise on the Family*. Cambridge, Mass.: Harvard University Press.

Berk, Sarah Fenstermaker. 1985. *The Gender Factory: The Apportionment of Work in American Households*. New York: Plenum.

Bernhardt, Eva. 2005. "No, We Should Not Worry about the Future of Europe's Population." Paper presented at meetings

| BOX 11-1 | *(Continued)* |

of the International Union for the Scientific Study of Population, France, July 2005.

Bernier, Christiane, Simon Laflamme, and Run-Min Zhou. 1996. "Le travail domestique: tendances à la désexisation et à la complexifaction." *Canadian Review of Sociology and Anthropology* 33,1: 1-21.

Coltrane, Scott. 1998. *Gender and Families.* Thousand Oaks, Cal.: Pine Forge Press.

Engelhardt, Henriette and Alexia Prskawetz, 2004. "On the Changing Correlation Between Fertility and Female Employment over Space and Time." *European Journal of Population* 20: 35–62.

Hochschild, Arlie Russell. 1989. *The Second Shift.* New York: Viking.

Lundberg, Shelly and Elaine Rose. 1998. "Parenthood and the Earnings of Married Men and Women." University of Washington: Seattle Population Research Center Working Paper, no. 98–9.

McDonald, Peter. 2000. "Gender Equity in Theories of Fertility." *Population and Development Review* 26, 3: 427–439.

Olah, Livia. 2003. "Gendering Fertility: Second births in Sweden and Hungary." *Population Research and Policy Review* 22, 2: 171–200.

Oppenheimer, Valerie K. 1988. "A Theory of Marriage Timing." *American Journal of Sociology* 94,3: 563–91.

Adapted with permission from Policy Research Initiative (Government of Canada), *Horizons*, 2006, Vol. 8, No. 3: 24-26.

INTENSIFIED MOTHERING

One key cultural change in gender and family is the issue of parenting and our cultural conceptions of mothering. Because most people have a mother who was more or less involved in their lives, they have an idea about what mothers are and what mothers do. But *mother* is a status that is in large part socially constructed. Giving birth is biological, but the raising of children is social and is therefore heavily influenced by culture. Not surprisingly, child-rearing has been gender-polarized in many cultures. Certainly, our whole notion of the "traditional family" was based on the premise that women are the people who should be entrusted with the rearing of children. This notion is seen as having its basis in biology—only women have the biological capacity to breastfeed infants. Moreover, the gender-based normative expectations of emphasized femininity highlight the importance of nurturing; for women with children, these expectations extend to their role as mothers.

Those who have studied families, both historically and cross-culturally, have discovered that perceptions about children and notions about appropriate child-rearing have varied dramatically across time and place. The methods and qualities involved in mothering are not based on universal biological imperatives, but on sets of normative expectations, specific to particular cultures. For example, common practices of the past—such as the swaddling of infants to prevent movement and using opium to quiet distressed babies—are now considered barbaric in Canada. In addition, not long ago, most people believed that the best method for teaching children obedience was through the use of physical discipline. But today, corporal punishment of children is considered abusive. On the other hand, more recent approaches to mothering based on a rationale of child-centred care (or permissiveness, as some people call it) are judged by some as having led to the corruption of children and the creation of the "me generation." Just as ideas of appropriate gendered behaviour change over time, so too do ideas of appropriate mothering.

With the emergence and then decline of the two-sphered family arrangement, notions of mothering have changed in complex ways. Prior to the "traditional family," most children worked. And certainly fathers as well as mothers were actively involved in disciplining their children and teaching them the skills necessary to work in the family-based economy. In those days, there were no expectations that mothers would devote all or even most of their attention to rearing their children. Women's economic activities were vital to the survival of the family. Child-rearing simply involved keeping the children fed and out of harm's way until they were old enough to participate in economic activities. Even in the wealthiest classes, where women's labour wasn't necessary for the survival of the family, mothers still didn't regard their children as their primary focus: wet nurses, governesses, and tutors were employed to look after children. However, as the Industrial Revolution spread and the middle class grew, and more and more families adopted the "traditional family" arrangement. These economic changes led to a change in the division of labour between women and men and ultimately influenced modern ideas about child-rearing. Mothering became the primary focus of women.

The widespread cultural belief in the profound importance of mothering was bolstered by some psychologists who drew attention to the significance of early childhood development and the need for effective nurturing and teaching (see, for example, Bowlby, 1969). In her discussion of mothering, Hays (1996) traces the development of this trend, showing the rise of what she calls **intensive mothering**. Intensive mothering is a cultural construction based on the premise that raising her children is the most important undertaking of a woman's life. While men can and do parent, the expectation is that raising children is primarily a woman's responsibility—women are the nurturers. Men who are involved parents are typically viewed as wonderful fathers, but they are not seen to be following the norm. Conversely, when fathers are not fully involved, they are not perceived as irresponsible or inadequate; their lack of participation in parenting is considered normal in this cultural context. Women with children, on the other hand, are judged by their success as mothers. If a mother is anything less than wonderful, her children are perceived to pay an extreme price for her failure.

Through in-depth interviews with mothers, as well as analysis of historical texts and best-selling childcare advice books, Hays found that Western cultural standards place high demands on mothers. The expectation is that mothers should invest as much time, energy, and money as possible into providing an ideal environment for their children. Definitions of "ideal" vary by class and subculture. For example, in the middle class, the ideal might include music lessons, sports activities, and private schools; whereas in the under class, it often means keeping children safe from violence and drugs and encouraging them to pursue their schooling. But despite these variations, there is a common theme: women control their children's destinies, and a "good mother" does not fail her children.

The mass media reinforces these intensive mothering ideals by bombarding us with images and messages about how to raise children properly, and by detailing the severe costs of failing to do so (for example, sensational accounts of children abused or neglected by paid caregivers). Douglas and Michaels (2004), in their book *The Mommy Myth: The Idealization of Motherhood and How It Undermined Women*, explore the media's influence. They are convinced that the media has reinforced standards of mothering that are all-consuming for women and that are actually impossible to achieve. So mothers who "fail" to measure up—be they stay-at-home moms or working for pay outside the home—feel guilt and anxiety over their choices and actions.

Even though mothers have entered the paid labour force in large numbers, there has not been a corresponding decline in the cultural phenomenon of intensive mothering. The pattern of women doing the child-rearing that emerged during the era of the "traditional family" has not really transformed. Working outside the home has not meant that women have been granted the same flexibility around parenting that men enjoy. In fact, Hays argues, the work of mothers has become even more intense. While there has been more gender equity in some of the household work and also in paid work, there continues to be an expectation that women are still primarily responsible for child-rearing; and as the standards of good mothering increase, the demands on mothers continue to intensify.

CONCLUSION

The family is not merely a unit of individuals relating to one another; it is also a social institution, often polarized and idealized, defining norms and strongly influencing the ways in which gender is done in Canada. It is also, however, an institution shaped and defined over time by the individuals within it.

CHAPTER SUMMARY: KEY POINTS

1. A social institution is a practice that has evolved over time to meet the needs of the society. Family patterns in Canada reflect the history, culture, and environment, as well as the gendered socio-cultural landscape of this country.

2. There have been dramatic changes in the demographic patterns of families in Canada, including a decline in the fertility rate, a huge increase in divorce rates, a rapid increase in common-law unions, and a resurgence in lone-parent families resulting from the rise in divorce rates.

3. The notion that the two-sphered "traditional family" existed throughout history is incorrect. Prior to the Industrial Revolution, women, men, and children were all involved in earning income except in the most affluent families.

4. The "traditional family," where men worked outside the home for pay and women worked at home without being paid, emerged after the Industrial Revolution and was eventually supported by law.

5. The *homemaker/breadwinner family arrangement* was a middle-class phenomenon that resulted in the perception of men as providers and disciplinarians while women were seen "unproductive" nurturers, focused entirely on their husbands and children.

6. The "traditional family" began disappearing during the Depression and World War II. It was further undermined by demographic, and economic value changes, as well as divorce patterns during the 1950s and 1960s.

7. The division of unpaid labour within heterosexual families reflects the tension of changing gender roles. Women have tended to increase their paid work activities more quickly than men have expanded their domestic contributions.

8. LaRossa argues that there is a disconnect between changing *culture* (ideas about the contributions of women and men) and *conduct* (the actual contributions of women and men). This disconnect results in inequity and conflict.

9. Beaujot outlines a variety of social programs that might lead to a more balanced sharing of paid and unpaid work including improved parental leave and benefits for part-time work.

10. *Intensified mothering* is a hegemonic pattern that suggests that the ideal type of mothering involves intense levels of time, energy, and money to provide children with an "ideal" environment. Women who do not live up to this normative expectation are perceived to be failing their children. But the expectation actually contributes to gender inequity.

DISCUSSION QUESTIONS

1. Why is the myth of the "traditional family" so powerful, given that it only reflected the lives of a narrow range of people for a short period of time? How has the pervasiveness of this notion of family shaped our socio-cultural landscape and our gendered interactions?

2. We have seen the close links between gender arrangements and demographic patterns. Given these links, what do you think family arrangements will look like twenty years from now?

3. This notion of intensive mothering seems to be hegemonic—a standard against which all mothers are measured. But it too may reflect a narrow range of mothers based on social class and ethnicity. How is this arrangement supported within our socio-cultural landscape and through interaction? How and where is it resisted?

4. If you could establish the "ideal" division of labour with a long-term partner, what would it look like? How could it be achieved and maintained? What shifts in the larger society would be needed to support this pattern?

5. Identify three changes that you think would have the most impact on energizing the "stalled revolution." Justify your choices.

KEY TERMS

blended family
common-law unions
culture/conduct
expressive role
gender strategy
hierarchical relations
homemaker/breadwinner
Industrial Revolution

instrumental role
intensified mothering
maternity leave
paternity leave
separate spheres/cooperative relations
sexual territory

shared spheres/ changing relations
social institutions
stalled revolution
step family
total fertility rate
"traditional family"

chapter twelve

Gender and Paid Work

As already outlined in Chapter Eleven, the links between gender and work are integrally related to families. When we consider work, we need to remember that much of the work that people do is unpaid, and that unpaid work often occurs within family households. Think about all the work you have completed in the past few days. How much of it did you get paid for? Sometimes children get paid for doing chores around the house, but most adults complete domestic work with no expectation of monetary reward. People teaching small children to tie their shoes and cross the road safely are working, as are those sorting laundry, carrying out the garbage, shoveling the snow, and aiding great-grandma if she needs help with her chores.

Historically, unpaid work has been undertaken by family members of all ages and genders. Only since the Industrial Revolution has there been a large-scale separation of home and workplace. Because of rising standards of living during the nineteenth century, many women and children (mainly from the emerging middle class) were able to leave the paid labour force in large numbers. Under those particular circumstances, women were most likely to take over the majority of unpaid work.

This separation of home and work led to the notion of women's work being primarily focused on mothering and homemaking, while the paid workplace came to be seen as male *sexual territory* (Bernard, 1981). The implications of this separate-sphere arrangement have been far-reaching for both women and men, as well as for the paid workplace itself.

TABLE 12.1	Gender-Linked Workplace Patterns	
Masculine Workplace Characteristics	**Feminine Workplace Characteristics**	
Competing	Collaborating	
Relying on Argument	Relying on Dialogue	
Commanding	Empowering	
Ladder/Pyramid/Hierarchy	Network/Community	
Directing	Inspiring	
Compliance	Commitment	

Source: Maier, 1999, pp. 76-77

Our culture has developed in such a way as to define masculinity, in part, with success in the paid workplace and the accumulation of goods (a direct result of earnings). As Kimbrell (1995) argues, masculinity has been transformed into an unhealthy proposition (see Chapter Three). Kimbrell believes that the pressure on men to achieve in the workforce has had a negative impact on their physical and mental health (high rates of heart disease and suicide), on their relationships with other people (pressure to compete and win versus cooperation and compassion), and on the earth itself (increasing profit versus effectively managing natural resources).

This two-sphered arrangement has also shaped the workplace itself. Arrangements in many workplaces have been characterized as masculine because of the organizational practices that have evolved. For example, Maier (1999) found that "a lasting consequence of the industrial revolution of society (and the related sex segregation of human activity) has been the creation of a bureaucratic social order grounded in the norms conventionally ascribed to men" (p. 74). He juxtaposes a series of qualities and interaction styles and concludes that the "masculine" ones predominate over the "feminine" ones in most corporations (see Table 12.1).

Many workplaces perpetuate these patterns because the leadership excels in them: people were promoted upwards in a corporate environment that rewarded the "masculine" behaviour patterns. Thus, when these leaders are looking to hire and promote others, they look for similar qualities, which they usually find in men. This results in continued gender inequities in hiring and promoting. But Maier argues women certainly can succeed in this kind of climate. To do so, he says, they have to "internalize the requirements of their position, becoming like men" (p. 89). He concludes that as long as the corporate culture retains its "masculine" qualities, hiring more women will not lead to change: women either have to adapt to the expectations or they will have difficulty thriving.

Nonetheless, one of the most dramatic changes in the Canadian workplace in recent decades has been the rapid increase in women working in the paid labour force. In the 1960s, only one quarter of women over the age of 15 worked in the paid labour force (full or part time). Now almost 60 percent of women earn an income from work (see Figure 12.1). But this large-scale entrance of women into areas that had previously been understood as male territory has not been without problems. One of the most troubling patterns is the continuing earnings gap. Women still only earn about 70 percent of what men earn. This persistent disparity in the **earnings ratio** contributes to higher levels of poverty and lower spending power among women.

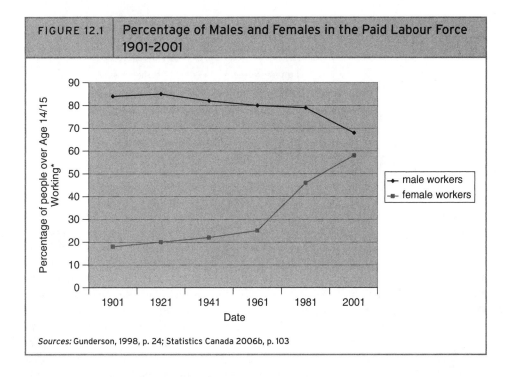

| FIGURE 12.1 | Percentage of Males and Females in the Paid Labour Force 1901–2001 |

Sources: Gunderson, 1998, p. 24; Statistics Canada 2006b, p. 103

This chapter examines labour force patterns and explores reasons why gender affects earnings. It also examines national policies designed to address these issues. However, this chapter does not directly answer the question: why do women earn less than men? Instead, it reviews many hypotheses and theories to inspire discussion about the issues and possible solutions, along with their attendant difficulties.

GENDERED PATTERNS OF WORK AND WAGES

The labour force participation rates of women and men in Canada over the last century have changed markedly, as Figure 12.1 shows (the working-age population was measured from age 14 and over in the 1901–1961 statistics; and 15 years and over for 1981 and 2001). In addition to the dramatic increase in the percentage of women in the paid labour force in recent decades, there has also been an almost 10 percent decline in the proportion of males working for pay. There is a logical explanation for these differences. The demographic pattern of increased life expectancy and the widespread retirement of older workers (see Chapter Six) creates a greater proportion of adults who are classified as "not working." This trend explains the decline in men's labour force activities. There are women in this category as well, but these retired women do not have an obvious impact on the graph because their numbers are more than offset by the huge increase in numbers of women who have entered the paid labour force over the same time period.

While women's labour force participation has increased, women have not adopted work patterns identical to men. For example, in 2004, a full 27 percent of female workers held part-time jobs, while only 11 percent of men did. As Table 12.2 shows, this pattern of part-time work varies by age.

TABLE 12.2	Percentage of Total Workers Employed Part-Time, by Sex and Age	
	Female workers	Male workers
15-24 years	52%	37%
25-54 years	21%	5%
55-64 years	30%	11%

Source: Statistics Canada 2006b, p. 100

Clearly, younger workers are much more likely to have part-time occupations than are middle-aged workers, with an increase again among older workers. This is likely a reflection of young people's education activities and a slow easing into retirement of older adults. When women and men were asked why they did not work full-time, an interesting pattern emerged (see Table 12.3). Women of all ages were much more likely to work part-time because of responsibilities related to their families than men, and men were more likely explain their work arrangements based on education commitments. Close to one quarter of men and women chose to work part-time. And just over one quarter of men and women were not working full-time because they were unable to find full-time employment. Clearly, family commitments have a greater impact on women than on men, and a very similar number of both women and men freely chose to hold part-time instead of full-time positions.

One of the most serious of gender-based inequalities is the issue of earnings. Women earn significantly less than men (see Table 12.4).

The good news is that the gap is closing. Women earn a higher percentage of what men earn than they did 35 years ago. But as this table makes obvious, there is still a huge gap: women earned 60 cents on the dollar in the 1970s, and now they earn just over 70 cents on the dollar. It is important to note that this earnings ratio is not explained by the difference in part-time and full-time employment: Table 12.5 only includes full-time/full-year workers. Table 12.5 breaks down the wage differentials by age to show the pattern more clearly.

TABLE 12.3	Reasons Given for Working Part-Time, by Sex	
Reasons	Female Workers	Male Workers
Child/family/personal responsibilities	18%	2%
School commitments	25%	42%
Personal illness	3%	4%
Couldn't find full-time work	26%	28%
Personal preference	27%	23%

Source: Statistics Canada, 2006b, p. 126

This breakdown of income differentials shows the depressing reality that at no point do women earn as much as men, not even at entry-level positions. The earnings gap begins when people start to work and widens throughout adulthood.

Of the many workplace issues that relate to gender, the earnings gap is one of the most important, because it has very real economic consequence for women and men. What causes this pattern, and how can we change it?

EXPLAINING THE PATTERNS

Perhaps the most obvious explanation why women in Canada earn less than men is that in past decades, men have largely held the powerful positions and have dictated who has been hired, for what positions, what they have been paid, and how far they have been promoted. Meanwhile, women's work was understood to be in the home, and women had less access to higher education and the network of business associates. The slow narrowing of the gap in earnings since the 1970s may simply reflect the reality that since the second wave of feminism, women insisted on having rights to higher education and careers, and worked to bring about—albeit slowly—institutional and legislative change. This explanation for the wage differential is tied closely to the **Dual Labour Market** theory (see below). There are, however, other attempts to explain the pattern.

A. Biological Differences

One of the oldest arguments for why women and men earn different amounts is that they have unique physiological capacities that lead them to undertake different jobs and result in unequal pay levels. This argument is based on the notion that essential biological differences between the sexes predispose them to succeed or fail at different occupations.

In this theory, the most basic difference between the sexes is that females are the ones who have the potential to be pregnant. Women have been excluded from some jobs on the grounds that they may be pregnant and fetuses should not be exposed to toxic substances or dangerous conditions *in utero*. On the surface, this might seem like a sensible argument: we wouldn't want to expose a fetus to harm unnecessarily. But, of course, not all women are pregnant all the time. To exclude an entire sex based on the possibility that some of them might at some time be pregnant is simply unjust. This argument was the centre of a major court battle finally resolved when U.S. Supreme Court unanimously ruled that discriminating against women because they might become pregnant is not legal. However, there is some evidence that such discrimination based on possible pregnancy continues to occur (see Kalish & Latif, 2005, for a discussion of the Supreme Court ruling and the ongoing discrimination). Interestingly, there are many harmful substances in hospitals to which nurses are exposed (Wroblewskito, 1993); yet the argument that nursing is dangerous for fetuses and that men should be solely responsible for this type of work is seldom raised. Moreover, if a work environment is dangerous enough to damage a fetus, chances are that it is potentially toxic enough to have a negative impact on any human. In the interest of all the workers' health, be they women or men, pregnant or not, it is important to make every effort to create the safest possible working conditions, especially when toxic substances are present.

TABLE 12.4	Average Income for Full-Time/Full-Year Workers by Year and Sex (constant $2003)		
Year	Female Average Income	Male Average Income	Earnings Ratio: Women/Men
1971	$ 25 700	$ 43 000	59.7%
1976	$ 30 700	$ 51 900	59.1%
1981	$ 30 200	$ 47 600	63.5%
1986	$ 30 900	$ 47 100	65.6%
1991	$ 33 000	$ 48 100	68.7%
1996	$ 34 300	$ 47 400	72.3%
2001	$ 36 500	$ 52 300	69.9%
2003	$ 36 500	$ 51 700	70.5%

Source: Statistics Canada, 2006b, p. 152

One frequently heard explanation for why women earn less is that they are not as strong or fit as men; therefore, they can't do the same kind of intense physical labour. Two aspects of this notion are considered below. First, are men stronger than women, and do jobs dependent upon strength depend on such differences? Second, is there any obvious justification for valorizing physically demanding unskilled labour over other equally important unskilled labour?

Certainly, on average, women are not physically as strong as men, but only *on average*. Chapter Two discussed overlapping normal curves. If the average ability of two groups is different, that does not mean that everyone in the high-scoring group has superior strength to everyone in the low-scoring group. There is a significant amount of overlap between the sexes. In short, a person's sex is certainly not the sole contributor to their physical abilities. Not all men are capable of doing heavy physical work, and not all women are incapable of it. Moreover, it is incorrect to assume that the reason men get hired and women don't is because women are not capable for biological reasons. Reversing the selection criteria shows

TABLE 12.5	Earnings Ratio by Age, 2003		
Age	Female Income	Male Income	Earnings Ratio: Women/Men
16-24	$ 19 700	$ 24 400	80.9%
25-34	$ 32 100	$ 43 100	74.4%
35-44	$ 40 000	$ 54 900	72.8%
45-54	$ 40 300	$ 60 200	67.0%
55+;	$ 36 100	$ 52 700	68.6%

Source: Statistics Canada, 2006b, p. 154

the arbitrariness of biologically based arguments. For example, consider the notion that women should be hired in occupations that require intensely demanding physical labour instead of men because women are less prone to heart attacks—prior to menopause women's bodies are less vulnerable to cardiovascular problems. This argument is no more or no less absurd than the argument that men deserve jobs because of greater physical strength: both are examples of sex-based discrimination.

In fact, many women do engage in heavy physical work. For example, consider two occupations predominantly considered to be women's work: childcare and nursing. Daycare workers routinely pick up and carry young children, many of whom weigh 40 pounds (not to mention that they are often squirming and trying to get down). Nurses also need physical strength to maneuver their patients, many of whom are incapacitated and unable to move without assistance. Yet no one advances arguments that women are too frail to do these jobs, that men should be childcare workers and nurses because of their superior strength. What is interesting is that when we compare wages of women who do heavy work with those of men who do heavy work, we discover that regardless of the strength required, the women's work typically pays less.

Moreover, often physically demanding jobs have guidelines in place to protect workers from injury. In many cities, garbage bags may not weigh more than 20 kilos. The vast majority of both women and men find this weight manageable. So, in fact, men and women are equally capable of being sanitation workers. But check out your garbage collection team next time you get a chance: few women do that job.

Many factors influence the amount of physical exertion different occupations require. Some jobs can only be completed by the strongest individuals, but the vast majority of physical work is not too demanding for all women. If women, or men for that matter, opt not to work in physically demanding occupations because they feel unable or are unwilling to engage in that kind of work, there is no problem—they have freely exercised their right to choose. But when a group of people is excluded from those jobs based on the incorrect belief that they aren't capable of such work, that is discrimination. This kind of discrimination keeps women out of some high-paying blue-collar work and contributes to the wage gap between the sexes. Retail jobs, for example, typically pay significantly less than low-skilled construction jobs ($7 versus $14 per hour). Neither job requires a great deal of training, but one pays twice the other. Unfortunately, these patterns are not just a result of individual choice. Assumptions about the suitability of women and men for particular kinds of work often determine who gets hired. Underlying the whole discussion of physical labour is the as yet unasked question: why, in the twenty-first century, should there be a link between strength and income? Is garbage collection a higher priority than childcare? Or is it that "men's work" is valued over "women's work"?

B. Dual Labour Market

A second explanation for the inequitable distribution of pay is the *dual labour market*. Based on an economic theory, it suggests that there are two kinds of jobs: **primary sector** jobs and **secondary sector** jobs (also known as *career jobs* and *dead-end jobs*, or *good jobs* and *bad jobs*). You may have worked in a dead-end job while you saved money for your education. Or maybe you have a dead-end job right now as you juggle the conflicting demands of school, work, and family. Dead-end jobs are those that have little upward mobility. They are frequently low paying with little long-term security. There are plenty of these jobs available when the economy is booming. (In Alberta, for example, as this text is being written, there are more jobs than people to fill them: stores and companies are struggling to retain employees because there is such a high demand.) These jobs are typically filled by young people just entering the labour force, new arrivals to the area, people with little education who may not be perceived to have the skills necessary for more challenging work, and people who have other demands on their time, like raising/caring for family members.

In contrast, primary sector jobs are longer-term career jobs. The common pattern is for people to begin at an entry-level position and then work their way up into more challenging positions, as long as their skills and desire meet expectations. Based on hard work and accumulated experience, these jobs typically offer opportunity for advancement and pay raises. Unlike McDonalds counter workers, who likely learn all they need to know within the first few days (how to make french fries, how to serve customers with a smile, etc.) and whose chances of getting a raise are slim unless the minimum wage is raised, a primary sector job involves increasing levels of challenge. One never learns it all and often has opportunity to be promoted up the ladder.

According to the dual labour market theory, the most desirable employees are more likely to be chosen for the primary sector jobs: those with the requisite education or the appropriate skill set, those who are perceived to have potential to be promoted and, importantly, those who are considered to be valuable long-term assets for the company. In other words, employers want to hire people with sufficient potential who will also reflect well on the company. Historically, when the two-sphered family arrangement was in full force, these jobs went to educated or skilled white men. Women were excluded because of the belief that they belonged in the home. They were not perceived to have the skills, ability, or ambition necessary to succeed in primary sector jobs. Bluntly, there was very little room for women in the primary sector. Cultural beliefs have evolved, with the growing recognition that women are fully capable of excelling in primary sector careers, but this does not mean that the original pattern has completely disappeared.

Many women still end up in dead-end, secondary sector jobs. Over the last few decades, more women have attained management and professional positions. Equal numbers of women and men are gaining higher levels of education. However, the entrance of women into primary sector jobs did not occur (and is not occurring) naturally and easily, simply because more women are drawn into the paid labour force. Because the paying workplace and primary sector jobs in particular have typically been perceived as reserved for men, women seeking such work had and still have an uphill battle to gain admittance.

In the United States, *affirmative action* policies were created and enforced to ensure that those who had traditionally been discriminated against (such as non-white people and women) were given equal opportunity to education and employment. These policies helped women gain a foothold in male-dominated professions. However, efforts to consolidate women's rights in by adding an **Equal Rights Amendment** to the United States constitution were defeated—not everyone agrees that full legal equality for women is desirable. Canadians have enacted various laws to ensure that women are not discriminated against in the workplace. Canada has had equal pay policies in place for decades, the first established by Ontario in 1951. This legislation guarantees that people must be paid equally for the same or substantially similar work. When the Charter of Rights and Freedoms became law in 1982, discrimination against people because of specific characteristics, including sex, age, religion, and ethnic origin, became illegal. Having equality rights entrenched in law, however, clearly does not mean that discrimination no longer exists. While more women are actively working in primary sector jobs than ever before, we still see sex-based patterns in positions with greater authority, responsibility, status, and pay. In almost every sector of the Canadian economy, the higher one goes up the career hierarchy, the fewer women one sees. Think about your own education experiences. You were much more likely to have had female teachers in the lower grades and male teachers at higher levels. Consider the faculty at your current university or college. Chances are there are more men with full-time tenured positions and more men designated as full professors. If you are working for pay while you go to school, think about the power hierarchy where you are employed. Are there more women at the top?

C. Human Capital

A third explanation for the differential employment positions of women and men is based on the idea of **human capital**. Whereas the "biological differences" theory is more often connected to wage differentials in unskilled labour, the human capital explanation is more closely tied to skilled work. Human capital can roughly be defined as all the education, training, and experience people have that enhance their desirability as employees. Certainly, historical patterns bolster the argument that human capital accounts for women's lower earnings. In the past, women as a group did tend to have less education than men. They also often had truncated or interrupted work histories as a result of time off for family-based responsibilities. And they did have fewer opportunities for on-the-job training in areas that would advance their careers. However, times have changed. As noted earlier, more women than ever are getting post-secondary education. Indeed, in 2001–02, women outnumbered men at Canadian universities (see Table 12.6).

So the idea that women currently earn less because they are less qualified is inaccurate for recent entrants into the labour force. In some professional schools, there are more women than men qualifying—for example, as doctors and lawyers. But Table 12.7 shows that the human capital argument falls short as an explanation for gender differences in income by comparing the incomes of workers who have similar educational backgrounds.

Table 12.8 further breaks down degrees and diplomas to highlight the disparities. These statistics show that if you graduate with a undergraduate degree, and so does the other-sexed person sitting next you, chances are whichever one of you is the woman is going to earn less.

Gunderson (1998) undertook a complex analysis of the impact of human capital on wages, controlling for a long list of variables. His goal was to compare workers who were similar on wide a wage range of characteristics, where the only difference was their sex. The variable list included age, education, marital status, language spoken, immigrant status, hours worked, occupation, and industry sector. Using weekly earnings data, where the earnings ratio was 63.3 percent (women earned $63.30 for every $100 men earned), he found that, while human capital factors explained some of the differential (47 percent), 53 percent of the gap remained unexplained (Gunderson, 1998, p. 114). Clearly, the human capital theory leaves much unexplained.

One final statistical report does provide reason for optimism (Statistics Canada, 2006). Table 12.9 compares the incomes of young, university-educated women and men in the same occupations. Listed are the top seven occupational categories for each group. The data shows that in this particular group, women earn almost as much as men. But, even here a wage gap persists. Only in the unionized teaching positions do the women earn within 5 percent of the men's incomes.

Judging from these data, the wage gap for educated young adults is closing. It appears that young people with similar amounts of human capital in middle-class jobs and professions are getting close to wage parity. In fact, in the ninth most common occupation for these women—social work—the women actually out-earned the men ($36 555 compared to $35 011; that is, women's earning are 104.4 percent of men's earnings). If this trend continues and expands to other age, occupational, and human capital categories, the persistent earnings differential may close. However, this possibility will not be realized if women and men are not equally hired and promoted in similar positions. If simply educating and training women were enough to eliminate the wage gap, then the earnings of these young adults should be equal—and they are not.

D. Occupational Segregation

A fourth explanation for the gap between women's and men's earnings is the phenomenon of **occupational segregation**. Occupational segregation refers to the different places where people work and the different jobs they do. Think about the working people you have observed recently. Have you taken a car in for repairs? You were unlikely to have had a female mechanic fixing the alternator. What about shopping at the grocery store? More men work in the produce and meat departments, while more women in the bakery and as cashiers. Daycare? Hardware store? Construction site? Library? Sex segregation in the workplace is so common that we barely notice it unless we see someone who doesn't seem to belong. (For example, a young man worked at my child's daycare, and some of the parents were uncomfortable with the idea of a male caring for their infants, believing there had to be something wrong with a man who chose such a job, similar to the men studied in Chapter Eight who are nurses.) The term **pink collar ghetto** was coined to describe the secondary sector clerical jobs where so many women work.

In fact, empirical research suggests that occupational segregation is a powerful explanation for the earnings differential. Women and men may have similar degrees and similar years of work experience; but if one is employed as a nurse in a doctor's office and the other as a geological engineer working in the oil industry, their pay will be significantly different. Even within the same profession, if female medical doctors are more likely to pursue family medicine practices and males are more likely to train as surgeons, people with similar credentials will earn disparate wages. Drolet (2002) undertook a study utilizing 1999 data to assess how well occupational segregation explains the earnings ratio. Her

TABLE 12.6	Percent of University Degrees Earned by Women			
Education Level	1972-1973	1981-1982	1991-1992	2001-2002
Bachelor/1st Professional Degrees	38.4%	46.7%	53.5%	57.7%
Master's Degrees	27.1%	41.1%	46.2%	51.4%
Doctorates	18.8%	31.0%	35.2%	45.9%
All University Degrees	37.0%	45.8%	52.2%	56.7%

Source: Statistics Canada, 2006b, p. 100

TABLE 12.7	Income by Education, Full-Time/Full-Year Workers, 2003		
Education Level	Female Average Wage	Male Average Wage	Earnings Ratio: Women/Men
Less than Grade 9	$ 21 700	$ 31 200	69.4%
Some High School	$ 22 900	$ 40 000	57.3%
High School Diploma	$ 30 500	$ 43 000	71.0%
Some Post-Secondary	$ 31 500	$ 41 600	75.6%
Post-Secondary Diploma/Certificate	$ 34 200	$ 49 800	68.6%
University Degree	$ 53 400	$ 77 500	68.9%

Source: Statistics Canada, 2006b, p. 153

study measured over 24 000 employees on a long list of variables, roughly broken down into four categories: 1) who they were (human capital and demographic characteristics); 2) where they worked (workplace size and industry); 3) what they did (occupations, work group arrangements); and 4) when they worked (regular hours, flex time hours).

Drolet's findings clearly show the relevance of workplace location in addition to human capital. When only human capital characteristics were measured, these characteristics explained about 23 percent of the wage differential. But when Drolet added workplace features and occupations, these additional characteristics explained just over 60 percent of the wage differential. Drolet's analysis still leaves almost 40 percent of the difference in women's and men's wages unexplained, but her results are informative nonetheless. They suggest that for women to improve their financial position, they need to think very carefully about where they want to work and what kind of work they want to do, beyond just attaining their qualifications. Moreover, to change occupational segregation within the workplace,

TABLE 12.8	Income by Qualification, 1990		
Type of Qualification	Female Average Wage	Male Average Wage	Earnings Ratio: Women/Men
Trade Certificate	$ 19 621	$ 34 161	57.4%
Other Non-university Certificate	$ 22 384	$ 36 035	62.1%
Bachelor Degree	$ 29 429	$ 44 874	65.6%
Master's Degree	$ 39 020	$ 54 331	71.8%
Doctorate Degree	$ 45 962	$ 64 311	71.5%

Source: Gunderson, 1998, p. 94

TABLE 12.9	Average Earnings in the Seven Occupations Most Commonly Held by Those Aged 25-29 with a University Degree Working Full-Year, Full-Time, by Sex, Canada, 2000		
	Average Earnings		Earnings Ratio:
	Men	Women	Women/Men
Seven occupations most commonly held by young men			
Computer and information systems	$ 54 052	$ 45 915	84.9%
Financial auditors and accountants	$ 42 913	$ 39 990	93.2%
Sales marketing and advertising managers	$ 56 440	$ 46 047	81.6%
Retail trade managers	$ 38 122	$ 31 596	82.9%
Secondary school teachers	$ 36 201	$ 35 546	98.2%
Financial and investment analysts	$ 52 208	$ 44 864	85.9%
Retail sales persons and sales clerks	$ 33 167	$ 26 211	79.0%
Seven occupations most commonly held by young women			
Elementary school and kindergarten teachers	$ 36 243	$ 35 535	98.0%
Computer and information systems	$ 54 052	$ 45 915	84.9%
Financial auditors and accountants	$ 42 913	$ 39 990	93.2%
Registered nurses	$ 44 688	$ 41 088	91.9%
Secondary school teachers	$ 36 201	$ 35 546	98.2%
Sales, marketing, and advertising managers	$ 56 440	$ 46 047	81.6%
General office clerks	$ 30 339	$ 28 348	93.4%

Source: Statistics Canada 2006a

our society needs to think about the structural causes of this segregation and create effective strategies for minimizing them.

However, knowing that occupational segregation is a significant cause of the earnings ratio still leaves us with a critically important question. Why do women and men end up working in different industries and locations? Why, for example, do more women choose to practice family medicine, while men are more likely to choose surgery? And, maybe more importantly, why is the workplace structured in such a way to provide differential opportunities and obstacles for women and men? As discussed in other chapters, gender is not done solely on the individual level. Gender issues permeate society and social institutions. In effect, not all employment options are available to women and men at the same cost.

Two types of occupational segregation relate to the gender wage gap: vertical and horizontal. **Horizontal segregation** refers to the pattern of people working in completely different fields (daycares versus construction). Table 12.10 illustrates horizontal segregation. It lists the top ten most common occupations for women and men. More than 60 percent of

Canadian women and just under 50 percent of men work in these jobs. Only for two occupations do the sexes overlap

Vertical segregation is based on hierarchies within an organization: more women are in clerical positions, and more men in managerial roles. One of the key issues in vertical segregation is the notion of the **glass ceiling**. If women and men are similarly qualified, why do so many more men make it into top management positions than women? Canadian data shows that about one third of men work in supervisory positions, while only one quarter of women do. In fact, the difference in supervisory positions explains almost 7 percent of the gap in hourly wages (Statistics Canada, 1999). The glass ceiling suggests that there is an invisible barrier keeping women from being promoted into the upper ranks of an organization. This phenomenon has been widely studied.

In his review of the literature on the glass ceiling phenomenon, Powell (1999) explores a variety of explanations for it. We will focus on three of these. First, he argues that "women's presence in top management positions violates the societal norm of men's higher status and superiority to a greater extent than women's presence in lower-level management" (p. 334). Quite simply, our workplaces reflect the patriarchal roots of our socio-cultural landscape: we expect men to be in positions of power, and we are uncomfortable with women at the top of the hierarchy. The *masculine work environment* discussed earlier in the chapter reflects this same phenomenon. Hiring and promotion practices reflect the expectations of those in power about workplace performance and desirable qualities. Empirical research supports this idea. Managers interviewed about their perceptions of employees were more likely to believe that men more than women have the necessary qualities and characteristics to succeed in upper management positions (p. 335). While employers may not be specifically looking at a person's gender when making decisions about promotions, they do look for specific attributes that are most often associated with masculinity—for example, ambition and competitiveness. In addition, psychological theory suggests there is a *similarity-attraction* phenomenon at play. Research suggests that people evaluate others who they perceive to be like themselves more favourably than those they perceive to be unlike them (Byrne & Neuman, 1992). If men are already in positions of power, they are more likely to hire men, by virtue of this subconscious preference. Second, Powell explains that status expectations influence the way people act and assess others (see also Chapters Two and Eight). If men and women in the workplace act in accordance with normative expectations to avoid unfavourable assessments, this can contribute to the perception that men are more competent and more able to make valuable contributions. Thus, behaving in a way that helps women avoid censure based on gender expectations may simultaneously project the wrong image for promotion. And third, the glass ceiling creates an absence of female mentors, which then perpetuates the problem of very few women being promoted. Because there are so few women in the upper realms of most organizations, there are few people available to fill mentoring roles. As Powell describes it, "Mentors significantly contribute to their protégés' career success and satisfaction. In addition, mentors buffer women from both overt and covert discrimination and help them to overcome obstacles" (p. 337). Of course, women don't have to have female mentors; but the similarity-attraction phenomenon works in mentoring relationships as well as in promotion decisions.

When women do break through the glass ceiling or are hired into a situation where there are very few other women, they face unique challenges. In her classic research on gender and work, Rosabeth Kanter (1977) detailed what she called **token dynamics**—the

TABLE 12.10	Percentage of Workers in Top 10 Jobs by Sex, 1991		
Male Occupations	**Percent**	**Female Occupations**	**Percent**
Other Sales	6.93%	Clerical	17.34%
Clerical	5.50%	Other Sales	8.49%
Transport/Equipment Operator	5.07%	Secretaries	7.91%
Machine Operator	4.89%	Retail Sales	5.76%
Trade Helpers	4.41%	Teachers and Professors	5.19%
Other Managers	4.33%	Childcare and Home Support	4.02%
Mechanics	4.30%	Nurse Supervisors and RNs	3.71%
Agricultural Occupations	4.21%	Occupations in Food and Beverage	3.42%
Construction Trades	4.08%	Cashiers	3.38%
Professional in Natural/Applied Science	3.62%	Manager: Retail, Food, Accommodation	2.84%
Total	**47.34%**	**Total**	**62.06%**

Source: Gunderson 1998, pp. 137–139, 145

workplace dynamics involved in experiencing different treatment than the majority of employees in a specific work environment. If there is a serious imbalance in the sex of employees, minority workers tend to face additional challenges that the majority do not face. Thus, women who choose to work in male-dominated occupations are subject to these dynamics. Kanter describes two key challenges. First, there is more *performance pressure.* If you are one of many, then no one pays particular attention to your work. However, if you are marked as different in some way, your work is more likely to be scrutinized. The work of the lone female on the assembly line or on the oil rig is going to be noticed. And her work is going to be judged by those around her, to assess whether she really deserves her job. Second, because a woman in such a situation is effectively an outsider, the majority tends to identify with one another and marginalize the one who is different. Kanter suggests people in such a position are often socially isolated. Empirical studies of Kanter's ideas show that low-status minorities are much more subject to these dynamics than high-status minorities. That is, the lone woman on the construction site will face these challenges, but the lone male on the nursing staff is much less likely to be isolated or experience additional performance pressures. In fact, some have suggested there is a *glass escalator* for men in nontraditional occupations which helps them get hired and promoted ahead of their female colleagues (a phenomenon noted in Chapter Eight). The result of this phenomenon is troubling. "Most women who take nontraditional (male dominated) jobs tend to move to more traditional jobs when they change jobs; in fact, for every 11 women who work in nontraditional jobs, about 10 will eventually move to a female dominated job" (Gutek, 2001 p.1196).

A third problem women face in the labour force is the nature of the work environment itself. A significant body of research has documented the existence of a **hostile work environment**, sexual harassment, and/or a **chilly climate** for women. *Hostile work environment* is an American legal term referring to sexual conduct that is sufficient to make the workplace offensive or intimidating for employees. The term *chilly climate* includes this sexual component but also incorporates the lack of mentoring and unequal experiences of employees. Jo-Anne Kirk's research (2002) effectively illustrates the problem of chilly climate for women in nontraditional jobs. She undertook a qualitative study of students at a Canadian medical school and found that many factors contributed to the medical specialties students chose. Even though the students (women and men) had all been accepted into the medical school (therefore, presumably, their qualifications were comparable), most of the women students did not feel comfortable at medical school. Beginning with the admissions interviews, many of the women were questioned about their family intentions. Would they be having children? How did they think they would balance their practice with the demands of a family? No one had ever heard of male students being asked such questions. The admissions committee consisted mainly of senior male doctors, often with an upper-year student or resident as the sole female member.

From the outset, the position of women in the medical faculty appeared to be lower than that of men. There were few female role models, and many of the female students reported that they were actively discouraged from pursuing surgical specialties. One student stated that she was bluntly and condescendingly told not to try orthopedic surgery, that a family practice would make it easier for her to have and raise children. In addition, these students perceived surgery as a macho specialty where the "old boys" worked hard to keep women out. In fact, the perception that women weren't welcome was pervasive. Kirk quotes one student who said that surgery rotation was "a month and half of them trying to make you cry" (p. 177). In addition to these experiences, which contributed to occupational segregation, Kirk also found many examples indicating that medical school was a hostile work environment for females. For example, she found that the language and humour used in classes belittled women. In some classes, anatomical differences were clearly differentiated: male genitalia was referred to as a "penis" while women's breasts were called "'tits." Women students were frequently referred to as "girls" and "skirts" (see Chapter Three for a discussion of slang and belittling language). Moreover, when women students complained about misogynistic experiences, the administration trivialized their concerns. In fact, it was suggested that if they couldn't handle sexism in school, they'd never make it as medical doctors. The administration did not address the problems, and the women were effectively silenced, since they didn't want their careers jeopardized. Kirk noted that certainly not all of their experiences and professors were misogynistic, but there were enough problems for the women students to feel marginalized and distressed. Given these examples, it is hardly surprising that many women choose not to go into specialization that would involve more rotations in this type of hostile environment.

Yet another hypothesis about occupational segregation has suggested that differential socialization leads women and men to choose different jobs. Chapter Five explained that girls were much more likely to be given dolls and domestic toys while boys were more likely to play with trucks and building toys. Can horizontal segregation be explained by differences such as boys wanting to drive trucks while girls wanting to play house? Jacobs (1999) found that socialization isn't sufficient to explain the occupational segregation. He notes that young people frequently change their career aspirations, and there is little connection between aspirations and actual educational and occupational choices. More importantly, the socialization hypothesis suggests that changes in occupational segregation only occur over time as new generations who had been socialized in less gender-polarizing ways entered the paid labour force. But data shows that changing occupations of women and men aren't simply arising from new workers entering the job market. Certainly, the youngest groups have shown the greatest reduction in segregation, but there have been reductions in segregation in every age group. As explained in Chapter Five, early gender socialization does not entirely explain subsequent choices and behaviours. Thus, gender socialization is insufficient for explaining occupational segregation.

A second hypothesis to explain sex differences in occupations involves the nature of the work itself. Some have suggested that women get paid less because they choose to do jobs that are more agreeable. In essence, they trade off higher wages in order to enjoy better working conditions. Researchers have assessed the nature of work and the working conditions to see if these undesirable qualities, euphemistically called **workplace disamenties**, can explain sex-based earnings differentials. The answer appears to be *no*—this does not explain why women earn less (Jacobs & Steinberg, 1995). While men may work in unpleasant surroundings (the heat of a foundry or the chill of a winter construction site), jobs that are considered to be women's work also have disamenties (cleaning up after others, blood and feces).

A third explanation is based on the notion that men and women simply have different job preferences. They like doing different things and therefore they choose different occupations. Konrad *et al.* (2000) undertook a major meta-analysis involving data from over 200 samples and 600 000 respondents. They found that some differences do exist: women are more likely to prefer good hours and interpersonal relations, while men were more interested in challenge and earnings. However, they also found that these patterns change over time. By the 1990s, the aspirations of women appear to have shifted: sex differences regarding the desire for responsibility have disappeared, and women's interest in being challenged at work has risen (Konrad *et al.*, 2000). After analyzing all this data, the authors concluded that differences in workplace preferences between the sexes are very small. Their analysis showed a wider range of preferences *within each* sex group than there was *between* the groups. Thus, sex differences related to work preferences do not adequately explain the occupational segregation patterns that have led to the earnings ratio.

In their research on occupational segregation, Brooks, Jarman and Blackburn (2003) analyzed the changes in both vertical and horizontal segregation in Canada over a 15-year period (1981–1996). They found some positive changes but also some disturbing outcomes. The good news is that there has been a decrease in vertical segregation. Many more women are being hired and promoted in primary sector jobs today than in the past. And about 12 percent of the increase in female employees during that time period was women entering careers that remain male dominated (though the majority still entered into female-dominated occupations). The continuing problem is that even though vertical segregation is declining, it is still a significant issue. "Although these women may have been improving their position, men still dominate the higher-status, higher-paid jobs in the country" (p. 207). An even larger concern is that their analysis of part-time work shows that "while gender equality appears to exist in the part-time labour force, this seems to be due to men losing ground rather than women gaining, and earnings are well below those in full-time occupations. The majority of part-time workers are women, and the numbers are growing steadily" (2003 p. 207). They conclude that although there have been improvements, there are still real challenges to be overcome before occupational segregation disappears.

What emerges from this discussion of potential causes of the earnings ratio is the fact that multiple factors likely contribute to unequal wages. Individual employee characteristics, such as human capital, ability, preference, and socialization, likely play a role. Employer and co-worker behaviours also have an impact, through harassment and/or discrimination in hiring and promotion, or more positively by creating empowering, non-discriminatory workplaces. But institutional factors also play an important role; the existence of a glass ceiling, a hostile work environment, or a masculine corporate climate can limit opportunities for women and block their access to equal employment and earnings. The labour force and the workplace itself appear to be in transition from male-domination to more fully accepting and accommodating the participation of both sexes.

REDRESSING INEQUITIES: POSSIBLE SOLUTIONS

Thinking about the nature of and the reasons for gender inequity in Canada leads to the search for solutions. Just as systems that lead to the earning differential operate in the individual, interactional, and institutional levels, so too must the solutions. But while individuals can effect change, they do so most powerfully when they change policies, laws, and institutional gender regimes.

On the individual level, people can certainly improve their opportunities by developing as much human capital as possible. They also need to make fully informed choices about their careers, recognizing the very real financial consequences of their decisions. But just working hard and making careful choices is not enough to end occupational segregation—the institutional factors must also be addressed. A variety of policies have been developed and are being developed and implemented in Canada in an effort to reduce workplace inequities.

As already noted, equal pay policies "guaranteeing" that people are paid equally for substantially similar work have been in place for decades. However, the broader notion of equal pay for work of equal value, known as **pay equity** in Canada (termed *comparable worth* in the United States), was a much more recent initiative. The idea of pay equity is that even though two people working for the same employer do very different jobs, if those jobs require approximately the same level of intelligence, responsibility, and diligence, then they should be rewarded similarly. The purpose of pay equity is to redress the pay imbalance between jobs undertaken primarily by a single sex (food preparation jobs may be dominated by women while men may occupy the majority of janitorial jobs, for example). Prior to pay equity practices, "men's work" typically commanded higher wages.

Ontario enacted pay equity legislation in the 1980s, and since then most provinces have done the same. Alberta is the only province that does not have pay equity legislation. The pay equity rules require employers to investigate their wage structures—first to see if a single sex dominates any particular occupation (70 percent or more of workers of one sex). Then they assess the value of the jobs based on specific criteria (for example, skill, effort, responsibility, and working conditions). If there is an unequal relationship between job requirements and pay in single-sex-dominated positions, then they must adjust pay rates accordingly. For example, if food preparation and janitorial work are considered to be work of equal value, and the male janitors are paid more than female food workers, then there must be an upward adjustment to the female food service workers' pay. Pay equity was designed to eliminate discriminatory wage policies that led to lower incomes for women. But it is not a universal solution, because it compares incomes only within organizations, not between organizations. Thus, if only women are employed in a particular factory, they can be paid whatever the management wants (subject to minimum wage laws).

Even if the men in the factory next door do comparable work and earn twice as much, pay equity legislation doesn't apply. Also, not everyone is covered by pay equity legislation: people who work for small businesses are not covered, nor are people working in mixed-sex jobs. Most problematic, pay equity is difficult to establish and enforce: even provincial governments who enacted the legislation have not been quick to implement it for their own workers. Pay equity legislation certainly seems to be a step in the right direction—fighting institutional sexism in pay scales—but it won't solve all the problems.

A second kind of policy designed to address inequities in the workplace focuses on discrimination in hiring, promoting, and firing. This legislation was designed to create equal opportunities for specific groups and to provide a mechanism for solving problems when they arise. If there is reason to believe that discrimination is occurring, a worker can complain to the **Human Rights Commission**, who will investigate the problem. In addition, workers can use human rights legislation to fight sexual harassment in the workplace. When we ask our students about **sexual harassment**, almost everyone has stories about what has happened to them or their friends in the workplace. It appears that inappropriate sexual comments and/or pressures are a common feature of employment for many people. But when we ask how our students handled the situations, the responses varied significantly. While the majority of students who speak about these issues are women, men too can be subject to such harassment. Some people just quit their jobs—they don't believe it is worth their peace of mind to put up with such treatment. Others just ignore the problem hoping it will go away, even if they feel demoralized by the situation. Some students retaliate by belittling their tormenter, and the problem seems to disappear. Very few students report that they made a formal complaint about the situation. Even though there are protections under the law, many people are reluctant to initiate the complaint process. Therefore, human rights legislation is not sufficient for ending workplace harassment.

Moreover, sexual harassment has many definitions. This one comes from the Alberta Humans Rights Commission, charged with overseeing sexual harassment policy and complaints in Alberta:

> Sexual harassment is any unwelcome behaviour, sexual in nature, that adversely affects, or threatens to affect, directly or indirectly, a person's job security, working conditions or prospects for promotion or earnings; or prevents a person from getting a job, living accommodations or any kind of public service.

> Sexual harassment is usually an attempt by one person to exert power over someone else. It can be perpetrated by a supervisor, by a co-worker, by a landlord or a service provider. (Alberta Human Rights, 2002)

According to this legislation, all employers are required to create and maintain a work environment where sexual harassment is not tolerated. In fact, they can be held accountable if they do not undertake adequate actions to ensure the rights of their employees to be free from such harassment. However, one of the challenges of sexual harassment is that it is in some ways subjective. You know when someone is harassing you; but that someone may not know how destructive you find their actions. What one person finds humorous and harmless another might find offensive and threatening. This is one of the reasons so many of our students don't report mistreatment—they don't want to be seem like complainers who can't take a joke. Unfortunately, sexual harassment isn't a joke. It can have serious negative consequences, creating a hostile environment in which it is hard to be productive, threatening job performance and ultimate career success.

Another policy focused on workplace inequities is known as **employment equity**, designed to ensure equality of opportunity by focusing on hiring outcomes. Under this kind of policy, also known as **affirmative action**, certain groups (typically women, Aboriginals, visible minorities, and disabled persons) who have been discriminated against in the past and are currently under-represented within an organization, are targeted for hiring. Thus, if two well-qualified candidates apply for a single job, and the organization has very few people belonging to the target group already in its employ, they will be required to hire the person from that target group ahead of the other candidate. The Canadian government follows this employment equity policy in the public service, including Crown and all other public sector jobs. However, employment equity is not without controversy. (The Ontario government, for example, enacted a similar policy but then repealed it.) Many people believe that affirmative action is reverse discrimination and that able-bodied white men who cannot be members of a target group will not have an equal opportunity to be hired. On the surface, these critics are correct. Even if a white, able-bodied man is equal to the other candidate, he will not be hired if the qualified candidate is a member of an under-represented group. Do you think this is discrimination? If you were the man not being hired, I'm sure you would feel that this is unjust; however, others argue that men have enjoyed a hiring privilege for so long—by virtue of the gendered nature of our society—that this kind of policy simply removes their privilege, putting them on equal footing with people over whom they once had an advantage.

A third set of policies facilitates the participation of women in the labour force. These policies typically do not relate directly to hiring or salary; instead they focus on opportunity. Maternity leave, publicly funded daycare, family leave programs, and education policies to encourage women to pursue nontraditional jobs can reduce occupational segregation and close the earnings gap. Because women in our gendered society typically do have primary responsibility for caring for children and overseeing households, programs that make it easier to balance home and work responsibilities can be beneficial. Nevertheless, these policies are not without their critics. Guaranteeing a mother a full year at home with her infant after birth can have a negative impact on employers who must find temporary employees to fill her job during her absence. Moreover, publicly funded daycare is not universally supported in Canada. (At the time of writing this text, it continues to be a contentious issue in federal politics.) While universal daycare is beneficial for families with parents working outside the home for pay, some believe it disadvantages families where one parent does not work outside the home because they may not be eligible for comparable benefits.

One proposal for facilitating parenting and work is popularly known as the **Mommy Track**. The Mommy Track was proposed as an alternative career path in large law firms specifically for female lawyers who were challenged by the competing demands of work and family. In competitive law firms, young lawyers are hired to work as associates—they are expected to work long hours (80 hour weeks are not uncommon) to prove their skill and worth in the hopes that they will eventually "make partner." That is, they will join the owners and share in the profits and decision-making, rather than continuing as salaried employees. The partnership track is a lengthy endurance test/marathon (often 8–10 years long) during which associates must make work their top priority. One concern is that women with children cannot meet such onerous expectations because they can't devote their lives entirely to the practice of law. The creation of the Mommy Track was intended to recognize that highly competent lawyer/mothers were assets to a firm, even if they couldn't play the partnership game. This alternative track honours their joint commitment to family and career while lowering the demands and preserving their jobs. Women on this track are well paid, though they earn less than partner track associates, and they have lower annual targets which ultimately results in shorter work weeks. Can you see the problem inherent in this strategy? It appears to facilitate parenting, but it creates a two-tiered system that disadvantages both groups. Mothers are seen as less valued employees because they will not ever become partners, leading to ongoing occupational segregation for those with families. And those on the partner track cannot protest if unreasonable demands are placed upon them. They have been designated as career-focused (as opposed to family-focused); therefore, their attempts to place limits on their work demands are regarded as shirking. In effect, by choosing the partner track, they forfeit their right to place anything above their careers. Fortunately, not all policies designed to facilitate equity between the sexes have such negative consequences. But the lesson to be learned from the Mommy Track is that organizations must carefully consider the consequences of every policy and program, because sometimes unintended consequences negate their value.

The primary focus of this chapter has been on paid work and the disparate incomes of women and men. But keep in mind that there is another kind of essential work that improves the quality of life in our communities: volunteer work. Volunteers are not paid but that does not mean their efforts do not have economic value. In her essay on volunteer work, Muriel Mellow explores the links between gender and volunteering.

BOX 12-1	Women and Volunteer Work

by Muriel Mellow, University of Lethbridge

The feminist analysis of work has drawn attention to the connections between paid and unpaid work; but most of the focus has been on domestic work in the home. Sociologists have been slower to consider links to other forms of unpaid work. These would include "helping"—informal assistance to neighbours and friends—and "volunteering"—the provision of unpaid labour to an organization in a formally recognized and often ongoing position.

Helping is somewhat more difficult to study because of its informal or sporadic nature; we suspect women do a large proportion of this as an extension of their caregiving roles in the home. As for volunteering, the Canadian Census does not yet collect data on this activity, but we do have several national surveys on this topic, including the 1997 and 2000 National Surveys on Giving, Volunteering and Participating.

The proportion of the Canadian population who volunteer is shrinking. It dropped from 31% in 1997 to 27% in 2000 (Hall, McKeown, and Roberts 2001, p. 31). Historically, women were far more likely to volunteer than men; it was an acceptable form of public participation for women before it was common for the majority of women to work outside of the home. In recent years, the difference in the proportion of women and men who volunteer has narrowed. In 2000, 28% of Canadian women volunteered compared to 25% of men (Hall, McKeown, and Roberts 2001, p. 33).

| BOX 12-1 | *(Continued)* |

This shift in women's participation is linked to their entry into the paid labour force and the reduced amount of time that they have to contribute volunteer hours. It is probable that the likelihood of informal helping has also declined for the same reason.

Arlie Hochschild (1989) talked about "the second shift" that women work when trying to carry out their domestic tasks after a full day on the job; when one considers volunteer work, one might even talk about women putting in a triple shift. One of the ways that women have found to manage their double load of work has been to withdraw from volunteer involvements. However, some women may feel compelled to volunteer because of the way that it can help to support family members. For example, women may help with school or recreational events in which their children are involved or may even participate in activities that are related to their husband's career, such as charity work done by wives of politicians or singing in the church choir by wives of clergy. Thus, it may be simplistic to characterize volunteering as a free choice or pure expression of altruism for all women.

There appears to be a gendered division of labour in volunteer work just as there is in paid employment and in domestic work. Women are more likely than men to provide care or support as volunteers and are more likely to collect or deliver food whereas men are more likely to teach or coach or to maintain or repair facilities (Mailloux, Horak, and Godin 2002, p. 9).

A wide variety of organizations— for example, schools, hospitals, social service facilities, and churches—benefit from volunteer labour. Volunteers sometimes supplement the work that is done by paid individuals such as in the case of volunteers who provide practical or emotional support to hospital patients, thereby assisting nurses. Many of the areas where women are more likely to volunteer than men are in institutions where women are employed in large numbers, such as in education or in health care (Baldock, 1998). Some authors have expressed concern over the potential for volunteers to be used to replace lower-skilled jobs held by women in such institutions or to justify lower staffing levels or fewer increases in the wages of paid employees (Armstrong and Armstrong, 1994; Baldock and Mulligan 1999; Macduff, 1997).

Women are sometimes seen negatively as employees because of the amount of time required by unpaid tasks such as childcare. While volunteering does not seem to contribute to such negative associations for women, neither is it typically recognized in discussions of a worker's human capital. As volunteers, women (and men) may, for example, develop organizational or fundraising skills. This was particularly important for women in the past when they had fewer employment-related opportunities to develop such skills.

Since volunteering, by definition, is not paid, how else can we recognize the value of the contributions made by women and men in this area? Perhaps we could give volunteers a tax credit for the hours that they contribute or allow them to count their volunteer hours towards qualifying for maternity or parental leave and benefits. Another way would be to encourage more employers to recognize

(Continued)

| BOX 12-1 | Women and Volunteer Work (*Continued*) |

how volunteering contributes to a job applicant's human capital. It is interesting to note that employers have started to give people time away from their jobs in order to volunteer—for example, by giving an employee a few hours away from their desk every two weeks to help deliver Meals-on-Wheels. In 2000, 27% of volunteers who were employed reported that their employer had made such accommodations (Hall, McKeown, and Roberts 2001, p. 31). Given that men are more likely than women to be found in "good jobs"—those with attractive working conditions and benefits—it would be interesting to know whether men are any more likely than women to have access to such a benefit. On the other hand, since women are more likely to take time away from employment to attend to other forms of unpaid work, are they any more likely to negotiate with employers for time to volunteer?

References

Armstrong, P. and H. Armstrong. 1994. Health Care as a Business: The Legacy of Free Trade. In *Take Care: Warning Signs for Canada's Health System* P. Armstrong, H. Armstrong, J. Choiniere, G. Feldberg & J. White (eds.). Toronto: Garamond Press, pp. 31–51.

Baldock, C. 1998. "Feminist Discourses of Unwaged Work: The case of volunteerism." *Australian Feminist Studies*, Vol. 13, pp. 19–34.

Baldock C, and D. Mulligan. 1999. "Restructuring and women workers in Australian Home Care." *Resources for Feminist Research*, Vol. 27, Nos.3/4, pp. 13–26.

Hall, M., L. McKeown, and K. Roberts. 2001. *Caring Canadians, Involved Canadians: Highlights from the 2000 National Survey of Giving*, Volunteering, and Participating. Ottawa: Minster of Industry (Statistics Canada).

Hochschild, A. 1989. *The Second Shift*. New York: Avon Books.

Mailloux, L. Horak, H. and Godin, C. 2002. *Motivation at the Margins: Gender Issues In the Canadian Voluntary Sector, 5-11*. Ottawa: Voluntary Sector Initiative Secretariat.

McDuff, N. (1997, Fall). Solving the hazards of unions and volunteer relations in government organizations. *The Journal of Volunteer Administration*, 34–9.

CONCLUSIONS

This chapter has focused on the gender-based wage gap, exploring the causes and possible solutions to this persistent problem. As with the institution of family, the gendered institution of the paid workforce valorizes and idealizes some work over other work and establishes norms for "men's" and "women's" work. In so doing, it both shapes and is shaped by the understanding of gender of the individual members of society.

CHAPTER SUMMARY: KEY POINTS

1. With the rise of the homemaker/breadwinner family arrangement, the workplace came to be associated with men and to reflect masculine normative expectations. Workers were expected to comply with demands as though they had no family obligations.

2. In the last four decades, women have entered the paid labour force in large numbers, and men's labour force participation has declined slightly.

3. Women are more likely to work part-time than men, typically because of child/family/personal obligations.

4. Women—even those working full-time all year around—earn significantly less than men (approximately 70 cents for every dollar that men earn). This disparity holds true across all age categories.

5. One explanation for the earnings gap is biological: women aren't capable of the same physical work so they naturally don't earn as much. This argument is disputed by empirical evidence.

6. A second explanation for the discrepancy is based on the theory of the *dual labour market*. This theory suggests that, historically, married women have not been interested in working at career type jobs because of their unpaid responsibilities. Now that women are interested in the same career paths as men, this pattern should disappear, though it hasn't yet.

7. A third explanation for the wage gap relies on the perception of different levels of *human capital*. It suggests that men have more education, training, and experience, which translate into higher wages. Empirical evidence does not fully support this argument.

8. A fourth explanation is *occupational segregation*: men and women do different work and this is reflected in the wage gap. Evidence does support this argument, but begs the question: what causes occupational segregation?

9. Many factors appear to contribute to but don't fully explain occupational segregation, including socialization, choice, discrimination, token dynamics, and *workplace disamenties*. Because there are likely multiple causes of the wage gap, there is likely no simple policy solution to eliminate the problem.

10. Canada has created and implemented various policies to reduce the earnings differential. But people also need to create change on the individual level by fulfilling their potential through education and career training and making informed career and work decisions. Structures must also change to eliminate harassment and discrimination in hiring and pay and to facilitate the dual roles of parents and employees.

DISCUSSION QUESTIONS

1. Think about all the summer, part-time, and full-time jobs that you have had. Have you seen examples of vertical or horizontal gender segregation? What career do you plan to pursue when you finish your education? Will you be following the typical gender pattern or entering a "non-traditional" career? What factors influenced your decision to pursue this career?

2. Why in the twenty-first century is there a link between physical strength and income? Is garbage collection a higher priority than childcare? Or is it that "men's work" is valued over "women's?"

3. Think about the people you know or have observed who have not followed typical gender patterns in their choice of occupation (men in caring profession or women in "masculine trades and professions"). Have they been challenged by others, or have they experienced a chilly climate for resisting gender-based normative expectations?

4. Do you believe there is a glass ceiling keeping women from the highest positions in corporations and politics? If not, what do you think is the explanation for the lack of women in these positions?

5. If you had the power and resources to implement policies to address the persistent wage gap between women and men, what are the top three solutions you would implement? Explain and defend your choices.

KEY TERMS

affirmative action	horizontal segregation	pink collar ghetto
chilly climate	hostile work environment	primary sector jobs
dual labour market	human capital	secondary sector jobs
earnings ratio	human rights commission	sexual harassment
employment equity	Mommy Track	token dynamics
equal rights amendment	occupational segregation	vertical segregation
glass ceiling	pay equity	workplace disamenities

chapter thirteen

Law

Law is another institutional site that reproduces gender in a variety of ways. If we treat law as an arena for struggle, then it is arguably both a facilitator of the status quo and a vehicle for change. In other words, law can work to thwart change or it can facilitate change. In this context, it is important to not lose sight of the fact that "law" does not exist apart from human actors, and that its boundaries are shaped by struggle. Moreover, cases are not just won or lost, but they provide information about the way courts think about gender and the way it plays out in social settings—within the family or in political or professional life. This perspective is noteworthy, because too often people look only at the results of cases without examining more closely the nature of legal reasoning. The latter is as or perhaps even more important than the former.

This chapter covers two major themes: the gendered nature of law itself, and the way law can be used to change gender inequities. Historically, law has blatantly supported the patriarchal order, excluding women from property regimes and ensuring their control through the legal support of violence to keep women "in line." Men could not be charged with rape of their wives because women were regarded as property of men and thus could be forced to have sexual relations with no legal consequence. Women were conceptualized as being sexually available for their husbands at all times. Indeed, women were, and arguably still are, conceptualized as being sexually available for men generally. We will explore this latter idea more fully later in this chapter.

Like the response to religion, the response to law as a possible locus for shifting gender roles is mixed. This chapter draws on the work of several theorists to examine gender and law, starting with its absurdities.

THE *PERSONS CASE*: GENDER AND LAW IN HISTORICAL CONTEXT

If someone asked you whether men and women were included in the word *person*, you might think they weren't asking you a serious question. But in 1929, this exact issue was deliberated by Canada's highest court, and subsequently by the then court of highest appeal—England's Privy Council. At that time, the definition of *person* in the British North America Act had been interpreted to exclude women. The act permitted the governor general to appoint "Qualified Persons to the Senate." Following on the heels of the struggles of two women—Clara Brett Martin and Mabel French—to be admitted into the legal profession, a group of Alberta women, now known as the Famous Five, took up the challenge to have women included in the definition of person by launching what has become known as the *Persons Case*. However, the Supreme Court of Canada concluded that women did not fall within the definition of persons and therefore could not be appointed as senators. The Famous Five appealed the decision of the Supreme Court of Canada to the Privy Council, which allowed the appeal and decided that women were included within the definition of *person*.

The idea that women were not included in the definition of *person* in the first place may seem bit ludicrous to some readers. But the case is an important reminder how law (and language) reflects social and cultural values at the same time that it acts a site of struggle. Remember that at the time of the *Persons Case*, women were still fighting for the vote in some jurisdictions, and that property and estate laws still favoured men. Eighty years from now, people may look back at the fight to include same-sex unions in the definition of marriage with the same level of astonishment as we view the *Persons Case*.

Women were not, however, the only "non-persons" at law. Constance Backhouse (1999) documents the fascinating socio-legal history of the *White Woman's Labour Law*, first enacted in 1912, through the case of Yee Clun, a Chinese businessman who wanted—and indeed needed—to employ white women. This law and its application is thick with interlocking racial and gender implications. "No person shall employ in any capacity any white woman or girl or permit any white woman or girl to reside or lodge in or to work in or, save as a *bona fide* customer in a public apartment thereof only, to frequent any restaurant, laundry or other place of business or amusement owned, kept or managed by any Japanese, Chinaman or other Oriental person." White women were thus "protected" from Chinese businessmen, who, it was assumed, would lead them down the path of moral depravity in one form or another. The law assumed the vulnerability of women as the "frailer sex" (1999, p. 158). The act "functioned as a critical tool enabling racially dominant groups to prohibit Chinese men from participation freely in the economic and social communities in which they lived" (1999, p. 171). The combination of race and gender particularly disadvantaged Chinese men, who were painted as sexual predators and opium users, among other things.

The *White Woman's Labour Law* relied on racial and gender stereotypes. "It was the horror of female sexual slavery that the act was meant to remedy. The protection of white women, as the symbolic emblem of the 'white race,' became a crucial cornerstone in the attempt to establish and defend white racial superiority and white racism. White women were called into service in their reproductive capacity as the 'guardians of the race,' a symbol of the most valuable property known to white men, to be protected at all costs from the encroachment of other races" (1999, p. 141). This particular intersection of gender and race is one example of the ways that law re-enacted and contested men's and women's roles. Backhouse's analysis shows one of the ways that gender plays out in and weaves through law and society.

Haven't the ways that law presents men and women changed significantly since the *Persons Case*, and especially since Yee Clun challenged the *White Woman's Labour Law*? After all, several decades of cultural change have occurred. Yet gendered assumptions still affect the law in sometimes rather surprising ways. Such was the case in *R* v. *Ewanchuk*, a 1998 decision from the Alberta Court of Appeal that was eventually overturned by the Supreme Court of Canada. This is the famous "bonnets and crinolines" case, in which a justice of the Alberta Court of Appeal, McClung J. (the odd irony here is that he was the grandson of one of the Famous Five, Nellie McClung!), determined the credibility of the victim of a sexual assault by stating, "It must be pointed out that the complainant did not present herself to Ewanchuk or enter his trailer in a bonnet and crinolines. She told Ewanchuk that she was the mother of a six-month-old baby and that, along with her boyfriend, she shared an apartment with another couple" (1998, p. 245). The fact that the young woman involved was obviously not "chaste" was somehow relevant to McClung J.'s decision-making process in the case. In addition, from his perspective, the fact that she had consented to sexual relations with her boyfriend and that she was an "unwed mother" made her available to any man who wished to have sexual relations with her.

On appeal to the Supreme Court of Canada, L'Heureux-Dubé J. noted, "Even though McClung J.A. asserted that he had no intention of denigrating the complainant, one might wonder why he felt necessary to point out these aspects of the trial record. Could it be to express that the complainant is not a virgin? Or that she is a person of questionable moral character because she is not married and lives with her boyfriend and another couple? These comments made by an appellate judge help reinforce the myth that under such circumstances, either the complainant is less worthy of belief, she invited the sexual assault, or her sexual experience signals probable consent to further sexual activity. Based on those attributed assumptions, the implication is that if the complainant articulates her lack of consent by saying 'no,' she really does not mean it and even if she does, her refusal cannot be taken as seriously as if she were a girl of 'good' moral character" (1999, para. 89). L'Heureux-Dubé J.'s response to the point judgment captures the essence of the difficulties women have in reporting sexual assault and the reasons why women do not turn to the legal system for help when they are victims of sexual assault.

Unfortunately, there are many examples of cases like *R* v. *Ewanchuk*, which in part explains the low rate of reporting of incidents of sexual assault. The law re-victimizes women who come before it with sexual assault complaints, replaying patriarchal gender expectations about the sexual availability of women, and incorporating stereotypes about the reliability of women's evidence.

RESPONSES TO LAW AND THE POSSIBILITY FOR CHANGE

Like the responses to organized religion, a number of approaches have been used to respond to the use of law in gender issues. Both academics and community activists alike are skeptical about law's ability to effect change, particularly for issues like sexual assault. As mentioned above, victims of sexual assault are more often than not re-victimized by the legal process. This insight has prompted people like Carol Smart (1989) to argue for a *decentring* of law. Smart argues that law is at the *apex of discourses*, meaning that the power of law to organize knowledge and exclude voices is superior to other discourses, such as science or medicine. Law claims to be objective and neutral and to produce the "truth." Smart challenges these assertions (as do many other critical theorists). She proposes that we decentre law to respond to people's needs outside of resorting to the courts. This strategy has been used, for example, with cases of sexual assault. Victims seek healing through the services of sexual assault centres, rather than through formal legal proceedings. Decentring can be an effective strategy in some instances, but determining decentring strategies that meets all needs isn't always possible. Indeed, Smart has been criticized for the vagueness of this proposal. Nonetheless, her work is an important contribution to understanding the ways in which law reenacts gender and supports power relations that disadvantage women.

Although it may be obvious at this point, it is important to emphasize here that law is not neutral or objective. Some people respond to this by saying, "Yes, but what about precedent?"or "Statutes are clear about the law." Mary Jane Mossman (1987) details the process of legal method and examines its gendered nature through three case studies, including the *Persons Case*. She emphasizes that both precedent and application of statutes involve choice. If this weren't the case, women still wouldn't be persons! While perhaps more optimistic than Carol Smart about the possibilities of using law to produce change, Mossman is also extremely cautious. She frames her discussion around the question: is law impervious to feminism? She concludes that it may well be. In other words, she is pessimistic about the possibility of law to actually effect changes that benefit women or that shift the status quo. Nonetheless, the law's approach to gendered issues is gradually shifting.

Mossman's work raises critical points that relate to the authors' approach to law and gender. First, and perhaps most difficult for students to accept, law is not objective and neutral. This does not mean that legal decisions are dependent on the whim of judges. Rather, while clearly judges' beliefs can impact decisions, so too do social context and legal context, both of which are still highly gendered. Second the ways that legal issues are framed largely determines the way that law works to preserve the status quo. Within law, rules of relevance control and shape legal issues. These rules can act as a barrier to change, even when it is clear that change is necessary. For example, consider how the issues were framed in the *R* v. *Ewanchuk* case. While McClung J. relied on old stereotypes about women to frame the issue of consent and credibility, L'Heureux-Dubé J. reviewed the myths about sexual assault and used those same stereotypes to frame her decision about consent and credibility.

However, legal method begins prior to the courtroom; and in the same way that the process of interpreting statutes, choosing precedent, and reviewing the admissibility of evidence is gendered, so too are those sorting practices involved in the working up of the case. Carol Smart identifies this as the "mundane" aspect of law, which involves the translation of everyday processes into legal issues (1990, pp. 197–198). Beaman (1996) has argued that "the more pervasive and dangerous aspects of legal method do not occur in the courtroom, but behind the closed doors of the lawyer's office" (1996, p. 56). What does this mean? Legal frameworks and legal processes are gendered, and as such, they may render many women's experiences "unsayable." Certainly, women are not the only persons excluded from legal frameworks: members of other marginalized groups—such as First Nations peoples, the poor, or those who are mentally disadvantaged or challenged—are all potentially left outside of the framework and/or processes of law.

For example, suppose you are a twenty-two-year-old mother of two small children. You had worked in the paid labour force until you were 20 years old. You have a high school education and attended university for two years. Since age 20, you've been living with the father of your children (let's call him Bob, with apologies to all of the Bobs out there). Bob owns the house you live in, he earns $50 000 a year, and he does all the banking and gives you an allowance of $100 a week for groceries and the children's needs. For the past two years, Bob's behaviour has become more and more abusive. He criticizes you about your appearance, your mothering, and the cleanliness of the house. He has four times pushed you or slapped you during an argument. One night when you and Bob are having a serious argument, he becomes extremely violent. He dumps the dinner dishes in with the clean clothes in the basket in the kitchen, pushes your face into it, and yells at you, and when you "talk back," he punches you repeatedly. After the incident, your face is bruised, including a black eye. An hour later, Bob is contrite, but insists that you drove him to behave as he did.

The next day you call a friend at work, and she leaves work and comes over. She makes an appointment with her lawyer and you nervously go to her office. How does the law respond to your dilemma should you decide that you no longer wish to live in this abusive relationship with Bob? In some jurisdictions (provinces), you may be eligible for legal aid. Some jurisdictions insist that you will need to go through mediation with Bob first in order to access public assistance, unless you can offer evidence that the relationship was abusive. However, the legal aid eligibility process may assess Bob's assets as your own, even though you have no access to money and your name does not appear on any of the bank accounts or the house deed. This assessment will mean that you are not eligible for legal aid and will have to pay for legal services yourself. In addition, the court may not consider Bob's behaviour when determining custody the children, insisting that it is good for fathers to have access or joint custody of their children. The court will also not consider the possibility that Bob may use the children to continue to abuse and harass you. In addition, you will have to fight for the right to move from the community to live with relatives, which for you may be the best option, because your family, who would support you while you finish your university education, lives 500 kilometers away. Moreover, the legal processes that might help you, should you have access to them, will take a year or two.

This scenario is not unusual or unrealistic: it happens frequently to women who are young and isolated from their support networks, as well as to older women who have raised their families and find themselves in middle age with no job training and no means of support. Legal processes are often so unwieldy and so time-consuming that they leave women in poverty and even more helpless than they were in their marital relationship. Legal rules, such as the assumption that joint custody is good for children, ignore the reality that women still provide the majority of childcare, even when they are also employed full time in the paid labour force. This is relevant because the law awards custody based on the best interests of the child, and continuity and experience in providing care are important in considering how well a child will be cared for. If one parent has had limited involvement in providing care, that parent's ability to meet a child's needs may be compromised. However, as more and more men become involved in childcare, social reality may be able to catch up with law's optimistic vision of a world in which women earn as much as men do and men are capable of providing conscientious childcare.

This same scenario becomes even more complicated if the woman in question is a member of a minority group or other disadvantaged group. Immigrant women are especially vulnerable to legal difficulties, as are First Nations women. Miedema and Waccholz (1998) found that a variety of factors exacerbated the vulnerability of immigrant women, including social isolation, lack of information because of language barriers, and cultural patterns of accepting violence in the culture of origin.

VIOLENCE AGAINST WOMEN: IS THERE A SIMPLE SOLUTION?

Using law to shift the status quo is complicated because the consequences of a new legal response are often not fully and immediately obvious. One example is the legal response to violence against women. It was well known that police response to "domestics" has traditionally been inadequate. If the police were called, and even if there were a great deal of evidence that a woman had endured many incidents of battering before that day's abuse happened, the police often simply talked to the man, reassured the woman, and left the batterer to continue on. Charges were never laid, and the violence continued. As awareness about violence against women grew in the 1980s and 1990s, a cultural shift occurred which resulted in better education for police and a new approach to responding to calls involving "domestic violence." This involved laying charges against the batterer and reducing the need to have the victim give evidence against the abuser. However, this response had its disadvantages as well. The batterer was often the primary breadwinner in the home, and the victim was therefore left with few or no financial resources. Moreover, criminal sanctions were not what the victim desired—rather she often simply wanted the violence to stop. Some critics argued that a hard-line legal response simply continued the abuse of the woman and perpetuated a patriarchal response to violence by assuming that someone else knew best. In domestic violence situations, it is not clear how the law could best respond to reflect the state's position that violence against women is unacceptable as well as the needs of abused women.

Another complication on this same issue is reflected by the use of *Battered Woman Syndrome* (BWS). In some measure, legal recognition of BWS and the acceptance of the argument of self-defence to better reflect women's experiences was a victory against a patriarchal view of self-defence that was largely premised on the bar room brawl. This perspective was acknowledged by the Supreme Court of Canada in the first successful case using the defence of Battered Woman Syndrome in Canada. Twenty-two-year-old Angelique Lavallee had been living in a common-law relationship with her physically abusive boyfriend. She described the incident: "He said, 'wait till everybody leaves, you'll get it then," and he said something to the effect of "either you kill me or I'll get you," that was what it was. He kind of smiled and then he turned around. I shot him but I aimed out. I thought I aimed above him and a piece of his head went that way" (1990). In her judgment, written for the majority of the Supreme Court of Canada (six judges, three women and three men), Wilson J. acknowledged the difficulty many people have in understanding the dynamics of abusive relationships. She stated:

> Expert evidence on the psychological effect of battering on wives and common law partners must, it seems to me, be both relevant and necessary in the context of the present case. How can the mental state of the appellant be appreciated without it? The average member of the public (or

of the jury) can be forgiven for asking: Why would a woman put up with this kind of treatment? Why should she continue to live with such a man? How could she love a partner who beat her to the point of requiring hospitalization? We would expect the woman to pack her bags and go. Where is her self-respect? Why does she not cut loose and make a new life for herself? Such is the reaction of the average person confronted with the so-called "battered wife syndrome." We need help to understand it and help is available from trained professionals. (1990, pp. 871–72)

Wilson J. also acknowledged the gendered nature of the legal parameters of self-defence, which allows for the possibility of a mistake in assessing a situation based on what "an ordinary man using ordinary care could have made in the same circumstances." Wilson J. noted: "If it strains credulity to imagine what the 'ordinary man' would do in the position of a battered spouse, it is probably because men do not typically find themselves in that situation. Some women do, however. The definition of what is reasonable must be adapted to circumstances which are, by and large, foreign to the world inhabited by the hypothetical 'reasonable man.'" (1990, p. 874). The reasonable man is one of these examples. The "hypothetical reasonable man" has played a large role in the development of law in assessing all sorts of situations, and "he" has come under a great deal of fire in recent years as excluding many people, including women, people of colour, gays and lesbians, and those in lower socio-economic groups. The *R. v. Lavallee* SCR [1990] 852 case was significant because it helped to tranform the "reasonable man" measure into the "reasonable person," thus allowing Lavallee's actions to fall within the notion of self-defence.

The recognition of BWS is an acknowledgment that women experience life differently and that the law must reflect women's experiences of it if it is to offer them justice. But certainly, this "difference" approach to justice has its disadvantages. Some people argue that defences such as BWS, postpartum depression, or premenstrual syndrome (PMS) as mitigating factors in a crime simply reinforce stereotypes about women as the "weaker" sex. These people argue that we are not yet in an era when women can afford to go this route. "Women's defences, it is argued, are predicated on emphasizing women as victims, of both men and their own raging hormones, and present women as powerless. Women's defences have also been in many cases defined and shaped by men in the context of medical and legal discourses" (Beaman, 1998, p. 95). In other words, women still need men's "approval" to be able to use such defences. Ultimately, the question is whether the advantages of such defences outweigh the disadvantages for women as a group. This is a difficult question that does not have a straightforward answer.

This case raises one of the central dilemmas in legal responses to gender: should the law treat men and women the same or differently? In other words, should equality be conceptualized in a manner that accounts for gender differences or ignores them? If so, then how should law respond to the needs of gays and lesbians and same-sex couples?

A CASE STUDY: SAME-SEX MARRIAGE

On July 20, 2005, Bill C-38 received royal assent and was passed into law amidst much controversy and protracted public debate. The *Civil Marriage Act* allowed same-sex couples to marry and thus brought them within the legislative purview of various other pieces of legislation, including the *Divorce Act*. The official legislative summary of this act states: "This enactment extends the legal capacity for marriage for civil purposes to same-sex couples in order to reflect values of tolerance, respect and equality, consistent with the Canadian Charter of Rights and Freedoms. It also makes consequential amendments to other Acts to ensure equal access for same-sex couples to the civil effects of marriage and divorce" (see http://www.parl.gc.ca/38/1/parlbus/chambus/house/bills/government/C-38/C-38_1/C-38-2E.html). Sexual orientation had already been "read in" to s.15 of the Charter of Rights and Freedoms, and so in many ways, the *Civil Marriage Act* simply brought marriage into conformity with the charter. What, then, was the source of contention?

At the heart of the matter was a debate about gender. Marriage, argued some groups (predominantly but not exclusively religious groups), was and should be exclusively reserved for one man and one woman. Part of this argument also included the idea that only men and women can procreate, which, it was argued; was central to the notion of marriage. The gender expectations tied up in these arguments are dense: that women and men want to or should procreate; that human value is tied up in the ability to procreate; and perhaps more specifically, that female value is linked to the ability to procreate. The valorization of "one man, one woman, to the exclusion of all others" as implicit in this vision underscores the notion of heteronormativity. Same-sex marriage challenges basic assumptions about the role of men and women in society, which some people link to their own religious ideologies and see as god-given. But not all religious groups held a heteronormative position in this debate, with some celebrating marriage as a union of two people who love each other. The *Civil Marriage Act* makes provision for religious clergy who do not want to marry same-sex couples, excluding them from any obligation to do so and protecting them from sanction under human rights legislation.

Given the passage of the *Civil Marriage Act*, the reading in of sexual orientation into s. 15 of the Charter might suggest that law can be used to alter gender expectations and to facilitate equality. Certainly, the past decade has seen some very rapid change in the law. But social attitudes are not the same as legal changes, since homophobia continues to exist; thus, law may in this instance be more "progressive" than the social reality.

The issue of same-sex marriage is not uncomplicated within the gay and lesbian community. While there has been a strong lobby for same-sex marriage, there are counter-currents as well. Some gays and lesbians have argued that they do not want to have access to a patriarchal institution like marriage, which, they say, is inherently flawed. Moreover, the enactment of legislation that allows same-sex marriage has the effect of bringing gays and lesbians under a state regime which some argue simply allows the state better opportunities for surveillance. The argue that the benefits of marriage could be accessed in other ways.

The legal provision for same-sex marriage does not solve all of the problems for gays and lesbians within law. Custody and access continues to be challenging for women and men who live in same-sex relationships. There are deeply ingrained assumptions in law and in society about who makes a good mother or a good father and what a good parent looks like. The good mother is still assumed to be heterosexual, as is the good father.

THE CHARTER OF RIGHTS AND GENDER

The Charter of Rights and Freedoms was enacted in 1982. The equality provisions in the charter were expected to have such a great impact that they did not come into force and effect until two years after the rest of the charter. Of particular significance were the sections that seemed to address gender inequities. These sections include the following:

15. (1) Every individual is equal before and under the law and has the right to the equal protection and equal benefit of the law without discrimination and, in particular, without discrimination based on race, national or ethnic origin, colour, religion, sex, age or mental or physical disability.

(2) Subsection (1) does not preclude any law, program or activity that has as its object the amelioration of conditions of disadvantaged individuals or groups including those that are disadvantaged because of race, national or ethnic origin, colour, religion, sex, age or mental or physical disability.

28. Notwithstanding anything in this Charter, the rights and freedoms referred to in it are guaranteed equally to male and female persons.

Note that the charter uses the word *sex* instead of *gender*. Note also the allowance for what are often called affirmative action programs in 15(2). These programs and laws are intended to redress the systemic disadvantages faced by women. Unfortunately, some people cannot see that there is any disadvantage to be redressed. They label such programs "special treatment" and, despite a great deal of evidence, deny the existence of inequality and discrimination (often not just against women, but any disadvantaged group). If you remember the description of *misery justice* in Chapter Seven, such a position adopts a vision of justice that says, "I didn't get that, so then why should she?" The people who argue, "I pulled myself up by my own bootstraps" often ignore the fact that they were given boots to begin with!

| BOX 13-1 | Bodies, Spaces, stories and Law |

by Rebecca Johnson

At its core, law is enmeshed in a world of stories: there is no law, rule, or regulation that does not rest on a deep foundation of (often unarticulated but nonetheless powerful) stories. The stories tell us who "we" are, describe the things and people that most threaten us, tell us how best to respond to the world around us, encourage us to accept or challenge "the way things are." These stories seek to persuade: they sketch out the world of threat and desire in ways that encourage us to willingly live our lives in certain ways. And where voluntary compliance breaks down, the force of law steps in to fill the gap, structuring the world in ways that reproduce the bodies, spaces, and realities in the story law is invoked to tell.

But all that sounds unsatisfyingly "academic" doesn't it? Is there a more direct way to talk about the links between bodies, spaces, stories, and law? A more direct way to argue that it is important to ask questions about the shapes of our own lives, the places we inhabit, the ways experience those places and bodies, and to think about how both law and stories are wrapped up in those experiences? Let me begin again by sharing an experience and posing some questions about it.[1]

In 1998, carrying my newborn baby with me, I left Canada to join my partner, who had taken a contract in England. Weeks later, Canadian Supreme Court Justice Claire L'Heureux-Dubé came to Bristol to speak at a conference. Having worked for her some years earlier, I was excited to have a chance to see her. She suggested that I bring my partner and baby and join her for dinner at a great

(Continued)

| BOX 13-1 | Bodies, Spaces, stories and Law (*Continued*) |

pub she had found. I was hesitant. New to motherhood, I was feeling awkward both with breastfeeding in general and public breastfeeding in particular. I couldn't see any alternatives. I had an 8-week-old baby who seemed to nurse constantly. If we were to go to dinner, the baby would have to come with us.

We met at the pub and took a table near the back. When the waiter finally approached us, it was not to take our order, but to order me out of the pub. The problem? The baby I had been discretely nursing. Their liquor license was clear: no minors allowed. I was stunned and unable to form a coherent response. The judge, stepping into the void, blurted out in a tone of outrage, "You can't kick her out! That is a violation of her human rights!" But, as sometimes happens, Justice L'Heureux-Dubé was in dissent. We found ourselves on the street, looking for some other place to eat.

What had happened? From a purely legal point of view, in our attempt to share a meal, the group of us had failed to attend to law's distinction between the licensed pub and the licensed restaurant. Though both places provide food and liquor, the law specifies that children may be present only in the latter, and *not* in the former. At the base of this distinction lies a set of stories that construct the pub as a site of danger and contagion, and another set of stories about parents (mothers?) that can't be trusted to adequately protect their children. Certainly, in the moment of my expulsion, the weight of those stories felt very real. The event was humiliating, and I felt very much that I had been publicly singled out as a bad mother,

one who had failed to give appropriate care to her child. The pub now felt like a hostile place, one in which I was no longer entitled to be.

Now, one might argue that I was *not* denied entry to the pub: the legal texts deny entry only to the *child*. I remained entitled to be there. This is true if one attends only to the words. But things are more complicated when one considers the kind of work texts actually do (Smith, 2001). As these particular legal texts move into the social world, they work to deny entry not only to children, but also to those who have persistent (or "sticky") connections to children. This happens through the operation of three different kinds of discriminatory adverse effects.

First, there is a set of "gender-neutral" discriminatory effects. Though the primary target of the law is the child, the effect is the exclusion of any adult who is accompanied by a child. Here, the rule will operate to exclude men and women alike. The pubs that denied me entry would also have denied entry to my brother, travelling with his little boy, or to my father, out for the day with his grandchild. Second, there are "gender-specific" adverse-effects. On the work/family front, our society continues to create different headwinds for men and women—headwinds that push and tug men in the direction of "the ideal worker" and women in the direction of "domesticity" (Williams, 2000). To the extent that women remain more *likely* than men to be travelling in the company of children, the "neutral" exclusion of children will also produce some gendered effects, having a disproportionate

| BOX 13-1 | *(Continued)* |

impact on female caregivers. Third, we can return to the body of the breast-feeding woman, to see how the law also generates a set of "sex-specific" adverse effects. To the extent that her body is materially interwoven with the body of her nursing infant (meaning that not only does the child need to remain close to her, but she needs also to keep the child close at hand),[2] the exclusion of the child necessarily entails the exclusion of the nursing woman. In short, a liquor regulation excluding children from the "pub"' has the effect of also disproportionately excluding caregivers of either sex, mothers, and nursing women.

It is hard not to see a certain odd irony in this story. Activism has long since dismantled laws which explicitly denied women entry to bars and public houses, laws based on certain stories about the proper places for women to be found. Contemporary liquor licensing regimes are written in the language of gender neutrality, and aim ostensibly at the social good of child protection. And yet, these regimes sustain the boundaries of a still-gendered public space and social roles. Women may be present in pub space, but they may not carry in with them the visible markings of maternity. Nor may fathers make visible any changes in their practices of parenthood by entering the pub in the role of primary caregiver. The space of the pub retains its character as a (gendered and sexualized) space of leisure and release from the visible marking of obligation, particularly of those obligations that are wrapped up with the bodies of children. The liquor-licensing regime makes participation in and enjoyment of some forms of public

space contingent on the ability to sever (or at least put to the side) evidence of connection to those who require care. The body of the nursing mother makes visible some of the persistent gender- and sex-based exclusions of our current distributions of public obligation and public leisure. And there is a story worth thinking more about.

Bibliography

Harris, Pamela. *Faces of Feminism* (Toronto: Second Story Press, 1992)

Johnson, Rebecca. "Bars, Breasts, Babies: Madame Justice L'Heureux-Dubé and the Boundaries of Belonging." Elizabeth Sheehy, ed., *Adding Feminism to Law: The Contributions of Justice Claire L'Heureux-Dubé* (Toronto: Irwin Law, 2004) 139–157.

Johnson, Rebecca. "Law and the Leaky Woman: The Saloon, the Liquor Licence, and Narratives of Containment." (2005) 19:2 *Continuum: Journal of Media and Cultural Studies* 181–199.

Johnson, Rebecca. "Blurred Boundaries: A Double-Voiced Dialogue on Regulatory Regimes and Embodied Space." (2005) 9 *Law, Text, Culture* 157–176.

Smith, Dorothy E. "Texts and the Ontology of Organizations and Institutions." (2001) 7 *Studies in Cultures, Organizations and Societies* 159–198.

Williams, Joan. *Unbending Gender: Why Family and Work Conflict and What To Do About I.t* (New York: Oxford University Press, 2000).

Endnotes

Here, I point in the direction of some questions this particular experience raised for me,

(Continued)

BOX 13-1	Bodies, Spaces, stories and Law (*Continued*)

questions that I have explored in three other articles. Those interested in further details about the story, and the law which pervades, it can look at "Bars, Breasts, Babies: Madame Justice L'Heureux-Dubé and the Boundaries of Belonging." Elizabeth Sheehy, ed., *Adding Feminism to Law: The Contributions of Justice Claire L'Heureux-Dubé* (Toronto: Irwin Law, 2004) 139–157; "Law and the Leaky Woman: The Saloon, the Liquor Licence, and Narratives of Containment." (2005) 19:2 *Continuum: Journal of Media and Cultural Studies* 181–199; and "Blurred Boundaries: A Double-Voiced Dialogue on Regulatory Regimes and Embodied Space." (2005) 9 *Law, Text, Culture* 157–17. The first of these pulls the story in the direction of human rights discourse; the second in the direction of tax law and popular culture; and the third in the direction of space and embodiment. On a personal note, I might add that working through "the experience" three times (three shots at exorcism?) has given me an increased appreciation of feminist activists and academics who have insisted on the value of using complicated embodied experience to ground theoretical inquiry. It has also taught me that there is no "one" explanation for any given experience, and that there is real value in allowing oneself to return to past difficult experiences with new questions.

The fear of just such an experience is very real to any woman who has nursed a child. Lawyer Elizabeth Cusack-Walsh, then the nursing mother of a three-and-a-half-week-old baby, writes about the experience of being in a trial and having the judge refuse her a lunch break long enough to go home and nurse her child. She writes: "By mid-afternoon I was in deep distress, mentally and physically. Milk began spurting through my clothes, all over my cross-examination notes. The courtroom was crowded with spectators. I was standing, cross-examining an RCMP scientist on a very technical point. The judge was enraged when I requested a few minutes adjournment. When he cooled down, I explained that I was leaking milk, that my notes were wet and that I would like a few minutes to deal with the situation. The justice remembers the incident as a joke. I remember how women and motherhood were degraded." See Pamela Harris, *Faces of Feminism* (Toronto: Second Story Press, 1992) at 46.

Can law alleviate discrimination? Pay equity legislation gives cause for only a small bit of optimism. Affirmative action in hiring is the same: unless there is a desire to deal with discrimination, such programs are easily condemned and sabotaged by those who wish to preserve the status quo. And sometimes discrimination is less obvious to some than to others. Guest essayist Rebecca Johnson examines the ways that laws that seem to apply equally to everyone are in fact discriminatory.

There are broader debates underlying the struggle over how to achieve equality. One of them is the "sameness/difference" dilemma. The key question is: should men and women be treated the same by law? Your immediate response might be, "Of course." But we need to go a bit deeper to sort out the complexities of this question. If we think about law as a mechanism for the achievement of equality, which is arguably one of the things law is supposed to do, we need to ask how we regard equality. When we treat everyone the same, we ignore structural disadvantages faced by some people or groups of people. Quite simply, sometimes in order to achieve equality, we must treat people differently. What does this mean in practice? Here's one example: only women give birth; and thus maternity benefits (as distinguished from parental leave) can accrue only to women.

The complexity of gender issues as they play out in law is illustrated by the work of guest essayist Rebecca Johnson (2000b), whose analysis of the Symes case in Chapter Seven points to the often hidden ways that law is gendered. Law draws on assumptions about women and men to reinforce the status quo. People must often work hard to identify these assumptions, since such assumptions become as natural to us as the air we breathe. Some groups, such as LEAF (Legal Education and Action Fund for Women), engage in strategic intervention, which means identifying gendered assumptions and then challenging them to attempt to make important shifts in legislation or policy.

Of course, as shown in Chapter Seven, people don't always experience disadvantage as a single point of discrimination; instead, it may involve multiple intersections of such factors as gender, ethnicity, and age. This is perhaps where law faces its greatest challenge in terms of effectively addressing inequality.

However, application of substantive law is not the only concern. The very access to justice is often limited for some groups of people. There is a great deal of evidence to suggest that women and men have different levels of access to law and justice, whether through their ability to access criminal and domestic legal aid or through the availability of prison programs and resources for males and females convicted of crimes. Until relatively recently, there was only one prison in Canada for federally sentenced women, which meant that women from outside of central Canada had to leave their families, friends, and children, who often provided support during the prison term; in effect, they had to live in greater isolation than did their male counterparts.

WOMEN IN LAW-RELATED PROFESSIONS

To what extent has the entry of women into the legal system (as police, lawyers, or judges) improved the chances of shifting old patriarchal relations, eliminating unfair or unequal gender relations? Do women judges judge differently? Do women lawyers practice law differently, treat their clients differently, or present cases differently? Do female police officers handle situations in a manner that is different from their male counterparts?

Carol Gilligan's (1982) work on women and justice suggests that they do. Gilligan argues that women think about justice differently than do men: in short, they are less willing to reduce justice to hard and fast rules. Gilligan's work on justice and gender is well known because she raised some important questions about the ways in which gender affects both the theory and practice of justice. Part of the reason to strive for equal participation of women in policing, lawyering, and judging is that women do bring another view to law. However, these efforts are also based on a more basic wish to erode patriarchy that has preserved positions of power for men.

Now that women make up almost half of law school admissions, has this enrollment increase had any impact on the legal profession? Apparently very little has changed. "The process of exclusion is far-reaching, involving all stages of a woman's career from law school, to articling, to achieving partnership. Women lawyers report a variety of barriers to advancement that include sexual harassment, blocked opportunities to leadership positions, limited access to articling positions, difficulties balancing family and work responsibilities and gender bias in the courtroom. The barriers experienced by racialized women, lesbians and women with disabilities are particularly severe. That women continue to experience exclusionary pressures in law is a sensitive issue within the profession, despite the vast amount of empirical evidence documenting its existence" (Kainer, 1995, p. 120).

Joan Brockman (2001) has done a detailed study of gender in the legal profession by talking to both women and men about their work lives and experiences. Brockman considers gender through the lenses of the issue of quality of life, recalling predictions in the 1950s of a two- to three-day work week and increased leisure time. Obviously, if anything, we've moved in the opposite direction, with women and men struggling to balance work, family and leisure activities with ever-increasing demands on their time and energy. Although data suggests that women are disproportionately burdened with juggling these demands, men too are caught on the treadmill. It is in this context that Brockman explores why law in particular perpetuates the "workaholic" treadmill.

Brockman found that women actually earn more money than men at the outset of their legal careers, but that men quickly catch up and surpass them. Women are also more likely to be passed over for promotion and less likely to be given high-profile or important cases to work on. In addition, Brockman examines the issue of sexual assault and harassment, noting that over one third of the women she interviewed had been sexually harassed by colleagues, judges, and clients. Women also had to endure comments from clients like, "What's a nice girl like you doing not married and having kids?"

Krakauer and Chen (2003) note that even though women make up at least half of law school classes, they leave the legal profession at a much higher rate than their male peers. However, Krakauer and Chen point out that the situation is even worse for ethnic and racial minorities generally and for women specifically: "Women who belong to minority groups have reported facing barriers to success while in law school, lower levels of career satisfaction on entry into the profession and greater incidence of discrimination throughout their careers" (2003, p. 67). Krahauer and Chen examine the ways in which the *chilly climates* of law schools impact on women's career choices and trajectories. Although things are changing, Krakauer and Chen argue that special attention must be paid to the disadvantaged position of women law students generally and to women from minority ethnic and racial backgrounds in particular.

Do women judges judge differently, or make a difference? In her article "Will Women Judges Really Make a Difference?" (1991), then justice of the Supreme Court of Canada Bertha Wilson wrote: "If the existing law can be viewed as the product of judicial neutrality or impartiality, even although the judiciary has been very substantially male, then you may conclude that the advent of increased numbers of women judges should make no difference, assuming, that is, that these women judges will bring to bear the same neutrality and impartiality. However, if you conclude that the existing law, in some areas at least, cannot be viewed as the product of judicial neutrality, then your answer may be very different" (1991, p. 159). Judicial neutrality is itself a nebulous concept, and it is highly likely that a justice system that has been predominantly run by men will not account for, value, and understand women's experiences as fully as it could.

Maryka Omatsu (2005), a judge, believes that women judges both do and don't make a difference. While being cautious about *women* as an essentialist category bringing a particular insight or position to judging, Omatsu argues that "the presence on the bench of heretofore under-represented people can help to balance an existing tilt" (2005, p. 74). And the existing "tilt" she refers to is the fact that only 11 percent of Canada's judges are women (2005, p. 72). Omatsu was the first (and only, so far) East Asian Canadian woman to be appointed to the bench.

It is important that the bench reflect the diverse population of Canada. Moreover, there must be at least some proximity between the demographics on the street and the make-up of the bench. Omatsu also notes the intersection of class with judicial appointments, point-ing out that judges "lack of experience of the daily lives of working-class people and the circumstances and functioning of specifically working-class institutions, such as trade unions, deprives them of potentially relevant information on which to make impartial judg-ments" (1997, p. 75).

Moreover, women judges may bring sensibilities to issues such as sexual harassment and sexual assault. This increased focus may be overt or subtle. In the *R* v. *Ewanchuk* case discussed at the beginning of the chapter, the judgment of the male justices of the Supreme Court was decidedly different in tone than that of the two female justices. L'Heureux-Dubé, J. begins her judgment by placing sexual assault in context: "Violence against women takes many forms: sexual assault is one of them. In Canada, one-half of all women are said to have experienced at least one incident of physical or sexual vio-lence since the age of 16" (1999, para 68). And further, "Violence against women is as much a matter of equality as it is an offence against human dignity and a violation of human rights" (1999, para 69). On the other hand, the male justices state, "In the present appeal the accused was acquitted of sexual assault. The trial judge relied on the defence of implied consent. This was a mistake of law as no such defence is available in assault cases in Canada. This mistake of law is reviewable by appellate courts, and for the rea-sons that follow the appeal is allowed" (1999, para 1). Although the judgments reach essen-tially the same conclusion, the tone is important in situating the incident either as one incident disconnected from the treatment of women generally (the approach taken by the males justices), or as something that happens to many women and as a social problem that the law must actively participate in stopping.

Unfortunately, as Omatsu documents, diversity on the bench has not come without a backlash. Sometimes, those judges who bring the very sensibility we are lacking—whether to race issues or gender issues—are themselves accused of bias. As Omatsu concludes, "A one-sided homogeneity of the judiciary cannot help but carry with it a narrowness of vision and of life experiences that is bound to create unconscious biases. How ironic, indeed how sad, if the potential of an expanded bench is impeded by allegations of the very shortcom-ings in our judicial system that the appointments were meant to correct" (2005, p. 83).

CONCLUSIONS

Shifts in law do not necessarily result in shifts in gender relations. When we study law, it is important to look beyond the letter of the law to examine the way courts interpret it and the way law is "lived" in day-to-day life. Too frequently, discussion focuses on law as it is writ-ten without examining law as it is enacted "on the ground." Affirmative action initiatives are a good example, because they are attempts to address the structural inequality of women and men. There has been much criticism of these sorts of policies, despite being constitutionally protected; yet at the same time, there is still very little naturally occurring improvement in inequality based on gender. For example, in 2001–02, only 16 percent of full professors at universities were women, according to the report "Ivory Towers: Feminist and Equity Audits 2005" prepared by the Canadian Federation of the Humanities and Social Sciences. The fact that women are still paid on average about 75 percent of what men earn for the same or similar work is evidence that there is still a large disparity between the treatment of women and men in our society.

So does this mean that we should abandon law as a mechanism for changing the unequal treatment of women and men? Can law ever redress wrongs based on gender stereotypes or assumptions? Answers to these questions are not easy or necessarily straightforward. Law certainly can be a tool for groups seeking to shift the status quo. However, it is equally available to those who would prefer to keep things just as they are. An additional caution might be that law as an institution favours the status quo. A less instrumentalist view of law might simply conclude that law is an arena of struggle. Either way, the outcomes of legal struggle are not easily predicted.

CHAPTER SUMMARY: KEY POINTS

1. Law has played a pivotal role in preserving gender inequality and in shifting gender imbalance

2. Sexual assault has been one area in which gender stereotypes about men and women have been and continue to be especially prevalent in law

3. Some feminist theorists are skeptical about the ability of law to ever be changed so that it does not reify gender inequality. They even view the possible differences that female judges can make with caution.

4. Contrary to popular belief, the law is not objective and neutral. Rather, it is embedded in a social and cultural context that includes notions about how men and women should behave.

5. Legal method—the process by which legal decisions are made—offers many opportunities for discretion in the characterization of issues, the choice of precedence, and the interpretation of statutes.

6. Legal language often excludes the voices of marginalized peoples, making their claims unable to be articulated.

7. Legal recognition of Battered Woman Syndrome represents an acknowledgment that women's realities are different from men's and that it as such requires specific legal responses.

8. Legal approaches that recognize difference are not without costs, because they essentialize particular groups in ways that may not ultimately advantage them.

9. The Charter of Rights and Freedoms contains a number of provisions that guarantee equality between men and women.

10. Law alone cannot eliminate discrimination. Shifts in law are not necessarily result in shifts in gender relations.

11. Legal responses to discrimination must deal with the intersection of multiple points of disadvantage: for example, race, class, and gender.

DISCUSSION QUESTIONS

1. What is the difference between formal and substantive equality? Can law help to achieve substantive equality?

2. One of the problems with "difference" thinking is that inevitably "difference" is interpreted as "different from men." This leaves men as the baseline from which all else is measured. Discuss this problem.

3. What are the advantages and disadvantages of "affirmative action" programs that seek to correct past inequities?

4. Do women judges make a difference to the outcome of cases involving gender issues? Do their rulings help improve justice for women?

KEY TERMS

affirmative action	LEAF	persons case
decentring law	legal method	precedent
difference approach	mundane aspects of law	reasonable man

Religion

Religion has certainly played a role in the creation and preservation of gender boundaries. As we write this chapter, the battle over same-sex marriage rages, with some religious groups arguing that to allow same-sex marriage violates the traditional notion of marriage and family, which they argue is based on biblical text. Such views draw on the rhetoric of "family values" and the idea that there exist standard family formats and gender scripts. The Apostle Paul's famous instruction recorded in the Christian bible to wives to submit to their husbands has provided the basis for gendered prescriptions for behaviour within family life and has prompted a great deal of criticism for the ways in which Christian churches frame gender relations.

We must be cautious, though, about interpreting all religious groups in the same way, because not all religious groups see gender in similar ways. Even within each group (such as Christians, Muslims, or Jews), there is great variation on the ways in which gender plays out. Moreover, it is important to look beyond superficial presentations of gender roles, because *lived religion* often looks quite different from official religion. Thus, for example, women are not permitted to be priests in the Roman Catholic church; and yet as the ranks of the male priesthood have diminished, religious women have taken on more and more of the roles formerly allocated to male priests.

Moreover, like any social institution, religion is dynamic. For example, as we write this book, a swell of conservatism is occurring in both Christianity and Islam. In addition, the religious world order is shifting as Africa becomes a stronghold for religious conservatives of a variety of faiths. And tension is growing around issues such as the ordination of gays, lesbians, and (in some religions) women. Further, interpretation of religious teachings is very much a matter of local and specific concern, not simply across national boundaries, but within counties and regions as well. Thus, when we make comments about "the church," these comments must be taken in context and with the recognition that emergent and ongoing tensions and struggles play out in a variety of ways.

In Canada, religion is slowly changing its demographic face. While the majority of Canadians identify as Christian, even if they don't actually attend a church, this statistic is changing. At the very least, the percentage of those who adhere to faiths other than Christianity is likely to increase significantly as population growth occurs through immigration from countries whose populations are not predominantly Christian. This demographic change will result in new challenges in the gender-religion dynamic and will necessitate a careful examination of religious practices in the context of legal documents, such as the Canadian Charter of Rights and Freedoms, which guarantees both freedom of religion as well as equality between sexes and sexual orientations.

This chapter explores both the gendered nature of religious institutions and the ways in which women and men live out gendered lives in their religious practice. It examines five issues that illustrate the possibility for change in gender-religion intersections: the emergence of Wicca, the development of new religious movements, the use of religion to combat violence against women, the wearing of the hijab, and polygamy as religious practice.

RELIGIOUS INSTITUTIONS AND GENDER

Social scientific research has revealed that women's roles within organized religion have often replicated their traditional roles at home. In other words, women polish the sanctuary silver, hold the bake sales, run the church nurseries, and act as "helpmates" to the men in the church, who fill positions of power to the exclusion of women. The ordination of women has been a point of contention in many religions, some of which still exclude women from the pulpit or positions of leadership even as they demand a great deal of time and energy from women in the day-to-day operations. Perhaps surprisingly, women outnumber men in terms of church attendance, despite the fact that the church can largely be characterized as a patriarchal institution, which often denigrates women while claiming to elevate them.

Religious organizations are sometimes surprised when they are accused of perpetuating women's inequality: they argue that they value women and see them as different, but equal, to men. Thus, while women may not have access to the same positions of leadership as men, churches claim that they are valued for being women. Embedded in this "valuing" are expectations that reinforce patriarchal limits on women's potential; that, for example, a woman's most important role is mothering.

This issue is further complicated by women's perceptions that society does not value them as mothers. One of the authors (Beaman, 1999) researched and interviewed evangelical women and learned that many of them felt that society devalues the role of women as mothers. While many of these women were also involved in the paid labour force, working the double and triple shifts discussed in Chapter Twelve they received validation for their mothering through their churches. Their situation is made more complex by the fact that their churches often communicate that good mothers do not work in the paid labour force. This results in feelings of guilt by evangelical women for not mothering adequately. They are, in a sense, caught between a rock and a hard place, feeling pressure to work and pressure to stay at home.

Women's responses to gender inequities in organized religion can be divided into roughly four types:

1. Advocacy of complete *abandonment* of traditional organized religion;
2. Advocacy for *radical structural transformation* of existing religious organizations;
3. Movement toward *reshaping* religious organizations;
4. Attempts to *reframe* religious doctrine to better reflect equality between men and women.

We will examine each of these four types in turn.

Mary Daly (1968), a former Roman Catholic nun, argues that the church and organized religion are so fundamentally patriarchal that there is no possibility that they can be transformed into an institution that empowers women or accords them equal status. Women, she argues, should not bother to try to transform an institution that is by nature patriarchal and will remain so. Thus, she advocates **abandonment** of traditional religion is the only possible solution. Radical in her strategy, Daly pictures women in a separate sphere of religious and spiritual fulfillment. Daly's argument challenges us to consider gender seriously in the context of organized religion, but her position is not without difficulties. For example, her argument could be extended to other social institutions, such as law and education. By Daly's reasoning, women should withdraw from these institutions as well. Hence, while groundbreaking at the time, Daly's observations have been met with some criticism.

The second approach advocates focusing on solutions to meeting spiritual needs by developing woman-only spaces or by creating practices in which the needs of women are the central focus. This represents a **radical transformation** strategy: it is based on an assumption that women's spiritual needs are important and need special attention in the face of patriarchal religious institutions. While this approach would require major surgery on the body of religious institutions, it would leave the body intact. Arguably, the emergence of ecumenical women's spirituality groups represents an attempt to create woman-only spaces while at the same time acknowledging women's involvement in more traditional religious spaces. But radical transformation is not without its limitations. Women-only spaces may not do much to shift patriarchal relations. While they may facilitate consciousness-raising, they may reinforce existing organizational and relational patterns, resulting in a preservation of the status quo.

A third approach is a **reshaping** strategy: changing the structure of religious organizations to better reflect gender equality. This approach may involve strategies such as scriptural reinterpretation, ordination of women, and an opening of all roles within the church to women. Reshaping is an attempt to adjust the structure of the church in what might be described as a gentle way (although certainly debates over such issues as ordination can become rather heated). However, reshaping does not guarantee equality. Even ordained women do not always have access to the key positions and are often instead relegated to music or children's ministry.

While reshaping strategies develop to shift structural patterns of inequality, a fourth strategy—**reframing**—occurs at the individual and interpersonal levels. This is not to say that reframing activities do not work through structure, but that their locus is more overtly individual. Reframing means reworking what may at first appearance seem like oppressive doctrine to reinterpret it in ways that reinforce equities based on gender. A large body of literature examines women's experiences in conservative religious groups, including Orthodox Judaism (Kaufman, 1993; Davidman, 1991), charismatic Catholicism (Neitz, 1987), and evangelical and fundamentalist Christianity (Ammerman, 1987; Beaman, 1999; Gallagher, 2003). For example, women in these groups often emphasize the ways in which the teachings of their faiths highlight the responsibility of men to their families. Thus, they reinterpret the call for their "submission" to their husbands into a call for equal partnership with their husbands in day-to-day life. They interpret teachings on strict divisions between genders as liberating, rather than confining. However, the main criticism of reframing is that is does not shift structural gender inequality in any profound way.

To be sure, none of these approaches is discrete; they overlap in interesting ways. Reshaping and reframing may occur at the same time. For example, the emergence of a Wiccan group might be based on separatist notions advocated by Daly, rather than a transformation in terms of reshaping or reframing ancient Wicca spirituality. In the end, each of these strategies is designed to address issues of gender roles and their performance.

Further, none of these strategies is linear, nor do any exist independently of individual actors, whose own life histories influence the emergence and shape of strategies. Consider the following example of an individual in the context of these change movements.

> Joan is a 52-year-old woman who describes herself as a feminist Latter-Day Saint (Mormon). However, her definition of herself as a woman within this religion has shifted over her life course. Raised as a Mormon, with a family history of involvement with the Church dating back to the beginning days of Latter-Day Saint history in the United States, Joan is proud of her religious heritage. But she is not happy with the church's position on women's issues. She has at times been a "good Mormon woman," raising five children, being involved in church activities, and acknowledging her husband's priesthood. But her consciousness has shifted and with it her discontent with church policies and teachings about women.
>
> She started a women's spirituality group in her mid-thirties, and she began to take university courses when her youngest child started school. Eventually, this women's spirituality group came into direct conflict with church administration when the group recommended changes in their local congregation that would open opportunities for women. After being chastised for being a troublemaker, Joan stopped attending church. Today, she continues to meet the spirituality group outside of the church and—as Joan describes it—"under the radar screen" of the administration. She is also part of an Internet discussion group for both women and men working to shift ways that the Mormon church deals with gender relations.

Thus, Joan's interactions with her church have included three of the four strategies discussed above. In addition, these strategies have existed simultaneously and have intersected with other events in Joan's life. She has engaged in radical transformation by creating a women-only space. She questioned church policies and the ways in which scriptural text had been interpreted in relation to gender. She tried to reshape the structure of her church, both locally and at a broader level. Further, she reframed religious teachings in her own life to re-conceptualize church teachings that seem to suggest she is less than equal with her husband. While it is conceivable that Joan might leave the church entirely (abandonment) at some point, according to her account, her faith is still an important part of her life, as is her religious heritage. This singular example illustrates the complexity of strategic responses to gender issues in the context of religion.

How have men thought about their roles in the context of religion? As discussed in Chapter Ten, there is little impetus for those in positions of power to renegotiate power relations. Yet men have not remained oblivious to their position within religious institutions too. The Promise Keeper movement is an evangelical organization of men whose self-definition includes being loving, involved, and faithful husbands and fathers. It addresses both institutional structures (changing the role of men in their churches and families), as well as individual religious practices (exclusionary club-type activities). Although the concern of the Promise Keepers has not been the inequality of women, they have paid attention to racial inequality among men. The section below discusses Promise Keepers and their position on men and religious practice.

Organized religion has had a profound influence on how women see themselves within families. Religious controversies surrounding sexual orientation are based on gendered beliefs about how men and women should be. By characterizing "homosexuality," common-law arrangements, and childbearing outside of marriage as "sins," some religious groups seek to reinforce the status quo of the "traditional family." By valourizing one image of the family over others (mother, father, children), they ignore the historical presence of many models of family. Further, such a romanticization fails to acknowledge the harm that many people have suffered as a result of the family model that is held up as ideal. For example, many women and children especially have suffered abuse in the traditional family model that is supposed to be the bedrock of society. Finally, the claim that one model of family is the right model ignores the possibility that people can be nurtured in a variety of types of families.

WOMEN, MEN, AND RELIGIOUS PRACTICE

Different religious traditions obviously have different gender expectations for men and women. In the Christian tradition, women are often categorized in one of two ways: as virginal innocents or as sinning temptresses. This *virgin-whore complex* of course does not accurately reflect the lives of most women. Moreover, male-centred language dominates Christian text and teachings, with god being referred to with exclusively masculine pronouns. However, even though the ability of language to shape interpretive frameworks should not be underestimated, part of what makes religion a fascinating area of study is the way in which **lived religion** breathes life and unexpected turns in the day-to-day practice of religious beliefs. Thus, the masculine bias in the official religion does not necessarily translate into a masculine bias in the religious lives and beliefs of the adherents of that religion. How do evangelical men make sense of their headship within their families? Does headship, in their opinions, make them "boss" or "partner"? Does a Latter-Day Saint man see his priesthood as a gift to be used in consultation with his wife or as a right to rule others? How do women "submit" to their husbands? Beaman's research (1999) on evangelical Christian women revealed that many women defensively claim, "I am not a doormat," when asked about submission. When asked about the priesthood, Latter-Day Saint women sometimes interpreted this uniquely male license as necessary for men to "keep them in line." These statements reveal the lived religion that breathes life into the official or apparent religion. Thus, lived expressions of gender roles are perhaps more important than official teachings for revealing how religion and gender intersect in everyday life.

Moreover, the voices of conservative Protestant women reveal a great deal about their concept of gender in their lives in the context of their faith. Historically, women from conservative

Christianity have had a significant role in social development. Evangelical women have a history of activism that often remains obscured in present-day accounts. In particular, they were key activists in the fight to gain women the right to vote during the first wave of feminism. They based their support on a maternal feminist stance that posits women as the moral guardians of society. In many ways, this argument played on gendered stereotypes of women's nurturing role as mothers; nonetheless, these groups helped women gain the right to vote. Moreover, they were also active in establishing social welfare programs. This involvement in the public sphere was premised on the idea that women, as mothers, and as morally superior beings (playing on traditional stereotypes again), had a duty to become involved in the public sphere. How do evangelical women see themselves and their roles in today's society?

One of the authors (Beaman, 2001) researched evangelical women in the Atlantic provinces and identified three types of women: traditionalists, moderates, and feminists. Each type belongs to a church that teaches conservative Protestant doctrine about the gendered nature of god's plan; and yet, each sees women and their roles very differently. Interestingly, Beaman's research with Latter-Day Saint women revealed the same three types: *Molly Mormons* (a term used by the women themselves to describe a "good" Mormon woman who follows church teachings), moderates, and feminist Mormons. Each of these categories represents the degree to which women negotiate the boundaries in their faith traditions.

A. Traditionalist Women

Traditionalists adhere to the notion that women are first and foremost mothers and homemakers. They are often more literal in their interpretation of scriptural texts and might be described as fundamentalist. They are opposed to women's involvement in the paid labour force and readily adopt the notion that men are uniquely chosen by god to be the head of the household. Does this mean they do whatever their husbands say or that they are "doormats"? Not at all. Yet traditionalists are quite hostile toward feminism, characterizing feminists as selfish and as "ruining" things for women. The following is a summary of an interview of a traditionalist woman from Beaman's (2001) research:

Mary meets me at the door of her bungalow in a rural area of Nova Scotia. She has baked muffins in honour of my visit; and two hours later when I leave her home she will send me away with two, expressing concern that I will not have a chance for a proper meal during my long day of traveling and interviewing. She offers me a pair of slippers because she has not built a fire and is afraid my feet will get cold. We talk about where we can most comfortably do the interview; and although Mary has set up the dining table for this purpose, she offers to move if that does not suit my needs. She has stacked the quilt pieces she is working on a chair in the corner of the room. We talk a bit about how I have come to be interested in the research I am doing, and then we switch the focus to a discussion of the importance of her faith to her.

Mary is a sixty-eight-year-old widow who works part-time as a clerk at a local government office in order to make ends meet. Her husband died twenty years ago, leaving her to raise their three boys alone. When I ask about her Christian commitment, she describes some of the miracles God has performed in her life. Her unswerving belief that God loves her stems from an experience she had many years ago, which she shares with me: "And I thought, Lord, you know, I have confessed to everything I know of, I repent, and I am truly sorry. And it just happened like—the song says 'sparks from smitten steel just so quick salvation reached me, praise God, I know it's real, it's real, it's real.' And that's just the way it was with me, beyond a shadow of a doubt, and that was years and years ago, and that's never left me." Mary is active in her church as well as in a local interdenominational Bible study group.

In her comments about modern life, she is critical of parents who do not use physical punishment on their children and cites the biblical wisdom "Spare the rod and spoil the child." She says, "I think Christian parents or parents who really love their children shouldn't be reprimanded or put in jail because they discipline their children with a spanking—as long as the child isn't bruised." She is also critical of women who work outside the home for reasons other than absolute financial necessity. She notes that if women would stay at home, then perhaps there would be more jobs for men who have to provide for their families: "You know, if she wants to work at home, like make quilts or something like that, but I think it would make for a much happier home if she were home and it would make him feel good. He would feel 'I'm providing for my family.'" She worries about the effects of women in the workplace on men: "A man might feel inferior because perhaps her education, and you know, she may make a bigger salary and all kinds of things that tend to make her feel that she is the one who is running the show."

When we talk about submission, she is unequivocal in her support for male headship. Men are, in her view, God's intended leaders, and as such have the right to make the final decisions related to family life. Though women are weaker than men, they have a special role as God's caregivers and nurturers, and as such are "equal" to men. "I feel that the man should have a stronger, how should I put it?. . . well, he's the leader in the home and I just feel that. . . . I know some homes a wife can balance the chequebook much better than the husband can, and so I think those things, I'm not saying he has to be the head of everything. But, I think when it comes to . . . well, like buying a new car . . . I want a certain kind, and he feels another kind would be more for our budget and more economical, so I think his word has to be the final word." To Mary, if women accept their role as a helpmate, they will have a happy home, with no "pull as to who runs the show." Divorce, in her view, is simply not an option for Christians.

To Mary, Christian commitment is evidenced and witnessed through an unselfish attitude, which sometimes means letting someone else "have the advantage." Her day begins with prayer: "Prayer and praise—I always try to thank the Lord first thing in the morning for my night's rest and for this new day and ask for his help throughout the day." She doesn't watch "junk" on television, particularly anything with "cursing and swearing," she tries to eat in restaurants that don't serve liquor, and she tries to be considerate of others, although she acknowledges that there are considerate non-Christians as well.

We can see from Mary's comments a complex interweaving of religious beliefs and gender role ideology. We might also note that she situates her beliefs quite clearly in her faith; thus, religion provides an explanatory as well as prescriptive guideline. Despite her belief in male headship, it is quite clear that Mary is very capable of taking care of herself, and in fact has for the past 20 years. It is also important to note that not all evangelical women see the world as Mary does, and it is also interesting to note that there are those who share her views who are not evangelicals.

B. Moderate Women

Moderates, who make up the bulk of evangelical women who participated in this research, believe in submission in headship but are careful to qualify it as being accompanied by companion duties from their husbands. They show a greater openness to feminism, acknowledging its contributions, especially in more liberal versions—equal pay for equal work, for example. The following is an example of a moderate voice in Beaman's (2001) research:

Jane races into her driveway in her minivan and jumps out, beckoning to me while she helps two children disembark. As she hustles them into the house, which is in a middle-income neighborhood in a small city, she tells me to make myself at home in the family room while she puts the children down for their naps. The home (or what I can see of it) is neat and nicely decorated, a fact that becomes incredible when Jane tells me that she has five children. Before she sits down to join me, she invites me to join her in a glass of lemonade; and while she pours, she tells me about her daughter's track and field meet, from which she has just come, and for which we have had to postpone the interview by a half hour. She apologizes for the delay, but explains that it was important for her to be there to support her daughter.

It's a hot day, and Jane is dressed in a sleeveless tank top, shorts, and running shoes. She is wearing a modest amount of makeup. We begin the interview; and during the course of the next two hours, the two children who were napping reemerge and three older children return home from school. Jane deals with each in turn, instructing them to change their clothes and telling them where the snacks are. The phone rings, and I overhear Jane negotiating her contribution to the church supper—two pies, fine, she can do that.

During the course of the interview, Jane tells me how important being an evangelical Christian is to her; she doesn't know how people can manage to get through life without Christ. "An evangelical to me means someone that's a little more intense about their Christianity, a little more excited about it, wanting to make it more than just a Sunday thing. I am not just interested in teaching my children Bible stories, but how they can have Christ as their personal Savior and Lord." For Jane, God is involved in every aspect of her life, including her marriage: "I firmly believe the circumstances in which Dan and I came together were such that we really feel that God brought us together." Her Christian worldview frames her life—most of her friends are Christian, she witnesses to her children, and she is extensively involved in her church: she sings in the choir, is involved in the missionary guild, attends Bible study, and participates in a couples group. She seeks the Lord's guidance and forgiveness through prayer on a daily basis, and she feels comforted by her personal relationship with Jesus: "It gives me comfort knowing that God cares about me and my husband and my children, and it makes me feel assured that anything that is going to happen is not outside His realm of control, so it just gives me peace that whatever comes my way then I know that God already knew about it first, and that He is there to support me."

Jane says that although she understands that some women want or need to work outside the home, for her it is simply not a desirable option, and, with five children, not really a choice at all. She sees herself as being very lucky to have a supportive husband who earns a good income. She is comfortable in her role as "just" a homemaker: "I stay at home, and the reason I stay at home is because Dan and I decided before we were married that we were going to have a big family, and we both knew that I wanted to be home. He wanted me home, but even before he told me he wanted me home I said, you know, I would be home. That was the home that we had grown up in, our Moms had been home. I never even thought of anything other than that, and neither had he." They have just come back from a rare escape weekend, and she sees the recent time by themselves as valuable. Jane is uncomfortable with feminism because she feels that feminists promote too much of their own agenda and not enough of God's.

Although her evangelical husband is head of their household, and she would describe herself as a submissive wife, decisions are always made jointly. She thinks that men have the more difficult biblical role: "I have had some discussions with women who have a real difficult time with that—'Wives submit to your husbands.' Now I don't have difficulty with that at all, because in the next breath it says 'Husbands love your wives as Christ loved the church.' In my mind, we've got the easy end of the job, they've got the hard one. I mean, they've got to love like Christ. If they love like Christ, it can't be difficult to submit to that. I mean, that's perfect love."

Jane is clearly living out what we might consider a "traditional" role for women—homemaker and mother. But, her vision of herself and women's and men's roles employs a notion of equality. Rather than framing her decision to be a homemaker in terms of what is right for women, it translates as a personal decision that is supported by her faith.

C. Feminist Women

Finally, evangelical feminists are also likely to reject the notion of headship and submission and see no reason to attempt to reshape that doctrine to fit their lives. Feminist evangelicals see themselves as equal partners with their husbands, and they have no reservations about women's involvement in the paid labour force. Here is one evangelical feminist from Beaman's (2001) research:

> Beth is a thirty-six-year-old nurse and mother of two small children. I arrive at her house a bit earlier than scheduled, but she is very welcoming. Her house is in a suburb of a small city. She has just returned from Bible study. Beth works part-time and says that she would not be happy unless she was in the labour force. "I don't want to be just here and just thought of as a mother, although I think that's a very important job, and I want to do it the best I can, but I want to have other interests outside of that role." Her part-time status allows her the best of two worlds—time to spend with her children, and an opportunity to remain active in her profession. Her husband is a firefighter who works shift work, so he is often able to spend time with their children. In fact, as I am interviewing Beth, he comes home at the end of his shift and makes lunch for the children. Though she grew up in a Christian home, Beth does not feel that her real commitment to Christ happened until her mid-twenties. She describes herself as an evangelical Christian. She feels that "as a woman, it's our duty to promote the gospel when we have opportunity to present it to people if they are willing to receive it." She attends church regularly and is also involved in two church groups, one of which is the Thursday morning women's Bible study where I first met her. She tells me that since my research team visited her women's group, she has started praying for abused women. While she feels that her life is church-centred, she does have many non-Christian friends. She is troubled by the Godless society she feels we are becoming.
>
> When I raise the issue of submission, Beth declares that she does not buy into "that submission stuff." She explains that she is an equal partner in her marriage and is unwilling to call her husband "the head" of their household. "We are both the head," she declares, and their household is run as a "team effort." She says, "Baptists are so brought up in the fact that the man is the head of the home, and the head of the house and what he says goes. And that's changing more and more, I think that the younger women today, that it's not considered, it's you, you really should consider God the head of your home, and you two are an equal team." She refers to marriage as a "covenant" with God as well as one's spouse, although she believes there are times when separation and divorce are acceptable. She says that although a lot of people would describe her as a feminist, and she would describe herself as one, "I don't really feel I'm a true feminist because I like to stay at home, and I like to take care of my children, and I get a lot of enjoyment out of that, but I also like to be in the work force too." She is grateful for the feminist movement and the advances that she feels it has brought for women.

Beth sees no conflict between her beliefs as an evangelical Christian and feminism, and is uncomfortable with the doctrine of submission, which she sees as outdated and not especially relevant to running a Christian home.

These three portraits illustrate the intersection of religious beliefs, practices, and gender. Moreover, these women are situated in a particular social and cultural context—a further intersection. But even though these intersections provide insight, identity construction is a continuous process. Thus, establishing causal relationships between religious beliefs and attitudes about women's roles is very difficult. In other words, many people of Mary's generation share her beliefs about the "permissive" parents of today's generation, even those who are not evangelical. Thus, even though Mary frames her beliefs about parenting in terms of her Christian commitment, we should be careful not to interpret this as a causal relationship. In other words, her religious beliefs do not necessarily cause her behaviour. Among other things her age, the fact that she lives in a rural area, and her widowhood at a relatively young age all contribute to her current beliefs.

D. Promise Keepers

How do men link their beliefs and practices regarding their religion and gender? John Bartkowski has done extensive research on the **Promise Keepers**, an evangelical men's group. Bartkowski's (2003) work offers another perspective on gender—how conservative Christian men translate biblical teachings into day-to-day expectations of themselves as men. But even within Promise Keepers, belief is not made up of a single strand, but of multiple strands. Situated in the broader "Christian men's movement," Promise Keepers emerged during the 1990s as a strong voice among evangelical men. It began with a "small" meeting of 4000 men in Colorado in 1991, and culminated in its "finest hour" in 1997 when 600 000 to 800 000 men gathered in Washington, D.C., "to offer somber prayers, sing manly hymns, and most famously, share tearful embraces" (2003, p. 2). Canadian evangelicals also participate in PK gatherings. Bartkowski describes a typical Promise Keepers gathering, which combines sport, gender, and religion: "As the contemporary heir to *Muscular Christianity*, the Promise Keepers appropriate and evangelize sport rituals at their conferences. Chanting, cheering and screaming erupt during each break period between conference speakers' addresses. At several points during the San Antonio conference, men were challenged to cheer for Jesus at the top of their lungs by men on stage. 'Come on! That's not loud enough,' boomed someone up front with his hand cupped behind his ear. 'I can't hear you! Jesus can't hear you!' What is all of this screaming about? In part, Promise Keeper gatherings are simply opportunities to affirm and celebrate masculinity"(2003, p. 68).

But Bartkowski cautions against an overly simplistic reading of the PK agenda on gender, arguing that "there is not one definitive gender ideology articulated by Promise Keepers leaders" (2003, p. 12). The use of patriarchal language and ideas such as the notion that men must "take back" their roles as leaders in family life has certainly contributed to the idea that Promise Keepers have an authoritarian and regressive mandate. Their use of *godly-man archetypes* have added to this perception. But Bartkowski situates the Promise Keepers in the ideal of the nineteenth-century *self-made man*, arguing that "the chaos and confusion faced by men in the early twentieth century paralleled that confronting men at the century's end" (2003, p. 33). The Promise Keepers, then, is a group that in part aims to give men a sense of their purpose in an era in which their roles have become less clear.

Bartkowski identifies the four archetypical forms of the godly man that emerge in Promise Keeper literature:

1. The *Rational Patriarch* (traditional masculinity). In this version, men and women have divinely ordained different roles, with women being especially capable for caregiving to young children (2003, p. 47). Men are the heads of households. Gender blending and homosexuality are misguided at best, sins at worst.

2. The *Expressive Egalitarian* (men's liberationism). This evangelical man embraces an androgynous approach to gender, highlighting the artificiality of gender differences. He emphasizes the common humanity between men and women. "Traits commonly associated with being male (*e.g.*, bravery, strength, stoicism, an insatiable sex drive, a preoccupation with achievement) are not really masculine at all" (2003, p. 50). Similarly, "women's" traits are not the exclusive terrain of females. Marital egalitarianism, rather than submission and headship, are emphasized by this group of men.

3. The *Tender Warrior* (poeticized manhood). These evangelicals draw on symbolism to explore men and masculinity, positing men's role as somewhat between the first two types in their belief in the "servant-leader." Gender difference in this type is more fluid; but there is a sense that masculine and feminine essences are brought together in the Tender Warrior.

4. The *Multicultural Man* (interracial masculinity). This type focuses on racism and the reconciliation of racial difference to emphasize men's singularity. (2003, p. 62)

Like the evangelical women, evangelical men voice different strands of gender ideology that weave their way through their faith and its expression. Understanding gender in this context means recognizing that the ways people "perform" gender are fluid and variable, not only over the life course, but from circumstance to circumstance.

THE EMERGENCE OF WICCA

During the past three decades, there has been a resurgence of woman-centered religious practices, such as those found in Wicca. Wicca is a goddess-based religion that focuses on the rhythms of nature. Because of misconceptions about "witches" and who they are, and conflations of Wicca and Satanism, Wiccans keep a low profile. Wicca appeals to both men and women, but women make up the bulk of Wiccan practitioners (65 percent, according to Berger, 2005). Interestingly, "the New Age, Witchcraft, Neopagan, non-Native American Shamanism and women's spirituality have mostly attracted white middle-class individuals" (Berger, 2005, p.3). Some of these individuals combine more mainstream religious participation (such as attendance at a church) with "alternative" spiritual practices. Wicca falls within the broader umbrella of neopaganism, which "is an umbrella term for spiritual practices that share a view of the world as enchanted and the earth as sacred" (Berger, 2005, p. 29).

Wendy Griffin (1995), Helen Berger (2003, 2005), and Tanice Foltz (2000) in the United States and Sian Reid (2006) in Canada have conducted research on Wiccan communities in an attempt to understand how women and men see themselves within the context of a religion whose revival has been situated in the *Goddess movement*. Griffin's (1995) research demonstrates that Wiccan groups cannot be characterized in a singular manner: some are separatist, for women only, following the *abandonment* strategy discussed above, while others are more inclusive, intending to offer woman-centred space which may not be woman-only space in some cases. Witches practice in a variety of ways, including as sole practitioners, whose religious beliefs and practices differ in some measure from organized religion's sense of community. Naomi Goldenberg puts it succinctly: "By celebrating both women and the natural world, the Craft sets itself up as both competitor with, and critic of, mainstream religions" (2004, p. 206).

Wiccan rituals often focus on the celebration of women's experiences, including menstruation and childbirth, but also the different phases of women's lives, which include the maiden, mother, and the crone. While they do use magic, witches are bound by the following maxim: "Do as you will as long as thou harm none." Moreover, there is a price to pay for sending out negative energy. "The energy one sends out will return to one with three times the force with which it was sent" (Berger, 2003, p. 36).

Wicca is an important vehicle that addresses some of the negative gendered aspects of traditional religions. The "evoking of women's life stages allowed women to identify with deity in a way that had not been possible since the advent of patriarchal religions" (Griffin, 2003, p. 62). For male witches, Wicca shifts patriarchal interpretations of the deity and opens the possibility for a new conceptualization of women and the divine.

GENDER AND NEW RELIGIOUS MOVEMENTS

While Wicca is arguably a **new religious movement** (a non-traditional religious group by North American standards), most scholars recognize its connection to past practices and paganism more generally, which has ancient roots. New Religious Movements (NRMs) are usually considered separately from ancient traditions, although that too is too arbitrary a distinction. Included in NRMs might be groups such as the Raelians (who are perhaps most famous for their announcement that they had successfully cloned a human being), Scientologists (often mentioned in the media in association with its "famous" members, such as John Travolta), and the Hare Krishna (more properly known as ISKCON or the International Society for Krishna Consciousness). These groups are sometimes referred to as "cults," a term that is most often used in a disparaging manner to distinguish these groups from more traditional religions.

Like any religious group, NRMs can both break down and/or reify gendered patterns. For example, in her research on children in Sahaja Yoga families, Judith Coney (1999) documents the gendered division of toys encouraged by the group's leader (girls with dolls, boys with trucks) and notes "the girls tend to be dressed in pretty feminine clothes" (1999, p. 114). In contrast, Susan Palmer found in her research on Messianic communities that "childrearing is a manly vocation," observing that "fathers are as actively involved as mothers in raising children . . . the men frequently meet to discuss problems and policies in childrearing, even discussing various cures for diaper rash" (1999, p. 159). As is the case in society generally, NRMs employ a variety of strategies around gender and sexuality, including polyamourous relationships and celibacy, traditional "mother" roles and authoritarian "fathers." Susan Palmer explored gender among the Raelians (2004). She noted that "The Order of Rael's Angels" highlights women's feminine charisma and emphasizes free love, and people remain in relationships only as long as both parties are happy. "Rael gives women permission to be unmarried mothers and sexually active single mothers" (2004, p. 137). Palmer notes that pre-1998 gender roles were egalitarian; but in 1998, after Rael created "The Angels" (an elite women's caucus within the movement), Raelian views of gender shifted, placing an emphasis on women's unique qualities, thereby polarizing the sexes in the movement (2004, p. 139).

It is difficult to generalize about gender within NRMs for a variety of reasons. First, NRMs are extremely diverse. Secondly, there is limited research that explores day-to-day life in NRMs in Canada. Thirdly, as NRMs evolve, their approach to gender often shifts.

Finally, religion is lived, and as such, the ways that religious groups set out their teachings and the ways that those teachings are actualized by individual believers are often quite different. Consider the three evangelical women we introduced earlier in the chapter: three strands of belief/practice in relation to gender emerged from one religion.

THE HIJAB: SYMBOL OF GENDER SCRIPTS?

While this chapter has focused primarily on gender within the Christian tradition, one of the most fascinating debates taking place in Canadian society centres on the importation of religious traditions other than Christianity and the way those traditions fit in the context of Canadian society. Of particular interest are Muslim traditions that seem to reproduce patriarchy. And yet, like the examples discussed above, it is imperative that we move beyond appearances and examine the ways in which Muslims themselves interpret such "gendered" symbols. This debate is particularly heated in Québec, in part because some people there interpret religious freedom along France's secular model, which abolishes religious symbols from the public sphere.

Consider the **hijab**, also known as the headscarf or veil, and its gendered symbolism. Some people regard the hijab as a cultural symbol, rather than a specifically religious symbol. Layers of meaning around this religious/cultural symbol are perhaps best uncovered by exploring the ways in which women themselves think about its meaning. Homa Hoodfar (2003) has conducted extensive research into the ways in which young women themselves interpret their wearing of the hijab and its gendered symbolism. In her research, Hoodfar has come to describe the wearing of the hijab as an "adaptive strategy." Surprisingly, Hoodfar found that contrary to popular perceptions, young women often had to fight with their parents to wear the veil. Their parents saw the decision to "veil" as regressive, and moreover, they did not associate it with "being Muslim." As Hoodfar points out, the Qur'an does not specifically discuss or recommend the covering of one's hair (2003, p. 6). However, as she also points out, "The veil, and to a lesser extent clothing in general, formed the symbolic battlefield on which the modernists and conservatives fought out their differences" (2003, p. 8).

Hoodfar's research also points to the importance of considering both the global and the local meanings of symbolic religious practices and symbols. In Canada, the young women she interviewed often saw wearing the veil as a way to negotiate space between religious tradition and "modern" life, creating what we might describe as a postmodern solution. As one woman put it, in describing a friend who had decided to veil: "She said that since she started wearing the veil, she feels so much happier and freer. It is as though she has suddenly matured in the eyes of her parents and everyone else. Now she is allowed to drive, to go to her friends' or to have them come home" (2003, p. 20). For this woman and some of her friends, the veil is a way to negotiate their freedom. By wearing a headcover, the woman convinces her parents that she takes her faith seriously. In a community where family often exercises a great deal of influence, this action is extremely important for young women to gain a sense of autonomy and freedom. For them, it is a small price to pay. Many headscarfed women are genuinely committed not only to their faith, but also to their culture.

THE DEBATE ABOUT POLYGAMY

Is **polygamy** inherently patriarchal? Is it necessarily oppressive to women? Does the criminalization of polygamy harm women more than it helps them? First, as described in

Chapter Nine multiple sexual and relationship partners is not a practice that is limited to polygamists. Moreover, polygamy cannot be reduced to sexual practice; rather, it is a particular kind of family arrangement. Why should we concern ourselves with these questions and this issue?

Religiously motivated polygamy has been in the news lately. But polygamy as a manifestation of religious beliefs is not a new phenomenon nor is it relegated to one religion. As an issue of public concern, it emerged in the United States with Joseph Smith's (the founder of the Church of Jesus Christ of Latter-Day Saints, or Mormons) teachings in favour of polygamy. The United States banned polygamy, and Mormon polygamists went into hiding or fled the country, some coming to Canada. Debates about polygamy in the 1890s led to the Canadian Criminal Code provision which specifically banned polygamy and specifically mentioned "the persons commonly called Mormons." Fears of moral corruption prompted the ban of polygamy. Yet the practice has persisted, and today, polygamy is being revisited as an issue of religious freedom and as a gender issue (see Beaman, 2004).

Some people portray polygamy as inherently abusive of women. But how do women themselves describe polygamy? The answer to this question is not simple. The community of Bountiful, British Columbia, is made up of 700 people who are "Fundamentalist Mormons," many of whom live in polygamous relationships. The community has come under increased scrutiny as several ex-members have alleged abuse within the community. Yet other women in the community have made public statements about the positive experience of living in polygamous relationships. An organization called "The Women of Bountiful" ("Bountiful Women," 2005) emphasizes the benefits of plural marriage, including shared labour and higher family incomes. Those women refute allegations that very young girls are married against their will, noting that there have only ever been two plural marriages of girls under sixteen. This group also identifies issues of concern within their own community, such as lobbying for a ban on marriage for women under eighteen.

While accounts of abuse within polygamous communities must be taken seriously, as should any allegations of abuse, they do not necessarily indicate systemic abuse. Moreover, as noted above, polygamous women have themselves identified the problem of girls marrying men as an issue they would like to see legally addressed. Women in polygamous relationships have been particularly disadvantaged by the law, which refuses to see them as entitled to the protections and rights normally offered to parties to a marriage, including, for example, equal division of marital property. This seems to be in some measure a punitive stance toward women who choose to live in this form of relationship. In the recent report commissioned by Status of Women Canada, 2006, Bailey *et al.* stated that in order to better protect women and children, polygamy should be decriminalized, not legalized.

The issue of polygamy raises interesting questions about the intersection of religion and gender. Recently the Supreme Court of Canada held in the case of *R* v. *Labaye* that a private swingers club (a club in which men and women engage in sexual activities with multiple partners) in Montreal could operate legally. Those who were participating in the activities at the club were characterized as freely consenting adults. The notion of consent is perhaps the issue on which many people focus when they think about polygamy. Some people argue that girls who are raised in communities such as Bountiful cannot freely consent to polygamous relationships. To date, there has simply not been enough social scientific research to fully understand the dynamics of polygamous relationships that are religiously motivated. It is important to remember that polygamy is not just about sex, but also about a particular family structure. Whether it is any more or less oppressive to women than so-called traditional family structure is not easily answered.

RELIGION AND VIOLENCE AGAINST WOMEN: RELIGION IN ACTION

One of the most serious concerns about teachings such as the doctrine of submission has been that is perpetuates not only inequality but violence against women, by encouraging punishment of women who do not "obey" their husbands. Abused women report that they have themselves interpreted religious teachings as a licence for their husbands to do whatever they please in marital relationships and as an indication that they deserved the abuse they received. In recent years, even conservative religious groups have begun to recognize that these sorts of interpretations are leading to behaviour that is not part of Christian teaching.

Nancy Nason-Clark, head coordinator of the Religion and Violence Research Team at the Muriel McQueen Fergusson Centre for Family Violence Research at the University of New Brunswick, has spent the last decade researching the ways in which religious ideology, based in part on men's and women's roles in the context of family life, perpetuates violence against women. They have examined women's, men's, and clergy's understanding of and attitudes toward religious teachings and violence against women. They have also worked to increase understanding within religious organizations about the ways some teachings perpetuate violence against women, and have developed pragmatic resources, such as workshops bringing clergy and transition house workers together to formulate strategies. The good news in this action-oriented research is that church women have been activists on this issue for a long time, raising money for transition houses, or donating goods and services to help abused women in their local shelters. Women of faith together with community groups have worked together to shift the ways that religions see and respond to violence against women.

BOX 14-1	Can Hope Really Change People? Violent Religious Men and Their Journey of Accountability

by Nancy Nason-Clark
Fieldnotes: February, 2006; Location: Northwest, USA.

Some arrive early to watch the Olympics on the screen of the big TV mounted high in one corner of the room. Others appear just before class begins. As they enter, alone or in pairs, they sign in—a reminder that for most of the men assembled on this Tuesday evening, attendance is not optional. At first blush, they look like any other group of working-class men. Yet their soiled jeans, rugged workboots, peak caps and tattoos cover up ever so dimly secrets very close to the surface. As they begin the process of "check-in," the men call out their names and the ages of their children. Most appear much older than their years: as a group, they have been hard on their own bodies and abusive to the

BOX 14-1	*(Continued)*

bodies of others. In consequence, the judicial system has processed their cases, handed down prison sentences, mandated separation from their partners and/or children, and required attendance at a batterers intervention program.

For the most part, the men are very attentive to the group facilitator and to the other men whose stories are similar to their own. On this particular evening, the focus is on interacting in healthy ways with loved ones. Few assembled here have experienced such positive interactions in their childhood homes. And, by their own accounts, they have lived their lives in ways that perpetuated the very activities they vowed to themselves early in life never to commit. *I hated my old man,* says one man in his mid thirties, *he beat us kids and mom. And now I have become the spittin' image of him.*

The language of contemporary culture provides the basis for the curriculum and the men's court-mandated attendance at the group. With skill and determination, staff attempt to help men to help themselves. Yet, in powerful ways, the language of faith is woven through the dialogue. *There is hope. Change is possible.*

This is a faith-based program for men who have acted abusively.

One Man's Story

Bill[1] is a 40-something, soft-spoken, manual labourer who has always held steady employment. He has lived in several U.S. locations, which might be interpreted as running from his problems. *I have had a problem with substance abuse in my life, there's a lot of alcoholism and drug addiction.*

He began the intervention program after 15 months in prison for domestic violence. *I had domestic issue problems in my life many different times with my partner of 13 years and I ended up going to prison.*

In consulting with his probation officer, Bill chose to attend a faith-based intervention program *because of my faith, faith-based and I made the right choice.*

I realized I wasn't living my life the way God intended me to live my life and when I came to that realization and that surrender, it's like God removed the blinders from me . . . Everything I have learned from past treatments and all the years of going to NA and AA all made sense to me for the first time in my life and I started being honest with people . . . it's all in God's plan, that's all I can figure . . . I give my life to the Lord everyday . . . it's been a blessing, the Lord has blessed me and I am on the verge of getting custody of my daughter back . . . by God's grace alone, because I know I could never have done it. And it's by doing the next right thing, by being honest, by being accountable, by living on life's terms and doing the right thing rather than hiding in a bottle which I did from the time I was 14 years old . . .

Through the program, learning life skills, by continued accountability, Bill lives each day through the lens that so quickly he could give up all he has gained. *I just live my life one day at a time . . . And it is a big struggle. Its like the old cliché, you have to be sick and tired of being sick and tired. And until you get to that point, until you have made that decision on your own, you can't do it . . . hope is to me, it's like this is my thing on hope—helping other people every day. That gives hope. It's hard, every individual is different . . . nobody hands you anything, you have to work for it and I am*

(Continued)

BOX 14-1	Can Hope Really Change People? Violent Religious Men and Their Journey of Accountability (*Continued*)

going to tell you something else—when you have led lives like most of these men led and I have led myself, it takes time, it doesn't happen over night, you have to prove yourself, you have to show by your actions on a daily basis . . .

Hope is a central construct in Bill's struggle to keep clean, sober, and abuse-free. If he is successful, he believes the reward will be obtaining custody of his daughter, who is living temporarily with one of his siblings under state supervision.

For almost twenty years of my professional life, I have been researching the interface between religion, culture, and violence. Through questionnaires, in-depth interviews, focus groups, observation, community consultations, and the content analysis of case files and documents, I have come face to face with the suffering caused by violence in the family context. It is a multi-faceted story and I have been attempting to tell it from a variety of perspectives—the victim, the perpetrator, family members and friends as well as those within or beyond the faith community who have been attempting to give assistance.

For many victims, their faith sustains them through long periods of domestic crisis: it empowers them ultimately to flee their abuser and to seek refuge and safety where they begin a new life free of the violence of the past (Nason-Clark and Kroeger 2004). There are others who never find the inner strength or practical support to leave the fear or reality of battery behind (Nason-Clark 1997). As religious women, they might believe that this is their *cross to bear*. But no matter how celebrated family life is in religious traditions around the world, there is no

place for abuse (Kroeger and Nason-Clark 2001).

As a social scientist, my task is to understand the world clearly using the tools of my professional life and to communicate that knowledge as best I can. Yet, I must never forget that with knowledge comes social responsibility. Every home should be a safe place, a place of refuge and shelter. There is no place like home. When abuse is present, there is no home.

"Can hope really change people?" the title of this essay asks. The answer depends on who you ask.

When women and men around the globe catch a vision that they can help to reduce abuse in all its ugly forms, the world will be a safer place. For people of faith, that dream is empowered by religious hope.

References

Kroeger, C. Clark and N. Nason-Clark. (2001). *No Place for Abuse: Biblical and Practical Resources to Counteract Domestic Violence.* Downers Grove, IN: InterVarsity Press.

Nason-Clark, N. and C. Clark Kroeger. (2004). *Refuge from Abuse: Hope and Healing for Abused Religious Women.* Downers Grove, IN: InterVarsity Press.

Nason-Clark, N. (1997). *The Battered Wife: How Christians Confront Family Violence.* Louisville, KY: Westminster/ John Knox Press.

Endnotes

The name is a pseudonym and a few specific details have been altered to protect his identity. Words in italics are direct quotes from the interview.

CONCLUSIONS

Religion has a powerful impact on the way women and men make sense of their world and their gender. The connection cannot be stated in general terms but must be considered in light of other intersections, including the specific religious group involved, the dynamics of the local group, the life history of the individual, and the social space in which the religion is located. The ways that religions as institutions define roles for men and women have also had an impact, but so too have the ways that women and men have decided for themselves to live their faith. Some religions specifically address "gender shortcomings" that people have experienced in other religious groups (Wicca in particular); but at the same time, other religious groups which emphasize traditional ways of thinking about gender because they are uncomfortable with less defined gender roles. This is often the case in more orthodox understandings of faith traditions. The point here is that gender is intertwined with religion in complex ways.

Finally, a note on method. General surveys show some broad patterns of religious affiliation, whereas detailed research that examines individual life histories reveals the ways that individuals create meaning as men and women. Religion can provide both prescriptions for how men and women should be and also explanations for why things are the way they are. Through a careful exploration of the intersection of religious beliefs and practices with gender, social scientists can discover the ways in which gender is negotiated on a day-to-day basis. They can also learn how gender shifts as religious beliefs and practices shift.

CHAPTER SUMMARY: KEY POINTS

1. Religious groups are diverse. For example, to speak about Christianity is to group many diverse strands of religious belief and practice together.

2. Examining *lived religion* (the ways people practice their faith) is essential to understanding the ways that gender is performed in that religious context.

3. Religions and religious culture in Canada is in a state of transition.

4. Organized religion often mirrors patriarchal ideas about women's and men's roles.

5. Women have generally used four strategies—*abandonment, radical restructuring, reshaping,* and *reframing*—respond to gender inequality within religious groups.

6. Even groups that may appear to have fixed gender boundaries still negotiate and interpret gender in multiple ways.

7. Gender boundaries in "traditional" religions have sometimes been challenged by *new religious movements,* which often rewrite gender scripts.

8. *Wiccans* celebrate the life cycle of women and nature, positioning themselves in opposition to religious beliefs which maintain patriarchy.

9. Religious and cultural symbols such as the *hijab* and religious practices such as *polygamy* cannot be studied only at the level of ideology. They must be explored through the eyes of those who are members of those religious communities.

10. Religion can both oppress and empower women and men.

DISCUSSION QUESTIONS

1. Which religious traditions are you familiar with? How do people in those religions think about how men and women are and should be?
2. Do you think polygamy is oppressive to women? Does it advantage men?
3. Can religion be changed to promote gender equality?
4. Should religious groups have a say in who can be married?

KEY TERMS

abandonment	new religious movements	reframing
cults	polygamy	reshaping
hijab	Promise Keepers	
lived religion	radical transformation	

Conclusion

chapter fifteen

Crime as Case Study

It is a most abstract conundrum, to wrap one's mind around the fact that a killer and/or prisoner could also be a good person.

(Gayle K. Horii, 2000)

If there is a forum in which stereotypes about gender and its various intersections are likely to be publicly played out, surely it is in relation to the criminal justice system. When we hear the word "criminal" in relation to men, we think of aggression and assault and feel fear. In relation to women, we think of media images of "women gone wrong" or of prostitutes. We may feel revulsion or curiosity. Yet for the most part, being "criminal" usually involves activities associated with property offences—minor theft, such as shoplifting. In other words, the vast majority of crime is made up of those activities that do not make the news and are relatively uneventful and non-dramatic. This empirical fact—that crime is mostly made up of petty or less serious offences—is even more the case for women than for men, but is nonetheless true for men as well. Why then do we have gendered images of dangerous criminals when we think about crime?

While we acknowledge the role the media plays in the perpetuation of these images, media's influence is only part of the story. Theories of crime themselves have perpetuated popular stereotypes and images. Theorists have long argued that criminal men "look" a particular way (Lombroso, 1911). They have reified the notion of women as passive and therefore unable to "mastermind" crime. Interestingly, while theories of crime have been based predominantly on men, they do not focus on gender as an analytical framework. This means that men are in many ways the default position—the assumed perpetrators of crime. Thus, most criminality theories have focused on men, without ever identifying gender as an important focus!

Crime provides us with a case study to explore multiple levels of gender within one social phenomenon. Note that these "levels of gendered activity" are simply analytical tools, rather than reflections of any sort of categorical reality. Crime illustrates how difficult it is to separate these levels. How individuals define themselves—"good girls don't" or "real men do"—has an impact on how people engage in crime, or to what extent they even define their activities as crime. Self-definition is complex, as already discussed, because identity is not a fixed category, but rather, one that is constantly negotiated, re-enacted, and redefined. Identity also intersects with other levels, such as race and class. These intersections have profound implications for self-definition and the living of gender. Moreover, society and culture are other levels of gendered activity, ones that provide the context for gender.

Moral panics seem to govern the way officials "deal with" crime. For example, a few years ago "girls gone wild" was the panic of the day, caused by a few incidents of girl bullying and violence that made national media coverage. Although these were isolated incidents, the "increased violence of girls" became a full-blown panic that translated into a problem that needed to be solved. To better understand the power of moral panic, examine today's media reports about crime and identify the current moral panic. Ask how this panic is created, how it is perpetuated, and how the state and community groups respond. Consider carefully the ways in which the problem is gendered—the different implications for men and women. Look for the power relations that seem to construct and define the problem. Moreover, consider the ways in which men and women interact or act out their gender in the context of these crimes. Crime analysis of this type becomes especially complex when it involves challenges to fixed categories, such as transgendered prostitutes.

DEFINITIONS OF CRIME AND GENDER

The definition, processing, and punishment of crime offers an interesting case study for examining the ways in which gender is enacted, negotiated, and constructed in our society. Gender is woven through crime in complex and often obscure ways. We have already seen examples of this in earlier chapters: the **battered woman defence** is one example of the ways in which law and the criminal justice system positively acknowledge the gendered nature of experiences. But acknowledging gender difference is not without costs: woman-specific defences also reify women's difference, sometimes at the cost of being "different from" men, which often is interpreted to mean "inferior to" men.

Certainly crime is defined in the Criminal Code of Canada, and from this standpoint, we might think its definition is relatively straightforward. However, the Criminal Code is a document that changes: behaviour deemed to be criminal in nature today may or may not have been criminal 30 or 50 years ago. There are numerous theories about how certain acts become criminal. Some people believe that the state acts at the behest of the powerful in society, especially corporate interests. Others argue that the state acts as a neutral arbiter in the crime definition process. No matter how we think about the creation of crime (for *no* behaviour is *inherently* criminal), we may be certain that gendered expectations are woven through definitions of crime once it is defined.

The processing of crime—*i.e.,* identification of criminal behaviour, charging with an offence, and so on—is highly discretionary. Consider the following example. A woman known to the authors was driving home from the beach in convoy with her son, and both were speeding. She was driving a family minivan, and he was driving a large pick-up truck. When both were stopped by police, the woman received a warning to slow down, whereas the young man received a ticket for speeding. What accounted for the difference in treatment? One person was a younger male, and the other was an older female. While this example does not focus on a criminal charge, similar sorts of discretion are used in relation to criminal processing as well. Sometimes discretion is related to how the person responds to police inquiries. Is the person under surveillance perceived by the police as "respectful"? Is she or he known to the police? What is her social class and status? What is his age? Is she or he Aboriginal? And, as the speeding ticket example shows, is the accused a "mature woman" or a "young man"? While police, crown prosecutors, and judges don't like to think of themselves as exercising discretion on these bases, they sometimes do, and gender plays a part in this process in the criminal justice system. Another aspect of this discretion can be seen in violence against women. The failure to take this problem seriously is due not so much to Criminal Code provisions as it is with the discretion exercised by police and crown prosecutors in preparing files for prosecution.

To talk about a *criminal justice system* here is somewhat simplistic. More accurately, the various agencies involved in the definition of crime, its enforcement, its processing, sentencing, and punishment are often in tension or outright conflict with one another. Think about the recent debates about Criminal Code revisions relating to marijuana use. The police are opposed to any decriminalization of possession; Parliament was (until recently) in favour decriminalization; and citizens have voiced opinions on both sides of the debate. Contests over the definition of crime often involve gender assumptions.

Until the late 1960s, there was very little attempt to seriously and critically address the issue of gender and criminalization. Most theories of crime focused on men's activities. This is not to imply that men fared especially well in crime theory. In 1876, Lombroso, one of the world's first criminologists, theorized in *The Criminal Man* that criminals are born biologically predisposed to crime and that in fact body types were a good indicator of that predisposition (Lombroso also argued that when uncontrolled by men, women are "more vicious, more dangerous and monstrous than any man" (Faith & Jiwani, 2002, p. 82). Lombroso's biological theory ignored social factors and focused on body type. The biological explanation for both crime and deviance has continued to have explanatory power, particularly in the medical model understanding crime and deviance. The biological model was revived in relation to explanations for women's crimes by Otto Pollack, who argued in his 1950s book, *The Criminality of Women,* that "women were more deceptive than men, due to having both to hide their monthly period and to fake orgasm. Biology thus equips women with the skill of deception (Faith & Jiwani, 2002, p. 87).

Of course, this criminalization of women could have been worse. And indeed it was during the Middle Ages, when for approximately 100 years, women were systematically targeted as witches. Estimates are that 90 percent of those identified and executed as witches during this period were women. Estimates of the number of people killed range from several hundred thousand to nine million (Noonan, p. 212, footnote 4). Sheila Noonan (2001) states that this process began in the Inquisition and Crusades and had the overall aim of eliminating heresy. The roots of Lombroso and Pollack's beliefs about women existed even here. The *Malleus Malificarum,* the church's official book describing the crimes of witchcraft, which formed the basis for the Church's recognition of witches and witchcraft, portrayed women as "more credulous and hence more easily corrupted. Feebler both in body and in intellect, women are more impressionable and therefore make easy targets for the Devil" (2001, p. 95). Women's insatiable lust made them evil and urged them into relationships with the devil.

Women out of the "control" of men—widows and single women—were considered especially likely to succumb to the devil and witchcraft. Torture was often used to evoke a confession from the accused witch, which resulted in a high rate of confessions.

But Noonan's work goes beyond documenting a historical period of extremism. She makes important links between historical patterns of viewing women's sexuality and the ways in which women are viewed in the criminal justice system. Noonan states, "Variations upon the theme of woman as temptress have been among the most powerful and pervasive in legal discourse. It finds expression particularly in rape and child custody cases. The evil of women threatening to consume or otherwise destroy children is deployed in debates around abortion, infanticide, and in child-welfare statutes that problematize women's failure to protect children or provide adequate nurturance in the face of male violence" (2001, p. 117). In these debates "good women" stand up to oppose abortion, condemn "bad mothers," and seek to rescue their fallen sisters from themselves.

Feminist theories of crime have sought to address the woman-as-bad, woman-as-mad conceptualizations of criminalization. In this process, feminist theories have called into question all gendered stereotypes about gender and crime by highlighting the critical consideration of social and cultural location. As a result, feminist theories have made several achievements in relation to women and crime. First, they have started to address the "systematic neglect of women/gender in criminological theory" (Hannah-Moffat & Shaw, 2000, p. 12). Second, they have explored women's everyday lives to understand women's offences and power relations, gender as an issue of social control, and ways that women experience the criminal justice system (Hannah-Moffat & Shaw, 2000, p. 13). Third, they have challenged the gendered and oppressive nature of both family and criminal law. These challenges are not easy, since women are diverse in their socio-cultural positions, thus making theorizing about "woman" as a category extremely difficult (Hannah-Moffat & Shaw, 2000, pp. 13–14). Statistics Canada shows some of the distinctions between men and women in the context of crime:

- In 2004, women made up 18 percent of adults charged with criminal offences.
- In 2004, 32 percent of adult women were charged with a property offence compared with 22 percent of men.
- Men are more likely to be charged with break and enter than women.
- Women are more likely to be charged with theft under $5000 or fraud than men.
- For both men and women, assault constitutes the majority of violent charges.
- Women are charged with 11 percent of robberies and only 2 percent of sexual assaults.
- Women make up 15 percent of those charged with drug offences.

INDIVIDUAL DIMENSION: GOOD GIRLS, AND BOYS WILL BE BOYS

Theories about crime have often differed for men and for women, based on notions of the "good girl" and "bad boy." This section focuses primarily on women, for the most part, because women as criminals have been problematized in a manner that sees their behaviour as somehow being exceptional. This notion of exceptionality is as problematic for men as it is for women, because concomitantly the theory normalizes crime among men. Thus, curiously, while most theories of criminal behaviour have been based on men, their maleness is rarely a focus of study.

Because of notions of the "good girl," society has tended to treat women's behaviours that seem to violate social norms as mental illness, rather than as crime. The same behaviours in men are more likely to be treated as criminal behaviour. Hilary Allen's (1987) classic study of cases processed in Britain gives interesting insight into this phenomenon. She documents a case in which a man and a woman, both middle-aged, black, and unemployed, carried out a robbery together. They were jointly charged, tried, and convicted. For both suspects, a psychiatric report was prepared. The woman was found to have no psychiatric illness; but the man was reported to have a "considerable" psychiatric history, as well as evidence that he suffered from a serious mental illness. However, despite the report's evidence that the woman was not mentally ill, the court sentenced her to probation with the condition that she receives psychiatric treatment; while the man, who had been diagnosed with mental illness, was sentenced to two years in prison. Allen's research details the discursive production of decision-making processes that go to "working up" a woman as mentally ill. In other words, mental illness is constructed from bits of information that produce a file as textual proof of mental illness. This file is often based on discretionary selection of facts. Allen focuses on the power relations that produce medico-legal decisions. She argues that "the pattern of sexual discrepancy is a product of the interaction of structure of medico-legal provisions and a structure of gendered understandings about the nature of human beings" (1987, pp. 116–17). Ultimately, Allen challenges a system that consistently criminalizes men and diagnoses women.

Kathy Kendall's (2000) work examines the treatment of women prisoners and their mental health issues within Canadian prisons. Kendall based her work on her experiences working in the corrections system. She presents women prisoners' descriptions of the pain of imprisonment and the negative impact of incarceration on therapy, rehabilitation, and emotional health. However, these experiences were translated into "evidence of the women's lack of ability to adjust to and with the prison environment. In shifting responsibility onto the women, not only were moral judgments being made about them, but the research was also depoliticized" (2000, p. 82). In other words, systemic issues were deflected back onto individual prisoners as their own pathologies. Kendall describes the difficulties she experienced trying to document the mental health treatment of women in prison. She includes a history of "medical" incidents, including the administration of LSD on an experimental basis in the 1960s, as a method of behavioural control (largely believed to have been done without consent or with coercive consent because of the circumstances under which it was given), as well as studies on drug addiction and pain intolerance, and one story of a hysterectomy performed to "rid a prisoner of her premenstrual tension" (2000, p. 88).

Kendall (2000, citing Motiuk & Blanchette, 1998) points out that the protocol used to determine women prisoners' health (and other) needs is "rife with moral judgments. For example, some of the indicators include: unemployment, 'family is unable to get along as a unit,' resides in a criminogenic area, has no credit, has used social assistance, takes risk inappropriately and has difficulty performing sexually" (2000, p. 91). If we consider the socio-economic circumstances in which many women who are criminalized find themselves, as well as the fact that many serious offenders have been sexually abused, we can begin to see the systemic individualization of gendered patterns.

In addition, women have also been conceptualized as the moral guardians of society, as if women were better than men at living within normative expectations. Women are thus less likely to be characterized as "criminal." However, when women "misbehave" in ways that are defined as criminal, they are more likely to be constructed as "bad." A Quebec Superior Court judge commented about a woman who had just been sentenced to life in prison for the second degree murder of her husband, "People say, and I believe it, that when they fall, women reach a level of baseness that the most vile man couldn't reach" (Boritch, 1997, p. 6, citing the *Edmonton Journal*). Women who offend are seen as being especially deviant, characterized as "monsters." The flip side for men is that we expect them to be criminal: in other words, male criminality is to some extent normalized.

Biological and psychological theories about women and crime construct women as weak-minded and passive; thus, women are seen as not being capable of masterminding criminal activities and are easily coerced into participating. Many people believe this way of thinking has largely died out, but the research of Kelly Hannah-Moffat (2004) indicates otherwise. She studied how parole boards make decisions to release female offenders and found that in assessing risk levels in relation to danger posed by the women on release, board members considered women's relationships with men. "The presence of men in these women's lives is often associated with an increased potential for violent recidivism. Given that board members often construct the men in women's lives as negative influences, women's relationships are heavily scrutinized." (2004, p. 372).

In many ways, the case of Karla Homolka epitomizes this type of approach. In 1995, she and her husband were convicted of murdering two young women after sexually assaulting and torturing them in the early 1990s. Homolka was and still is portrayed both as a victim and as womanly evil run amok. The courts have linked her criminality to the presence of her husband, Paul Bernardo, whom they considered the main offender, and she has therefore been ordered to stay away from all men with criminal records. Her involvement with a male prisoner while she was in prison has been reported by the media. Holmolka is especially problematic in the public imaginary because she is blonde and pretty and looks like "the girl next door." The problem is she participated in the torture and murder of young women while she was living *next door*. Moreover, to most people, she doesn't look like a criminal (think again about Sheldon's criminal body types). As Helen Boritch describes it, there was "little that was unusual or mysterious about Bernardo" (1997, p. 2). It was Homolka who presented the puzzle: how could a *woman* do such things?

The construction of women as sick and irrational has helped fuel this view of woman offenders, given that women have also fought for acknowledgment that their live experiences are different from the experiences of men. Thus **postpartum depression**, **premenstrual syndrome (PMS)** and **battered woman syndrome** reflect women's experiences, but also play into those notions of women as being somehow sick, deficient, or "less than" men. Women themselves come to think about who they are as women in these terms. The use of these defences and conditions as mitigating factors is thus a double-edged sword. While they acknowledge women's unique life experience, they also reify ideas about women that may not reflect the experiences of all women and contribute to women's inequality.

However, individual pathologization is inadequate for explaining the overrepresentation of Aboriginal men and women in the prison system. It is thus essential to consider socio-cultural context for a more complex analysis that employs a multilayered and intersectional approach.

SOCIO-CULTURAL DIMENSION OF CRIME

What is the socio-cultural context in which crime is defined and processed, and how is that context gendered? So far, this book has discussed gender in its socio-cultural context; but this section examines how culture works to frame the ways we perceive men's and women's "deviant" behaviour. Images of masculinity and violence form an important part of the socio-cultural context that expects men to be men. Socio-cultural context frames the ways in which men are encouraged to behave and to react. Similarly, women's anger and aggression is expected to be manifested (or not) in particular ways that do not include violence. Gendered messages impact on the construction of, reaction to, and punishment of criminal behaviour. The links are complex and not always clearly linear, but are subtle patterns of power relations that pose interesting challenges for social scientists who wish to map them.

As earlier chapters have explained, the media plays an important role in defining gender and its intersections. Media influence is particularly important for notions about women and crime. The media tends to focus on "dangerous women," who become the symbolic representation of all women who commit crime. This story angle misses the reality of criminalized women, most of whom are poor, have histories of abuse, and are most likely to be involved in the crime of shoplifting. Thus, the public comes to picture the criminalized woman in terms of Karla Homolka, rather than in terms someone who is socially disadvantaged. As Faith and Jiwani point out, "This phenomenon prompts fear, outcry, more aggressive prosecution of girls and women, harsher punishments for all women convicted of crime and a backlash against feminist and womanist movements" (2002, p. 84).

Faith and Jiwani also examine the "girl crisis" perpetuated by the media a few years ago. While rates of girl violence were steady or declining by statistical measures, the media focused on a few incidents of violence among girls to paint a picture of rising violence among young women. The case of Kelly Marie Ellard did little to offset this perception. In 2000, Ellard was convicted of killing Rena Virk, a 16-year-old girl who was taunted and assaulted by a group of young people, then followed by Ellard, beaten again to the point of unconsciousness, then held under water and drowned. Ellard acted with a male accomplice. Faith and Jiwani point out that one of the critical elements of the murder—the fact that Rena Virk was of South Asian origin—was left out. The intersection of race with gender in this case was largely omitted by the media, and, as Faith and Jiwani point out, by the courts as well. The titillation of the "girls gone wild" element of the case was the central focus for the media.

As Faith and Jiwani point out, much of the hype of "killer girls" was based on a single study that interviewed only six girls! The fact remains that data predominantly suggests that rates of violence among women and girls remain steady (as they do with men). Moreover, when rates of violence do occur, a closer examination reveals that it is the social response to these acts, rather than the actual frequency of incidents, that has shifted. Further, research has shown that "when girls and women are violent they are most commonly defending themselves or fighting back, with a man initiating the violence" (2002, p. 89). Isolated incidents cannot and should not be the basis on which we base "facts" about violence among women and girls, no matter how sensational they are.

What about assumptions about men and crime? As with women, poverty and race influence male criminality, with an overrepresentation of men from lower socioeconomic backgrounds in the criminal justice system, as well as Aboriginal men and men of colour. However, Comack *et al.* (2002) point out that messages about masculinity that are not linked to class or race influence the picture of men and crime. They argue that messages from the media, including violent films and games, define ways of being masculine. "Indeed, police reports are replete with cases of young men 'taking it outside' at the local bar to settle their differences with friends or acquaintances" (2002, p. 248). Comack *et al.* are critical of any approach that simplifies crime as "men as offenders" and "women as victims," arguing that such generalizations reify notions of women as "by nature nurturing, caring, and sensitive" and men as "assertive, aggressive, and competitive" (2002, p. 249). Drawing on Messerschmidt's notion of **hegemonic masculinity**, the authors argue that cultural messages translate differently depending upon social location. In other words, the ways that a man will translate masculine messages depends on whether he is poor, middle class, a person of colour, and so on.

INTERACTION DIMENSION

How do women and men act out their gender roles in the commission of crime in relation to the four dimensions of gender—the individual, interactional, socio-cultural, and institutional? Overemphasizing institutional and socio-cultural influences would be inaccurate: women and men also exercise agency in their identity negotiation which shifts gender roles and patterns. Moreover, gendered patterns influence how men and women interact with each other, but they don't determine those interactions. This may seem like a subtle distinction, but it is an important one. Thus, the interaction dimension is important in discussions of gender and crime.

In the 1970s, Freda Adler proposed an explanation of women's crime that prompted considerable debate. Adler's *Sisters in Crime* (1975) argued that women's liberation had triggered a corresponding shift in the rates of women's crime and in the way women committed crime. In her "liberation thesis," not only were women freed from the bonds of marriage, children, and economic dependence on men, but they were also free to commit crimes that had typically been thought of as "men's crimes." Women were moving outside of their traditional roles in all kinds of ways, argued Adler. She argued that the gap in rates of crime between women and men was rapidly declining because of "changes in traditional sex roles, greater equality for women and an increase in the female labour force" (Akers, 1997, p. 197). Adler's work was important for another reason: it essentially dismissed hormone-based theories of male aggression. Her argument emphasized a social rather than a biological explanation for crime (Boritch, 1997, p. 63).

Ultimately Adler's theory has not been proven in the thirty years since she first proposed it. The difference in rates between men and women has remained relatively stable, as is illustrated by Figure 15.1. Only a 4 percent increase in women charged with Criminal Code offences occurred between 1977 and 2004. This increase could be attributed to several causal factors, including poverty or increased prosecution of certain offences, rather than an actual increase in crime by women. Moreover, scholars have rejected the notion that there is a correlation between increased legitimate opportunities (*e.g.,* jobs) and increased illegitimate opportunities (*e.g.,* crimes) (Boritch, 1997, p. 65). The underlying logic of Adler's theory was also problematic, because it implied that women's freedom from the domestic sphere and their equality would lead to crime and to social chaos (Boritch, 1997, pp. 66–67). But despite the fact that Adler's thesis was unfounded, the media latched on to it and have replayed it in numerous variations ever since. Adler's work prompted research exploring the differences between men's and women's crime and its rates of commission. Her research played an important role in generating discussion about the socio-cultural context (the feminist movement) and the interactive aspect (how individual women act on their so-called freedom) of gender and crime.

John Hagan (1989) has developed another theory that incorporates a gender analysis focused on interaction. His "power-control" theory considers family structure and social class as keys to understanding how males and females are socially controlled. Egalitarian families (both mother and father are employed in the paid labour force) and patriarchal families (the father is the "head" of the household) have an impact on the delinquency patterns of the children. Hagan predicts that there will be greater gender differences in delinquent behaviour in patriarchal families (1989, p. 158). But as Akers points out, while Hagan's own data supports this thesis, other research has not been as conclusive. Moreover, his thesis is only predictive of girls' behaviour, not boys (Akers, 1997, p.199). Thus, research on the question of family impact on crime is not conclusive.

Prostitution is a fascinating example of the intersection of gender with social interactions. Some people argue that because prostitution is work, it should be decriminalized and regulated in a manner that would promote the safety and health of those who work in the trade. Others argue that prostitution is exploitative, and that everything should be done to prevent it, including the harsh imposition of penalties for prostitutes, their customers, and pimps. Prostitutes themselves have weighed in on this debate, calling for state intervention that enhances their work conditions but does not impede their ability to do their work. COYOTE (Call Off Your Old Tired Ethics—an organization based in the United States) as

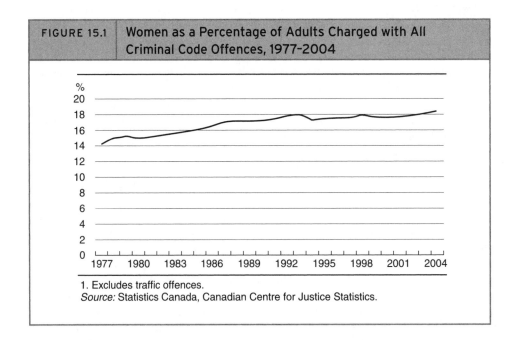

| FIGURE 15.1 | Women as a Percentage of Adults Charged with All Criminal Code Offences, 1977-2004 |

1. Excludes traffic offences.
Source: Statistics Canada, Canadian Centre for Justice Statistics.

well as GAATW (Global Alliance Against Trafficking in Women) are rights organizations that lobby for health benefits, decriminalization, and generally better working conditions for prostitutes. They argue that attempts to eliminate prostitution only serve to make working conditions more dangerous (Larsen, 2000, p. 56). Despite the gender-neutral wording of prostitution or "anti-solicitation" laws, it is widely argued that prostitution has been for the most part "fundamentally a female crime. As well, the moralist impetus for laws to control prostitution remained at the heart of statutes and of public perceptions of prostitution itself. Prostitutes were bad women, unless of course they were forced into prostitution, in which case they were the innocent victims of bad men" (Brock, 2000, p. 85). Gayle Mac-Donald and Lesley Jeffrey (2006) have conducted research on sex-trade workers in the Maritimes. They employ a sophisticated definition of sex work, addressing directly some of the problems raised by people who are unsupportive of such a characterization. "The useful term 'survival sex work' has been introduced by the sex-worker-run Prostitution Alternatives, Counselling and Education (PACE) Society to distinguish those prostitutes with less control over working conditions because of heavy addictions, for example. The term acknowledges that sex work is still work, and that workers would all benefit from better conditions, but that there are some for whom the job is more problematic than for others" (2006, p. 6).

Of course, men do work as prostitutes as well, but the majority of prostitutes are women who provide sexual services for men. And indeed, male prostitutes are predominantly selling their services to men. Note that the majority of research on prostitution has focused on the 'supply side" of this transaction, rather than on the "demand side." In other words, there has been only a limited focus on the gendered aspects of those who purchase sexual services.

INSTITUTIONAL DIMENSION

Gender remains relatively meaningless until we consider it as something that is *brought* to human interaction, either overtly and or subtly. Just as power is relational and situated in institutional contexts, so too is gender.

A. The Court Process

Institutional expectations about gender play out in relation to crime. These expectations take many forms: in fact, even the legal system itself is gendered, with an over representation of men in law enforcement, crown prosecutors, and judges (see also Chapter Thirteen). Key legal concepts are often gendered, sometimes without explicitly saying so. Consider the court's traditional use of the "reasonable man" criteria, as discussed in Chapter Thirteen. In general, two themes have dominated the treatment of women by the criminal justice system: one asserting that women have it harder than men, and another that asserts that women have it easier than men.

The argument that women are treated more harshly by the criminal justice system than are men is linked to the omnipresent dichotomous cultural binary in which women are often situated—as virgins or as whores, the good girl or the temptress/bad girl. When women "turn bad," they are monsters, and people expect that they should be treated as such. Alternatively, this way of thinking about women in the criminal justice system recognizes that women are less powerful than are men in our society and as such do not have the same resources to deal with crime. For the most part, data shows that there is little difference in the way women and men are treated by the criminal justice system.

However, more sophisticated analysis of particular legal situations, such as access to justice, challenges assumptions about women's equality before the law. **Legal aid** illustrates how women and men have different access to justice. When a person is charged with a criminal offence, he or she is considered innocent until proven guilty. Have you ever thought about how you might defend yourself if you were accused of a criminal offence? Since the majority of people charged with crimes come from lower and middle socio-economic backgrounds, they need to consider the costs of access to justice. How many of us have several thousand dollars to pay for legal services to defend ourselves if we are charged with a criminal act? The defence of more serious crimes may cost tens of thousands of dollars. Legal aid—the provision of financial assistance for such a defence by the state—is available only for more serious matters and is based on income and assets. Certainly, both impoverished men and women are disadvantaged under this system if they are charged with a less serious offence. However, because the majority of women who commit criminal offences are charged with relatively minor offences that are not eligible for legal aid assistance, women are disproportionately disadvantaged for legal aid. The solution to this problem is not for women to commit more serious offences, but for legal aid to be more readily available for a wider range of offences.

The gendered aspects of legal aid become even more complex when we consider domestic legal aid. **Domestic legal aid** is legal aid for the resolution of separation and divorce issues. Patricia Hughes (1995) argues that women have a greater need for domestic legal aid than do men, and thus the state's failure to support domestic legal aid is a matter of gender inequality. Hughes puts it this way: "Men receive the assistance of the state in defending their abuse of women, while women receive less assistance fending off the abuse or removing themselves from it" (1995, p. 206). Access to justice is a gendered issue that intersects with class and race to mean that often those who most need the legal system cannot access it.

The second theme about women and crime is the *chivalry paternalism thesis*, which argues that the criminal justice system treats women less harshly. "This hypothesis proposes that predominantly male police, prosecutors, and judges have a traditional, chivalrous attitude toward women and extend this attitude even to women offenders; therefore, they treat them with more leniency than men" (Akers, 1997, p. 191). The "paternalism" part of this thesis is the argument that has emerged from the feminist critique that chivalry and paternalism are not the same thing, and that a "father knows best" attitude can actually result in harsher penalities for women as they are conceptualized as having violated the "submissive" roles women are supposed to enact (1997, p. 191). There is some evidence to support this contention, as Kelly Hannah-Moffat's (2004) research on parole boards discussed below shows.

B. Prisons and Parole

Women make up only a small percentage of the Canadian inmate population. There are only a handful of federal prisons for women, while there are 45 for men. Until the 1990s, there was only one federal institution for women, located in Kingston, Ontario. The practical result of this was that any woman sentenced to federal imprisonment was often far away from her family and social support network. While women were sometimes permitted to serve their sentences in provincial institutions, provincial facilities and programs were not as extensive as the federal prison.

Women make up only about 2 percent of federally sentenced offenders. To understand this statistic more fully, keep in mind only those people sentenced to two years or more serve their time in federal prison. Sentences under two years are served in provincial jails. "The small number of women receiving a prison sentence, compared with men, reflects the less serious nature of their offending as well as incidence of offending overall" (Correctional Service of Canada, 2006). Repeated sentencing for women tends to be for offences related to drinking, property crimes, and prostitution (Correctional Service of Canada, 2006). Women are also much less likely than men to have a prior criminal record. "Three out of every 10 are admitted for failure to pay a fine; others are admitted for breaches of court orders or probation orders that do not involve a further offence. Overall, their offences involve fairly minor infractions and present little threat to public safety" (Correctional Service of Canada, 2006). Note that for men, the picture is similar: many of those who serve time in prison are there for relatively minor offences.

Correctional Service of Canada notes that men and women in prison have similar profiles, but there are several key differences. First, women generally have fewer economic resources than their male counterparts. Second, women in prison are even less likely than men to be able to earn a living after release. Third, women inmates tend to have more responsibility for children than do men. Finally, "They are also more vulnerable to the effects of alcohol and drugs, tend to have more physical health problems, and are more likely to have experienced both physical and sexual abuse" (Correctional Service of Canada, 2006). But both women and men suffer ill effects from imprisonment that only exacerbate their often-disadvantaged position in society (see Morris, 1995).

Kelly Hannah-Moffat's (2004) study of parole board decision-making illustrates the institutionalization of what she calls "gendered risk frames" to determine eligibility for parole. She found that a number of *gendered knowledges* operate simultaneously in this process. She quotes one of the people board members she interviewed: "There is a sense in many of these cases that the women are not ever really encouraged to take responsibility for their behaviour—I get the feeling that they are encouraged to consider themselves as victims in some way—and along with that goes an inability to accurately name what their risk issues are and take responsibility for addressing the issues. We expect that from the men but some how for the women it does not seem to be a focus" (2004, p. 367). Hannah-Moffat concludes, "Parole board members' normative gendered risk frames target women's identities in a way that simultaneously infers responsibility, choice, and the capacity to change. The notion of taking responsibility for offending, as well as stereotypical and dichotomous construction of the passive versus resistant victim, conflate freedom and agency—they equate the capacity to choose one's actions without external constraints with the power to act" (2004, p. 381).

In addition, institutionalized women are often held to a different standard then are men in a similar position. Faith and Jiwani note that women who are labeled "dangerous" in prison are often simply unco-operative. Of the two women who have been labeled dangerous offenders in Canada, neither has killed anyone. "Men require much more serious criminal histories, usually involving rape and/or murder, before being designated a dangerous offender" (2002, p. 91). Moreover, Allen's arguments that women tend to be labeled mentally ill is relevant for describing life for women inside prisons.

Another institutionally gendered issue intersects with the broader problem of the over-representation of First Nations peoples in prisons. In 2006, First Nations women made up 83 percent of the female prison population in Canada. Why is this? It is not because they are "more criminal"; rather, the unique combination of disadvantages faced by First Nations peoples contributes to their over representation in Canadian prisons. Here the socio-cultural dimension explicitly intersects with the institutional: we cannot consider the over representation of First Nations peoples within the prison system without considering their socio-cultural position. **Systemic disadvantages** rather than individual action is the most important explanatory variable. Systemic disadvantages refer to poverty, the reservation system, substance abuse, and poor education, as well specific systemic disadvantages within the criminal justice system, including negative application of discretion by police.

Students from white middle-class backgrounds sometimes have difficulty understanding the complicated ways in which systemic disadvantage intersects with individuals' lives, especially regarding serious crimes. Like using the phrase "white middle-class," making assumptions about individuals because they belong to a disadvantaged group requires caution. Group identification should not preclude an acknowledgment of the many textures of lived experience. Nonetheless, systemic disadvantage needs to be acknowledged and accounted for. Many books narrate the ways that such disadvantages become insurmountable obstacles, such as in Elizabeth Comack's *Women in Trouble* (1996) and Rudy Wiebe and Yvonne Johnson's *Stolen Life: The Journey of a Cree Woman* (1999). Comack's work is not exclusively centred on Aboriginal women, but Aboriginal stories are certainly an important part of her work. Comack argues, "We cannot fully grasp their lives without maintaining a sensitivity to the historical forces which have shaped contemporary aboriginal communities: the processes of colonization; of economic, social, and political marginalization; and of forced dependency upon a so-called 'benevolent' state" (1996, p. 122). *Stolen Life* (1999) follows the life of one Cree woman, Yvonne Johnson. The book begins with her letter from prison to Rudy Wiebe and then documents the harsh reality of her life, which includes sexual assault, abuse, and the circumstances of her first-degree murder conviction. Her story is not presented as an "excuse" for any wrongdoing on her part, but rather gives a contextualizing account of the human potential and harsh reality of her situated-ness as an Aboriginal person. Yvonne shows how the Canadian prison system has become part of "normal" for many First Nations people—a reality that is gendered for First Nations women.

Patricia Monture-Angus (2000) writes about the shift from Aboriginal culture to a Corrections Canada mentality that has gradually taken place at the Okimaw Ohci Healing Lodge in Saskatchewan, which happens to be the facility in which Yvonne Johnson is currently serving the latter part of her sentence. Akomaw Ohci is supposed to be an Aboriginal-centred facility. But Monture-Angus states bluntly, "I did not experience an Aboriginal place or space" (2000, p. 53). She is critical of the failure of the Corrections Canada to continue to involve or incorporate the local Nehaneet First Nations Cree community in this institutional attempt to use Aboriginal culture and traditions to heal Aboriginal women offenders. The (medium) security designation of the Lodge has worked to exclude many Aboriginal women, who are often sentenced to minimum security, and is based on "risk management" principles that Monture-Angus argues are "contrary to how I was raised as an Aboriginal person to think about relationships" (2000, p. 56). Finally, Monture-Angus points out that a focus on the Aboriginal offender for their wrongdoing and healing can divert attention from the more important issue of systemic racism.

Finally, as Chapter Thirteen already discussed, some of aspects of the legal system see women only as victims of crime. The virgin-whore dichotomy in the *Ewanchuk* case shows institutional rejection of the day-to-day realities of women's lives. Because of institutional moral views and gendered notions, sex-trade workers are often left without legal protection as they are portrayed as somehow "deserving it" when they are sexually or otherwise assaulted. Women are not the only excluded victims in the sex trade, for men engaged in sex work also face a double stigma of performing sexual services for same-sex customers as well as "deserving it." In effect, male sex-trade workers face a third stigma, because scripts about masculinity suggest that not only does one not have sex with men, but also that a "real man" can defend himself.

CONCLUSION

The example of crime provides some interesting insight into the ways that gender plays out in our society and in our cultural motifs. Individuals bring their own conceptualizations of who they are as men and women into their actions, which sometimes motivates them to commit crimes. But these individual conceptualizations shape and are shaped by socio-cultural sedimentations about gender, including expectations about how women and men should behave. In addition, these notions play out in the interaction of women and men, which produce and reproduce cultural and social patterns.

Gendered patterns are also embedded in institutions, including the very composition of law enforcement and processing agencies (police, judges, and probation officers), as well as the services offered to women and men in prison. But institutional patterns can shift. They do not represent a cultural straitjacket but rather are fluid and flexible. Changing family forms, legal shifts in marriage laws and sexual prohibitions, and workforce trends show that gender patterns can change. For many people, institutional forms do not change quickly enough to reflect notions of equality. For others, change is frighteningly rapid.

Perhaps most striking is the fact that crime and gender cannot be easily separated from poverty, race, and ethnicity. These intersections mean that any theories about crime must take into account patriarchy and its impact, as well as the ways that power relations replay racialized sedimentations and reify poverty. Gender is not an isolated concept that can be carved off and examined in any meaningful way apart from its context. For social scientists, the challenge is to think about gender on multiple levels when studying society and the way it works.

CHAPTER SUMMARY: KEY POINTS

1. Theories of crime should take into account and problematize gender differences. At the same time, women and men often commit crime from similar socio-cultural locations of poverty.

2. While most theories of crime are based on male behaviour, very few of them actually consider gender or maleness as an important concept

3. Media portrayals and popular beliefs about crime still employ gendered notions of who commits crime and why. Society still expects criminals to be male. To some extent, our society normalizes male criminal behaviour.

4. Female criminals are more likely to be characterized as abnormal than are male criminals.

5. Male criminals are more likely to be characterized as being criminal rather than as mentally ill, while women are more likely to be characterized as mentally ill rather than criminal.

6. Aboriginal men and women are over represented in the Canadian criminal justice system.

7. While gender is an important focus in theories about crime, it cannot be easily separated from poverty, race, and ethnicity.

8. Access to legal aid is limited to serious crimes, which leaves both women and men unable to defend themselves when charged with a lesser criminal offence.

9. The *chivalry paternalism thesis* holds that women are either treated more leniently by the law when they are charged and convicted of criminal offenses, or they are treated much more harshly because they have stepped outside of cultural expectations. They are viewed as either innocents caught up in the actions of others or as aberrations from womanhood.

10. Crime, prosecution, and punishment combine with gendered notions to determine how men and women will be defined and treated as criminals.

DISCUSSION QUESTIONS

1. Why is it important to distinguish between men and women when theorizing about crime?

2. Would you be able to pay for a defence if you were wrongly accused of a criminal offence?

3. Why do you think Canada has one of the highest rates of incarceration in the Western world?

4. As a society, how could be better meet the needs of women and men who are charged with a crime?

5. Why do you think it is predominantly men who are charged and convicted of crimes related to sexual assault and child pornography?

6. Do you think prostitution should be eliminated or regulated?

KEY TERMS

battered woman defense	hegemonic masculinity	power sedimentations
battered woman syndrome	legal aid	premenstrual syndrome
domestic legal aid	postpartum depression	systemic disadvantages

Glossary

Abandonment An approach that argues that organized religion is so fundamentally patriarchal that there is no possibility of transforming it into an institution that empowers women or accords them equal status. This approach advocates abandoning organized religions.

ADHD (Attention Deficit Hyperactivity Disorder) A developmental disorder or condition characterized by hyperactive behaviour and learning difficulties.

Adulthood A stage of life that marks the end of adolescence and the beginning of the second phase of life. The markers of entry into adulthood are socially constructed and vary from culture to culture.

Affirmative action A legal mechanism for correcting past wrongs related to discrimination based on sex, race, or dis/ability.

Agency The power of human beings to act freely.

Agentic/communal dichotomy The opposition of normative expectations for men and women. Men are supposed to be agentic (active, instrumental), and women communal (nurturing and empathetic).

Agents of socialization People and groups in a child's environment who have the greatest effect on socialization, including family, peers, and schools.

AIDS (Acquired immune deficiency disorder) A viral illness of the immune system. In the early 1980s and into the 1990s, there was no effective treatment for AIDS. Developments in drug effectiveness have meant that an AIDS diagnosis does not necessarily mean death, although the drugs have life-changing side effects.

Alpha bias The policy of refereed journals that posits that studies chosen for publication should make a valuable contribution to the knowledge base. Studies that do not make discoveries (*e.g.*, finding significant sex differences) are not seen as making the requisite contribution. Thus, refereed journals are biased toward proving trends and differences, rather than disproving them.

Ambiguous genitalia The term used to describe the genitals of intersexed persons, combining a mixture of male and female characteristics.

Apartheid The legally entrenched system of segregation or discrimination on grounds of race in force in South Africa between 1948 and 1991.

Backlash An adverse reaction to a social change from people who prefer the status quo. In the case of education, there is a backlash against curriculum changes to diminish sexism against girls, since these changes are seen to disadvantage boys. In the case of feminism, it refers to the belief that equality has already been achieved and there is no need for further concern or attention to issues of gender equality.

Battered woman defence The expansion of the notion of self-defence to account for the unique circumstances of women who are abused by their husbands or partners.

Battered woman syndrome A condition caused by prolonged domestic abuse at the hands of a partner. Sufferers become depressed and feel unable to escape their abuse.

Between-group variation The difference in the average scores and distributions of a measured variable between two identified groups.

Beauty bias The social advantages of attractive people over unattractive people. From infancy through adulthood, good-looking people receive better treatment in society.

Beauty myth Intense pressure on women to conform to particular appearance standards, despite the women's movement's efforts to gain women freedom from narrowly defined roles. Some women spend so much effort on appearance that they have little energy left for developing their other potentials.

Blended family   A family in which one or both spouses have children from previous unions or children from the current union and children from previous unions.

Blurred exit   A retirement process involving at least two changes in labour force status over 24 months: for example, a bridge job which spans the end of a person's main career prior to full retirement creates a blurred exit.

Bois   Androgynous biological females whose gender identity is fluid.

Boy turn   A notion in education that suggests that the educational system has been restructured to remove discriminatory components that disadvantaged girls and now it is the "boys' turn". Changes in resources and classrooms are necessary to enable boys to reach their full academic potential.

Causality   The proven relationship between a cause and an effect. Causality is dependent upon three criteria: a consistent pattern; a consistent time order; and lack of an alternate explanation.

Charter of Rights and Freedoms   Part of the Constitution of Canada formed in 1982, which replaced the Canadian Bill of Rights. The charter's intention is to support the rights and freedoms of Canadian citizens from the actions of the government and agencies of Canada. It protects against discrimination based on ascribed characteristics including sex, age, race, and sexual orientation.

Childfree   A strategic use of a terminology to reshape childlessness as a positive state.

Chilly climate   Challenges and hostilities women and minorities sometimes face in the paid workplace. Overt sexism, harassment, and subtle micro-inequities create an unwelcoming and discriminatory working environment.

Chronological aging   Measuring age by the passage of calendar time, not accounting for individual health factors.

Cognitive development theory   A theory suggesting that thinking skills develop sequentially through a series of stages. Children's understandings of themselves as gendered beings are shaped by their stage of development. Cognitive development is a self-socialization process in the sense that once children acquire knowledge of gender, they strive to behave in gendered ways.

Common-Law Unions (CLU)   Legally recognized unions by two adults who form a long-term, intimate relationship without participating in a legal or religious ceremony.

Comparative act   Adolescents assess their "selves" by measuring themselves against their peers. By socializing with peers, they gain insight into the possibilities and the social consequences of various actions.

Content analysis   A measurement technique for examining specific messages encoded in the media. It typically involves identifying and counting the number of specific images or messages that occur.

Correlation   A mutual relationship between two things or events that may or may not be causal.

Counterhegemonic acts   Acts of resistance that challenge the hegemonic order or the status quo.

Covert intimacy   Intimacy expressed through joking behaviour, physical gestures, and/or reciprocal assistance, rather than through open affection or self-disclosure.

Crisp exit   A retirement strategy through which workers end their main economic activity and do not re-enter the paid workforce.

Cults   Pejorative term to describe new religious movements to emphasize their "dangerous" nature.

Cultivation theory   A theory suggesting that consistent yet restricted media messages construct a distorted portrait of the social world that influences the viewers' attitudes and beliefs. The more media audiences consume, the more likely they are to cultivate these beliefs.

Cultural feminism   A strand of feminist theory that argues that women have unique and valuable characteristics that should be celebrated.

Culture/Conduct   Conceptual model that explains change in normative expectations and behaviours. Essentially, these two components must shift for social change to occur, but they rarely evolve simultaneously. In some cases our ideas (culture) change before our actions (conduct) and in others the reverse is true. For example, mothers entering the paid labour force marked a shift in conduct that occurred prior to the cultural acceptance of this practice.

Decentring law   A strategy proposed by Carol Smart to avoid using the law as a mechanism for problem solving. For example, victims of sexual assault can seek healing through the services of sexual assault centres rather than through formal legal proceedings.

Decoding   Reception and interpretation of media messages by the individual audience member.

Deficit relationship   A term sometimes used to describe men's friendships. This notion of deficiency is based on the idea that men are less interested in or able to disclose emotions or reveal personal information.

Difference approach   An approach to equality that takes into account differences between women and men.

Diminutives   A form of linguistic sexism whereby suffixes are added to nouns to distinguish one group from the main group, thereby devaluing that group in comparison (for example, hero*ine*, act*ress,* and comedien*ne*).

Discrimination   Differential treatment of a person or group based on their membership in a social category rather than on individual qualities or merits. Sexism is a particular kind of discrimination that valourizes men over women.

Discursive frameworks   Ways of organizing knowledge that produce "truths" or "facts."

Division of labour   The organization of people into separate but integrated activities of production or reproduction. The gender-based division of labour in traditional families involved men working outside the home for pay and women working inside the home without being paid.

Domestic legal aid   Financial assistance to pay for legal services to settle matters related to divorce or separation, including child support, child custody, access, and spousal support.

Dominant/preferred meaning   One way of decoding media messages based on perceptions of the intended meaning created by the encoders. The dominant meaning typically reflects the mainstream cultural order.

Dramaturgical analysis   A means of studying social interaction using terms and concepts drawn from theatrical performance.

Dual labour market   A theory suggesting that most occupations fall into one of two sectors: primary jobs that are well-paying, secure, and offer upward mobility to employees; and secondary jobs that tend to be low-paying, insecure, and have little room for advancement.

Earnings ratio   A comparison of the wages of two groups. The earnings ratio of women to men in Canada reveals that women still earn only approximately 70 percent of men's incomes.

Emphasized femininity   The dominant form of femininity in Western culture. It focuses on empathy, nurturance, and appearance, rather than on power or physical strength. This set of normative expectations reinforces gender inequalities because it encourages women to accommodate others' needs rather than pursuing their own.

Empirical research   Data gathered through direct observation, experiments, survey research, and/or experience.

Employment equity   Policies introduced in the 1980s that prohibited occupational discrimination against disadvantaged groups for hiring, promoting, and firing. It also ensured that employers would identify and eliminate barriers to employment for these groups.

Encoding   The creation of carefully structured media messages through scripting, editing, and posing. This is an integral part of the production of virtually every form of media.

Equal Rights Amendment (ERA)   A proposed amendment to the United States constitution that would have guaranteed that civil rights could not be denied on the basis of sex. Despite intensive lobbying efforts, it did not pass.

Essentialism   The making of assumptions about a group of people based on an identifying characteristic, such as *man* or *woman*. Essentialism assumes that all members of a group share the same characteristics, or that there is some unifying element to being *men* or *women*.

Eugenics   The scientific eradication of perceived human defects based on intellectual ability, race, or other factors.

Expressive role   In functionalist theory, the role of looking after the socio-emotional (expressive) needs of family members, historically relegated to women. Functionalist theory largely ignored the practical physical labour of women.

Face-to-face relationships   Friendships that involve sharing activities, talking together, and sharing intimate disclosures.

Feminine   A word used to describe qualities generally associated with women, including appearance and expressiveness.

Feminization of love   The historical process of transforming the notion of *love* into a quality associated with women. Open expressions of affection and disclosure of intimacies (more commonly associated with women's relationships) are considered loving, while practical assistance (more commonly associated with men's relationships) is not. This understanding is rooted in the separation of home and workplace and the resulting division of labour between women and men.

First wave of feminism   The women's movement of the late nineteenth and early twentieth centuries that focused on women's right to vote, own property, and participate in public life.

Formal curriculum   A set of subjects officially and explicitly taught to students in school.

Front stage/backstage   Concepts from dramaturgical analysis that suggest we are much more likely to manage our impression when we are on stage—in front of an audience—than when we are when in our personal space (backstage).

Gender   A system of social properties within society that constitutes people as different in socially significant ways and organizes relations of inequality on the basis of the difference.

Gender is sometimes also defined as personality traits and behaviour patterns, understood to correlate with sex-based differences.

Gender blenders   Women who choose not to conform to societal expectations of femininity. They are sometimes mistaken for men as their appearance conveys more masculine signifiers not contradicted by any feminine cues.

Gender constancy   The stage in cognitive development theory (usually at about five or six years of age) when children become aware that their gender is permanent and unchanging.

Gender depolarization   A process whereby the difference between the behaviour of elderly men and elderly women tends to become less polarized over time. Men may engage in activities or display emotions considered to be feminine, and women may exhibit patterns perceived to be masculine.

Gender identity   A person's sense of their self as a gendered person. Once considered to be a relatively stable property of all individuals, gender identity is now seen by many sociologists as a relational, situational, and fluid quality that intersects with other identities that shape the self.

Gender perspective   A term for the multi-dimensional approach to understanding gender patterns.

Gender polarization   The pervasive organization of social life around gender differences. Gender polarization refers to the exaggerated differences between masculine and feminine that pervade virtually every aspect of human experience, including roles, emotions, and appearance.

Gender regime   The many features of an institution that create, maintain, or undermine specific gendered practices.

Gender roles   A set of behavioral expectations based upon a person's perceived gender. These roles are perceived to influence the ways in which people are supposed to think, feel, appear, and behave.

Gender schema theory   A theory which states that children develop cognitive categories, or schema, to understand gender patterns beginning at a very early age. These schema become increasingly elaborate as children mature.

Gender sedimentations   Repeated patterns of gender relations. The term emphasizes that these patterns can change, but that they do exist to shape gender relations.

Gender socialization   A lifelong process of socialization through which people learn gender normative expectations. It also contributes to a person's gendered identity.

Gender strategy   A plan of action for creating workable arrangements (*e.g.*, the household division of labour) based on cultural and individual notions of gender.

Glass ceiling   An unacknowledged barrier to advancement within an occupation or profession, especially affecting women and members of minorities. The glass ceiling explains why there are very few women in positions of power in many occupations and professions.

Glass ceiling of age   Discrimination in the paid workplace, linking ageism with sexism, that limits women's opportunities to be hired or promoted relative to men of similar age.

Hegemonic femininity   A specific appearance-based version of femininity that privileges beautiful women over those who do not comply with the cultural ideal.

Hegemonic masculinity   The form of masculinity adopted by dominant cultural or group leaders. This type of masculinity oppresses those of any gender who don't conform to its standard.

Heteronormativity   A term referring to society's normative assumptions about heterosexuality and the way they are reinforced in societal institutions and policies.

Hidden curriculum   The values, norms, and beliefs that children learn in school that are not included in the formal curriculum.

Hierarchical power   A modernist conceptualization of power which views power as oppressive, held, and top-down.

Hierarchical relations   Heterosexual relationships where both adults believe that women should make the household their sole priority, and men should not be responsible for domestic activities.

Hijab   The headscarf sometimes worn by Muslim women.

Homemaker/breadwinner model   The division of labour between wives and husbands in the "traditional" family. The husband earns the income, and the wife manages the household.

Horizontal segregation   A pattern of occupational segregation that results in a concentration of men and women in different jobs: for example, most nurses are women and most engineers are men.

Hostile work environment   A legal term referring to situations where unwelcome sexual conduct is severe and/or pervasive enough to create a hostile, intimidating, or offensive work environment.

Human capital   The skill set, based on education, training, and experience, acquired by an individual that contributes to their value as an employee. Workplace experience is considered to be human capital while skills attained in non-paying activities, such as household management, are often discounted.

Human Rights Commissions   Provincial and federal agencies that guarantee that people are protected from discrimination. Most jurisdictions establish a commission to administer the rules and to hear complaints about rights violations.

Identity construction   The development of a sense of self during adolescence. A child's sense of self develops mainly through family interactions and expectations; but adolescents seek to recreate their own self-definition through interaction with peers and others.

Ideology of motherhood   A hegemonic position that regards motherhood as something that women should want and ultimately desire. It also includes the notion that women are primarily responsible for childcare. The ideology of motherhood assumes that mothering takes place in a heterosexual coupled setting.

Impression management   A term to describe the dramatic devices—appearance, props, mannerisms, and setting—people use to create a specific image.

Incorrigible male-female binary   A feature of many languages that positions people as belonging to one of *only* two sexes, for example, by providing only two pronouns: *he* and *she*.

Individual dimension   One dimension in the multi-level approach to understanding gender patterns, referring to the ways people as individuals learn to be gendered. The individual dimension also intersects with other identities, such as race and class.

Industrial Revolution   A shift from a primarily agriculture-based economy to a manufacturing economy. This transition created large-scale changes in social arrangements, including urbanization, a long-term rise in the standard of living, and growth of the middle class.

Informational power   Management of knowledge as an important facet of power.

Institutional dimension   One dimension in the multi-level approach to understanding gender patterns, referring to the ways that gender is organized in social institutions, such as the education system, law, government, the economy, and families.

Institutions   Normatively sanctioned social practices. In most cases, institutions evolve as societies find ways to cope with ongoing needs and concerns. Systems of government, economy,

and education are all part of these social coping mechanisms.

Institutional ethnography   A methodological approach developed by Canadian sociologist Dorothy Smith, which begins with the standpoint and voices of the oppressed, and then considers the organizing mechanisms of social structure in the shaping of their experiences.

Instrumental Role   In functionalist theory, the role of earning incomes and making decisions, historically held by men in families.

Intensified mothering   A cultural construction about motherhood based on the premise that being a mother is the most important undertaking of a woman's life. While men can and do parent, the normative expectation is for women to take primary responsibility for raising children. In effect, her obligation as mother is to devote all her resources to this task.

Interactional dimension   One dimension in the multi-level approach to understanding gender patterns, referring to the ways in which people do gender, including presentation of self and interaction with others.

Internalization   The degree to which an individual adopts cultural ideals. Internationalization is one of two factors that determine whether a viewer will be influenced by an encoded message.

Internalized oppression   The notion that women who spend a great deal of time, effort, and money to achieve cultural standards of beauty are striving to meet a patriarchal ideal and potentially harming themselves in the process. Women police themselves to meet an unachievable goal that does not earn true respect or power and may distract from other activities.

Intersectionality   The ways that people's lives intersect using a variety of points of identity, such as gender, race, class, ability, and sexuality.

Intersexed   A person whose body combines a mixture of male and female physical markers or reproductive organs. Empirical research suggests that 1.7 percent of humans do not fit fully within the male or female sex-typed categories.

Invisibility   In linguistics, masculine generic language conventions that focus on one sex, thereby minimizing or concealing others.

Labour force participation   People's paid work activities. In Canada, people who are unemployed but currently seeking work are also considered to be labour force participants.

LEAF   Legal Education and Action Fund for women.

Legal aid   Financial assistance from the state (*i.e.,* provincial government) to qualifying individuals to cover the cost of defending against criminal charges.

Legal method   The process by which law reaches decisions.

Legitimacy effect   In status expectations theory, gender-based expectations that lead people to evaluate the behaviour of others. Because men are held in higher esteem and are considered more rational and/or more assertive, they are seen to be legitimately deserving of opportunities. Women face more resistance when entering domains believed to be legitimately "masculine" because people believe they don't deserve to be there.

Liberal feminism   A branch of feminism that emphasizes inequality of opportunity. It is based on the argument that women have largely been excluded from positions of power in the workplace and social institutions.

Life expectancy   A statistical calculation of the number of years a person can expect to live, measured from a specific age. In Canada, life expectancy at birth is over 80 years.

Linguistic determinism   The notion that language determines the way people perceive and think.

Linguistic sexism   An umbrella term referring to the ways that language devalues women.

Lived religion   Religion as experienced by a practitioner in everyday life. For social science,

it is as important to study lived religion as it is to study religion at an organizational or ideological level.

Macro approach   An approach to studying society which focuses on larger structures that constrain and guide individuals.

Male-centred   A focus of attention upon the activities of men more so than on the activities of women.

Male-dominated   The prevalence of men in powerful positions in social institutions.

Male-identified   The influence of men and masculinity in defining what is considered to be normal and good.

Masculine   A word used to describe qualities associated with men, including dominance, assertiveness, competitiveness, and inexpressivity.

Masculine generic form   A language convention that uses masculine forms to include people of any sex. This convention was once entrenched in law, such that legal documents, using the terms man or he could actually refer to all people, regardless of their sex.

Maternity leave   A social policy that allows women freedom from their paying jobs to recover from childbirth and to care for their infants for a limited period of time. During this leave, they are eligible for income, and their job is guaranteed upon their re-entrance into the labour force.

Micro approach   An approach to research which seeks to understand social patterns through studying the actions and choices of individuals.

Micro-inequities   Barely noticeable patterns of communication and interaction that privilege one group over another. In the case of education, teachers who interact differently with girls and boys are engaging in micro-inequities.

Misery justice   "[M]isery justice always looks at ways of taking away from the one with more, not giving more to the one deprived. Thus misery justice never looks at improving the lot of the victims, but only victimizing offenders so they will be equally miserable" (Morris, 1995, p. 72).

Modeling   An element of social learning theory in which children learn by observing and imitating the roles and behaviours of others.

Mommy track   An arrangement (either formal or informal) that allows women to combine work and parenting responsibilities by forgoing promotions and pay raises to ensure that they may devote time to raising their children.

Mortality differential   A comparison of death rates between social groups, showing that some categories have higher or lower life expectancies than others (*e.g.*, women tend to live longer than men).

Mundane aspects of law   The everyday functioning of legal processes.

Nature *vs*. nurture debate   The debate which asks how much of who people are is predetermined by physiology and how much is created by social experiences.

Negotiated/resistant meaning   A contradictory method of decoding media messages wherein the viewer has the potential to adopt or oppose the dominant message. The viewer can see the dominant encoded meaning but can also see other possibilities.

New religious movements   Religious groups characterized by their small size and marginalization by society. Frequently they defy the mainstream in their conceptualization of sexuality, family arrangement, and interactions with the larger social whole. Many of these groups are not necessarily new, but were not previously seen in North America, and their congregations are largely composed of converts.

Normal curve   A statistical term for a symmetrical probability distribution (also called a bell curve) with the most common scores concentrated around the mean (average) and progressively less common scores occurring further from the mean.

Normative expectations   Elements of the socio-cultural landscape that guide our behaviour and our assessments of others. Gender-based normative expectations define cultural standards of masculinity and femininity.

Occupational segregation   The different locations of women and men in the paid labor force. Occupational segregation can be either horizontal (based on careers patterns) or vertical (based on positions of power).

Oppositional meaning   One way of decoding media messages, in which the viewer recognizes the dominant message but opposes it.

Overlapping normal curves   Two normal curves that overlap when a single variable is measured and graphed for two social categories (*e.g.*, men and women). The graph may reveal a difference in average scores and also the degree of similarity between groups.

Paternity leave   A social policy that allows men freedom from their paying jobs to care for their young children for a limited period of time. During this leave, they are eligible for income and their job is guaranteed upon their reentrance into the labour force.

Pathologized   Rendered into a disease or made to seem abnormal. The medical model has come to dominate much of social life and pathologizes sexual functioning in both men and women, which assumes that there is a "normal" against which we define the abnormal.

Patriarchal dividend   An often unnoticed advantage afforded to men because of the patriarchal elements within society. Because of status expectations and male dominance, the patriarchal dividend genders opportunities. Even men who do not oppress others still profit from this dividend.

Patriarchy   The hierarchical organization of a society, with males dominating most of the positions of power and wealth, while a disproportionate number of females fill subordinate positions with little wealth or control.

Pay equity   Policies designed to ensure that people doing work of equal value are paid similarly. Its purpose was to counter the common pattern in which occupations dominated by men were paid more highly than those dominated by women, even though the work was no more difficult and did not require more skill.

Peer arena   The social location where young people evaluate, model, imitate, experiment, critique, observe, and judge the people around them.

The personal is political   A slogan that emerged in the context of the second wave of feminism. It essentially meant that so-called private issues (such as violence against women in the home) were not private at all.

Persons Case   A famous 1929 court case in Canada which determined that women were considered *persons* under the law.

Physiological aging   Measuring age based on physical health and fitness, rather than on the passage of time.

Pink collar ghetto   Work typically associated with women that is low paying and has little opportunity for promotion and advancement.

Polyamorous relationships   Long-term relationships that are not monogamous.

Polygamy   Marriage in which there are two or more wives, or two or more husbands.

Postpartum depression   A form of depression experienced by some women after giving birth.

Power sedimentations   Patterns of power relations that recur over time and place.

Precedent   The use of previous court decisions to help guide judgments in subsequent related cases.

Prejudice   Assumptions based on unfounded judgments of others because of their group membership. Often prejudice can be adverse or irrational.

Premenstrual syndrome   Symptoms that may occur in some women preceding and during menstruation that can be both physical and emotional.

Primacy effect   The family's crucial role in socialization and a child's first learning experiences.

Primary sector jobs   In the dual labour market theory, jobs that are well-paying, secure, and offer the potential for upward mobility.

Primary socialization   The initial learning process that occurs in early childhood and arises from our first interactions with others.

Promise Keepers   A large Christian men's movement that encourages men to take on traditional family roles at the head of the household. It is strongly opposed to racism.

Psychosocial theory of adolescence   A theory which emphasizes the importance of peers, the peer arena, and comparative acts for identity construction and personal development during adolescence.

Race   A socially constructed term for human differences. Even though the term has no basis in biology, race is often used as an identifying characteristic, frequently in negative ways.

Radical feminism   A strand of feminism that focuses on oppression and patriarchy as the fundamental explanation for inequality.

Radical transformation   A strategy for dealing with patriarchy in organized religion. It focuses on solutions to meeting spiritual needs by developing woman-only spaces and by developing ways of transforming the needs of women into a more central focus.

Reasonable man   A legal assumption that all behaviour follows a male norm.

Reflection hypothesis   This theory that suggests that media messages do not shape society or influence audiences: they merely reflect the existing culture.

Reframing   A strategy for dealing with patriarchy within organized religion, involving reworking what may at first appearance seem like oppressive doctrine.

Reinforcement   From social learning theory, the process of rewarding certain behaviours and punishing or ignoring others. Gender behaviors are shaped through reinforcement as children are encouraged to follow stereotypical gender patterns.

Relational aggression   A type of aggression that uses gossip, rumour, and exclusion to harm others, rather than using direct or physical aggression.

Relational power   A postmodernist conceptualization of power that does not regard power as something that is held, but rather as something that is exercised.

Relationship experts   A term sometimes used to describe women's friendships because they are perceived to have more intimate relationships than men.

Reshaping   A strategy for dealing with patriarchy within organized religion that uses scriptural reinterpretation, ordination of women, and an opening of all roles within the church to women.

Retirement   An institutionalized pattern allowing older adults to permanently exit from paid employment.

Second wave of feminism   The revival of feminism and the women's movement in the 1960s and 1970s. Issues of concern included equal rights and reproductive autonomy.

Secondary sector jobs   In the dual labour market theory, those jobs that that tend to be low-paying, insecure and have little room for advancement.

Semantic derogation   The process through which meanings of words become more negative over time, reflecting dominant cultural values. A word that began as neutral (*e.g., mistress* as the lady of the house) developed negative connotations (*e.g., mistress* as a kept woman of ill-repute).

Separate spheres/co-operative relations
Heterosexual relationships where both adults believe that men and women should have separate priorities (paid work and domestic duties) but both believe that it is appropriate to help each other with these tasks: women contributing to the family income and men undertaking household chores.

Sex   Biological characteristics that are considered significant in distinguishing between males and females including the presence of ovaries or testes and external genitalia.

Sex role strain   The strain experienced by those who attempt to live up to the difficult-to-achieve sex roles set out by society.

Sex role   The historically accepted idea that men and women behave differently because of their biological capacities in concert with learned behaviour deemed appropriate for their sex.

Sexism   Discrimination, prejudice, or stereotyping based upon assumptions about a person's sex.

Sexual division of labour   A biologically justified division of labour. Because sex is believed to be biologically determined and static, the sexual division of labour is also seen as unchangeable, the "natural" outcome of biological differences.

Sexual harassment   Any unwelcome behaviour, sexual in nature, that adversely affects, or threatens to affect directly or indirectly a person's job security, working conditions, or prospects for promotion or earnings; or prevents a person from getting a job, living accommodations, or any kind of public service. Sexual harassment is usually an attempt by one person to exert power over someone else. It can be perpetrated by a supervisor, by a co-worker, by a landlord, or by a service provider.

Sexual orientation   One's sexual, emotional, or romantic interest in a person of the same or opposite gender.

Sexual power   The use of sexual favours to control situations.

Sexual territory   The association of certain locations of work with the sex of the dominant group of workers (women in the household and men in the paying workplace). A person's masculinity or femininity was measured by the individual's ability to perform well in that territory.

Sexuality   Sexual expression, including norms, identity, and performance.

Shared spheres/ changing relations Heterosexual relationships where both adults believe that women should have an equal right to pursue paid work opportunities. The two should be equal partners in all areas of life.

Side-by-side relationships   Friendship that involve sharing activities together rather than talking and sharing intimate disclosures.

Single-sex schools   A school exclusively for boys or for girls.

Slang   Informal and often group-specific language, more common in speech than writing.

Social aging   Social constructions and social experiences attached to the physiological and chronological reality of becoming old.

Social comparison   The degree to which we evaluate ourselves in comparison to others. Social comparison is one of the two factors that determine whether a viewer will be influenced by an encoded message.

Social construction   A theory that states that gender is not based on biological characteristics but is a result of social experience.

Socialist feminism   A strand of feminism that focuses on the intersection of sex and class to explain oppression. It argues that women are doubly disadvantaged because they are expected to undertake non-waged domestic labour, which hinders their earning capacity. Men are doubly privileged because someone else fulfills their domestic needs, and they are relatively free from the competition of women in primary sector jobs.

Social institutions   Stable, well-established patterns of social relationships that result from enduring ideas about how to accomplish specific goals. The education system is a social institution that has evolved to enable young people to develop their potential and learn the necessary tools to become productive members of their communities.

Social learning theory   A theory that suggests humans learn and develop through observation, modeling, and reinforcement.

Social support   Receiving tangible or emotional assistance as well as frequent communication and contact with others. Social support has a positive impact on both physical and emotional well-being.

Socialization   A process by which individuals develop selfhood and acquire the knowledge, skills, and motivations required for participation in social life.

Society of widows   A term used to describe the strong practical and social support networks which many widowed women share.

Socio-cultural landscape   A term to denote the sociological and cultural landscape in which all action occurs. It consists of values, norms, beliefs, and ideologies, and is transmitted through language and mass media.

Spoiled identity   A concept in dramaturgical analysis to describe qualities that may be judged as disreputable or undesirable. In some cases, people seek to manage their impression so that this stigma is hidden.

Spotlighting   A type of linguistic sexism whereby an adjective is added to a noun to identify the sex of an individual in an occupation that is commonly associated with the other sex (*e.g.*, a female judge or male nurse). Spotlighting provides additional information but reinforces the notion of differential positions for women and men.

Stalled revolution   The large-scale entrance of women into higher levels of education and the paid labour force without the necessary adjustments in domestic arrangements, social policies, and programs for working parents. This contradiction causes difficulties for parents, families, and communities.

Statistical significance   A condition in which the measured results found within a sample are likely to be reflective of the larger population. However, statistical significance does not imply that the finding is socially relevant: as a result, it should not be assumed to signify importance.

Status expectations theory   A theory which states that expectations of individuals differ based on the status ranking of the group to which they belong. These expectations are widely shared cultural beliefs that often lead people to value men over women because of their hierarchically ranked statuses.

Status expectations theory   A theory which states that people interact with awareness of the status of each other. If some people belong to a social group that it is considered to superior or inferior to the rest, all people involved in the interaction adjust their actions accordingly, even when status is not relevant.

Step family   A family which contains at least one child from a previous relationship of one of the adults.

Stereotype   Fixed, simplistic, often incorrect, and often negative ideas about the behaviours and characteristics of a social group.

Subculture   A unique cultural group within a larger culture, often having norms, values, or beliefs at variance with those of the larger culture in which it is embedded.

Systemic disadvantages   Socio-cultural factors that work to marginalize particular groups of people.

Third Wave Feminism   A shift in feminism in the 1990s with the recognition that being a woman intersects with other statuses, such as class, sexual orientation, and ethnicity. Thus, feminism now strives to address a broad spectrum of issues rather than narrowly defined "women's issues."

Token dynamics   Different treatment from that received by the majority of employees in a specific work environment, due to membership in a minority group.

Total fertility rate   A measurement of the average number of children born to women when they are between the ages of 15 and 49.

"Traditional" family   A family in which the division of labour is such that husbands earn the income and wives manage the household (also known has homemaker/breadwinner arrangement).

Transsexual   An individual whose gendered identity is contrary to the normatively assigned gender based upon biology.

Two worlds approach   A theory that suggests that women and men do gender differently in social interaction because they have been socialized to fit into different gendered worlds. Difference is not simply a case of gender performance and/or living up to expectations, nor is it even a case of overwhelming physiological sex-based differences; it is an enduring property of individuals arising from gender based socialization.

Vertical segregation   The separation of men and women into different levels of authority and pay in the labour force hierarchy. Men are more often found in higher-lever, better-paying positions.

Within-group variation   Variation that focuses on the range of values when measuring characteristics of an identified group.

Workplace disamenties   The characteristics of a workplace or activity that might make it undesirable. For example, extreme temperatures, noise, dirt, or odour make some jobs unpleasant.

References

Abercrombie, N., Hill, S., & Turner, B. (1984). *The Penguin Dictionary of Sociology* (2nd ed.) London: Penguin Books.

Adam, B.D. (2006). Relationship Innovation in Male Couples. *Sexualities, 9*(1), 5–26.

Adler, F. (1975). *Sisters in Crime: The Rise of the New Female Criminal.* Toronto: McGraw-Hill.

Akers, R.L. (1997). *Criminological Theories, 2nd Edition.* Los Angeles: Roxbury Publishing.

Allen, G. (2005, April 30). X Factor: Is the Art Market Rational or Biased? *The New York Times.*

Allen, H. (1987). *Justice Unbalanced: Gender, Psychiatry and Judicial Decisions.* Philadelphia: Open University Press.

Ammerman, N.T. (1987). *Bible Believers: Fundamentalists in the Modern World.* New Brunswick: Rutgers University Press.

Anderson, M.L. (2005). Thinking about Women: A Quarter Century's View. *Gender & Society, 19*(4), 437–55.

Arber, S., & Ginn, J. (1995). *Connecting Gender and Ageing: A Sociological Approach.* Philadelphia: Open University Press.

Aries, E. (1998). Gender Differences in Interaction: A Reexamination. In D. Canary & K. Dindia (Eds.), *Sex Differences and Similarities in Communication: Critical Essays and Empirical Investigations of Sex and Gender in Interaction* (pp. 65–81). Mahwah: Lawrence Erlbaum Associates.

Backhouse, C. (1999). *Colour-Coded: A Legal History of Racism in Canada, 1900–1950.* Toronto: University of Toronto Press.

Bailey, M., Baines, B., Amani, B., & Kaufman, A. (2006). Expanding Recognition of Foreign Polygamous Marriages: Policy Implications for Canada. *Status of Women Canada.* Retrieved from the World Wide Web: http://www.swc-cfc.gc.ca/pubs/pub-spr/0662420683/200511_0662420683-3_1_e.html

Baltes P.B., & Mayer, K.U. (Eds.). (1999) *The Berlin Aging Study: Aging from 70 to 100.* New York: Cambridge University Press.

Bankey, R. (2001). La Donna é Mobile: Constructing the Irrational Woman. *Gender, Place & Culture: A Journal of Feminist Geography, 8*(1), 37–54.

Bartkowski, J.P. (2003). *The Promise Keepers: Servants, Soldiers, and Godly Men.* New Brunswick: Rutgers University Press.

Bartky, S. (1998). Foucault, Femininity, and the Modernization of Patriarchal Power. In R. Weitz (Ed.). *The Politics of Women's Bodies: Sexuality, Appearance and Behaviour* (pp. 25–45). New York: Oxford University Press.

Beaman, L. (1996). Legal Ethnography: Exploring the Gendered Nature of the Legal Method. *Critical Criminology, 7*(1), 53–74.

——— (1998). Women's Defences: Contextualizing Dilemmas in Difference and Power. *Women & Criminal Justice, 9*(3), 87–115.

——— (1999). *Shared Beliefs, Different Lives: Women's Identities in Evangelical Context.* St. Louis: Chalice Press.

———— (2000). (Ed.) *New Perspectives on Deviance: The Construction of Deviance in Everyday Life*. Scarborough: Prentice Hall Allyn and Bacon Canada.

———— (2001). Molly Mormons, Mormon Feminists and Moderates: Religious Diversity and the Latter-Day Saints Church. *Sociology of Religion, 62*(1), 65–86.

———— (2004). Church, State and the Legal Interpretation of Polygamy in Canada. *Nova Religio, 8*(1), 20–38.

Beaujot, R. (2000). *Earning and Caring in Canadian Families*. Peterborough: Broadview Press

Beaujot, R., & Liu, J. (2005). Models of Time Use in Paid and Unpaid Work. *Journal of Family Issues, 26*(7), 924–46.

Beaujot, R., & Ravanera, Z. (2005). Family Models for Earning and Caring: Implications for Child Care. *University of Western Ontario, Population Studies Centre*, Discussion Paper May, 2001. Retrieved from the World Wide Web: http://www.ssc.uwo.ca/sociology/popstudies/dp/dp05-01.pdf

Beaumeister, R., & Leary, M. (1995). The Need to Belong: Desire for Interpersonal Attachments as a Fundamental Human Motivation. *Psychological Bulletin, 117*, 497–529.

Becker, G.S. (1981). *A Treatise on the Family*. Cambridge: Harvard University Press.

Belsky, J. (2001). Aging. In J. Worell (Ed.) *Encyclopedia of Women and Gender: Sex Similarities and Differences and the Impact of Society on Gender* (pp. 95–107). San Diego: Academic Press.

Bem, S. (1993). *The Lenses of Gender: Transforming the Debate on Sexual Inequality*. New Haven: Yale University Press.

Bennion, J. (1998). *Women of Principle: Female Networking in Contemporary Mormon Polygymy*. Oxford: Oxford University Press.

Berger, H. (2005). *Witchcraft and Magic: Contemporary North America*. Philadelphia: University of Pennsylvania Press.

Berger, H., Leach, E.A., & Shaffer, L.S. (2003). *Voices from the Pagan Census. A National Survey of Witches and Neo-Pagans in the United States*. Columbia: University of South Carolina Press.

Berger, J. (1972). *Ways of Seeing*.
Hammondsworth: Penguin.

Berk, S.F. (1985). *The Gender Factory: The Apportionment of Work in American Households*. New York: Plenum.

Bernard M., Itzen, C., Phillipson, C., & Skucha, J. (1995). Gendered Work, Gendered Retirement. In S. Arber & J. Ginn (Eds.), *Connecting Gender and Ageing: A Sociological Approach* (pp. 56–68). Philadelphia: Open University Press.

Bernard, J. (1981). The Good-Provider Role: Its Rise and Fall. *American Psychologist, 36*(1), 1–12.

Bernhardt, E. (2005). *No, We Should Not Worry about the Future of Europe's Population*. Paper presented at Meetings of the International Union for the Scientific Study of Population, France, July 2005.

Bernier, C., Laflamme, S., & Zhou, R. (1996). Le travail domestique: tendances à la désexisation et à la complexifaction. *Canadian Review of Sociology and Anthropology, 33*(1), 1–21.

Biggs, S. (1999). *The Mature Imagination: Dynamics of Identity in Midlife and Beyond*. Buckingham: Open University Press.

Blackwell, J. (1998). Making the Grade against the Odds: Women as University Undergraduates. In J. Stalker & S. Prentice (Eds.), *The Illusion of Inclusion* (pp. 60–71). Halifax: Fernwood Publishing.

Blaubergs, M.S. (1980). An Analysis of the Classic Arguments against Changing Sexist Language. *Women's Studies International Quarterly*, 3, 135–47.

Blumstein, P., & Schwartz, P. (1983). *American Couples: Money/Work/Sex*. New York: Willian Morris.

Boonzaier, F., & de La Rey, F. (2003). 'He's a Man, and I'm a Woman' Cultural Constructions of Masculinity and Femininity in South African Women's Narratives of Violence. *Violence Against Women*, 9(8), 1003–29.

Borisoff, D., & Hahn D. (1995). From Research to Pedagogy: Teaching Gender and Communication. *Communication Quarterly, 43*, 381–93.

Boritch, H. (1997). *Fallen Women: Female Crime and Criminal Justice in Canada*. Toronto: Nelson Canada.

Bountiful Women Defend Polygamy: 'Silent no more': Wives allow unprecedented peek at lifestyle. *National Post* (21 April 2005), A3.

Bowlby, J. (1969). *Attachment and Loss*. New York: Basic Books.

British Columbia Human Rights Commission, (2001). *Factors Affecting the Economic Status of Older Women in Canada*. Retrieved from the World Wide Web: http://www.llbc.leg.bc.ca/public/PubDocs/bc-docs/344377/MandatoryRetirementReport.pdf

Brock, D. (2000). Victim, Nuisance, Fallen Woman, Outlaw Worker? Making the Identity, Prostitute, in Canadian Criminal Law. In D.E. Chunn & D. Lacombe (Eds.), *Law as a Gendering Practice*. Don Mills ON: Press Gang Publishers.

Brockman, J. (2001) *Gender in the Legal Profession: Fitting or Breaking the Mold*. Vancouver: UBC Press.

Brooks, B., Jarman, J., & Blackburn, R. (2003). Occupational Segregation in Canada 1981–1996. *Canadian Review of Anthropology and Sociology, 40*(2), 197–213.

Browne, I., & Misra, J. (2003). The Intersection of Gender and Race in the Labor Market. *Annual Review of Sociology, 29*(1), 487–513.

Brownmiller, S. (1984). *Femininity*. New York: Linden Press/Simon & Schuster.

Butler, J. (1989). *Gender Trouble: Feminism and the Subversion of Identity*. New York: Routledge.

Butler, J. (2004). *Undoing Gender*. New York: Routledge.

Byrne, D., & Neuman, J.H. (1992). The Implications of Attraction Research for Organizational Issues. In K. Kelley (Ed.), *Issues, Theory, and Research in Industrial/organizational Psychology* (pp. 29–70). Amsterdam: Elsevier Science.

Calasanti, T., & Slevin, K. (2001). *Gender, Social Inequalities, and Aging*. Walnut Creek CA: Altimira Press.

Calasanti, T. (2003). Masculinities and Care Work in Old Age. In S. Arber, K. Davidson & J. Ginn (Eds.), *Gender and Aging: Changing Roles and Relationships* (pp. 15–30). Philadelphia: Open University Press.

Canada. (2006). *Women in Canada: A Gender Based Statistical Report*, 5th Edition. Ottawa: Statistics Canada.

Canadian Psychology Association. (2003). Gays and Lesbians Make Bad Parents: "There is No Basis in Scientific Fact for this Perception." Retrieved from the World Wide Web: www.cpa.ca/documents/GayParenting-CPA.pdf

Canary, D., & Dindia, K (Eds.). (1998). *Sex Differences and Similarities in Communication: Critical Essays and Empirical Investigations of Sex and Gender in Interaction.* Mahwah: Lawrence Erlbaum Associates.

Cancian, F. (1989). Love and the Rise of Capitalism. In B. Risman & P. Schwartz (Eds.), *Gender in Intimate Relationships: A Microstructural Approach* (pp. 12–20). Belmont: Wadsworth.

Caplan, P. & Caplan, J. (1994). *Thinking Critically About Research on Sex and Gender.* New York: Harper Collins.

Cavanagh, S.L. (2003). Teacher Transsexuality: The Illusion of Sexual Difference and the Idea of Adolescent Trauma in the Dana Rivers Case. *Sexualities, 6*(3–4), 631–83.

Chadwick, W. (1990). *Women, Art, and Society.* London: Thames and Hudson.

Chafetz, J.S. (1999). The Varieties of Gender Theory in Sociology. In Chafetz, J.S. (Ed.), *Handbook of the Sociology of Gender* (pp.

3–23). New York: Klewer/Plenum Publications.

Cheal, D. (1989). Women Together: Bridal Showers and Gender Membership. In B. Risman & P. Schwartz (Eds.), *Gender in Intimate Relationships: A Microstructural Approach* (pp. 87–93). Belmont CA: Wadsworth.

Cherian, V.I., & Seweya, J. (1996). Gender Achievement in Mathematics. *Psychological Reports, 78,* 27–34.

Choi, P. (2000). *Femininity and the Physically Active Woman.* London: Routledge

Colapinto, J. (2000). *As Nature Made Him: The Boy who was Raised as a Girl.* Toronto: Harper Collins.

Collins, P.H. (1990). Black Feminist Thought in the Matrix of Domination. In *Black Feminist Thought: Knowledge, Consciousness, and the Politics of Empowerment.* (pp. 221–38). Boston: Unwin Hyman.

Coltrane, S. (1998). *Gender and Families.* Thousand Oaks: Pine Forge Press.

Comack, E. (1996). *Women in Trouble: Connecting Women's Law Violation to their Histories of Abuse.* Halifax: Fernwood.

Comack, E., Chopyk, V., & Wood, L. (2002). Aren't Women Violent, Too?

The Gendered Nature of Violence. In B. Schissel & C. Brooks (Eds.), *Marginality and Condemnation: An Introduction to Critical Criminology.* Halifax: Fernwood.

Condry, J., & Condry, S. (1976). Sex Differences: A Study in the Eye of the Beholder. *Child Development, 47,* 812–19.

Coney, J. (1999). Growing Up as Mother's Children: Socializing a Second Generation in Sahaja Yoga. In. S.J. Palmer & C.E. Hardman, *Children in New Religions* (pp. 108–23) New Brunswick: Rutgers University Press.

Connell, R. (2002). *Gender.* Cambridge: Polity Press.

Connell, R.W. (1987). *Gender and Power.* Stanford: Stanford University Press.

Correctional Service of Canada. Long Term Offenders. (2006, February). *Women in Prison: A Literature Review.* Retrieved April 18, 2006 from the World Wide Web: http://www.csc-scc.gc.ca/text/pblct/forum/e06/e061d_e.shtml

Cottingham, L., & Jones, A. (1996). *Sexual Politics: Judy Chicago's Dinner Party in Feminist Art History.* Berkeley: University of California Press.

Cusson, S. (1990). Women in School Administration. *Canadian Social Trends*. Autumn, 24–25.

Daly, M. (1968). *The Church and the Second Sex*. New York: Harper Colophon Books.

Davey, M. (2006, April 16). Ripples From Law Banning Abortion Spread Through South Dakota. *The New York Times*, 14.

Davidman, L. (1991). *Tradition in a Rootless World: Women turn to Orthodox Judaism*. Berkeley: University of California Press.

Davies, B. (2003). *Frogs and Snails and Feminist Tales*. Cresskill: Hampton Press.

Davis, K. (1984). Wives and Work: The Sex Role Revolution and Its Consequences. *Population and Development Review*, *10*(3), 397–417.

Davison, K. (2000). Boys' Bodies in School: Physical Education. *Journal of Men's Studies* *8*(2), 255–66.

Degler, C. (1980). *At Odds: Women and the family in America from the Revolution to the Present*. New York: Oxford University Press.

Devor, H. (1989). *Gender Blending: Confronting the Limits of Duality*. Bloomington: Indiana University Press.

Dictionary.com

Diekman, A.B., Goodfriend, W., & Goodwin, S. (2004). Dynamic Stereotypes of Power: Perceived Change and Stability in Gender Hierarchies. *Sex Roles*, *50*(3–4), 201–15.

Dill, K. E., Gentile, D.A., Richter, W.A., & Dill, J.C. (2005). Violence, Sex, Race, and Age in Popular Video Games: A Content Analysis. In E. Cale & J. H. Daniel (Eds.), *Featuring Females: Feminist Analyses of Media* (pp. 115–30). Washington: American Psychological Association.

Douglas, S. J. (1995). *Where the Girls Are: Growing up Female with the Mass Media*. New York: Times Books/Random House.

Douglas, S., & Michaels, M. (2004). *The Mommy Myth: The Idealization of Motherhood and How It has Undermined Women*. New York: Free Press.

Drakich, J., & James, D. (1993). Understanding Gender Differences in Amount of Talk: A Critical Review of Research. In Tannen, D. (Ed.), *Gender and Conversational Interaction* (pp. 281–312). New York: Oxford University Press.

Drolet, M. (2002). *The Who, What, When and Where of Gender Pay Differential.*

Statistics Canada. 71-584-MPE no.4

Duck, S., & Wright, P. (1993). Re-examining Gender Difference in Friendship: A Close Look at Two Kinds of Data. *Sex Roles*, *28*, 709–27.

Eagly, A., Wood, W., & Johannesen-Schmidt, M. (2004). Social Role Theory of Sex Differences and Similarities: Implications for Partner Preferences of Women and Men. In A. Eagly, A. Beall, & R. Sternberg (Eds.), *The Psychology of Gender* (pp. 269–95). New York: The Guilford Press.

Education Quality and Accountability Office (2005, October). *Grades 3, 6, and 9 Provincial Report 2004-2005: English Language Schools.* Retrieved from the World Wide Web: http://www.eqao.com/pdf_e/05/05P026e.pdf p.19

Eichenbaum, L., & Orbach, S. (1987). *Between Women: Love, Envy, and Competition in Women's Friendships*. New York: Viking.

Eichler, M. (1988). *Families in Canada Today: Recent Changes and their Policy Consequences*. Toronto: Gage Educational Publishing.

Eller, C. (2003). *Am I a Woman: a Skeptics Guide to Gender*. Boston: Beacon Press.

Engelhardt, H., & Prskawetz, A. (2004). On the Changing Correlation Between Fertility and Female Employment over Space and Time. *European Journal of Population, 20*, 35–62.

Etaugh, C., & Liss, M.B. (1992). Home, School, and Playroom: Training Grounds for Adult Gender Roles. *Sex Roles, 26*, 129–47.

Evans, J., & Blye, F. (2003). Contradictions and Tensions: Exploring Relations of Masculinities in the Numerically Female-Dominated Nursing Profession. *Journal of Men's Studies, 11*(3), 277–92.

Evans, J. (2002). Cautious caregivers: Gendered Stereotypes and the Sexualization of Men Nurses' Touch. *Journal of Advanced Nursing, 40*(4), 441–48.

Eves, A. (2004). Queer Theory, Butch/Femme Identities and Lesbian Space. *Sexualities, 7*(4), 480–96.

Fact Sheet: Statistics On Violence Against Women In Canada. (2004). *Status of Women Canada*. Retrieved December 6, 2004 from the World Wide Web: http://www.swc-cfc.gc.ca/dates/dec6/facts_e.html

Fagot, B., & Leinbach, M.D. (1993). Gender Role Development in Young Children: From Discrimination to Labeling. *Development Review, 13*, 205–24.

Fagot, B., Hagan, R., Leinbach, M.D., & Kronsberg, S. (1985). Differential Reactions to Assertive and Communicative Acts of Toddler Boys and Girls. *Child Development, 56*, 1499–1505.

Faith, K., & Jiwani, Y. (2002). The Social Construction of Dangerous Girls & Women. In B. Schissel & C. Brooks (Eds.), *Marginality and Condemnation, An Introduction to Critical Criminology* (pp. 83–107). Halifax: Fernwood.

Fausto-Sterling, A. (1985). *Myths of Gender: Biological Theories about Women and Men.* New York: Basic Books.

Fausto-Sterling, A. (2000). *Sexing the Body: Gender Politics and the Construction of Sexuality.* New York: Basic Books.

Fehr, B. (1996). *Friendship Processes.* Thousand Oaks: Sage Publications.

Feise, B.H., & Williams, G. (2000). Gender Differences in Family Stories: Moderating Influence of Parent Gender Role and Child Gender. *Sex Roles, 44*(5–6), 267–83.

Ferraro, K.F., Mutran, E., & Barresi, C.M. (1984). Widowhood, Health, and Friendship Support in Later Life. *Journal of Health and Social Behaviour, 25*, 245–59.

Fillion, K. (1996). *Lip Service: The Truth about Women's Darker Side in Love, Sex, and Friendship.* Toronto: Harper Collins,

Finnie, R. (1993). Women, Men, and the Economic Consequences of Divorce: Evide. *The Canadian Review of Sociology and Anthropology, 30*(2), 205–30.

Fishman, P. (1978). Interaction: The Work Women Do. *Social Problems, 25*, 397–406.

Fivush, R. *et al.* (2000). Gender Differences in Parent-Child emotion Narratives. *Sex Roles 42*(3–4), 233–53.

Foltz, T. (2000). Women's Spirituality Research: Doing Feminism. *Sociology of Religion, 61*(4), 409–18.

Foucault, M. (1978). *History of Sexuality, Volume 1: An Introduction.* Toronto: Random House

——— (1985). *History of Sexuality, Volume 2: The Use of Pleasure.* Toronto: Random House.

———— (1986). *History of Sexuality, Volume 3: Care of the Self*. Toronto: Random House.

Fracher, J., & Kimmel, M. S. (1995). Hard Issues and Soft Spots: Counseling Men about Sexuality. In M. Kimmel & M. A. Messner (Eds.), *Men's Lives* (pp. 365–74). Boston: Allyn & Bacon.

Freedman, R. (1986). *Beauty Bound*. Lexington: D.C. Heath and Company.

Friedan, B. (1963). *The Feminine Mystique*. New York: Dell Publishing.

Gallagher S., & N.Gerstel, N. (1993). Kin-Keeping and Friend Keeping among Older Women: The Effect of Marriage. *The Gerontologist, 33*, 675–81.

Gallagher, S.K. (2003). *Evangelical Identity and Gendered Family Life*. New Brunswick: Rutgers University Press.

Gannon, L.R. (1999). *Women and Aging: Transcending the Myths*. London: Routledge University Press.

George, L. *et al.* (2005, April 30). Belinda and Peter, The Whole Story. *Maclean's*, 22–27.

Gerbner, G., Gross, L., Morgan, M., & Signorelli, N. (1986). Living with Television: The Dynamics of the Cultivation Process. In J. Bryant & D. Zillmann (Eds.), *Perspectives on Media Effects* (pp. 17–40). Hillsdale: Lawrence Erlbaum.

Giacommi, M., Rozee-Koker, P., & Pepitone-Arreola-Rockwell, F. (1986). Gender Bias in Human Anatomy Textbook Illustrations. *Psychology of Women Quarterly, 10*(4), 413–20.

Giddens, A. (1986). *Central Problems in Social Theory*, London: Macmillan Press.

Gilbert, S. C., Keery, H., & Thompson, K. (2005). The Media's Role in Body Image and Eating Disorders. In E. Cole & J. H. Daniel (Eds.), *Featuring Females: Feminist Analyses of Media* (pp. 41–56). Washington: American Psychological Association.

Gillespie, R. (2003). Childfree and Feminine: Understanding the Gender Identity of Voluntarily Childless Women. *Gender & Society,* (17)1, 122–36.

Gilligan, C. (1982). *In a Different Voice: Psychological Theory and Women's Development*. Cambridge: Harvard University Press.

Gilmore, D. (1990). *Manhood in the Making: Cultural Concepts of Masculinity*. New Haven: Yale University Press.

Ginn, J., & Arber, S. (1995). 'Only Connect': Gender Relations and Aging. In S. Aber & J. Ginn (Eds.), *Connecting Gender and Ageing: A Sociological Approach* (pp. 1–14). Philadelphia: Open University Press.

Gladwell, M. (2005). *Blink: The Power of Thinking Without Thinking*. New York: Little, Brown & Company.

Goffman, E. (1959). *Presentation of Self in Everyday Life*. New York: Anchor Books.

Golden, C. (1997). Diversity and Variability in Women's Sexual Identities. In J. Corvino & M.D. Lanham (.), *Same Sex: Debating the Ethics, Science and Culture of Homosexuality* (pp 149–66) Maryland: Rowman & Littlefield.

Goldenberg, N. (2004). Witches and Words. *Feminist Theology: The Journal of the Britain & Ireland School of Feminist Theology, 12*(2), 203–11.

Gould, L. (1992). "X": A Fabulous Child's Story. In J.A. Kourany, J.P. Serba, & R. Tong. (Eds.), *Feminist Philosophies* (pp. 43–48). Englewood Cliffs: Prentice Hall.

Gray, J. (1992). *Men are From Mars, Women are From Venus: a Practical Guide to Improving Communication and*

Getting What You Want in Your Relationship. New York: HarperCollins.

Green, L. (2000). Attention-Deficit/Hyperactivity Disorder: Constructing Deviance, Constructing Order. In L.G. Beaman. (Ed.), *New Perspectives on Deviance: The Construction of Deviance in Everyday Life* (pp.263–82). Scarborough: Prentice Hall, Allyn and Bacon Canada.

Grekul, J., Krahn, A., & Odynak, D. (2004). Sterilizing the 'Feeble-minded': Eugenics in Alberta, Canada, 1929–1972. *Journal of Historical Sociology, 17*(4), 358–84.

Griffin, W. (1995). The Embodied Godddess: Feminist Witchcraft and Female Divinity. *Sociology of Religion. 56*(1), 35–48.

Guendouzi, J. (2001). 'You'll Think We're Always Bitching': The Functions of Cooperativity and Competition in Women's Gossip. *Discourse and Society, 3*(1), 29–51.

Gunderson, M. (1998). *Women and the Canadian Labour Market: Transitions Towards the Future.* Statistics Canada 96-321-MPE no.2.

Gutek, B.A. (2001). Working Environments. In J. Worrell (Ed.), *Encyclopedia of Gender*

(pp. 1191–204). San Diego: Academic Press.

Gutman, D. (1987). *Reclaimed Powers: Toward a New Psychology of Women and Men in Later Life. New* York: Basic Books.

Hagan, J. (1989). *Structural Criminology.* New Brunswick: Rutgers University Press.

Han, S-K., & Moen, P. (1999). Clocking out: Temporal Patterning of Retirement. *American Journal of Sociology, 105,* 191–236.

Hannah-Moffat, K., & Shaw, M. (Eds.). (2000). *An Ideal Prison? Critical Essays on Women's Imprisonment in Canada.* Halifax: Fernwood.

Hannah-Moffat, K. (2004). Losing Ground: Gendered Knowledges, Parole Risk, and Responsibility. *Social Politics, 11*(3), 363–85.

Hardesty, C., Wenk, D., & Morgan, C.S. (1995) Paternal Involvement and the Development of Gender Expectations in Sons and Daughters. *Youth and Society, 267*(3), 283–97.

Harding, S. (1986). *The Science Question in Feminism.* Ithaca: Cornell University Press.

Harvey, S. (1999). Hegemonic Masculinity, Friendship and Group Formation in an Athletic

Subculture. *Journal of Men's Studies,* 8(1), 91–108.

Hays, R. (1988). Friendship. In S. Duck, D.F. Hay, S.E. Hobfoll, W. Ickes, & B.M. Montgomery (Eds.), *Handbook of Personal Relationships: Theory, Research, and Interventions* (pp. 391–408). Chichester, England: John Wiley.

Hays, S. (1996). *The Cultural Contradictions of Motherhood.* New Haven: Yale University Press.

Hayward, M.D., Friedman, S., & Chen, H. (1998). Career Trajectories and Older men's Retirement. *Journal of Gerontology: Social Sciences, 53*(2), S91–103.

Henley, N.M. (1989). Molehill or Mountain? What we know and Don't Know about Sex Bias and Language. In M. Crawford & M. Gentry (Eds.), *Gender and Thought* (pp. 59–78). New York: Springer-Verlag.

Henretta, J.C. (2001). Work and Retirement. In R.H. Binstock & L. K. George (Eds.), *Handbook of Aging and the Social Sciences* (pp. 255–71). San Diego: Academic Press.

Herbst, C. (2004). Lara's Lethal and Loaded Mission: Transposing Reproduction and

Destruction. In S.A. Inness. (Ed.), *Action Chicks: New Images of Tough Women in Popular Culture* (pp. 21–45). New York: Palgrave MacMillan.

Herdt, G. (1990). Developmental Discontinuities and Sexual Orientation across Cultures in Homosexuality Heterosexuality. In D.P. McWhirter, S. Sanders, & J.M. Reinisch (Eds), Concepts of Sexual Orientation (pp. 208–36). New York: Oxford University Press.

Hochschild, A., & Machung, A. (1989). *The Second Shift*. New York: Viking-Penguin

Hoodfar, H. (2003). More than Clothing: Veiling as an Adaptive Strategy. In A. Sajida, H. Hoodfar, & S. McDonough (Eds.) *The Muslim Veil North America: Issues and Debates* (pp. 3–40). Toronto: Canadian Scholars' Press.

hooks, bell. (1981). *Ain't I a Woman: Black Women and Feminism*. Boston: South End Press.

Horii, G. K. (2000). Processing Humans. In K. Hannah-Moffat, & M. Shaw (Eds.), *An Ideal Prison: Critical Essays on Women's Imprisonment in Canada* (pp.104–16). Halifax: Fernwood.

Hort, B.E., Leinbach, M.D., & Fagot, B.I. (1991). Is There Coherence among the Cognitive components of Gender Acquisition? *Sex Roles, 24*,195–207.

Howland, C.A., & Rintala, D.H. (2001). Dating Behaviors of Women with Physical Disabilities. *Sexuality & Disability. 19*(1), 41–71.

Hughes, P. (1995). Domestic Legal Aid: A Claim to Equality. *Review of Constitutional Studies, 2*(2), 203–220.

Hunt, Alan. (1993). *Explorations in Law and Society: Toward a Constitutive Theory of Law*. London: Routledge.

Huntemann, N.B. (2004). Pixel Pinups: Images of women in Video Games. In R.A. Lind (Ed.), *Race/Gender/Media: Considering Diversity Across Audiences, Content, and Producers* (pp. 251–57). Boston: Pearson Education Inc.

Hyde, J.S. (1984). Children's Understanding of Sexist Language. *Developmental Psychology, 20*, 697–706.

Interactive Digital Software Association, (2001). *State of the Industry, 2001*. Washington DC.

Ivory Towers: Feminist and Equity Audits (2005). Canadian Federation for the Humanities and Social Sciences. Retrieved May, 2005 from the World

Wide Web: http://www.fedcan.ca/english/pdf/issues/indicators2005eng.pdf

Jacobs, J.A., & Steinberg, R.J. (1995). Further Evidence on Compensating Differentials and the Gender Gap in Wages. In J.A. Jacobs (Ed.), *Gender Inequality at Work* (pp. 93–124). Thousand Oaks: Sage.

Jacobs, J.A. (1999). The Sex Segregation of Occupations: Prospects of the 21st century. In G. N. Powell (Ed.), *Handbook of Work and Gender* (pp. 125–41). Thousand Oaks: Sage.

Jeffrey, L., & MacDonald, G. (2006). *Sex Workers of the Maritimes Talk Back*. Toronto: UBC Press.

Jenkins, H. (1999a). Complete Freedom of Movement: Video Game as Gendered Play Spaces. In J. Cassell. & H. Jenkins (Eds.), *From Barbie to Mortal Kombat: Gender and Computer Games* (pp. 262–99). Cambridge: MIT Press.

Jenkins, H. (1999b). Voices from the Combat Zone: Game Grrlz Talk Back. In J. Cassell & H. Jenkins (Eds.), *From Barbie to Mortal Kombat: Gender and Computer Games*. (pp. 328–91). Cambridge: MIT Press.

Johnson, A. (1997). *The Gender Knot: Unraveling*

our Patriarchal Legacy. Philadelphia: Temple University Press.

Johnson, R. (2000a). Leaving Normal: Constructing the Family at the Movies and in Law. In L. Beaman (Ed.), *New Perspectives on Deviance: The Construction of Deviance in Everyday Life* (pp. 163–79). Scarborough: Prentice Hall.

——— (2000b). If Choice is the Answer, What is the Question?: Spelunking in *Symes v. Canada*. In D.E. Chunn & D. Lacombe (Eds.), *Law as a Gendering Practice* (pp.199–227). Oxford: Oxford University Press.

——— (2002) *Taxing Choices: the Intersection of Class, Gender, Parenthood, and the Law*. Vancouver: UBC Press.

Johnson, Y., & Wiebe, R. (1999). *Stolen Life: The Journey Of A Cree Woman*. Toronto: Vintage Canada.

Kainer, J. (1995). Pay Equity Strategy and Feminist Legal Theory: Challenging the Bounds of Liberalism. *Canadian Journal of Women & the Law*, 8(2), 440–69.

Kalish, J., & Latif, N. (2005). Pregnant Employees. *Professional Safety*, 50(6), 32–35.

Kanter, R. (1977). *Men and Women of the Corporation*. New York: Basic Books.

Kaplan, L. J., & Bernays, A. (1997). *The Language of Names*. New York: Simon and Schuster.

Kaufman, D.R. (1993). *Rachel's Daughers: Newly Orthodox Jewish Women*. New Brunswick: Rutgers University Press.

Kaufman, M. (1993). *Cracking the Armour: Power, Pain and the Lives of Men*. Toronto: Penguin Books.

Kendall, K. (2000). Psy-ence Fiction: Inventing the Mentally Disordered Female Prisoner. In K. Hannah-Moffat and M. Shaw (Eds.), *An Ideal Prison? Critical Essays on Women's Imprisonment in Canada* (pp. 82–93). Halifax: Fernwood.

Kilmartin, C. (1994). *The Masculine Self*. New York: Macmillan.

Kimbrell, A. (1995*). The Masculine Mystique: The Politics of Masculinity*. New York: Ballantine Books.

Kimmel, M.S., & Mahler, M. (2003). Adolescent Masculinity, Homophobia, and Violence: Random School Shootings, 1982-2001. *American Behavioural Scientist*, 46(10), 1949–58.

Kinsman, G. (1995). Men Loving Men: The Challenge of Gay Liberation. In M.S. Kimmel & M.A. Messner (Eds.), *Men's Lives. 3rd ed*. (pp. 406–17). New York: Macmillan.

Kirby, S. (2000). Sexual Orientation and Images of Deviance: Report on a Needs Assessment Survey of Senior Gays and Lesbians. In Beaman, L.G. (Ed.), *New Perspectives on Deviance: The Construction of Deviance in Everyday Life* (pp. 109–18). Scarborough: Prentice Hall.

Kirk, J.A. (2002). Gender Inequality in Medical Education. In M. Jacobs (Ed.), *Is Anyone Listening? Women, Work, and Society*. Toronto: Women's Press.

Konrad. A. M., Ritchie, J.E., Lieb, P., & Corrigall, E. (2000). Sex Differences and Similarities in Job Attribute Preference: a Meta-Analysis. *Psychological Bulletin*, 126(4), 593–641.

Koop, H. (2005). Mass Information. In L.W. Roberts, R. A. Clifton, B. Ferguson, K. Kampen, & S. Langois (Eds.), *Recent Social Trends in Canada 1960–2000* (pp. 488–92). Montreal: McGill-Queens University Press.

Krahauer, L., & Chen, C.P. (2003). Gender Barriers in the Legal Profession: Implications for career development of female law students. *Journal of Employment Counseling*, 40(2), 65–79.

Kunkel, A., & Burleson, B. (1998). Social Support and the Emotional Lives of Men and Women: An Assessment of the Different Cultures Perspective. In D. Canary & K. Dindia (Eds.), *Sex Differences and Similarities in Communication: Critical Essays and Empirical Investigations of Sex and Gender in Interaction* (pp.101–125). Mahwah: Lawrence Erlbaum Associates.

Kushner, H.I. (1985). Women and Suicide in Historical Perspective. *Signs, 10,* 537–52.

LaRossa, R. (1988). Fatherhood and Social Change. *Family Relations, 37,* 451–57.

Larsen, N. (2000). Prostitution: Deviant Activity or Legitimate Occupation? In L.G. Beaman (Ed.), *New Perspectives on Deviance: The Construction of Deviance in Everyday Life* (pp. 50–66). Scarborough: Prentice Hall.

Lee, G.R., Willetts, M.C. & Seccombe, K. (1998). Widowhood and Depression: Gender Differences. *Research on Aging, 20,* 611–30.

Leinbach, M.D., & Fagot, B.C. (1993). Categorical Habituation to Male and Female Faces: Gender Schematic Processing in Infancy. *Infant Behavior and Development, 16,* 317–32.

Lerner, G. (1986). *The Creation of Patriarchy.* New York: Oxford University Press.

LeVay, S. (1991). A Difference in Hypothalamic Structure Between Heterosexual and Homosexual Men. *Science, 253,* 1034–37.

Levy, A. (2004, January 12). Where the Bois Are. *New York, 37*(1), 24–27.

Levy, A. (2005). *Female Chauvinist Pigs: Women and the Rise of Rauch Culture.* New York: Free Press.

Lombroso, C. (1911). *Criminal Man.* New York: Putnam.

Lopata H.Z. (1999). Gender and Social Roles. In J.S. Chafetz (Ed.), *Handbook of Sociology of Gender.* New York: Plenum Publishers.

——— (1994). *Circles and Settings: Role Changes of American Women.* Albany: SUNY University Press.

——— (1996). *Current Widowhood: Myths and Realities.* Thousand Oaks: Sage.

Lorber, J. (1994). *Paradoxes of Gender.* New Haven: Yale University Press.

——— (2000). *Using Gender to Undo Gender: A Feminist Degendering Movement. Feminist Theory, 1*(1), 79–95.

Lowe, P. (2005). Contraception and Heterosex: An Intimate Relationship. *Sexualities, 8*(1), 75–92.

Lundberg, S., & Rose, E. (1998). *Parenthood and the Earnings of Married Men and Women.* University of Washington: Seattle Population Research Center Working Paper, no. 98–9.

Luxton, M. (1980) *More than a Labour of Love: Three Generations of Women's Work in the Home.* Toronto: The Woman's Press.

Lytton, H., & Romney, D. (1993) Parents' Differential Socialization of Boys and Girls: A Meta-Analysis. *Psychological Bulletin, 109,* 267–96.*M.* v. *H.* [1999] 2 S.C.R. 3.

MacKinnon, C.A. (1989). *Toward a Feminist Theory of the State.* Cambridge: Harvard University Press.

MacKinnon. C.A. (1987). *Feminism Unmodified: Discourses on Life and Law.* Cambridge: Harvard University Press.

Mahoney, M. R. (1994). Victimization or Oppression? Women's Lives, Violence and Agency. In M.A. Fineman & R. Mykitiuk (Eds.), *The Public Nature of Private Violence: The Discovery of Domestic*

Abuse (pp. 59–92). New York: Routledge.

Maier, M. (1999). On the Gendered Substructure Of Organization: Dimensions and Dilemmas of Corporate Masculinity. In G.N. Powell (Ed.), *Handbook of Gender and Work*. Thousand Oaks: Sage.

Malacrida, C. (2001). Motherhood, Resistance and Attention Deficit Disorder: Strategies and Limits. *Canadian Review of Sociology and Anthropology*, *38*(2), 141–65.

Marshall, B. & Katz, S. (2002). Forever Functional: Sexual Fitness and the Ageing Male Body. *Body & Society*. 8(4), 43–70.

Martin, P. Y. (2004). Gender as a Social Institution. *Social Forces*, *82*(4). 1249-73.

Maticka-Tyndale, E. (2001). Twenty Years in the AIDS Pandemic: A Place for Sociology. *Current Sociology, 49*(6), 13–21.

Matossian, L. A. (1998). Masculine Generic Language and the U.S. Women's Rights Movement, 1850–920. In L. Longmire & L. Merrill. (Eds.), *Untying the Tongue: Gender, Power, and the Word* (pp. 5–12). Westport, Connecticut: Greenwood Press.

Matthews, B. (2000). The Body Beautiful:

Adolescent Girls and Images of Beauty. In Beaman, L.G. (Ed.), *New Perspectives on Deviance: The Construction of Deviance in Everyday Life* (pp. 208–19). Scarborough ON: Prentice Hall

McConnell A. R. & Fazio, R.H. (1996). Women as Men and People: Effects of Gender-Marked Language. *Personality and Social Psychology Bulletin, 22*(1), 1004–13.

McDonald, P. (2000). Gender Equity in Theories of Fertility. *Population and Development Review, 26*(3), 427–39.

McGarry, K. (2005). Passing as a "Lady": Nationalist Narratives of Femininity, Race, and Class in Elite Canadian Figure Skating. *Genders: Presenting Innovative work in Arts, Humanities and Social Theories*. 41(1) Retrieved from the World Wide Web: http://www.iiav.nl/ezines/web/GendersPresenting/2005/No42/genders/g41_mcgarry.html

Meyers, D.T. (2002). *Gender in the Mirror: Cultural Imagery and Women's Agency*. New York: Oxford University Press.

Meyers, M. (2004). Crack Mothers in the News: A Narrative of Paternalistic Racism. *Journal of Communication Inquiry*, *28*(3), 194–216.

Michalski, J.H. (2004). Making Sociological

Sense Out of Trends in Intimate Partner Violence. *Violence Against Women, 10*(6), 652–75.

Miedema, B., & Wachholz, S. (1998). *A Complex Web: Access to Justice for Abused Immigrant Women In New Brunswick*. Ottawa: Research Directorate Status of Women Canada.

Miller, A.J., Bobner R.F., & Zarski, J.J. (2000). Sexual Identity Development: A Base for Work with Same-Sex Couple Partner Abuse. *Contemporary Family Therapy: An International Journal, 22*(2), 189–200.

Millett, K. (1977) *Sexual Politics*. London: Viraago.

Mitchell, D., & Snyder, S. (2003). The Eugenic Atlantic: Race, Disability, and the Making of an International Eugenic Science, 1800–1945. *Disability & Society, 18*(7), 843–65.

Mitchell, G., Obradovich, S., Harring, F., Tromborg, C., & Burnes, A.L. (1992). Reproducing Gender in Public Places: Adults' Attention to Toddlers in Three Public Locales. *Sex Roles, 26*(7–8), 323–30.

Mitchell, R. (2003) Ideological Reflections on the DSM-IV-R (or Pay No Attention to That Man Behind the Curtain,

Dorothy!). *Child & Youth Care Forum, 32*(5), 281–98.

Monture-Angus, P. (2000). Aboriginal Women and Correctional Practice: Reflections on the Task Force on Federally Sentenced Women. In K. Hannah-Moffat & M. Shaw (Eds.), *An Ideal Prison? Critical Essays on Women's Imprisonment in Canada.* Halifax: Fernwood.

Morris, R. (1995). *Penal Abolition, the Practical Choice: A Practical Manual on Penal Abolition.* Toronto: Canadian Scholars' Press.

Mossman, M.J. (1987). Feminism & Legal Method: The Difference It Makes. *Wisconsin Women's Law Journal, 3,* 142–168.

Mutchler, J. Burr, J. Pienta, A., & Massagli, M. (1997). Pathways to Labour Force Exit: Work Transitions and Work Instability. *Journal of Gerontology: Social Sciences.* 52B, S4–S12.

Nakonechny, L.E. (2003). Spousal Support Decisions at the Supreme Court of Canada: New Model or Moving Target? *Canadian Journal of Women and Law,* 15, 102.

Neitz, M.J. (1987). *Charisma and Community: A Study of Religious Commitment within the Charismatic Renewal.* New

Brunswick: Transaction Press.

Neugarten, B.L. (Ed.). (1968). *Middle Age and Aging.* Chicago: University of Chicago Press.

Nochlin, L. (1988). *Women, Art and Power and Other Essays,* New York: Harper and Row.

Noller, P. (1993). Gender and Emotional Communication in Marriage: Different Cultures or Differential Social Power. *Journal of Language and Social Psychology, 12,* 132–52.

Noonan, S. (2001). Of Death, Desire and Knowledge: Law and Social Control of Witches in Renaissance Europe. In G. MacDonald (Ed.), *Social Context and Social Location in the Sociology of Law.* Peterborough: Broadview Press.

Office of Research on Women's Health (2006). Home page. Retrieved from the World Wide Web: http://orwh.od.nih.gov.

O'Shea, J. (2005, August). *Re-Defining Risk Behaviours among Gay Men: What Has Changed?* Master's Thesis: Department of Sociology, McGill University, Montreal.

Olah, L. (2003). Gendering Fertility: Second Births in Sweden and Hungary. *Population Research and Policy Review, 22*(2), 171–200.

Omatsu, M. (2005). The Fiction of Judicial Impartiality. In G. MacDonald, R.L. Osborne, & C.C. Smith (Eds.), Feminism, Law, Inclusion: Intersectionality in Action (pp. 70–88). Toronto: Sumach Press

Omi, M. & Winant, H. (1994). *Racial Formation in the United States: From the 1960s to the 1990s.* 2nd Edition. New York: Routledge.

Ontario Women's Liberal Commission. (2005). *Liberal Party of Canada.* Retrieved December 2, 2005 from the World Wide Web: http://www.lpco.ca/owlc/photogallery.aspx

Oppenheimer, V.K. (1988). A Theory of Marriage Timing. *American Journal of Sociology* 94(3), 563–91.

Oppliger, P. (2004). *Wrestling and Hypermasculinity.* Jefferson: MacFarland and Company Inc.

Pachecco, S., & Hurtado, A. (2001). Media Stereotypes. In J. Worrel (Ed.), *Encyclopedia of Women and Gender* (pp. 703–709) San Diego: Academic Press.

Palmer, S.J. (1999). Frontiers and Families: The Children of Island Pond. In. S.J. Palmer & C.E. Hardman, (Eds.), *Children in New Religions* (pp. 153-71). New Brunswick: Rutgers University Press.

Palmer, S.J. (2004). *Aliens Adored: Rael's UFO Religion.* New Brunswick: Rutgers University Press.

Parke, R.D. (1996). *Fatherhood.* Cambridge: Harvard University Press.

Parsons, T., & Bales, R.F. (1955). *Family Socialization and Interaction Process.* Glencoe: Free Press.

Persell, C. H., James, C., Kang, T., & Snyder, K. (1999). Gender and Education in Global Perspective. In Chafetz, S. (Ed.), *Handbook of the Sociology of Gender* (pp. 407–40). New York: Kluwer Academic/Plenum Publishers.

Pirie, B. (2002). *Teenage Boys and High School English.* Portsmouth: Heinemann.

Pleck, J. (1981). *The Myth of Masculinity.* Cambridge, Massachusetts: The MIT Press.

Pollak, O. (1950). *The Criminality of Women.* Philadelphia: University of Pennsylvania Press.

Pollock, G. (1988). *Vision and Difference: Femininity, Feminism and Histories of Art.* New York: Routledge.

Pope, H.G., Phillips, K.A., & Olivardia, R. (2000) *The Adonis Complex: The Secret Crisis of Male Body Obsession.* New York: Free Press.

Powell G.N. (Ed.). (1999) *Handbook of Work and Gender.* Thousand Oaks: Sage.

Proctor, J. (2004). *Stuart Hall.* New York: Routledge.

Queen, C. (1997). Strangers at Home: Bisexuals in the Queer Movement. In J. Corvino (Ed.) *Same Sex: Debating the Ethics, Science and Culture of Homosexuality* (pp. 258–66). New York: Rowman and Littlefield.

R. v. Ewanchuk, [1999] 1 S.C.R. 330.

R. v. Labaye, [2005] S.C.C. 80.

R. v. Lavallee, [1990] 1 S.C.R. 852.

R. v. Morgentaler, [1988] 1 S.C.R. 30.

Revelli, B. (2005) Exploring Canadian Sociology. Canada: Pearson Prentice Hall

Razack, S. (2002). Gendered Racial Violence and Spatialized Justice: The Murder of Pamela George. In Razach, S. (Ed.), *Race, Space and the Law: Unmapping a White Settler Society* (pp. 121–56). Toronto: Between the Lines.

REALwomenca.com

Ridgeway, C., & Bourg, C. (2004). Gender as Status: An Expectation States Theory Approach. In A. Eagly, A. Beall, & R. Sternberg (Eds.), *The Psychology of Gender* (pp. 217–41). New York: The Guilford Press.

Ridgeway, C., & Smith-Lovin, L. (1999). Gender and Interactions. In J.S. Chafetz (Ed.), *Handbook of Sociology of Gender* (247–74). New York: Plenum Publishers.

Ridgeway, C., Johnson, C., & Diekman, D. (1994). External Status, Legitimacy, and Compliance in Male and Female Groups, *Social Forces, 72*, 1051–77.

Ried, S. (2006). Two Souls in One Body: Ethical and Methodological Implications of Studying What You Know. In L.G. Beaman (Eds.), *Religion and Canadian Society: Traditions, Transitions and Innovations.* Toronto: Canadian Scholars' Press.

Ripley, A. (2005, March 7). Who Says Women Can't Be Einstein? *Time*, 35–44.

Risman, B., & Schwartz, P. (1989). *Gender in Intimate Relationships.* Belmont: Wadsworth.

Risman, B. (1987). Intimate Relationships from a Micro-Structural Perspective: Men Who Mother. *Gender and Society, 1*, 6–32.

Ristock, J.L. (2002). *No More Secrets: Violence in Lesbian Relationships.* New York: Routledge University Press.

Rubin J.Z, Provenzano, F.J., & Lurra, Z. (1974). The

Eye of the Beholder. *American Journal of Orthopsychiatry, 44*, 512–19.

Sadker M., & Sadker, D. (1994) *Failing at Fairness: How Our Schools Cheat Girls.* New York: Simon and Schuster Inc.

Sagrestano, L., Heavey, C., & Christensen, A. (1998). Theoretical Approaches to Understanding Sex Differences and Similarities in Conflict Behaviour. In D. Canary & K. Dindia (Eds.), *Sex Differences and Similarities in Communication: Critical Essays and Empirical Investigations of Sex and Gender in Interaction* (pp. 287–302). Mahwah: Lawrence Erlbaum Associates, Publishers.

Sapir, B. (1956). *Culture, Language, and Personality.* Berkeley: University of California Press.

Sattel, J. (1976). The Inexpressive Male: Tragedy or Sexual Politics? *Social Problems, 23*, 469–77.

Sayers, J. (1982). *Biological Politics: Feminist and Anti-Feminist Perspectives.* London: Tavistock

Scott, J. (1998). Changing Attitudes to Sexual Morality: A Cross-National Comparison. *Sociology, 32*, 815–45.

Seltzer, V. (1989). *Adolescent Social Development: Dynamic Functional Interaction.* Lexington: Lexington Books.

Shaver, F.M. (2005). Sex Work Research: Methodological and Ethical Challenges. *Journal of Interpersonal Violence, 20*(3), 296–319.

Sheehy, G. (1995). *New Passages: Mapping Your Life Across Time.* New York: G, Merritt Corp.

Sheff, E. (2005). Polyamorous Women, Sexual Subjectivity, and Power. *Journal of Contemporary Ethnography, 34*(3), 251–83.

Shields, V.R., & Heinecken, D. (2002). *Measuring Up: How Advertising Affects Self Image.* Philadelphhia: University of Pennsylvania Press.

Signorelli, N. (1991). Adolescents and Ambivalence Towards Marriage: A Cultivation Analysis. *Youth and Society, 23*(1), 121–49.

Silveira, J. (1980). Generic Masculine Words and Thinking. *Women's Studies International Quarterly, 3*, 165–178.

Singh, I. (2004). Doing their Jobs: Mothering with Ritalin in a Culture of Mother-Blame. *Social Science & Medicine, 59*(6), 1193–1205.

Smart, C. (1989). *Feminism and the Power of Law.* London: Routledge.

——— (1990). Law's Power, the Sexed Body, and Feminist Discourse. *Journal of Law and Society, 17*(2), 194–210.

Smith, D.E. (1987). *The Everyday World As Problematic: A Feminist Sociology.* Toronto: University of Toronto Press.

——— (1990). *Texts, Facts, and Femininity: Exploring the Relations of Ruling.* New York: Routledge University Press.

——— (2005). *Institutional Ethnography: A Sociology for the People.* Walnut Creek: AltaMira Press.

Statistics Canada (1999, December 20) Survey of Labour and Income Dynamics: The Wage Gap between Men and Women. *The Daily.* Retrieved from the World Wide Web: http://www.statcan.ca/Daily/English/991220/d991220a.htm

———(2000, March 31). Health Reports: How Healthy are Canadians? *The Daily.* Retrieved from the World Wide Web: http://www.stat-can.ca/Daily/English/000331/d000331a.htm

——— (2002a, July 11). Changing Conjugal Life in Canada. *The Daily.* Retrieved from the World Wide Web: http://www.statcan.ca/Daily/English/020711/d020711a.htm

———— (2002b, December 2) Divorces. *The Daily*. Retrieved from the World Wide Web: http://www.statcan.ca/Daily/English/021202/d021202f.htm.

———— (2002c) *Census Dictionary*. 2001 Census Reference Material.

———— (2002d). *Profiles of Canadian Population by Age and Sex: Canada Ages*. 2001 Census Analysis Series.

———— (2003). The People: Household and Family Life. *Canada e-Book*. Retrieved from the World Wide Web: http://142.206.72.67/r000_e.htm.

———— (2005a, July 12) Births. *The Daily*. Retrieved from the World Wide Web: http://www.statcan.ca/Daily/English/050712/d050712a.htm.

———— (2005b February) *Suicide, and Suicide Rate, by Sex and Age Group*. Retrieved from the World Wide Web: http://www.40.statca.ca/01/cst01/health01.htm.

———— (2006a). *Earnings of Canadians: Making a Living in the New Economy*. 96-F0030-XIE-2001013.

———— (2006b). *Women in Canada: A Gender Based Statistical Report, 5th ed.* 89-503-XIE.

———— (2006c, August). *Persons in Low Income before Tax, by Prevalence in Percent (1999 to 2003)*. Retrieved from the World Wide Web: http://www40.statcan.ca/l01/cst01/famil41a.htm.

Stein, A. (2004). From Gender to Sexuality and Back Again: Notes on the Politics of Sexual Knowledge. *GLQ: A Journal of Lesbian and Gay Studies, 10*(2), 254–57.

Stern, S. (2004). All I really needed to Know (about Beauty) I Learned by Kindergarten: A Cultivation Analysis. In E. Cole & J. H. Daniel (Eds.), *Featuring Females: Feminist Analyses of Media* (pp. 22–29). Washington: American Psychological Association.

Stillion, J.M. (1995). Premature Death Among Males. In D. Sabo & D.F. Gordon (Eds.), *Men's Health and Illness* (pp. 46–67). Thousand Oaks: Sage.

Stockard, J. (1999). Gender Socialization. In Saltzman C.J. (Ed.), *Handbook of the Sociology of Gender* (pp. 215–28). New York: Kluwer Academic/Plenum Publishers.

Straus, M.A. (1979). Measuring Intrafamily Conflict and Violence: The Conflict Tactics Scale. *Journal of Marriage and the Family, 41*, 75–88.

Straus, M.A., & Gelles, R.J. (1986). Societal Change and Change in Family Violence from 1975 to 1985 As Revealed by Two National Surveys. *Journal of Marriage and the Family. 48*, 465–79.

Swain, S. (1989). Covert Intimacy: Closeness in Men's Friendships. In B. Risman & P. Schwartz (Eds.), *Gender in Intimate Relationships: A Microstructural Approach* (pp. 71–86). Belmont: Wadsworth.

Symes v. *Canada* [1993] 4 S.C.R. 695.

Tannen, D. (1990). *You Just Don't Understand: Women and Men in Conversation*. New York: William Morrow.

Tavris, C. (1992). *The Mismeasure of Women*. New York: Simon and Schuster.

Thornton, A., Alwin, D.F., & Camburn, D. (1983) Causes and Consequences of Sex-Role Attitudes and Attitude Change. *American Sociological Review,. 48*(2), 211–27.

Tiefer, L. (2002). Beyond the Medical Model of Women's Sexual Problems: A Campaign to Resist the Promotion of 'Female Sexual Dysfunction'. *Sexual & Relationship Therapy, 17*(2), 127–35.

Tong, R. (1989). *Feminist Theory: A Comprehensive Introduction.* Boulder: Westview Press.

Toobin, J. (2005, May 30). Girls Behaving Badly. *New Yorker, 81*(15), 34–35.

Trepagnier, B. (2001). Deconstructing Categories: The Exposure of Silent Racism. *Symbolic Interaction, 24*(2), 141–163.

Unger, R., & Crawford, M. (1992). *Women and Gender: A Feminist Psychology.* Philadelphia: Temple University Press.

Vanier Institute for Families. (2000). *Profiling Canada's Families II.* Nepean: Vanier Institute for Families.

Wagner, D.G., & Berger, J. (1997). Gender and Interpersonal Task Behaviours: Status Expectation Accounts. *Sociological Perspectives, 40*, 1–32.

Walker, K. (2004). Men, Women, and Friendship: What They Say, What They Do. In J. Spade & C. Valentine (Eds.), *The Kaleidoscope of Gender: Prisms, Patterns, and Possibilities* (pp. 403–413). Belmont: Thomson Wadsworth.

Ward, L.M., & Caruthers, A. (2001). Media Influences. In J. Worrel (Ed.), *Encyclopedia of Women and Gender* (pp. 687–701). San Diego: Academic Press.

Weatherall, A. (2002). *Gender, Language, and Discourse.* East Sussex: Routledge.

Weaver-Hightower, M. (2004). The 'Boy Turn' in Research on Gender and Education. *Review of Educational Research, 73*(4), 471–98.

Werking, K. (1997). *We're Just Good Friends: Women and Men in Nonromantic Relationships.* New York: The Guilford Press.

West, L. (2001). Negotiating Masculinities in American Drinking Subcultures. *Journal of Men's Studies, 9*(3), 371–79.

West, R. (1988). Jurisprudence and Gender. *The University of Chicago Law Review, 55*(1), 1–72.

Whitesell, N., & Harter, S. (1996). The Interpersonal Context and Emotion: Anger with Close Friends and Classmates. *Child Development, 67*, 1345–59.

Wilson E., & Ng, S.H. (1988). Sex Bias in Visual images evoked by generics: A New Zealand Study. *Sex Roles, 18*, 159–168.

Wilson, B. (1991). Will Women Judges Really Make a Difference? In Brettel, T. (Ed.), *Women, Law and Social Change: Core Readings and Current Issues* (pp. 157–63). North York: Captus Press.

Wilson, S. (1991). *Women, Families and Work.* Toronto: McGraw-Hill Ryerson

Winter, S.L. (1996). The 'Power' Thing. *Virginia Law Review, 82*(5), 721–834.

Wolf, N. (1990). *The Beauty Myth.* Toronto: Vintage Books

Wood, J., & Dindia, K. (1998). What's the Difference? A Dialogue about Differences and Similarities Between Women and Men. In D. Canary & K. Dindia (Eds.), *Sex Differences and Similarities in Communication: Critical Essays and Empirical Investigations of Sex and Gender in Interaction* (pp. 19–39). Mahwah: Lawrence Erlbaum Associates.

Wood, J. (1999). *Gendered Lives: Communication, Gender, and Culture, 3rd ed.* Belmont: Wadsworth.

Wood, J.T. (2004). Monsters and Victims: Male Felons' Accounts of Intimate Partner Violence. *Journal of Social and Personal Relationships, 21*(5), 555–76.

Woodward, K. (Ed.). (1999*). Figuring Age: Women,*

Bodies, Generations. Bloomington: Indiana University Press.

Worthington, E.L., & Buston, B.G. (1986). The Marriage Relationship During the Transition to Parenthood: A Review and a Model. *Journal of Family Issues, 7*(4), 443–73.

Wright, P. (1982) Men's Friendships, Women's Friendships and the Alleged Inferiority of the Latter. *Sex Roles, 8*, 1–20.

Wright, P. (1998). Toward an Expanded Orientation to the Study of Sex Differences in Friendship. In D. Canary & K. Dindia (Eds.), *Sex Differences and Similarities in Communication: Critical Essays and Empirical Investigations of Sex and Gender in Interaction* (pp. 41–63). Mahwah: Lawrence Erlbaum Associates, Publishers.

Wroblewski, S. (1993). Commentary on Adverse Reproductive Outcomes and Occupational Exposures among Nurses: An Investigation of Multiple Hazardous Exposures. *Nursing Scan in Oncology. 2*(4), 13.

Wrong, D. (1961). The Oversocialized Conception of Man in Modem Sociology. *American Sociological Review, 27*, 184–93.

Yates, S.J., & Littleton, K. (2001). Understanding Computer Game Cultures: A Situated Approach. In E. Green & A. Adam (Eds), *Virtual Gender: Technology, Consumption, and Identity* (pp. 103–23). New York: Routledge.

Yllo K., & Straus, M.A. 1990) Patriarchy and Violence against Wives: The Impact of Structural and Normative Factors. In Straus M.A., Gelles, R.J. (Eds.), *Physical Violence in American families: Risk Factors for Adaptations to Violence in 8145 Families* (pp. 383–99). New Brunswick: Transaction.

Index